Madame Roland and the Age of Revolution

Madame Roland and the Age of Revolution

Gita May

COLUMBIA UNIVERSITY PRESS

New York and London

1970

Gita May is Professor of French
at Columbia University.

Frontispiece:
MADAME ROLAND
Engraved portrait by F. Bonneville
Bibliothèque Nationale (Cabinet des Estampes)

PREFACE

MARIE-JEANNE PHLIPON, better known by her married name of Mme Roland, belonged to the generation that reached maturity in the shadow of Voltaire, Diderot, and Rousseau and that came into its own in 1789. She is remembered by those even superficially familiar with the history of the French Revolution, but her individuality, despite a certain fame, remains elusive, for it has been overshadowed by a legend born of the uncommon fortitude with which she met a harsh and untimely death. To some she summons forth the vague, and not quite reassuring, image of a gifted and charming woman who communicated her enthusiasms, passions, and hatreds to the impetuous and ill-fated Girondists. To most, however, she only evokes a figure standing at the foot of the guillotine and proudly uttering these eloquent words: "O Liberty, what crimes are committed in thy name!"

For a number of writers and historians of the nineteenth century, notably Stendhal, Lamartine, Michelet, Sainte-Beuve, and Carlyle, with their common interest in the French Revolution and their romantic tendency to admire and idealize women of passion and character, Mme Roland became the symbol of superior womanhood as well as of the generosity of spirit that distinguished the true revolutionaries.[1] Probably as a reaction against this romanticized and unrealistic picture, twentieth-century historians tend to view Mme Roland and her Girondist friends with undisguised hostility. On the one hand, exalted to an inordinate degree by her nineteenth-century admirers and, on the other, judged in a harsh light or almost totally neglected by modern historians, Mme Roland, as a personality, remains much of an enigma. A number of well-intentioned but Victorian accounts of her life have hardly revealed the woman behind the legend. To be sure, some of her beliefs and attitudes have been studied more penetratingly by French literary historians like Daniel

Mornet and André Monglond, but their analyses are perforce fragmentary since they occur in general histories of movements and ideas.[2]

In general, Mme Roland's biographers have tended to rely almost exclusively on her *Memoirs*—written in prison and under the shadow of the guillotine—and have paid scant attention to the all-important formative years. Having found that Mme Roland possessed an unusually retentive memory for facts and that the testimony of her autobiography was on the whole corroborated by the earlier correspondence, with only few and insignificant contradictions, they have been content to take her own reminiscences at face value without probing her evaluation of men and events. Yet the most instructive aspect of a biography would be not so much the recital of events along the lines of Mme Roland's own account as a study of those influences, intellectual as well as personal, that helped to shape her character. Such a study must also take into account the stresses and forces which, often unbeknown to the individual himself, go into the making of his conscious and unconscious attitudes. Moreover, as a member of the early Romantic generation, which eagerly patterned its thoughts and emotions according to a model popularized by Rousseau, Mme Roland more often than not reflects, in her stated beliefs as well as in her acts, the complex and sometimes opposing intellectual and emotional trends of her age. Like so many men and women who were to play a role in the revolutionary drama, it was in Voltaire that she at first discovered the ideas that would enable her to free herself from the prejudices and conventions of her class. In the end, however, it was Rousseau who came to dominate her mind and heart.

Some modern historians have taken Mme Roland to task for being inordinately proud and unbending. Proud she was, and not unjustifiably so, and there is no doubt that she could appear haughty and supercilious to those who failed to live up to her high intellectual and moral standards. She, who at the age of nine had read Plutarch and at eighteen had pondered over the best ancient and modern writers and philosophers, came to harbor, inevitably, a feeling of her own worth. She believed in the aristocracy of the intellect and looked with disdain upon the unthinking men and women perpetually chasing after facile pleasures and excitements. The fact that, at a time of acute crisis, she was given the opportunity of observing at close quarters those who held the destiny of a whole nation in their hands did not increase her respect for human nature. Yet she went on believing in the inherent nobility and goodness of Man. And even though she herself was of petit-bourgeois origin, she commiserated sincerely with the plight of the vast illiterate masses of France, whether it be in the great urban centers of Paris and Lyons, which she knew well, or in rural areas of the provinces, where she also spent a number of years as the wife of a hard-working inspector of manufactures under the Old Régime.

There are also those who point out Mme Roland's lack of worldly savoir-faire. To be sure, she was not one of those artfully seductive and easily accessible women, so common in any age but especially in hers. She was too intense and too passionate to be a coquette, and too opinionated to be a diplomatic salon hostess. A modest background, combined with an ill-disguised pride and shyness, made her somewhat impatient of mundane gatherings, where a witty repartee or an elegantly told anecdote is oftentimes more appreciated than a truly original idea. Unlike a Mme de Staël who, from early childhood, had been the focal point of the most brilliant salon life of her age, Mme Roland grew up in the home of an unassuming lower middle-class couple and had to seek out on her own the intellectual nourishment her precocious mind craved. But although books could impart knowledge, they could not teach such social graces as ease of manner, tact, and self-assurance. Not unlike Rousseau, who remained painfully self-conscious in Parisian society, Mme Roland was happiest when in the company of a good book or in the midst of a beautiful natural setting. In her own native Paris she remained, curiously enough, a provincial to whom was denied the sparkle of the theaters and fashionable salons.

Even when the Revolution brought Mme Roland into sudden, unexpected national prominence, she continued to long for the privacy of those obscure days when she had been free to devote the best of her time to the study of her favorite authors. "I like the shadows, and twilight is enough for my happiness. As Montaigne says, one is only at ease in the backshop," she confided to a friend.[3] And we have no reason to doubt the sincerity of this statement. Yet when circumstance brought her to the fore, she threw herself wholeheartedly into the struggle, for everything Mme Roland did, she did with passionate single-mindedness.

When the Revolution broke out, Mme Roland welcomed it with overwhelming enthusiasm. As a commoner imbued with the principles of the *philosophes,* she had grown increasingly restive with the existing social order. Wide-ranging readings only served to transform resentments of a personal nature into a coherent doctrine. Repeatedly, she was to taste the bitter fruits of corruption and injustice under the Old Régime. The dizzying pace of the Revolution, however, disappointed Mme Roland's fond hope that, once a representative form of government would replace absolute monarchy, justice and peace would prevail. The swiftness with which the Revolution moved towards a dictatorship of public safety left her groping desperately for those values she had always cherished. The violence evidenced by certain Parisian elements during the September massacres made her recoil in horror. Robespierre's tireless zeal, which at first had aroused her admiration, soon alarmed her; Danton's powerful rhetoric and shifty methods repulsed her; Marat's strident and persistent appeals to terror made her shudder. True Danton was willing enough to effectuate a rapprochement with the Girondists, but Mme Roland felt unable to overcome her physical and moral revulsion before the man's overwhelming animal exuberance and notorious venality. A shrewder, more seasoned politician would have perceived more readily the advantages of an association with the increasingly popular leader of the Paris masses and would have set aside personal antipathies. But Mme Roland equated compromise with weakness and regarded alliances founded on expediency as immoral and, in the long run, destructive. Convinced that the ideals of the Revolution were best exemplified by the Girondists, she gave them her unstinting support. This, however, did not blind her to their individual shortcomings and defects.

Swept into captivity by the Revolution that she had greeted so joyfully, Mme Roland saw those whom she had considered its most loyal defenders brought to trial and condemned to death. Realizing that she too would soon have to face the scaffold, she determined to set down her reminiscences so as to give transcendent meaning to her experience. Until now, she had always refrained from publishing her writings in the belief that a woman's destiny is best accomplished if she limits herself to the pursuit of personal happiness within the framework of home and family. Such prudence, however, no longer mattered since she was now willing to renounce life itself in order to uphold her convictions.

Mme Roland's *Memoirs* lay bare a soul with a candor and boldness which are often deeply moving, and sometimes disturbing. Inspired by the example of Jean-Jacques Rousseau, she resolutely unlocked the secrets of her heart for the benefit of posterity, her last resort against the injustice of men. And no one could accuse her of concealing or of dressing up the truth as she saw it. The result is a superbly indiscreet, spontaneous narrative, overflowing with a lyricism that is at once personal and sustained.

Throughout this biography, I shall seek less to pass judgment on Mme Roland than to understand what made her act the way she did. Using contemporary sources, specialized and general studies, and of course Mme Roland's own writings, I shall endeavor to trace her rise to the influential position as wife and active collaborator of the French Minister of the Interior during one of the most crucial periods in the history of France. By attempting to find out what manner of woman was at the root of the historical figure, I hope to reveal something of the spirit of a generation that repudiated the lesson of Voltaire and his call to reason and reform and turned instead to Rousseau's impassioned writings, finding in them the inspiration to topple the Old Régime. For it was Mme Roland's generation that laid the foundations of the French democratic state, but also

ushered in ideologies that made possible mass enthusiasms and
fanaticisms.

Not a single detail of time or place will be fictionalized in the
course of this narrative. This would hardly have been necessary, for
the biographer of Mme Roland is fortunate in having at hand an
abundance of sources in the form of personal as well as contemporary documents. References to works and manuscripts consulted will
be indicated in footnotes as well as in a selective bibliography. Much
of the material utilized here is new to the English-reading public,
since only Mme Roland's *Memoirs,* as well as a few youthful essays,
have been translated from the French. Moreover, there is a not in-
considerable body of still unpublished manuscripts and documents
that I have consulted at the Bibliothèque Nationale in Paris.

I should like to express my gratitude to the John Simon Guggen-
heim Memorial Foundation and to the Fulbright Program, which
made it possible for me to write this book. I also feel indebted to M.
Claude Perroud, the devoted student of Mme Roland, for what will
undoubtedly long remain the definitive editions of her *Memoirs* and
correspondence. For a careful reading of the manuscript and valuable suggestions, special appreciation is due to Professor Beatrice F.
Hyslop, of Hunter College. My greatest debt is to my husband,
Irving May, for unstinting encouragement and helpful advice.

                                                              Gita May

Columbia University
May 1969

CONTENTS

Preface, v

Part I The Formative Years

Part II Courtship and Marriage

Part III Passion and Politics

PART I

The Formative Years

ONE

A Child
of the Seine

ON THE TIP OF THE Ile de la Cité that lovely, boat-shaped island encircled by the two arms of the Seine, is the Pont-Neuf, the oldest of the Paris bridges and, in the eighteenth century, a far more active scene of popular life than now. Animated and colorful crowds of strollers paraded on it and from its parapets could enjoy a sweeping and unbroken view of the busy river traffic, the quays, and the city. Where the bridge crosses the island stood, as it still does today, the equestrian statue of good King Henri IV, and facing the statue is a small, triangular square closed off by old, dignified dwellings. It is named the Place Dauphine, after the Dauphin, Henri IV's son.

At the entrance to the Place Dauphine one can admire two hand-some, rose-colored brick buildings, almost unchanged since the time of Louis XIII. On one of them is a tablet reminding the passer-by that here grew up a heroine of the French Revolution, Mme Roland, born in 1754, executed in 1793. Unfortunately for historical accuracy, the commemorative tablet is wrongly placed, for it is in the third house from the bridge, on the Quai de l'Horloge facing the Seine, that M. Gatien Phlipon, Mme Roland's father, had his engraver's shop and living quarters. As a schoolgirl, Mlle Phlipon wrote to a friend: "I live on the edge of the Seine towards the point of this island where one sees the statue of the best of our kings." [1] Many years later, she reminisced nostalgically about the Pont-Neuf, near which was located the house where she lived.[2]

Not much in this section of Paris has changed since the 1760s, although it has acquired a more sedately residential character and is no longer the background for parading strollers; these have by now elected the more modern and spacious boulevards of the Right Bank. Whoever pauses in front of these venerable old buildings and small antique shops does not have to make a great effort of the imagination to feel transported to pre-Revolutionary days. Amid the many reminders of our own century, these older Paris neighborhoods retain an air of discreet gracefulness which gives concrete significance to Talleyrand's famous remark that "He who has not lived under the Old Régime knows nothing whatever about *la douceur de vivre.*" And indeed, to those who could afford the amenities of life, the last decades before the Fall of the Bastille offered an almost unique combination of intellectual excitement, social brilliance, and sophisticated luxury.

It was an age of reason and wit, but also one of growing sentimental fervor. The *philosophes* had popularized the art of expounding in an agreeable and piquant style metaphysical or technical subjects; and they had also applied their talents to lighter genres with a satirical and sometimes licentious flavor. It was an age when gifted artists like Boucher, Fragonard, and Greuze could simultaneously represent scenes of simple and virtuous domestic life, and pseudo-pastorals in which feminine nudity was the main feature. And it was plainly an age of restlessness, of mounting tension and discontent, for the notion of the pursuit of terrestrial happiness, advocated by the Encyclopedists and their followers, was making a deep impress on countless men and women who were growing impatient with the existing order of things.[3]

Under the surface veneer and rococo elegance, dissatisfaction seethed, inflamed by the writings of the *philosophes*. For this was a France in which passionate demands for reform crowded on the heels of new inventions. The frontiers of habit and thought were being pushed out and experience constantly enlarged. It was the France of Voltaire and Rousseau, of Diderot and the *Encyclopedia*, a France whose prestige and culture spread far and wide, penetrating into the courts of Frederick the Great and Catherine of Russia. But the caustic wit and impertinent repartee, so successfully practiced by Voltaire to the delight of both his admirers and his enemies, were now being supplanted by the brooding individualism and unshackled emotionalism of Rousseau. An overrefined society, surfeited with pure intellect, was eagerly seizing upon a new fashion—the cult of sensibility. Renewal was sought in the study of primitive tribes and in primeval instincts, and while the dignified, stable order of neoclassicism was giving way to the rebellious spirit of preromanticism, the Old Régime was imperceptibly disintegrating, becoming ripe for a drastic change.

It was an era of rapidly changing values, but never had Paris glowed more radiantly with intellectual and artistic activity. It was a city of striking contrasts, of imposing palaces and narrow alleys, of new town houses and crowded tenements, of glittering elegance and sordid poverty. With its teeming population of eight hundred thousand, it was not only the heart of France but also the largest city in Europe, a city where each succeeding epoch had left its mark and where the Middle Ages subsisted in spires and church towers. And once more the ancient metropolis was stirred by a spirit of opposition and defiance. In Versailles, however, an extravagant and pleasure-seeking court heedlessly continued to dance and fête, while the relentless, inexorable breakdown of tradition was insidiously sapping the already brittle foundations of the French monarchy.

It was in this turbulent and unstable France, in the year 1754, that Marie-Jeanne Phlipon, or Manon, as she would familiarly be called by relatives and friends, was born. In 1754, the *philosophes* were beginning to impose their ideas on a growing number of thinking men and women. Six years earlier, Montesquieu, the senior of the Encyclopedists, had completed his monumental and immensely influential *Spirit of the Laws*; he was now nearing his end. Voltaire, widely recognized as the greatest of eighteenth-century dramatists, poets, and philosophic writers, had hurriedly left Frederick's court under humiliating circumstances and was setting up his own at Ferney, safely removed from the reaches of authority. From then on would flow from his pen his most popular works, those racy tales and witty essays that would delight and shock contemporaries and, rather than his plays and poems, assure him immortality among future generations. In the same year, Rousseau, who was to become the oracle of the revolutionary generation, followed his prize-winning *First Discourse on the Sciences and Arts* with his still more daring and controversial *Discourse on the Origin of Inequality.* It was also in 1754 that Diderot, the bold thinker and dauntless editor of the *Encyclopedia,* endorsed scientific empiricism in his Baconian *Interpretation of Nature* and brought out the third volume of his dictionary amidst threatening rumbles of official censure. All these writers, and many more, would one day find their way into the tiny study of the engraver's daughter. For the time being, however, Manon lived mainly through her senses, absorbing the sights and sounds of a large city, watching her father's apprentices at work or curiously observing the customers chatting with her mother.

As was then the custom, even among the bourgeoisie, Manon had spent the first two years of her life in the cottage of a wet nurse, a robust peasant woman whom she occasionally continued to visit through the years. When she was brought back to the more comfortable apartment of her parents, she showed all the signs of being a healthy, alert child with an inquisitive and cheerful nature.

Manon's family belonged to the increasingly independent and ambitious French middle class. No remarkable trait distinguished the Phlipons: their interests centered exclusively on the home, business, and a narrow circle of relatives and friends. Their ancestors had all been thrifty, hard-working, but totally average tradesmen and artisans, with an occasional priest or vicar who conferred some prestige on the rest of the clan. Gatien Phlipon, Manon's father, could be called an artist, in the eighteenth-century sense of the term, since he was a master engraver by profession. In practice, however, he was little more than a skilled craftsman. The luxury trade, so prosperous in the reign of Louis XV, was his main concern. Phlipon ran a small but thriving business and employed several young apprentices who shared the family meals. His workshop turned out delicately decorated snuffboxes, jewel and watch cases engraved with emblems, frames for paintings and miniatures, and those large buttons, drawn with tiny landscapes and pastoral scenes, which were then the fashion.

The love for beautiful and highly ornamented artifacts, a distinguishing feature of rococo taste, favored Phlipon's trade. He could have earned a comfortable living for the rest of his days had it not been for a growing ambition to get rich quickly. More and more recklessly he would endeavor to increase his income by dealing in jewelry and diamonds and by risky speculation. In this respect, Phlipon's case was by no means exceptional. If one surveys eighteenth-century France and its highly flexible business ethics, one cannot help having the impression that in order to acquire great wealth a man merely had to speculate—on government bonds, on grain prices, on colonial holdings, even on royal lottery tickets. Subsequent to the notorious and ill-fated Law system, many a Frenchman of relatively modest origin, including such famous writers as Voltaire and Beaumarchais, had succeeded, thanks to a combination of astuteness and luck, in amassing a fortune. Phlipon probably thought that he too could take advantage of what appeared to be unlimited opportunities.

The trouble with Phlipon is that he speculated and lost. For many years, however, his shop sustained him handsomely, and Manon, being the only surviving child, grew up in pleasant, almost luxurious, surroundings which were no doubt disproportionate to her social rank. Some of the difficulty she would later experience in facing the limitations imposed by her sex and station no doubt stemmed from this favored childhood and from her father's expectation of wealth and influence.

Through his profession and contact with some of the best-known artists of the day Phlipon had acquired an appreciation for fine objects. Among those who occasionally visited his atelier to have their works engraved or properly framed were Jollain, a fashionable academic painter; the younger Falconet, son of the famous sculptor who was himself a painter of some renown; and the immensely popular Greuze, whose compositions, which deftly combined sly eroticism with moral pathos, dampened many a handkerchief. The penetrating portraitist Quentin de Latour was also a visitor, and it is believed that he painted the pastel portraits of M. and Mme Phlipon in their heyday.

The pastel portrait of the engraver, probably executed around 1760, at the time of his greatest prosperity, shows a young, self-assured man with regular although undistinguished features: the hair is carefully powdered, the mouth is full and well-shaped, and the cheeks are broad. There is a studied elegance in the gesture of the left hand lightly resting under the embroidered waistcoat, and the clothes are stylish, almost ostentatious. On the whole, the face is rather unsympathetic and the eyes have a direct, hard expression which denote neither marked intelligence nor great depth of sensitivity. Here is a masterly study of a successful tradesman and artisan with artistic and social pretensions, a dapper, stylish fellow proud of his appearance.

From her father Manon inherited a vigorous nature, good looks, self-confidence, and an understanding of the arts. Something of the engraver's stubborn and restless nature passed on to his gifted daughter. But her remarkable mental powers seemed to have been all her own, for Gatien's intelligence was quite ordinary and his formal education extremely limited. Absorbed with his shop, he took little interest in his daughter's training, leaving the main responsibility for her upbringing to his capable wife. In two or three cases of insubordination, his authority was invoked, but he soon discovered that the child had a will of her own that physical punishment could not break: "My father was rather brusque," writes Mme Roland in her *Memoirs*, "and he ordered like a master. As a consequence, obedience was tardy or nil. If he tried to punish me like a despot, his gentle little girl turned into a lioness." [4] Even a whipping could not bring submission; fiercely, Manon would bite the thigh over which she was bent in order to make her protest felt. One such scene she distinctly remembered thirty years later. She had been ill and her mother had tried in vain to make her swallow an ill-tasting potion. Phlipon, informed of this disobedience, proceeded to beat his recalcitrant daughter, for physical punishment was a common practice in those days. Instantly, Manon stiffened, silenced her protests and, turning toward the wall, stoically presented her derrière for further blows: "I would rather have been killed on the spot than utter a single sigh," she recollected. "It is a feeling I have since experienced in moments of stress, and today I would need make no greater effort to mount the scaffold proudly and die without being subdued." [5] The exercise of arbitrary authority would invariably awaken her combative instincts, for she was possessed with a fierce pride and a strongly developed sense of her own dignity.

After the memorable medicine scene, Phlipon never again ventured to lay hands on his daughter, preferring to entrust the ticklish task of disciplining the willful child to his wife. Rather, he assumed the more pleasant duties of teaching Manon the rudiments of drawing and engraving and of taking her to colorful fairs or to such fashionable promenades as the Tuileries Gardens.

Mme Phlipon differed sharply in character from her outgoing husband. A kindly woman, she nevertheless had a strong sense of duty. As was then customary, she had entered a marriage of reason and if conjugal life turned out to be something less than a state of bliss, she never uttered a complaint, for she was a good Christian who knew how to accept her fate in the proper spirit of humble resignation. Manon was the only surviving offspring of that marriage, several other children having died in early infancy.

Like most women of her class, Mme Phlipon divided her time between helping her husband in his business, managing the household, and fulfilling various family and social obligations. Under her quiet authority, harmony reigned in the Phlipon home, for she knew how to elicit respectful obedience. She was a religious woman, but without any exaggerated show of piety.

Latour's pastel portrait of Mme Phlipon shows a stoutish matron with a pleasing oval face enlivened by a faint smile. Like her husband, she is pictured in her best finery, consisting of a fur-trimmed mantle, a scalloped bodice, laced sleeves, and a flounced linen bonnet. Her appearance is one of seriousness, even austerity, but this impression is softened by her gentle eyes and sensitive lips. Upon comparing this portrait with its companion piece, one cannot help noting that Mme Phlipon's features bespeak a richer and more delicate nature than those of her dandified and yet common-looking husband.

From Mme Roland's own reminiscences one also derives the impression that she was more attached to her mother than to her father. Although she did not inherit Mme Phlipon's aptitude for self-effacement and quiet resignation, she admired and perhaps unconsciously emulated her stoical sense of duty and respect for decorum. Mme Phlipon had no special interest in formal learning, but she did not discourage her daughter's intellectual precociousness. Aside from teaching her the basic rules of morality and good manners, she did not force her personality into a conventional mold. Yet, in the presence of her mother, Manon never felt completely at ease, for Mme Phlipon's grave demeanor inhibited unreserved familiarity.

Although affectionate by nature, Manon's mother did not approve of effusive demonstrations of tenderness. Perhaps the child's high-strung temperament and turbulent moods gave her cause for concern. By a show of proper reserve she probably hoped to temper an all too volatile disposition. But to her dismay she found that the virtues she prized most—prudence, modesty, reasonableness, submission to authority—had little appeal for her daughter. She therefore maintained the aura of a kindly but strict parent to whom one speaks in respectful tones. As a result, Manon missed the companionship she craved above all else and, as is almost unavoidably the case of an only child surrounded by adults, came soon to experience loneliness and a sense of being apart from others.

Manon was taught to read at a very early age, probably when she was not quite four—in her autobiography she boasts that she knew how to read almost as far back as she could remember. Almost immediately she took to her books with such a passion that no one could tear her away from them. The Phlipons, despite their own cultural limitations, were shrewd enough to realize that theirs was no ordinary child and generously provided her with a host of tutors.

Manon therefore received an education far above that customary to her sex and social rank. Solemn-looking masters of grammar, history, geography, music, and even dancing came to the house in a steady procession. Manon absorbed and retained everything without apparent effort. No matter what book was placed into her hands, whether her catechism or an illustrated album of heraldry, she became completely absorbed in it. Indeed, her intellectual curiosity was such that she would rise in the early hours of the morning and steal, barefooted and in her nightgown, into her mother's bedroom where her writing table had been placed, and quietly work there while the rest of the household slumbered.

When she was seven, Manon was sent every Sunday to the parish church to prepare for her first communion. Once the rector came to the catechism and, in order to test the children's theological erudition, asked Manon how many orders of spirits there were in the celestial hierarchy. With a proud smile, the child replied that, though many were enumerated in the preface to the missal, she had found from other books that there were nine; and she marshaled before an admiring audience the whole host of angels in their proper order: archangels, thrones, dominions, and so forth. From that day on, Manon was held up by the matrons of the Place Dauphine as a prodigy and a soul predestined to salvation.[6]

Her music teacher soon discovered that his pupil had an unusually good ear but little aptitude for singing. He therefore taught Manon the viola and guitar, which she mastered with her customary facility. Later she also learned to play the pianoforte. Music affected her deeply, hardly a surprising trait for a future disciple of Rousseau.

Manon was fortunate in living away from the narrow, unpaved, and foul-smelling side streets so numerous in the Paris of the eighteenth century. Although her home was located in a busy intersection of the city, it faced an open area whose unbroken horizon she never tired of contemplating. From the windows of the apartment, she could survey the everchanging face of Paris. In the winter, the snow created a striking contrast between the white streets, the grayish rooftops with their myriad chimney pots, and the dark waters of the

Seine. On the other side of the house, the trees of the Place Dauphine, denuded of leaves, made a lacy pattern of silver branches.
In the summer, the quays were alive with strollers and the Pont-
Neuf, which could also be viewed from the windows of the Phlipon
flat, presented a variegated spectacle.

In Manon's time, the Pont-Neuf was the very heart of Paris: here
a colorful pageant was reenacted daily. Crowds of people assembled
to watch the royal coach and mounted courtiers pass by, for any
procession, either political or religious, invariably proceeded by way
of this crossing. Here too merchants hawked their wares, and outdoor
performers amused the onlookers with their stunts and droll acts. As
dusk fell, and the stream of carriages and humanity dwindled, Manon
would frequently sit at the window, spellbound by the spectacle of
Paris, resplendent in the sunset glow. A "child of the Seine," as she
was later to refer to herself, Manon dearly loved the river with its
indolent tide and magnificent setting. The panorama that she daily
beheld for many years made a profound impress upon her mind and
sensibility, and she would speak with nostalgia of "the vast deserts
of the sky, superbly vaulted, azured, magnificently designed, from
the east, far away beyond the Pont-au-Change, to the west behind
the trees of the Cours de la Reine and the houses of Chaillot." [7]

In the early morning hours, too, Manon liked to savor the special
magic of her city. Often the first in her house to arise, she would
throw open the window and watch the scene below. Outside the
light was still faint and the street had not yet come to life. Now
and then, a lone figure slithered across the road—perhaps some
vagrant or secret lover. Quite suddenly, church bells from nearby
towers rang out their matins as the uncertain dawn crept between the
staid dwellings of the Place Dauphine and the Quai de l'Horloge.
Shutters began to open and heads in white nightcaps cautiously
emerged. Trim maids scurried by, their shoes clattering on the cobble-
stones; shopkeepers readying for another day called familiarly to one
another; gangly valets started on their errands; and carriages began
clanking along on the Pont-Neuf, which gradually filled with its
usual throngs.

The apartment occupied by the Phlipon couple consisted of six rooms and was furnished with an eye to comfort and pleasure. One first entered a spacious antechamber, lighted from the courtyard. Here the family and apprentice engravers ordinarily took their meals. Curtains in red serge brightened the single window, and the walls were decorated with such prized status symbols as oil paintings and mirrors in gilded frames. The parlor had enough elegance to qualify as a salon, but Mme Phlipon modestly referred to it as the *salle*.[8] A large room, it directly faced the quay, and the reflections of the Seine filtered through two tall windows. A fireplace, veneered chests with marble tops on which there stood porcelain sets, a secretary, several armchairs, and a card table lent this room an air of luxury. Here the visitor could admire the fine pastel portraits of M. and Mme Phlipon, which are now in the Museum of Lyons. Tapestries, engravings, and later a painting of Manon at the age of ten executed by an unidentified but competent artist also decorated the walls. The portrait, now in the Musée Carnavalet in Paris, shows a strikingly handsome little girl with flowing long hair, healthy pink cheeks, and large expressive eyes.

Directly connected with the living room and also facing the street was Phlipon's studio. Plaster models of classical statuary hung from the walls, and beneath the window stood a large workbench cluttered with the tools of the engraver's craft. This room offered the best view of the Pont-Neuf, and Manon got into the habit of climbing on the workbench whenever an event of interest took place on the bridge. She liked the atmosphere of the studio, with its constant activity, lively young apprentices, and chatty customers. The room held a further attraction for Manon: she discovered that one of the employees, a more serious fellow than his boisterous companions, was also addicted to reading and kept his books in a drawer of his worktable. Manon surreptitiously borrowed these volumes, replacing them as soon as she completed her readings. If the apprentice ever uncovered the stratagem, he pretended not to notice. Since he had a taste for good literature, Manon was able to keep herself supplied with worthwhile books.

For the convenience of their daughter, the Phlipons converted a
recess in the parlor into a separate small room. Manon became very
fond of this cozy retreat, which she called her "cell." A tiny window
enabled her to look out onto the Seine and the Pont-Neuf. The furniture of this cubicle was of the simplest: a bed, a chair, a writing
tablet, and a few bookshelves. Manon's "cell" was the center of her
private, secret world. Here she avidly explored history, literature, and
philosophy. At first, religious works predominated, notably the *Lives
of the Saints,* followed by Bossuet, Fléchier, Bourdaloue, and Massillon, famed seventeenth-century preachers. Among the volumes borrowed from the apprentice was a Bible in an old French translation.
Manon delighted in its archaic yet vivid imagery and earthy descriptions. Some of the lessons from such edifying study, however, were
unexpected. When her grandmother once told her that babies were
found under cabbage leaves, she retorted: "My Ave Maria tells me
they come from quite another place." [9]

Not all books that fell into Manon's hands were of a ponderous
nature. She raced through the lighthearted and satirical *Roman
comique* by Scarron and the colorful *Memoirs* of the adventurous
Mademoiselle de Montpensier, daughter of Gaston d'Orléans and
granddaughter of Henri IV, better known as "La Grande Mademoiselle." Fénelon's prose epic *Télémaque,* a novel that enjoyed
immense popularity in the eighteenth century, also held her spellbound for many hours as she followed the travels of Odysseus' son in
a bucolic utopia along the banks of the Baetis in Spain.

One day, a friend with whom Mme Phlipon regularly played
piquet discovered to her dismay that Manon was engrossed in Voltaire's *Candide.* The lady's stern remonstrances, however, had little
effect. Manon was allowed to continue reading Voltaire and other
similarly controversial authors to her heart's content. Such permis-
siveness might have produced regrettable results had not Manon possessed innate good taste and a natural preference for works that presented an intellectual challenge. The spicy, licentious novels, so
keenly appreciated by a wide segment of the reading public, had
little appeal for one who, like Manon, was contemptuous of books
that offered no more than frivolous amusement.

At nine, Manon chanced upon a book that was to leave an indelible mark on her mind. It was Plutarch's *Lives* in Mme Dacier's highly successful translation. The Greek biographer's incisive portraits of the great men of antiquity, his narrative skill, and the loftiness of his moral judgments awakened the precocious reader to the heroic potentialities of the human spirit. In her *Memoirs,* Mme Roland states that, from the day she read Plutarch, she was a confirmed believer in the republican form of government, even though at that early age she did not quite know what this meant. Her conversion, in actuality, was probably far less dramatic. But viewed retrospectively from the vantage position of a militant revolutionary, the discovery of Plutarch no doubt acquired special significance, for had not Rousseau also been profoundly influenced by that writer? In the mind of Mme Roland and her contemporaries Plutarch came to symbolize the simple, virtuous ways of the ancient Stoics and early Romans. And this ideal, in turn, would be extolled by all those who were to oppose the principles of French absolutism.[10]

Without yet being able to discern clearly what it was that disturbed her, Manon began to cast a critical glance at her surroundings and to dream about those ancient times when men were born free and proud citizens of a republic. Like youthful Jean-Jacques himself, and like so many notable figures of the revolutionary generation, she first reflected on human character, on morality, and on the relation of the individual to the state through Plutarch's accounts of the noble deeds of the warriors and statesmen of Athens and Rome. And she was so fascinated by this book that she could not bring herself to part with it; even in church she continued reading it through the service, pretending it was her missal. Was it pure coincidence or unwitting imitation on Mme Roland's part? The revealing fact remains that Rousseau himself, in his *Confessions,* also declares that he first read Plutarch at about nine years of age and that it made him impatient of servitude for the rest of his tormented life. The lesson taught by Plutarch—love of freedom coupled with love of virtue—would, several years later, be reinforced in young Manon's mind by the passionate message of Rousseau's works.

When Phlipon realized that his daughter appreciated books more than toys or baubles, he endeavored to contribute to her little library. But his own limited education was no great help in selecting proper volumes for a ten-year-old girl. He reasoned that any work whose title included the word "education" would constitute a good choice. Thus Manon was presented with Fénelon's *Treatise on the Education of Young Girls* and Locke's *Essay on Education,* writings destined for the enlightenment of the pedagogue rather than that of the pupil! Thirty years later, when writing her *Memoirs,* she still could remember distinctly not only the contents of the volumes that had delighted her early years but also their physical shapes, the color of the bindings, and even the stains that marked some of their pages.

Since both M. and Mme Phlipon had numerous relatives among the lower Paris bourgeoisie, exchanging visits was an inherent part of their social ritual. After having been attired in her best clothes, Manon was instructed to behave with appropriate dignity and sit through interminable gossip sessions. It was no use trying to beg off these trying visits; Mme Phlipon insisted that it was her daughter's duty to participate in all family gatherings. There were two relatives, however, that Manon always enjoyed seeing: her paternal grandmother and an uncle on her mother's side. "Grandmama Phlipon" was a spry old lady with a ready wit and an education above her station. Widowed after a single year of marriage, she had been compelled to support herself and her son by raising the offspring of more opulent relatives and of nobles. Since her retirement she lived on the Ile Saint-Louis, sharing a small flat with a spinster sister and frequently inviting Manon, on whom she doted. The little girl was also very fond of Uncle Bimont, a kindly, cheerful ecclesiastic who ended his career as canon of the chapel of the famous Vincennes castle, a rather distinguished achievement for one of his modest background and who, moreover, had started as vicar in a lower-class district of Paris. Uncle Bimont, noting his niece's scholarly turn of mind, undertook to teach her Latin. But as a tutor he lacked assiduousness, either forgetting to show up at the appointed hour or taking his student on a walk instead of teaching her the declension of a noun. At this rate, Manon made little progress and never got beyond the first notions of Latin grammar.

So, in the cozy atmosphere of the Phlipon household, Manon grew, following her own will and fancy much of the time. Surrounding her were familiar, reassuring faces, and watching over her was the ever present Mme Phlipon, with her serious yet gentle eyes. And life flowed pleasantly on, a combination of well-regulated activities and adventures of the intellect. Early, Manon learned to combine her imaginary world with the realities of her middle-class environment.

Mme Phlipon liked to exhibit her girl in silk gowns and rich adornments. Such vanity in clothes was by no means unusual in the eighteenth century, when every tradesman's wife strove to emulate the glitter and stylishness of the nobility. Ostentation and luxury were not the monopoly of the aristocracy; many a bourgeoise went through ruinous expense for the gratification of being admired in church, on a Sunday outing in the Tuileries Garden, at a family gathering, wedding, or baptism. And nothing could flatter their *amour-propre* more than to be mistaken for a lady of rank. Thus Mme Phlipon delighted in outfitting Manon in the fashionable *corps-de-robe*, a dress resembling court gowns, close-fitting at the waist and with a long, sweeping skirt. To be sure, such a splendid appearance was not achieved without suffering: the toilette was excruciatingly long and painful, and one had to undergo the barbarous operation of having one's hair frizzed with hot curling irons. But it was all worth it when, upon appearing in church or on the street, Manon drew admiring glances and comments from relatives and neighbors. With a touch of vanity Mme Roland notes in her *Memoirs* that "this little person with her smart costume and good manners could easily have passed off for an aristocratic damsel who had just alighted from a coach." [11]

On ordinary days, however, Manon reverted to a routine more in keeping with her social rank. Dressed in a simple linen frock, she dutifully accompanied her mother and learned the art of bargaining and making wise selections. Frequently, she had to lay her book aside in order to purchase the parsley or lettuce Mme Phlipon had overlooked in her shopping rounds. True, she was not overly pleased with these menial chores, but she made the most of them by behaving with such adult dignity that the greengrocer always went out of his way to compliment the pretty, well-spoken customer. This everyday aspect of middle-class life has been admirably interpreted by the intimate art of the painter Chardin. The little girls he shows us in the process of performing homely duties all evoke Manon Phlipon, even down to their neat bodices, short-sleeved dressing jackets, and long skirts protected by ample aprons.

Mme Phlipon was determined to prepare her daughter for her future role in life, and Manon had enough common sense to accept this practical training with cheerfulness. She became as adept at making an *omelette aux fines herbes,* peeling potatoes and vegetables, or skimming the pot as she was at analyzing a literary passage or demonstrating a theorem of Euclid. And at family parties for young people, she outplayed and outdanced the other children.

Outwardly Manon appeared an active, spirited youngster, perhaps uncommonly bookish and at times the prey of fits of moodiness or obstinacy. Yet on the whole she did not seem out of place in her average entourage, and everything pointed to an uneventful existence, similar to that of generations of industrious Frenchwomen. Insidiously, however, the masterpieces of great writers and the works of the eighteenth-century *philosophes* were finding their way into the little study overlooking the Seine; they were sharpening Manon's critical sense and instilling in her mind ideas that challenged the way of life around her. All this intellectual activity, far from dulling her imagination and sensibility, only heightened an innate capacity to feel strongly. At the mere sight of a flower, she was sometimes overcome by a sense of delight and wonder, while a poem or a musical composition would call forth powerful yet undefinable emotions. For the attractive and intelligent daughter of the engraver-merchant, the horizons seemed to expand into a future full of promise.

TWO

Mystic Fervor

THE DAY THAT MANON WAS TO TAKE Holy Communion for
the first time was approaching. Her imagination exalted by the
solemn rites of the church, she spent her days rereading the *Lives of
the Saints,* wishing she had lived in the times of the early Christians
and martyrs. It was then that a rather scabrous incident, recounted
with characteristic bluntness in the *Memoirs,* caused something of a
revolution in the young girl's life.[1] It was her habit to visit her
father's workshop frequently in the course of the day, to show one of
her drawings, sharpen her etcher's needles, watch the apprentices at
work, or simply to look out the window on the Pont-Neuf. One of
the young boys, probably in the pangs of puberty, as he chanced to
be alone with Manon in the room took advantage of her unsuspecting familiarity to commit an act of exhibitionism and make obscene
remarks. Manon ran back to her mother, but did not at once denounce the apprentice's improper behavior. When he repeated his in-
decent advances, however, Mme Phlipon noted her daughter's bewilderment and elicited the whole story. If Manon had so far been
vaguely worried, she was terrified by her mother's violent reaction. A
close questioning at least reassured the engraver's wife that nothing
irreparable had happened. She nevertheless endeavored to paint such
a horrifying picture of the sins of the flesh that a totally confused
Manon was overcome by a sense of deep guilt and utter shame. It
seemed to her that she had just unwittingly committed a terrible
crime and that she must make amends for it. In addition, she was
sternly warned to exert henceforth the most extreme caution if she
wanted to safeguard her virtue and avoid an eternity in hell. To make

matters worse, Mme Phlipon hastened to lead her to confession, where she had to repeat once more the whole humiliating episode, this time to a solemn servant of God. No wonder that, from this day onward, she tended to look upon sex with fear. For many years to come, even after losing her religious faith, she thoroughly repressed all thoughts of physical love. Despite her passionate and sensuous temperament, she remained not only virginal but almost totally ignorant of sex until her wedding night. Even in her readings, she was so conditioned as to skip unconsciously those passages that might have enlightened her; in her *Memoirs* she humorously recalled hurriedly turning the pages of Buffon's *Natural History* that describe and illustrate the mechanics of reproduction.

Not without a touch of pride, Mme Roland compared her straightforward revelation of the incident in her father's studio with Rousseau's famed story of the stolen ribbon. Interestingly enough, when the first integral text of the *Memoirs* appeared in 1864, Sainte-Beuve, an enthusiastic admirer of Mme Roland and a keen student of manners and mores, nevertheless voiced disapproval of what he regarded as a lapse in good taste and feminine reserve. Mme Roland would have been well advised, he held, to keep silent about such matters.[2] But this was to forget the bold spirit of the eighteenth century and Mme Rowland's avowed principle to tell all.

At the age of eleven, Manon suddenly developed an overwhelming case of timidity and self-consciousness. It became well-nigh impossible to make her desert the tiny study, and her devoutness was such that she came to look upon her existence as still too worldly. The silence and austerity of monastic life assumed the most appealing colors; she fondly pictured herself in a convent. To be sure, the prospect of being removed from her family was painful, but this personal sacrifice, if accepted in the right spirit, could not fail to be pleasing in the eyes of God.

One evening after supper, a sobbing Manon threw herself at her parents' feet. Through her incoherent speech the Phlipons learned that it was her firm intent to become a nun and devote the rest of her life to the salvation of her soul. They knew their daughter well enough to realize that there was no point in resisting her will, but they nevertheless persuaded her to try convent life for one year before making a final decision. Their choice fell on the Convent of the Ladies of the Congregation, in the Faubourg Saint-Marcel. The convent had been established in the seventeenth century and combined instruction with a program of prayer and work that was austere, yet tempered by kindliness and congeniality. Here girls of the middle and lower classes lived in an atmosphere unadulterated by the mundane spirit that had pervaded so many religious institutions favored by a more elegant segment of society. Manon, choked with sadness but convinced that she was obeying the voice of God, on May 7, 1765, crossed the gates separating her from the outside world.

Many years later, her memories made all the more poignant by the fact that she was confined in a prison only a few streets away from the convent, Mme Roland recalled the feelings and thoughts that had filled her upon entering a religious community:

The first night I spent in the convent was agitated. I no longer found myself under the parental roof. I felt separated by a great distance from my good mother, who was doubtless thinking of me. A feeble light flickered in the room where I had been put to bed with four other children of my age. I silently rose from my bed, and went to the window. The moonlight enabled me to make out the garden that faced the room. The deepest silence prevailed around me; I listened to it, so to speak, with a sort of awe. Here and there great trees projected gigantic shadows. . . . I lifted my eyes to the sky, which was pure and serene. I thought I sensed the presence of the Deity benevolently smiling upon my sacrifice and already extending my reward in the consoling peace of a celestial abode.[3]

Such a description, with all its emotional intensity, is already typical of the Romantic mood as exemplified not only by the Rousseau of the *Confessions* but also by a host of nineteenth-century writers, from Chateaubriand to Musset, who wrote in similar style of their childhood experiences.

The convent provided room and board for thirty-four girls, aged from six to eighteen. The institution was unusually democratic, for children whose parents could not afford to pay the charge were treated the same as daughters of well-to-do families. The course of study, however, was typical of that offered to most young girls: it hardly went beyond a smattering of the three Rs. It was felt, especially among the bourgeoisie, that a woman needed very little book learning to make a good wife and mother. Manon's intellectual accomplishments astounded the sisters, who immediately placed her among the older girls. Her penchant for solitude had not diminished; she liked to walk about the spacious grounds of the convent, sometimes settling under a tree with a book, or pausing before the tomb of a nun.

In everything that surrounded her Manon saw the hand of Providence. But it was especially during Mass that religious sentiment took possession of her. The rolling music of the organs, the sweet voices of the young girls, the imposing spectacle of age-old rites, the mystery and solemnity of the divine service—all this penetrated her with awe and adoration. When the moment of her first communion came at last, during the feast of Assumption, she had to be helped to the altar. All those who saw this swooning young mystic were convinced that she was destined for the holy order; none could suspect that the day would come when this trembling communicant would press for the strongest anticlerical measures in revolutionary France. Yet, even after Mme Roland had rejected organized religion, she could not repress, when in the presence of a Catholic procession or service, a secret yearning for that rapture she had so frequently experienced during her pious years. On the whole, religion appealed to her imagination and sensibility more than it did to her intellect. Not long after her arrival, Manon witnessed a ceremony that made a strong impression upon her. In the presence of the whole congregation assembled for the occasion a young novice took the veil.[4] The chapel had been lavishly decorated with flowers, candles, and other adornments. At first wearing a sumptuous dress, symbol of the worldly things she was about to renounce forever, the novice was soon divested of her garments and covered with a white veil. She then intoned the traditional Latin verses and was finally made to stretch out on the cold pavement, a black veil shrouding her slender

form. Manon imagined herself as the victim of this sacrificial ceremony and found the thought unbearable. Perhaps the effect produced
by this scene had something to do with her eventual decision not to
become a nun.[5]

One of the nuns, shy and kindly Sister Saint-Agatha, developed an
intense affection for the brilliant but high-strung Manon. She was
born of a poor family and had received very little schooling; in the
convent she was given the lowly rank of lay sister and had to perform
all the menial tasks. But if her orthography was lacking, she had a
generous heart and was a cheerful companion. Not even the Revolution would affect her devotion for her protégée.

A few months after entering the convent, Manon was introduced
to two new boarders who immediately aroused her interest. They
were sisters who came from a fairly wealthy family of Amiens. The
eldest, Henriette Cannet, was about eighteen and paid scant attention to the eleven-year-old Manon. But Sophie, who was fourteen,
was obviously so unhappy at being separated from her family that
Manon was drawn to her, at first by sympathy but soon by friendship. Before long the two girls were inseparable. They had much in
common: a fondness for reading and a love of discussion. True,
Sophie was less impulsive and on the whole of a more phlegmatic
temperament, and being three years older she exercised a certain
ascendancy over her companion. But Manon's intelligence compensated for the difference in age, and in Sophie Cannet she found a
kindred soul, one able to share her innermost thoughts and aspirations. Henriette occasionally joined the two friends, but she remained an outsider. It was only several years later that she was included in their intimacy.

Manon, who as an only child had so far been surrounded by
adults, cherished Sophie with all the fervor of a passionate nature.
The eighteenth century, moreover, had an exalted conception of
friendship, which was at times placed on a higher plane than love.
While the latter was looked upon as a civilized expression of the
sexual instinct, friendship was praised as an ennobling relationship
between two beings sharing spiritual affinities. Some of the more

famous attachments of this kind were serene and durable like Voltaire's lifelong devotion to D'Argental or stormy and ill-fated like the association between Diderot and Rousseau.

After Manon's departure from the convent and Sophie's return to her home town of Amiens, their mutual affection was sustained by correspondence. It was while penning long letters to Sophie that Manon evolved a style of her own, sharpened her powers of observation, acquired the habit of setting down her comments on current political events, learned the art of summarizing and reviewing a book in a concise, pithy fashion, and perfected the art of self-analysis. To be sure, Sophie belonged to a wealthy, upper middle-class family which had risen to the nobility of the robe, and she remained faithful to tradition and respectful of opinion. But her ever more absorbing social obligations, which prevented her from keeping up with Manon's wide-ranging readings and studious habits, did not inhibit a trust and intimacy such as are rarely encountered among women. If the more conservative Sophie was often scandalized by her friend's bold reasoning and increasingly unorthodox views on society and religion, she was at least open-minded and eager to discuss important questions.

When the time came, in the spring of 1766, for Manon to leave the convent, it was decided that, rather than return to her parents, she would stay for one year with her grandmother Phlipon. The engraver had lately assumed so many commissions to alleviate his growing financial difficulties that his wife's assistance in the shop had become imperative; this left her insufficient time for other duties. Manon was not displeased with this arrangement; she enjoyed the company of the spry old lady and loved the serene atmosphere of the Ile Saint-Louis. Together they took leisurely strolls along the quays of the Seine and in the quiet streets of the island and attended Mass daily. Although Manon was still very devout, she no longer spoke of taking her vows and becoming a nun. Her first letters to Sophie are from this period, but it was not until three years later, in 1770, that she began writing almost daily and at length to the Cannet sisters.

The year on the Ile Saint-Louis provided a perfect transition from the seclusion of the convent to the bustle of secular life. Under the elder Mme Phlipon's affectionate supervision, Manon mastered the intricacies of needlework and naturally ransacked her grandmother's small library. The works of St. François de Sales and St. Augustine fed her religious meditations, but Bossuet's polemical writings, ironically enough, aroused her first doubts about certain dogmas. Through the eloquent bishop's onslaughts on the heresies of the Quietists, Jansenists, and Protestants she became aware of the objections that can be raised against Catholic articles of faith. Bossuet's rational approach to religion taught her to reflect about matters which she had so far accepted less through intellectual perception than through an emotional response. This was the first step, albeit a timid one, on the road to skepticism.

In the midst of all these books of piety Manon came upon the delightfully worldly Mme de Sévigné. The seventeenth-century epistolary writer's engaging sprightliness opened up for the young reader the intimacy of a glittering society. From that day on, the witty, sophisticated Mme de Sévigné would rank among Manon's favorite authors; and as she became increasing interested in correspondence as a form of expression, she emulated, often consciously, her manner. "The letters of Mme de Sévigné," she later wrote in her *Memoirs*, "determined my taste. I became as familiar with her entourage as if I had lived with her." [6]

Such critics as Sainte-Beuve and Brunetière, among others, have compared Mme Roland with her predecessor. Yet, as products of distinct eras as well as societies, the two women present more differences than resemblances. The aristocratic Mme de Sévigné's missives reveal a natural ease and elegance that reflect the best features of an age that prized grace enlivened by naturalness. As a noblewoman, she subscribed unquestioningly to the values of her class and, though sensitive and generous by nature, she could, like all her contemporaries, witness a scene of torture without wincing and report its horrifying details alongside the latest gossip from court. Mme Roland, on the other hand, dealt more frequently with serious, philosophical issues. Like many of her generation she was troubled by a metaphysical malaise, by a need to use letter writing as a means for self-expression and self-knowledge, rather than for communicating with others. Both women, however, share a common gift for humor and wit, a deft touch in relating an anecdote or sketching a portrait, although of the two Mme de Sévigné is undoubtedly more consistently flawless. Moreover, each was endowed with an intense nature and could be intemperate in a show of affection. At the same time, both captured the spirit of their respective worlds, one the sophistication of the high aristocracy of town and court under Louis XIV, the other the broadening horizons and restlessness of the enlightened bourgeoisie under Louis XV and Louis XVI and, after 1789, the high drama of revolutionary Paris.

Aside from family visits, the elder Mme Phlipon received little company. But being very sensitive to the social graces, she trained her charge in these amenities, beaming with pride whenever Manon succeeded in turning an elegant phrase or a witty compliment. Indeed, so pleased was she with her granddaughter's accomplishments that one day she decided to show her off to Mme de Boismorel, a wealthy noblewoman whose son and daughter she had raised in her younger days. After an elaborate toilette the two set off for the fashionable Marais sector where the Boismorels owned a town house. There Manon was to experience her first humiliating contact with haughty and pretentious aristocrats of the Old Régime. A tall, pompous lackey ushered the visitors into a drawing room, where the mistress of the house sat on a sofa, a lap dog at her side. Corpulent and outrageously rouged, she was all frills and laces, and her cold, shrill voice froze Manon. The hostess indicated a low stool to Mme Phlipon, whom, to the young girl's annoyance, she kept calling "Mademoiselle," a term which until the Revolution was reserved for women of low birth, no matter what their age or marital status. The direct and insistent manner in which Mme de Boismorel kept staring at the standing Manon while conversing in authoritarian tones with the former governess of her children made the sensitive girl feel uneasy. When a few questions directly addressed to Manon revealed to the gentlewoman that here was a plebeian youngster who knew how to reason and express herself, she sternly warned Mme Phlipon: "Take care that she does not become learned. That would be a great pity." [7]

It was not without a twinge of regret that Manon left the pleasant abode on the Ile Saint-Louis and returned to the house on the busy Pont-Neuf. In a way, rejoining the world of active grownups also meant leaving forever the enchanted world of childhood, for Manon was approaching adolescence.

THREE

A Disciple
of the Philosophes

MANON RESORTED TO CIRCULATING LIBRARIES, which were widespread in an age when the passion for reading had penetrated even the provinces. And so reluctant was she to part with the volumes that she found a way of at least appropriating their contents. Tirelessly she copied in her even, elegant hand long extracts and composed detailed summaries studded with personal observations.[1] In her letters to her friend Sophie she also commented upon and analyzed her most recent readings, a habit which developed the ability to bring out the gist of a work in precise terms. Later this discipline was to serve her in good stead, both as the collaborator of Roland in his many literary and administrative endeavors and as an unofficial but influential spokeswoman of the Girondins.

At the age of fourteen, Manon began having her first serious doubts about certain dogmas of her religion. In her systematic fashion, she submitted all the beliefs she had so far accepted on faith to the test of reason. While outwardly conforming to orthodoxy, out of deference to her mother's strong faith, she undertook an intensive study of all the significant religious and philosophic currents, from Jansenism to atheism, and in the course of her reading inevitably discovered the philosophic tenets of the Enlightenment. Never did she experience greater satisfaction than when, pen in hand and in the quiet seclusion of her tiny study, she could ponder an article from Voltaire's *Dictionnaire philosophique* or from Diderot's and D'Alembert's *Encyclopédie*. In her letters to Sophie she confided at length her restless search for truth and her doubts and her inner thoughts on the authors she was reading.

Manon, without following any outwardly imposed system and free to indulge in a personal preference for philosophy and history, devoured in succession an astounding number of works, from dry, obscure compilations to undoubted masterpieces in the field of ideas and letters. Nothing could dampen her abiding desire to find some logical explanations for a world that baffled her and for a society that oftentimes shocked her sense of justice. She almost wished she had been born a man so as to be able to give greater meaning to her existence. To Sophie she confessed: "If souls were preexistent to bodies and permitted to choose those they would inhabit, I assure you that mine would not have adopted a weak and inept sex which often remains useless."[2]

By taking refuge in private study, she could satisfy, at least in part, her need for intellectual challenge and activity. Her thirst for knowledge was such that she was not content poring over one book at a time. She therefore embarked upon contrasting and sometimes odd combinations of works: the satirical, light poems of Voltaire and the austere *Essais de morale* by the Jansenist Nicole; *Don Quixote* and the letters of Saint Jerome; Montaigne's *Essais* and Pascal's *Pensées*; Bossuet's orthodox *Histoire universelle* and Helvétius' controversial *De l'Esprit*; Descartes' *Discours de la méthode* and Locke's *Essay concerning Human Understanding*. Through Locke and his French followers she became acquainted with the Enlightenment and learned the meaning of natural law, empirical reasoning, religious toleration, and political liberalism. She copied long extracts from the Abbé Raynal's condemned *Histoire des deux Indes* and from D'Holbach's materialistic *Système de la nature*. Montesquieu's *Esprit des Lois* and the *Encyclopédie* completed her philosophic conversion. Oddly enough, all through her teens Manon remained largely ignorant of Rousseau's works, which she discovered only in 1776.

Voltaire at first became known to Manon as a poet, playwright, storyteller, and wit. Now he engaged her attention as a philosopher, historian, and scientific popularizer. The *Dictionnaire philosophique,* the *Questions sur l'Encyclopédie,* the *Essai sur les moeurs,* the *Histoire de Russie,* and the *Eléments de Newton* were analyzed in turn and copiously commented upon. With her contemporaries Manon shared an admiration for Voltaire's unique combination of profundity and wit. And like all Parisians of her time, she delighted in the latest bon mot, satiric epitaph, or resounding quarrel by the perennial and indomitable *enfant terrible* of the century. For even in Manon's bourgeois circle, Voltaire's astounding activity was a frequent topic of conversation, and Sophie was kept up-to-date on the goings on of the Patriarch of Ferney.

Voltaire became one of Manon's favorite authors, one whose sayings she was fond of quoting and whose repeated onslaughts against unquestioned traditions confirmed her own growing skepticism and independence of judgment. How enthusiastically she responded to his appeal to common sense, humanity, and tolerance, and how zealously she summarized his essays for the benefit of Sophie's enlightenment! More than once the engraver's daughter felt less isolated in her search for the truth thanks to the philosopher's courageous fight against bigotry and obscurantism. Voltaire sharpened Manon's critical faculties; Rousseau would one day reveal the depths of her heart.

Through the more outspoken atheists of the age like D'Holbach and Helvétius, Manon was brought into contact with naturalistic materialism and forced to question not only revealed religion but also the basis of philosophic deism, a position with which she tended to sympathize. Agnosticism and atheism, she found, were not incompatible with morality. "The atheist," she wrote, "is not, to my mind, an unsound intellect: I could live with him as well as and even better than with the devout man, for he makes more use of his mind." [3] Religious observance, she noted, failed to improve most men, since in practice they were impelled by their passions rather than by the principles or beliefs they professed. Yet, she somehow felt disconcerted by those thinkers who deny man's immortality as well as the existence of a Prime Mover and Deity who rewards the just and punishes the wicked. It seemed to her that the atheists, brilliant though they might be intellectually, were lacking in "a certain sense"—the ability to be moved by beauty or sentiment. Her mind could accept the reasoning of those who describe man in the light of his physical constitution and the origin of life as the result of matter in creative motion, but she found herself emotionally at odds with a philosophy that robbed her of all hope in the immortality of the human soul.

As she became imbued with the humanistic philosophy of the Enlightenment, Manon found it increasingly more difficult to accept certain Catholic dogmas, especially that of everlasting damnation. The thought that not only the wicked but also innumerable beings who, through no fault of their own, had never come into contact with Christianity would be called to account for their ignorance shocked her sense of justice. How, under those circumstances, could one reconcile the image of a merciful Savior who is all love with the notion of a God who has no compassion for the works of His own hands, just because of a geographical accident? How could one accept a dogma which excluded the largest portion of humanity from salvation? "I cannot digest, among other things," she reasoned with Voltairean logic, "the idea that all those who do not think like me will be damned for all eternity, that so many innocent beings, virtuous men, peaceful people will be cast into eternal flames because they have never heard of a Roman pontiff who preaches a severe morality which he does not always practice. I find this principle absurd, atrocious, and impious." [4]

In her mental anguish, she turned to her parish priest, the good Abbé Morel. The curé deployed all the resources of his rhetoric in order to bring back the lost soul to the fold. But in vain, for Manon, who now held that all articles of faith must be examined in the light of reason, remained unconvinced. The Abbé Morel then proceeded to put into Manon's hands the tracts of the best champions and apologists of the church—the Abbé Gauchat, Bergier, Abbadie, and others. She read them dutifully, making ample annotations.

They only confirmed her doubts by pointing out all too clearly the anticlerical arguments they were trying to refute. What is more, through these polemical works she came across the titles of contemporary books by Encyclopedists which she had not as yet read, and she hastened to get hold of them! The poor abbé was at his wits' end, especially when the troublesome girl, rather mischievously we may suspect, let him read some of her observations, which astounded him through their polemical dexterity.

Manon nevertheless determined not to publicize her unorthodox views, sharing them only with her confessor and with Sophie. The pious Mme Phlipon, whom Manon continued to accompany daily to mass, suspected nothing of her daughter's spiritual defection. Our young philosopher had resolved to follow, at least outwardly, religious practices so as not to upset her mother, arouse neighborhood gossip, or set a dangerous example to unenlightened and unlettered minds. For Mlle Phlipon shared Voltaire's principle that skepticism should be limited only to an aristocracy of the intellect and that the common folk should be allowed, for the sake of morality and public order, to practice their superstitious rituals.

There was another reason why Manon thought that the Christian religion was a useful and even necessary institution. She was too observant not to have taken notice of the plight of the common people, most of whom lived in wretched poverty and total ignorance. Her relatively sheltered existence did not blind her to the predicament of those who, in her own words, "groan under the innumerable hardships of miserable working and living conditions."[5] It was while commiserating with the poor that she came to the conclusion that for three-fourths of mankind religion is incontestably a great blessing, and often "the only blessing that can be had."[6] If Christianity was the ideal religion for the unfortunates and the hopeless, if it brought spiritual comfort and moral support to so many, Manon felt disinclined to reject it openly and kept her doubts to herself. To her parish priest she therefore bluntly announced: "I come to confession for the edification of my neighbor and the peace of mind of my mother."[7] The good Abbé Morel, who by now had given up his attempts to reconvert his charge through suasion, threw up his hands in despair and gave a little sermon on the dangers of intellectual pride.

Before long, Manon had adopted all the anticlerical arguments made popular by the *philosophes*. In an essay, which is strongly reminiscent of Voltaire's manner, she summarized all these arguments: there was nothing miraculous about the establishment and growth of the Christian religion, since other so-called heathen sects had just as many followers. Besides, the decadence of the Roman empire had facilitated the success of the new creed. And by appealing to the instinct of fear, by frightening men with the prospect of an eternity of bliss or torment, Christianity had had no trouble winning over numerous adherents. By using every device to strike the imagination and appeal to the heart, it had elicited widespread enthusiasm and zeal. And finally, by resorting to persecution and intrigue, it had imposed itself by force where it could not do so by conversion. As for the martyrs, whose lives she had at one time studied so reverently, they now appeared to Manon as foolhardy fanatics who "sometimes sought out punishment through the rash eagerness with which they broke up religious sacrifices and smashed the effigies of the emperors." [8] Manon even wondered whether the martyrology was not "exempt from exaggeration," for it seemed to her that "the greatest number of Roman bishops died peacefully in their beds." [9] This was indeed the reasoning of a worthy disciple of Voltaire!

She had to admit, however, that the Bible's version of the creation was poetic and beautiful. But she wryly added that it did not correspond with the latest discoveries of astronomy. And she could not reconcile herself with the doctrine of original sin. "What? this whole system, in which I admire the harmony and the meaning, is founded on an eaten apple?" she asked ironically. As for Christ, "what was the point in sending to our earth an incarnated God in order to save a few men in the general shipwreck? And what was the point in creating a man in order to condemn him with his whole race over such a trivial infraction? Adam is punished in the most horrible manner for having followed the counsel of the senses which had been given to him as guides." [10] And she ended her essay with a direct invocation to God: "Perfect Being, divine Intelligence, are these Your works? I cannot believe it. This whole system seems defective to me. What will then become of the edifice? I have the profoundest respect for Jesus-Christ, but I would believe much more firmly in Him if one did not fasten His story to that of Adam." [11]

Having rejected orthodox Christianity, Manon found herself hesitating between atheism and deism. On the one hand, how could one premise design, intention, and purpose in a universe so permeated with unhappiness, suffering, and unjust, incalculable death? But, on the other hand, how could one premise life itself without the existence of a Creator: "What is, then, this supreme Intelligence which acts in such an incomprehensible way?" Manon kept asking herself without finding a satisfactory answer. Yet, she could not bring herself to subscribe to the atheistic representation of man as a soulless machine projected in a universe devoid of supernatural intelligence and purpose. "I like to think there is a God," she mused. "I believe Him true, just and good. I revere in Him those qualities through which I would like to resemble Him. The ethical principles I have adopted must please Him, because they promote the general good." [12] Thus, like many an upholder of the Enlightenment, Manon leaned towards the principles of natural religion as divorced from external revelation and dogma.

As the engraver's daughter severed one by one the ties that held her fast to the traditions and beliefs of her class, she became increasingly aware of her intellectual isolation. Open defiance, however, did not seem a wise course of action, since there was so little that a person of her age, sex, and position could do to alter the order of things. Besides, she was not at all sure that her personal convictions were any better than the conventional ones. Under these circumstances, it was wiser to follow the example of Montaigne's cautious skepticism and prudent withdrawal from action: "Ignorance and lack of curiosity, these two pillows extolled by Montaigne," wrote Manon, who held the sixteenth-century essayist in the highest esteem, "appear rather comfortable to me. Skeptical indolence does not suit me badly and I confess that doubt and uncertainty seem the most appropriate state of mind for limited and weak beings like me." [13] A curiously mild and tolerant approach to life for one who would one day turn into a fiery revolutionary! And indeed until the Revolution was to jolt her into action, Manon would consistently seek her ideal in a private world of individual perfection and observe men and events with the cool and gently ironic detachment of a worthy admirer of Montaigne.

Being an optimist at heart, Manon was gratified to find in Voltaire and the Encyclopedists potent arguments against Pascal's somber portrayal of the human condition. If man was imperfect and frequently the prey of his passions, he was not, as Pascal had so eloquently maintained, a wretched creature blindly groping in an incomprehensible universe. How reassuring to learn that man was not half-angel and half-beast, but an essentially rational creature with the God-given right to find earthly happiness.

In her eagerness to discover irrefutable proofs of natural religion, Manon turned her attention to Pope's popular *Essay on Man,* which she first read in a French verse translation. But while she admired the poet's ability to set forth abstruse concepts in a lucid style and found his philosophic optimism "consoling," she remained acutely conscious of the objections that could be leveled against his justification of evil. "What I don't like in optimism," she explained to Sophie, "is that it confers limits to God's power. Console yourself, o Man! says Pope, submit to the order of things; good and evil, in morality as in physics, contribute equally to the general good." [14] What reconciled Manon, at least in part, to Pope's "all is well" was her growing conviction that the origin of most evils lay not in man's nature or in the order of the universe but in faulty social institutions. This enabled her to retain her belief in a benevolent, all-powerful Deity and the hope that, in time, man would learn to make better use of his will.

For several months Manon also applied herself to Descartes. Many aspects of his philosophy, however, left her dissatisfied. As a student of Locke and the Encyclopedists, she could not accept Descartes' rigid separation of mind and matter as well as his awkward theory of animal spirits as a sort of bridge between body and soul. Neither could she subscribe to the cartesian theory that animals are mere machines governed entirely by the laws of physics and devoid of all feeling or consciousness. Observing her cat, Manon simply found it impossible to believe that the little creature, when it meowed, was just a dumb automaton unwittingly playing its part. Such stern rationalism, she reasoned, led to the cold dissection of a lifeless world. How more inspiring it was to endow every living being with a spark of the divine spirit! In this respect she thought Spinoza's mystical pantheism far more reassuring than Descartes' rational dualism.

Of all the philosophic systems surveyed by our budding *philosophe*, Helvétius' systematic hedonism, which reduces all human actions to the pleasure principle, was the one that troubled her the most. Here she found the strongest challenge to her deism and to her belief in the innate goodness and nobility of man. With relentless logic Helvétius presented self-interest as the sole motive of human action, yet stressed the omnipotence of education and environment in overcoming our basic egoism. While adopting many of his pedagogical insights, particularly his theory that education can correct and direct natural inclinations, Manon was loath to accept his basic premise concerning human character. She would have considered herself debased, since she felt possessed of a generosity of soul whose existence Helvétius denied: "There are innate ideas of justice, a natural love for the beautiful," she argued, "that even the evil person respects inwardly while persecuting virtue. There are generous acts, admirable qualities which elicit my admiration without my self-interest finding in this tribute any remuneration. Yes, even if reason were not to demonstrate the absurdities uttered by the materialists, my heart would make me aware of their errors. For in spite of the arguments they accumulate, my heart feels itself more noble than they want to admit." [15]

Thus both in the sublime examples of great men and in what she called her "heart," Manon found sufficient evidence that self-gratification is not at the root of every human endeavor. This desire to demonstrate man's nobler attributes against Helvétius became a near obsession. Whenever she came across the recital of a heroic deed, she opposed it to the philosopher's materialism and fervently told herself: "I would have acted in the same manner." [16] That such an approach to metaphysics and ethics was more emotional than intellectual did not seem to have overly troubled her, for even before coming under Rousseau's influence she was already convinced that the ability to feel deeply is the test of a great soul. "Violent penchants, strong imaginations, firm characters, differently modified, make an individual sublime and energetic in virtue, or abominable and atrocious in crime," she noted, paraphrasing Diderot's apology of the passions in his *Pensées philosophiques*.[17] Without this intense sensibility, one did not run the risk of becoming a criminal, but neither would one ever be anything more than a very ordinary human being. Such was the attitude of the eighteenth-century forerunners of the Romantics.

From her study of the *philosophes*, Manon came away a resolute optimist and a firm upholder of the dignity of the individual. Not until the tragic events of the Terror many years later would she ever cast serious doubt on the idea that man is primarily a social animal with a natural propensity for good and that, given the right education and allowed to live in a just social system, he can achieve a high level of morality. But Manon was now faced with the immediate problem of choosing standards of conduct which would determine her own way of life. With regard to ethics, she resolved to try to find contentment in the rule of moderation and in the joys of the mind. Since there was very little that she could do to change the existing order of things, she could at least contribute indirectly to the betterment of mankind by practicing the tenets that she had learned from the Encyclopedists. And while she expected no recognition in a society that knew only distinctions of birth and wealth, she reasoned that by cultivating her intellect, patterning her behavior after the models she admired, and sharing her thoughts and feelings with a few friends like Sophie, she could not fail to attain that inner serenity without which happiness is impossible.

Whatever doubts Mlle Phlipon entertained about metaphysics or about the perfectibility of human faculties, at least she never had the slightest doubt that her main purpose on earth was to find happiness. But as a true daughter of the Enlightenment, she tended to equate happiness with moral excellence. The quest for individual fulfillment must be founded on one's responsibilities to the community at large and cannot be divorced from the general good. And as long as an absolute government made the individual powerless to act on the forces that shape his destiny, he ought nevertheless strive for personal accomplishment without expecting the rewards that should rightly be his. It should be obvious by now that, having renounced the spiritual comfort of religion, Manon found a measure of reassurance in the stern ethics of Stoicism. No wonder she held a secret sympathy for the uncompromising Jansenists, even though she was far from endorsing their theology. So much so that a visiting abbé once was greatly shocked to hear her say that, if forced to make a choice, she would prefer the heretical Jansenists, because of their moral integrity, to the worldly, all too accommodating Jesuits.

After much soul-searching, Manon finally opted for a sentimental form of deism, which she was the first to recognize as an answer to her emotional, rather than intellectual, needs: "In the silence of my study or in the course of a theoretical discussion, I shall agree with the atheist or materialist that certain mysteries are insoluble. But in the midst of the countryside and in the presence of nature, my heart soars to the vivifying principle that animates all things, to the intelligence that orders them, to the goodness that makes the scene so delightful to my senses." [18]

The reader should not be too surprised if he finds this profession of faith to be almost identical in content and style with Rousseau's own oft-expressed religious creed. "Sometimes in the privacy of my study," he confided to Mme d'Epinay, "with my hands pressed tight over my eyes or in the darkness of the night, I am of the opinion that there is no God. But look yonder: the rising of the sun, as it scatters the mists that cover the earth and lays bare the wondrous scene of nature, disperses at the same moment all darkness from my soul. I find my faith again, and my God, and my belief in Him. I admire and adore Him, and I prostrate myself in His presence." [19] Both the master and his disciple rejected intellectual proofs of God and relied on a theology of the heart and the senses. Such was the religion of Mlle Phlipon; such would be the religion of Mme Roland on the eve of her death. The Revolution by instituting the Terror would weaken her faith in man, it could never undermine her steadfast trust in divine justice.

Not all of Manon's time was taken up with the study of philosophy. Music continued to afford her many delightful hours of rewarding recreation. Her teacher, who prided himself on being something of a composer, undertook to instruct his gifted pupil in the theory of harmony. But Manon was much happier improvising on her guitar or violin a simple song with lyrics of her own composition than poring over the complicated mathematics of counterpoint. When the Abbé Jeauket, a renowned virtuoso of the harpsichord who had even taught Marie-Antoinette in Vienna, came to Paris and moved to Mlle Phlipon's neighborhood, he begged the young girl's mother to let him give her lessons: "What a shame," he exclaimed after having listened to Manon play, "to be humming over a guitar when one has the means of learning to invent and execute beautiful music on the first of all instruments!" [20] Jeauket was convinced that the engraver's daughter had the makings of an artist, but Mme Phlipon could not be persuaded to let her daughter be anything more than a competent nonprofessional. Women, in her opinion, were meant to be dutiful wives and devoted mothers—not objects of public exhibition.

Having all but given up her ambition of becoming a Latin scholar, Manon set herself the task of mastering one or two modern languages. Italian, the tongue of the great Renaissance humanists and poets, was selected first and before long she could read Dante and Petrarch in the original. And, of course, no disciple of the Enlightenment would consider his education complete without a good knowledge of English. The day Manon found that she could comprehend an English text without resorting to translations she experienced great satisfaction, for now she would be able to study at first hand all those dramatists, poets, and novelists about whom French writers spoke with such enthusiasm. In turn she discovered Milton and Shakespeare, Young and Thomson, Pope and Richardson.

The neoclassical conventions which still prevailed in France and caused Voltaire to say of Shakespeare that he was a "barbarian of genius" did not hamper Manon's appreciation of the Bard, whom she admired for following no other law than "nature and his own genius." Unlike many of her contemporaries, she was not unduly concerned with his neglect of the three unities, with his mingling of the noble and trivial, and with his many violations of what the French called *la bienséance* (propriety). Among the poets, Manon was fond of quoting Pope, but it was especially to the new lyricism of Young, Thomson, and Gray that her romantic sensibility eagerly responded. "If you want to know me," she wrote to Sophie, "read Young." [21] As for Thomson, he became her favorite poet and in the presence of a beautiful natural setting, she could think of nothing more appropriate than the *Seasons,* large portions of which she committed to memory. As for the English novelists, she looked upon Richardson and Fielding as "the undisputed masters in this genre." [22] It was especially Richardson's *Clarissa,* the six volumes of which she devoured with rapt interest, that revealed to her that novels need not be frivolous. "No one has written a novel capable of sustaining comparison with *Clarissa,*" was her comment, "It is the masterpiece in that genre, the model and despair of all imitators." [23] Richardson combined in a unique manner the ingredients that had special appeal for readers of Manon's generation: minute realism, sentimental moralism, and a skillful use of the epistolary form to create suspense and pathos. Diderot's dithyrambic essay on Richardson clearly shows what profound affinities there existed between the French reading public and the English novelist. It was Richardson who opened Manon's eyes to the exciting possibilities that lie in a faithful depiction of everyday life and ordinary humans confronted by a moral dilemma. How fervently she identified with the writer's virtuous character, Clarissa! How she wept over the hapless heroine's misfortunes at the hands of that rake Lovelace! And how earnestly she vowed to guard against her own sensibility so as not to allow some *roué* ever to get the better of her!

Nor was Manon's interest in England confined to its literature. Beginning with Montesquieu's *Esprit des Lois* and Voltaire's *Lettres anglaises,* she familiarized herself with the nation's political and social institutions. Other, more technical monographs, like Delolme's study of the English constitution, followed until she became thoroughly versed in English history from the Magna Carta to the reign of George III. Of special interest to her was the victory of parliamentarianism over absolute monarchy culminating in the Glorious Revolution of 1688. In English politics and economics Manon perceived a realistic and pragmatic approach to the dynamics of society, a rational utilization of the individual's creative abilities. And in English literature she admired the artistic manifestations of a bold and vigorous spirit of individualism, unconstrained by academic rules and conventions.

One day it occurred to Manon that her program of study was sorely lacking in the sciences. Surely, here was an opportunity to develop clarity of thought and perhaps to discipline those fits of moodiness of which she sometimes was the helpless prey. For while developing her mind, Manon noted with some concern that her temper remained excessively emotional and that her imagination had a way of casting a spell over her critical faculties. Melancholy, that bittersweet ingredient of precocious self-awareness, was working on a heart all too disposed to it by nature. Before having tasted the joys of life, Manon was on the point of becoming disillusioned with it, and intense study had only succeeded in feeding this world-weariness. History, quite frequently, showed her "nothing but the horrors which have been committed in every age and, under different names, none but rapacious conquerors and senseless victims." [24] Even her beloved writers and poets sometimes appeared as nothing more than clever deceivers who wove around her a magic web of glittering lies and illusions.

No, there was only one way to tame this tumultuous sensibility and to free herself from the beguiling and dangerous world of feelings and thoughts which invariably left her profoundly dissatisfied with the world of realities. And that was to occupy her mind with clear, objective propositions, with evident, indisputable truths. Laying aside poetry, fiction, and even history and philosophy, Manon first tackled the natural sciences. Buffon's combination of erudition and style enchanted her; she discovered that the *Histoire naturelle* was as readable as a novel. Réaumur's and Bonnet's studies of insect life and Maupertuis' observations on snails completed her investigation of this new area, one which was immensely popular in the eighteenth century.

It was time to turn one's attention to the pure sciences. Algebra, mathematics, geometry, and physics kept Manon occupied for long hours at a stretch. Among Mme Roland's manuscripts kept at the Bibliothèque Nationale, one can still see dozens of pages covered with algebraic formulas, geometry problems, and long extracts from the Abbé Nollet's *Leçons de physique expérimentale.* So possessed was she by this new enthusiasm that she copied the standard textbook on geometry of the time, Clairaut's *Eléments de géométrie,* from cover to cover, including the graphs. After mastering the equations of the first degree, however, Manon began to weary of xs and ys. It was more rewarding, she felt, to muse over a poem than to waste away over radicals. If the natural sciences, especially botany, would continue to hold attractions for her through the years, she gave up mathematics and physics for good and was never tempted to take them up again.

In her middle teens, Manon began composing essays on a variety of philosophical and moral subjects. Her desire for self-expression needed more than the critical summaries of readings or even the lengthy letters to Sophie. While deriving their inspiration from the works of the *philosophes,* and lacking true originality, these youthful writings possess an engaging charm and sincerity and evidence undeniable literary skill. As the spontaneous outpourings of an adolescent mind shaped by the Encyclopedists, they throw a revealing light not only on the intellectual and emotional evolution of Mme Roland herself, but on attitudes characteristic of the entire revolutionary generation. As such, these exercises, most of which are still in manuscript form at the Bibliothèque Nationale, constitute a fascinating document in the history of ideas.[25] For indeed, Mme Roland is the only member of her generation to have left such an intimate and complete record of her inner life. In these schoolgirl notebooks can be found all the commonplaces of the Enlightenment: man's right to terrestrial happiness, arguments in favor of natural religion, the benefits that are to be derived from political freedom and religious tolerance, even criticism of luxury and the unequal distribution of wealth and power. Here too are essays praising the simple, bucolic pleasures, true friendship and kindliness, an analysis of passionate love and its dangers, and a dissertation on Socrates and his heroic acceptance of an unjust death. Our young philosopher could hardly suspect that one day this lesson in Stoicism would stand her in good stead.

In more personal essays Manon also gave expression to moods that foreshadow the indefinable yearnings of the preromantics: here she celebrated the charms of rural life and the poignant melancholy that a beautiful natural setting can elicit in a sensitive soul. In her notebooks Manon, in short, could give free rein both to her fondness for analytical thought and to her penchant for introspection. Here she could pursue an idea or express a state of feeling in formal discourse, dialogue, allegory, or prose poem. Sometimes turning to verse to develop a theme, she would write charming, albeit somewhat naïve and amateurish, little poems. She even experimented with a fictional genre that was the rage of her day: the moral tale centered upon a conflict between love and moral duty. And her deft manipulation of pathos and didacticism shows that she understood the literary formula to perfection. Both in her prose and in her poems, Manon rendered, in richly descriptive imagery, a wintry scene, a fiery sunset, or the awakening of nature in the spring and the stirrings of a young girl's heart.

The tone of these writings is almost always serious and elevated, frequently a trifle sententious. Yet, even though they borrow heavily from well-known literary models, in them we perceive a mind and sensibility closely attuned to the aspirations of a changing and restless era.

With her literary facility and irrepressible urge to write, Manon might have considered becoming a woman of letters. But though she gave the matter much thought and was strongly tempted to make a name as an author and critic, she opted for obscurity and never came back on her decision. A combination of factors explains Mlle Phlipon's reluctance to embrace a literary career professionally. For one thing, Manon dreaded being looked upon as a *savante,* one of those overweening bluestockings who flaunt their intellectual superiority at the slightest provocation and who since Molière had become objects of universal ridicule. Even her limited social experience had exposed her to such ladies of learning, and she had always found them highly unsympathetic. And for another, she was by no means willing to defy openly the prejudices and conventions attendant to her sex in order to court fame. What chance for personal happiness did women of intellect have in a century where even the most liberal-minded men looked upon them with disfavor? "I have heard Diderot say," wrote Chamfort, an anecdotist and wit of some repute, "that a sensible man of letters might be the lover of a woman who writes books, but he ought to be the husband of one who knows only how to sew a shirt." [26] It was therefore not without justification that Mlle Phlipon shunned the dubious limelight of a literary career. In a society which regarded women artists and writers as freaks of nature, she was much better off, she reasoned, keeping her talent hidden and her notebooks carefully tucked away in her study.

To be sure, there were women in eighteenth-century France who had achieved renown in the world of letters, the arts, and even science. There was the brilliant Mme du Châtelet, mathematician, writer, and mistress of Voltaire. There were the promiscuous but gifted Mlle Clairon, the actress, the notoriously ugly but clever Mme de Puisieux, an essayist and former mistress of Diderot, whom Mlle Phlipon had occasion to observe during her stays at Vincennes, not to forget women novelists like Mme Riccoboni and Mme de Graffigny, who gained recognition as practitioners of a form of fiction that aptly mingled morality and sentiment. And from the days of the Regency, there had always been a number of popular hostesses who wielded an undeniable influence in literary circles—from the immensely clever and scandalous Mme de Tencin to the starchy, irreproachable Mme Necker, the mother of Mme de Staël.

For one who, like Manon, had much intelligence and energy, but no money or social connections, the difficulties involved in succeeding in the world would have been well-nigh insuperable. She might indeed have managed to escape her mediocre milieu by exploiting her charms, for she had the requisite good looks to select lovers among men of power and wealth. But nothing was more alien to her moral principles and retiring temperament. With her fastidious pride, she would have been totally incapable of seeking recognition by means of adroit scheming and well-publicized liaisons. She was quite content to cultivate whatever talents she had in the privacy of her study, lovingly polishing her essays and poems, occasionally lending her notebooks to a friend deemed worthy of such a privilege, but persistently refusing to submit her writings to public judgment or to attempt to make a name for herself in Parisian society.

FOUR

First Sorrow and New Friendships

WHILE TO AN OUTSIDER the Phlipon household appeared un-
clouded, forces were at work which would eventually make Manon's
financial position painfully precarious. The engraver, who had always had an undue fondness for beautiful, luxurious things, had of
late begun to speculate heavily, a fairly widespread trend among
the bourgeoisie as well as the aristocracy in the eighteenth century.
Lottery was the rage, and in order to raise the necessary money
Phlipon borrowed and freely drew from the family reserve and
from his daughter's dowry. And while the master pursued the chi-
merical dream of an easy fortune he deserted his shop and his apprentices became neglectful of their work. Customers dwindled,
preferring to place their orders with more reliable engravers after
noticing that assignments were poorly executed and after much delay. Manon stood by, helplessly watching her father ruin his business and squander her dowry. Yet she had to conceal her growing
anxiety so as not to alarm her mother, whose health was giving her
cause for added worry. Once a tirelessly active mistress of the house
and valuable overseer in the engraver's shop, Mme Phlipon now
sat for hours, silent and motionless, staring vaguely in front of her,
with an expression of sad resignation.

On the eve of Whitsuntide, in early June of 1775, the Phlipons
decided to spend the holidays in the nearby village of Meudon.[1]
It was hoped that this excursion and the fresh air would revive

the flagging spirits of the languishing Mme Phlipon. For more than a year she had been suffering from something resembling a bad head cold, which physicians were at a total loss to diagnose properly. The outing turned out to be a most pleasant affair. The weather was mild, the air full of summer promise, the boat trip delightfully leisurely and invigorating. Manon had always had a special fondness for the countrified atmosphere of Meudon, and she felt further encouraged upon seeing her mother's face take on some color and animation. When the family returned to Paris on the following Tuesday evening, the young girl was sufficiently reassured to leave the house and visit the good Sister Saint-Agatha at the Convent of the Congregation. But no sooner had she reached the convent than she felt oppressed by gloomy forebodings. Taking a hasty leave of the sisters, she rushed back home. As she approached the house, she noted several neighbors standing near the door and speaking in muffled voices. In the parlor her mother lay limply in an armchair, her head thrown back, her mouth open, and her eyes bulging. She had suddenly been struck by what appeared to be an attack of apoplexy. Doctors were summoned; a priest came and administered extreme unction. Holding a candlestick at the foot of the bed, Manon stood as though in a trance. When she was told that all was over, the violence of her sorrow frightened everyone. She fell into convulsions and had to be put to bed. Unable to weep or speak, she lay in a stupor. It was only a week later, when a letter of condolence from Sophie was read to her that, emerging from her dazed state, she broke out in violent, interminable sobs.[2]

Slowly, Manon regained a sense of reality and resumed her daily round of activities. But with her mother's passing the most carefree period in her life had abruptly come to an end. The lifelike portrait of Mme Phlipon by La Tour that hung in the parlor had to be taken down and placed out of Manon's sight; each time her gaze fell upon it she could not help weeping bitterly. Her father's insensitiveness and facile insouciance only aggravated her sorrow. Once he endeavored to console her by callously pointing out that Providence had done things for the best, even in this misfortune,

by decreeing that she should lose her mother, who had after all
fulfilled her task, rather than her father, who could still be very
useful to her.[3] More than ever Manon now retreated into her private world of books and dreams. Mme Phlipon had tempered somewhat the young girl's introvert tendencies. As Phlipon's absences
from the home became more frequent and prolonged—he even took
on a young mistress and stayed away for days on end—Manon was
quite alone for much of the time and also free to devote herself
completely to her intellectual pursuits. Soon father and daughter
were almost total strangers to each other and hardly ever exchanged
a word.

Mme Phlipon had been barely fifty at the time of her death, and
Manon, still unmarried at twenty-one, looked back on the previous
years as a paradise lost, comparable, in her own words, to "those
lovely spring mornings, when the serenity of the sky, the purity of
the air, the brilliance of the foliage, the scent of plants, enchant
everything that breathes, enhance one's awareness of life and bring
happiness by a sense of promise." [4] Four years later, in a letter to
Roland, she confided that the loss of her mother had been the most
shattering sorrow she had ever experienced and that it had left an
indelible hurt in her soul.[5]

Running the Phlipon household was simple enough. With the
capable assistance of Mignonne, the faithful family maid, Manon
managed to complete all her shopping and cooking by midday, re-
serving the afternoons and evenings for her favorite occupations.
Social calls were less frequent than during Mme Phlipon's lifetime;
Manon made no effort to encourage visits, except when the callers
shared her interests. Now that her mother was no longer there to
remind her of her obligations to the outside world, she ignored
them completely, taking as little part in the brilliant life of the
capital as if she had dwelled at the other end of the earth. An attitude of wariness became dominant in Manon's dealings with men.
To the company of young admirers she tended to prefer that of
more seasoned male friends. Young men were hotheaded and hence
dangerous for a dowryless single woman. Many of them, moreover,

in an age of cynical libertinage would have few scruples in beguiling and dishonoring the daughter of an unsuccessful engraver
and shopkeeper. Men past their youth, on the other hand, were for
the most part more reliable and appeared content to broaden her
horizons with their rich store of knowledge of the world and of
ideas. In 1776, having turned twenty-two, Manon came to the sober
realization that she had reached an age at which a still unmarried
girl could be considered a spinster. Together with the prosperity of
the Phlipon shop, candidates for the hand of his attractive daughter
had dwindled. Manon bravely summoned the teachings of the Stoics
in order to face the rather dim, cheerless perspective of a single,
solitary existence. The friendship of a few select beings would bring
her solace. She therefore poured all the repressed energy and emotions
of a passionate temperament into her epistolary effusions with Sophie
and Henriette and into her high-toned relationship with her elderly,
erudite admirers.

One of these was a liberal-minded nobleman with a strong interest
in good books and the proper sentimental appreciation of nature. M.
de Boismorel enjoyed one of those vaguely defined administrative
sinecures so numerous under the Old Régime, and this left him
with a great deal of leisure time to cultivate his private interests.
Manon had first met him when she was a twelve-year-old girl living with her paternal grandmother on the Ile Saint-Louis. M. de
Boismorel had been one of the old lady's charges when she still
worked as governess, and it was his mother who had so deeply
mortified young Manon with her haughty airs when Mme Phlipon
mère had decided to show off her grandchild to her former em-
ployers.[6] Far from sharing his mother's disdain for a girl of lowly
birth, Boismorel occasionally paid her visits, bringing books from
his library and describing the latest happenings in the social and
literary circles where he was a habitué. One day in June of 1775,
he called on Manon, probably to present his respects and condolences
over the recent loss of her mother. Manon happened to be out at
the time, but Phlipon, flattered at the interest shown by the aristocrat, boasted of his daughter's intellect and pointed to her writings,

which were lying on the table.[7] The visitor received permission to borrow the manuscripts so as to read them at leisure. When Manon returned she expressed displeasure over her father's indiscretion, but was soon reassured by a tactful and highly complimentary letter from Boismorel and an invitation, both for her and Phlipon, to his country estate of Bercy.[8] At first, she hesitated, remembering only too vividly how her pride had been made to suffer by the elder Mme de Boismorel's condescending words and patronizing manner. This time, however, she was graciously received by the host, his wife, and even by his imperious mother.[9] Thereafter, Manon occasionally visited the lovely country house, spending many hours in the well-stocked library and borrowing freely from it. Now and then, the old Mme de Boismorel would revert to her authoritarian ways, but Boismorel always interceded in time and soothed Manon's ruffled *amour-propre*.

It was thus that a warm intellectual friendship was established between the youthful bluestocking and the middle-aged nobleman, the "Sage of Bercy," as Manon liked to call Boismorel in a flattering analogy with Voltaire, the "Sage of Ferney." He took her to public sessions of the French Academy, where she heard the mathematician and Encyclopedist D'Alembert, the critic La Harpe, and the poet Delille deliver speeches.[10] D'Alembert's unimpressive appearance and squeaking voice made her realize that a philosopher's works are frequently more worth contemplating than his person. She was equally disappointed in the Abbé Delille, for whose poetry she had high regard, but who recited some of his verses in a monotonous, disagreeable tone. La Harpe's oratorical ability, on the other hand, made a more favorable impression on Mlle Phlipon. Being a great admirer of Rousseau, Boismorel organized an outing party to the valley of Montmorency, famous since the philosopher's stay there.[11] Sitting in the shade of the tall, century old trees, Manon made the appropriate reflections on the majesty of nature and on the genius of the man who had inhabited this valley. After a frugal dinner, the visitors proceeded to inspect the little house where Rousseau had composed some of his most famous works.

Because Boismorel resided in his country estate most of the year, he did not frequently come into the city and visit the shop on the Pont-Neuf, but he regularly corresponded with his young friend, exchanging with her comments on books, and encouraging her in her literary efforts. With tact and understanding, he guided her studies and endeavors. Indeed he was the first to advise Manon to consider seriously a career as a writer and to urge her to choose a literary genre that best suited her interests and talents. This gave her the opportunity of setting forth all her principles on the role of women in society and of justifying her aversion to becoming something of a public figure. Boismorel paid Manon the homage of delegating to her the task of composing an anonymous letter to his son, who was turning into a wastrel and heavy gambler, in order to impress him with a sense of his responsibilities and duties. The moral discourse Manon composed for this occasion has been preserved: in appropriately elevated style it portrays Duty, Virtue, and Happiness merging in a single, glorious apotheosis and, invoking Socrates, Demosthenes, Cicero, and many others, it urges the young man to forsake his wayward life and direct his steps toward the path of moral excellence, the only one that leads to happiness.[12] The "Sage of Bercy" judged the letter so perfect that he mailed it without a change to his son. When the young man received the anonymous epistle, he fancied it had been written by Duclos, the Academician and author, a conjecture that greatly flattered the real author's vanity.[13]

No doubt it was not just wit and erudition which attracted Boismorel to Manon. Her wholesome good looks had something to do with this kindly interest, but it must also be recognized that with her the aging and lonely nobleman could talk about intellectual and literary matters. Mme de Boismorel, a deeply pious person with not the slightest interest in philosophy or literature, did not envisage this friendship with too kindly an eye. But she had to resign herself, since Mlle Phlipon's conduct was so evidently beyond reproach or suspicion. Once, as the young girl was airing her opinion on the latest dress styles and condemning the frills and feathers which were the vogue, her hostess pointedly asked her whether she ever wore feathers herself. "I never wear them, Madame, because they would announce a condition in life and a fortune which do not suit an artist's daughter who goes about in the streets on foot." Mme de Boismorel must have been somewhat irritated by this polite but unmistakably defiant reply, for she persisted in her questioning: "But would you wear these frills if you belonged to a different class?" This time, Manon was beginning to bristle and she replied in icy tones: "I don't know; I attach little importance to such trifles. I only consider what is suitable to myself." Mme de Boismorel put an end to this exchange by exclaiming with barely disguised ironic hostility: "You are a real *philosophe!*" [14]

In September of 1776, Manon lost her friend, for M. de Boismorel died rather suddenly after a brief illness.[15] Perhaps more sincerely than his own son, she mourned the passing of one who had afforded her many hours of intellectual companionship and who had renewed her confidence in her ability. It goes without saying that Boismorel's family never made the slightest effort to keep in touch with the engraver's daughter and she, in turn, was much too proud to continue visiting these nobles, now that her sole link with them had been severed. Indeed Boismorel's widow took it upon herself to send for Phlipon in order to warn him of the dire consequences that would no doubt result from his daughter's dangerous readings. Manon, who learned of Mme de Boismorel's misgivings and of her father's visit, related the episode to Sophie in a half-humorous, half-irritated manner:

Speaking of adventures, I have lately discovered something which does not make me happy. My father was recently summoned to Bercy by the widow of Boismorel. She is excessively devout. She spoke a great deal of me and exhorted my father to protect me carefully from anything that might weaken my religious principles, declaiming against Jean-Jacques Rousseau, whom she does not like, and against Voltaire, whom she abhors, treating all those whose faith is not orthodox as miserable small pen-pushers, etc., and adding that all these fashionable authors had struck my fancy and that this would have to be watched. "I do not conceive," she added, "how M. de Boismorel, who was a reasonable man, took it into his head to lend Bayle to Mademoiselle Phlipon! Bayle, whose works I would burn on the spot if I could manage to pick them all up!" [16]

Another interesting newcomer among Manon's more constant visitors during the year 1776 was Joseph de Sainte-Lette, a sixty-year-old scholar and world traveler who had spent thirteen years in Louisiana, where he had traded with the Indians. He had also served as an administrator in India and had come back to Paris on a humane mission: to obtain enough money from the French government in order to facilitate the purchase of rice for the famine-ridden Indians.[17] Manon was impressed by Sainte-Lette's wealth of experience and knowledge, by his dignified yet warm manner, and by his profound understanding of the human heart. Sainte-Lette, moreover, had been a personal friend of Helvétius, and he declared himself an outright atheist, although he also admired Rousseau, an opponent of atheism. For hours they talked on all sorts of subjects. And since both were very fond of the sentimental poetry then in vogue, they would dampen their handkerchiefs over the more "sublime" verses of Jean-Baptiste Rousseau and the melodramatic scenes of Voltaire's tragedies. Or else, Manon would listen to Sainte-Lette's accounts of his travels along the Mississippi, of the life led by the settlers, or of the strange and fascinating customs of the natives. Sainte-Lette also painted a vivid picture of the abuses of colonialism, the cruel lot of the Negro slaves in America and the barbarous custom of trading children in India. At last Manon could speak with someone whose knowledge was not limited to one civilization and whose outlook on life was at once truly cosmopolitan and humanitarian. That an atheist should exhibit such generosity of spirit and compassion for his less fortunate fellow men confirmed Manon's conviction that one need not necessarily believe in reward and punishment after death to lead a virtuous and useful life on this earth. For her part, however, she found deism more emotionally satisfying than outright atheism. Thus it was the elderly and warm-hearted Sainte-Lette, a man physically worn out by an adventurous life but who had retained spiritual youthfulness and enthusiasm, who excited Manon's curiosity about foreign lands and particularly America. The outbreak of the American Revolution only intensified this interest. In November of 1777, Sainte-Lette set out for India after a ten-month stay in Paris. Manon never saw him again, for he died shortly after his arrival.

FIVE

The Revelation of Jean-Jacques Rousseau

THE LOSS OF A BELOVED MOTHER and the companionship of elderly, disenchanted men had exacerbated Manon's sensibilities, making her more prone than ever to bouts of melancholy and to that exaltation of feeling that was sweeping over much of Europe in the wake of the age of reason. The reign of Voltaire was imperceptibly, yet irrevocably, giving way to the cult of Rousseau.[1] Every book that passed through Mlle Phlipon's hands heightened this emotional mood, but it was left to Jean-Jacques Rousseau himself to open her eyes to the full implications of certain ideas and sentiments.

Curiously enough, until 1776, of all the eighteenth-century writers Rousseau had been the one with whose works Manon had had the most superficial acquaintance. Heretofore, she had read only his *Emile,* and that without the deep involvement she presently experienced. Rousseau renewed her faith in mankind by depicting the conjugal and domestic happiness to which a virtuous woman was entitled. Her mood of depression partially allayed, she dared expect something more from life than loneliness and disappointment. Rousseau, moreover, was the magician who threw a blazing light on the hidden causes of her malaise. He made her see that, by harboring aspirations which transcended her social rank, she was not some freak of nature. In a language she readily understood and to which she responded with both her heart and her mind he gave eloquent expression to those painfully repressed longings and resentments common to a whole class of serious intellectuals who felt hampered by their circumstances and who, on their own, had discovered and become committed to the philosophy of the Enlightenment. It is no mere coincidence that, at approximately the same time, obscure youths and students who would one day become famous, were experiencing a similarly decisive revelation. To Rousseau who, more boldly than any Encyclopedist, beheld and pointed out the social wrongs masked by rococo elegance and the brilliance of the *salons*, future leaders of the Revolution such as Robespierre, Danton, Brissot, and Marat turned for guidance.

In her *Memoirs* Mme Roland, reminiscing about her youth, wondered at the relative late date at which she first read all the important works of Rousseau, attributing this delay to her mother's watchfulness, for even though Mme Phlipon had exercised little control over her daughter's readings, she had somehow sensed that the highly impressionable Manon might draw a dangerous lesson from *La Nouvelle Héloïse*. Retrospectively Mme Roland approved of this cautiousness: "It was well for me that this was the case: he would have turned my brain, I should have read nothing else. Perhaps, as it is, I fear that he has strengthened my weak side, so to speak." [2] And by that she meant that Rousseau kindled an already passionate temperament, awakened too sensitive a heart to dreams of fulfillment that had so far been dormant.

Yet when Manon first set her eyes on *La Nouvelle Héloïse*, she was no longer a naïve, uninformed girl with emotions uncontrolled by reason. By 1776 she had read and assimilated the contents of a staggering number of books and mastered the philosophic and political theories of men like Locke, Montesquieu, Voltaire, Helvétius, to name but a few of the thinkers, writers, and critics she had successively studied in a most thoroughgoing manner. But it was Rousseau, rather than Montesquieu or even Voltaire, who shaped her whole moral being and, perhaps unbeknown to herself, determined her every important act both in her private and political life. Not that he taught her anything that was absolutely new. Most of his ideas she had already encountered in one or another form in the course of her previous readings. But he presented these ideas with such compelling eloquence and force that Manon Phlipon, together with most of her contemporaries, somehow acquired the conviction that he was addressing himself directly to her, that he alone had truly perceived the predicament with which she found herself confronted. She had already dimly perceived these thoughts and feelings but now could imbibe them so completely as to make them her own for the rest of her life. No wonder, then, that a historian like Michelet, whose own humble birth and background made him especially sensitive to the mentality of gifted plebeians impatiently chafing under prerogatives of birth and wealth, envisaged Mme Roland as a true daughter of Jean-Jacques Rousseau, one "perhaps even more legitimate than those that sprang from his pen," since, unlike the aristocratic Julie of *La Nouvelle Héloïse* and the high-born Sophie of *Emile,* she was a commoner in whose veins ran the rich, vigorous blood of the Frenchwoman of simple, popular stock whose line goes back to a Joan of Arc.[3]

It was a chance occurrence, for any event of apparently coincidental nature can change the course of an existence, that placed Rousseau's works in the hands of Manon Phlipon. She was still mourning her mother's death when a friend of the family brought her Rousseau's by then famous novel, *La Nouvelle Héloïse,* in the hope of distracting her from her sorrow. The book, with its brooding romanticism and sentimental atmosphere, its vivid depiction of passion pitted against familial and social duty, its idyllic scenes of marriage, country life, motherhood, and its lengthy digressions on manners and morals, made an unforgettable impression upon Manon.[4] At last she had found a kindred soul who also happened to be a transcendent genius and who knew how to speak directly to anguished, sincere women struggling in the difficult path of virtue. After completing *La Nouvelle Héloïse,* Manon wrote to Sophie Cannet: "Rousseau is the friend of humanity, its benefactor and mine. . . . I fully realize that I owe him the best part of myself. His genius has warmed me, I have felt elevated and ennobled by him. . . . His *Héloïse* is a masterpiece of sentiment."[5] Rousseau

had warned that the book should not be allowed into the hands
of young girls for fear that it might dangerously kindle their imagination and stir their senses.[6] Going further than her Master, Manon
stoutly upheld the morality of the novel and its usefulness to the
fair sex: "The woman who has read it without becoming a better
person, or at least without having that desire, has a soul of mud
and a listless spirit. She will never rise above the common level." [7]

In Saint-Preux, the idealized alter ego of Rousseau himself and
the hero of *La Nouvelle Héloïse*, she saw the perfect lover, but in
the elderly, world-wise Wolmar she recognized the perfect husband.
Secretly she yearned to be a Julie to some worthy Saint-Preux, yet
in her quest for a happy marriage continued to envisage a Wolmar-
type mate. She was, of course, quite unaware of this inconsistency
and many years later would discover it at her own expense. Curiously enough, this strong-willed, strong-minded young woman fancied herself another delicate, romantic Julie, and this confusion was
to contribute to her delusions, to her falsely sentimental interpretation of her own nature. In the blond, frail and aristocratic heroine
the vigorous, determined bourgeois girl thought she could mirror
her soul. In her *Memoirs,* she wrote nearly twenty years later: "It
seemed to me that I then found my true substance, that Rousseau
became the interpreter of feelings and ideas I had had before him,
but that he alone could explain to my satisfaction. . . . Rousseau
then made the same impression on me as had Plutarch when I was
eight. . . . Plutarch had predisposed me to become a republican;
he had inspired in me the true enthusiasm for public virtues and
liberty. Rousseau showed me the domestic happiness to which I had
a right to aspire and the ineffable delights I was capable of tasting." [8]

Avoiding as best she could those "amphibious beings" [9] one meets
in society, Manon sometimes experienced a discouraging feeling of
insignificance in this vast, indifferent cosmos. In those moments she
realized with an especially poignant acuteness her helplessness as a
woman of humble birth and no means. The world then seemed to
close in on her, and she experienced something akin to dread before
the unfathomable mysteries of life: "To my weary eyes the magnifi-

cent scene of the universe appears covered with a veil. I don't know what mist, similar to that of the mornings of autumn, surrounds and confuses the objects on which I would wish to fasten my gaze. . . . Already the sweetest illusions have vanished from me before I tasted all their charms." [10] The youthful Mme Roland was one of the first to suffer from that peculiar malady which the great Romantics in France would call *le mal du siècle*. Having cultivated her sensibility to a state of exquisite awareness, she noted with some dismay the results of constant introspection and self-analysis. Her letters and essays abound in references to a new state of mind which was sadness without grief. On some days she felt happy and cheerful, and then suddenly, with no apparent reason, her elation was followed by unpredictable fits of depression. Here again, Rousseau furnished her with an explanation for what had so far baffled her. Now she could savor her emotions in the knowledge that her moodiness was only the mark of an unusually sensitive soul.

Having found in Rousseau that exaltation of feeling and of self which finds justification in elevated ideas, Manon suddenly grew considerably more critical toward writers she had heretofore placed above all others. We note, in particular, a new and almost satirical tone in her comments on Voltaire, a change that hardly surprises us in view of the resounding Voltaire-Rousseau quarrel, of which no one in the eighteenth century could remain unaware. Like most of her contemporaries, the future Mme Roland came to look upon Voltaire as an extraordinarily witty, talented playwright, poet, and storyteller, and as a courageous denouncer of superstition and ignorance, but saw in Rousseau the "benefactor of humanity," [11] a new Messiah who had illuminated the secrets of the heart as well as of the mind. Voltaire, to be sure, appealed to one's critical sense, to one's judgment and intelligence, but who like Rousseau could stir one's sensibility? On the eve of the Romantic age, hardly anyone could resist the strangely moving voice of a man who dared lay himself bare to all, who dared reveal his mistakes and weaknesses with a mixture of pride and humility that made it so uniquely compelling.

While the immensely rich and successful Voltaire died in a blaze of publicity, Jean-Jacques, who had steadfastly refused pensions and honors, shunned the court and official recognition, and persevered amidst innumerable persecutions and painful physical ailments, would reach his end in the obscurity of voluntary retreat, his eyes fixed on the judgment of posterity rather than on the approval of a fickle public. No wonder, then, that this tragic and in many ways pathetic figure should become the object of a quasi-religious worship on the part of men and women of the revolutionary generation. We find a curiously intimate relationship between the Citizen of Geneva and his immediate disciples, a relationship that is borne out by the innumerable letters addressed to him by those who looked upon the author of *La Nouvelle Héloïse* as a trusted friend to whom one could confide delicate problems, especially problems of the heart.

After completing *La Nouvelle Héloïse,* Manon devoured all the other writings by Rousseau. Her religious convictions were directly influenced by Rousseau's "Profession of Faith of a Savoyard Vicar," as set forth in the famous chapter of the *Emile.* After her prolonged and anguished search for a religious belief, after the many doubts that had beset and troubled her, in Rousseau she found at last wholly satisfying answers to her questions. It was Rousseau who countered the effect of atheists like d'Holbach and Helvétius, as well as of personal friends like Sainte-Lette, by inducing her to turn to a benevolent God and to a divine, personal Providence. He justified her need for such consoling and reassuring beliefs. From that time until she would draw her last breath, even in the most trying circumstances, her trust in a just and all-powerful Deity that not only regulates the heavens and the stars, but that also judges man's actions and rewards the virtuous would no longer waver.

Voltaire's intellectualized concept of an impersonal and detached God that set the world in motion and thereafter rested, never interfering with his creation and with the affairs of men was as alien to Mme Roland's temperament as it was to Rousseau's. For the same reason, she could not resign herself to the atheistic notion of a universe governed by chance and matter in motion. In this respect,

as in many others, Rousseau encouraged her to follow her own feelings at the expense of purely intellectual arguments. Trusting no
longer the theologians and philosophers, she turned her gaze inward
to find a personal, compassionate God. By the same token, Rousseau
fostered an already strongly developed tendency to be self-centered.
Following her Master, Manon came to look upon herself as a being
apart, as a person who, to her delight and misfortune, had been endowed with great depths of perceptiveness and sensibility.

   Rousseau's political theories made as profound an impression on
the young woman as his more purely literary and personal works.[12]
Before chancing upon the *Discourse on the Origin of Inequality*
and the *Social Contract,* she had often felt, but in a confused sort
of way, that the French social system was sorely lacking. As the
daughter of a commoner, she had been exposed to the haughtiness of
aristocrats. She had come into contact with the nobility through her
paternal grandmother, who had served as a governess, and through an
uncle, who was an overseer on the vast estate of a prodigiously
wealthy farmer-general (tax collector under the Old Régime). Like
Rousseau, she had known the humiliation of being invited to dinner to find herself relegated to the pantry with the servants. She
had blushed with repressed fury and indignation upon hearing her
grandmother condescendingly called "Mademoiselle." Ever since
she had become aware of her surroundings and begun to reason she
had been painfully conscious of the inequities and unjust distinctions of a caste system.

   Quite naturally, Manon was eager to share her new insights with
her friend and confidante Sophie Cannet. To her disappointment,
however, Sophie, herself a well-born, wealthy young woman and one,
moreover, who did not possess Manon's rebellious turn of mind,
evidenced only coolness toward the radical thinker from Geneva.
For this daughter of provincial bourgeois who had found their way
into the nobility through magistracy and finance, Rousseau had a
dangerous heretic air. Manon was vexed to see her best friend, the
one whom she liked to regard as her spiritual alter ego, oppose banal
clichés to her enthusiastic comments. Summoning her most per-

suasive style, she repeatedly endeavored to win Sophie over to her
side, and to assuage her friend's fears she stressed the positive,
orthodox aspects of Rousseau's thought: his hostility to atheism, his
belief in a personal God and in the immortality of the soul, his rational approach to social evils. The *Emile*, she assured Sophie, sur-
passed all the erudite reasonings of theologians and metaphysicians
alike in demonstrating the existence of an all-powerful, benevolent
Deity, and his political doctrine was consistent with an enlightened,
forward-looking monarchy. She even stoutly upheld the morality
of his famous and controversial novel, claiming that it was the only
one of its kind that could both move and elevate a woman's soul.
And when Sophie, somewhat at a loss before Manon's relentless
rhetoric, shifted her criticism to the personal plane, citing Rousseau's
notorious quarrel with Voltaire and the other *philosophes,* the disciple, rising to the challenge, made an impassioned apology for the
character of Jean-Jacques:

All the faults that he is accused of amount to the vague charge of un-
sociability. But can we seriously expect a man who works hard in his
study to frequent society like our gentlemen of leisure? There is absurdity in wanting the same individual to possess contradictory qualities. . . . What is more, persecutions, injustices have almost given
Rousseau the right no longer to believe in the sincerity of men. Tormented in all countries, betrayed by those whom he regarded as his
friends, persecuted by his ungrateful motherland which he enlightened,
served and made illustrious, the butt of envy and spitefulness, is it
surprising that an obscure and secluded retreat should seem to him the
only desirable refuge? They very nearly put up a scaffold for this man
for whom another century would have raised altars! He is presently
about sixty-eight years old [Manon is in error; in 1776, Rousseau was
sixty-four]; his poor health, his infirmities would justify retirement,
even if there were no other reasons.[13]

Furthermore, Sophie was warned that any criticism of Rousseau,
no matter how mild or well-meaning, caused her friend chagrin and
unhappiness.[14] One can already perceive, in Mlle Phlipon's fanatic
espousal of Rousseauism, the emotionalism and obstinacy that would
mark Mme Roland's politics after 1789 and make compromise with

those who did not completely share her views well-nigh impossible. Although she commended Rousseau's love of privacy and solitude, she nevertheless resolved, in February 1776, to attempt to see him in person.[15] Perhaps the secret hope that the great man would readily recognize in her a kindred soul and offer words of encouragement, which she would treasure all her life, had something to do with this bold decision. Moreover, an unhoped-for opportunity presented itself: it so happened that one of Manon's more constant visitors at the time was a Genevan living in Paris, a certain Moré, who knew Rousseau and had the privilege of visiting him now and then in his garret apartment on the rue de la Plâtrière, today rue Jean-Jacques Rousseau.[16] It will perhaps be remembered that, in 1770, Jean-Jacques, after enforced wanderings following the condemnation of his *Emile*, had settled once more in Paris, a city he had so sternly condemned and that nevertheless tolerated his presence, albeit unofficially, with greater generosity than his native and much extolled Geneva. Cut off from his former associates and friends, he led an extremely retired existence, earning his living at his old trade of copying music. Like Rousseau's father, Moré was a clockmaker by profession. It was he who presented Mlle Phlipon with a complete edition of Rousseau's works.[17]

Manon decided to write to Rousseau in the name of their common acquaintance and, after a few days' wait, fetch an answer in person: a perfect pretext for rendering a personal homage to a man she revered more than any other. When Manon judged that Rousseau had had sufficient time to read her missive, she set off for the rue de la Plâtrière in the company of Mignonne, the family maid whom she treated as a companion more than as a servant.[18] It was with a sense of awe and rising expectation that she entered a shoemaker's alley and climbed the narrow, winding staircase to the third floor room where dwelled the aging writer. Unfortunately for the visitor, it was not Rousseau himself, but his common-law wife, Thérèse Levasseur, who half-opened the door, fixing upon the intruder a cold, hard stare. In a letter to Sophie, Manon has given a vivid description of the ensuing dialogue. Thérèse, she noted with feminine awareness, was neatly but simply dressed. She wore a plain gown protected by a large apron; an ordinary round but immaculately white bonnet covered her hair:

—Madame, is this where Monsieur Rousseau lives?
—Yes, Mademoiselle.
—Could I speak to him in person?
—What do you want from him?
—I came to fetch the answer to a letter I wrote him several days ago.
—Mademoiselle, you cannot speak to him, but you can tell the people who made you write, for surely it is not you who wrote a letter like that. . . .
—I beg your pardon. . . .
—Why, the handwriting alone shows that it is from a man.
—Do you want to see me write?

But Thérèse, keeping her hand on the doorknob all the while, remained adamant:

—All I can tell you is that my husband has absolutely renounced everything; he would like to be of service, but he is old enough to be entitled to a rest.
—I know, but at least I should have felt honored to have received this message from him personally. I would have taken advantage of this opportunity to present my homage to the man I esteem the most in the world. Please, accept it in his stead, Madame.[19]

Manon repaired home with the slight satisfaction that Rousseau had thought enough of her literary style, spelling, and handwriting to believe them to be the work of a man. But her disappointment at not having been admitted in the presence of the great man in no way dimmed her enthusiasm for him.

In 1776, Mlle Phlipon could not have yet known Rousseau's *Confessions,* since these would be published only after his death. Her later correspondence reveals, however, that she read the first six books as soon as they appeared in 1782.[20] When the second part came out in 1789, not even the dramatic events of that year could divert Mme Roland from plunging immediately into the last six books of the *Confessions.*[21] But even more significantly, when imprisonment and the shadow of the guillotine would reward her revolutionary zeal, Mme Roland would seek in the *Confessions* a source of consolation and moral strength and the necessary inspiration to write her own autobiography. To be sure, she could not fail to realize that to tell all is no easy matter. Not only does it entail the complex problem of sincerity, but also that of loyalty to friends, who might not always be projected in the most flattering light. After giving these questions some thought, Mme Roland, encouraged by Rousseau's example, resolved to be ruthlessly bold in her revelations. From her prison cell she was to write to a friend: "These [her *Memoirs*] will be, as you say, my *Confessions*, for I won't conceal anything. I have duly considered everything and made up my mind. I shall tell all, absolutely all. This is the only way one can be useful." [22] Only a true disciple of Rousseau could have subscribed with such total confidence to the value of reliving retrospectively one's existence, of revealing publicly the hidden recesses of one's inner world, of expecting posterity to be impartial in its judgment. She therefore set out to weave and compress the complex and often contradictory reality of human experience into the orderly fabric of a narrative, recounting in terms vivid and frequently poetic and with a gift for humor and pathos those apparently insignificant, yet highly meaningful, experiences that are common to all human lives. Like Rousseau, she is at her best when depicting in tenderly wistful scenes the delights and wonders of childhood, and the first sorrows and fits of rebellion before adult injustice and arbitrariness.

Like Rousseau, Mme Roland was endowed with a strongly self-centered and sensuous nature and, in her strivings for moral and religious excellence, was capable of complacent exhibitionism. Quite unconsciously, she constantly directed upon herself the spotlight and upon friends and foes alike she tended to look as supporting characters, for life to her was a drama in which she had been destined to play the main part. That this part was to turn out to be that of a tragic heroine she could not at first suspect, but when the time came to play that role, she would almost welcome the opportunity. And accomplished actress that she was, she would not fail to utter the right words and accompany these with the appropriate gestures.

Not that in this she ever lacked absolute sincerity and conviction. To Mme Roland the world was a stage, and she came to identify herself completely with the ideal she had constructed out of her readings and observations. Her sensibility fashioned by Rousseau and by the current atmosphere of self-indulgent exaltation and sentimentality, she thought herself the most candid and spontaneous of women, when in reality few thoughts and sentiments expressed by her had not at first passed the scrutiny of her critical faculties.

Of truth and sincerity this disciple of Rousseau would make a veritable cult and, as we have already seen, did not hesitate to sacrifice in the process some of the *délicatesse* expected of a woman of virtue. The modern reader is at times made to feel somewhat uncomfortable, not so much with what Mme Roland reveals in the course of her *Memoirs*, for it is relatively mild, but rather with her invariable aplomb and unruffled self-assurance. It is as though she derived such satisfaction from her blameless conduct and truthfulness that she did not find it necessary to exercise tact and savoir-faire. The great ladies of French letters, a Mme de Sévigné in her letters or a Mme de Lafayette in her novels, could not have committed such errors in good taste. There is something unmistakably petit bourgeois in much of Mme Roland's outlook that reflects on her literary style, an unconscious smugness which, it should be pointed out, is also evident in the best writers of the age such as Diderot and Rousseau himself. Well-born women of the eighteenth century, on the other hand, like Mme de Tencin or Mme du Châtelet, could be amoral; they were never priggish or complacent.

In 1776, the Academy of Besançon organized a literary competition on the question whether the education of women could contribute to making men better citizens. Certainly the subject could not have been better chosen to appeal to one who, like Manon, had been greatly concerned with this very same problem. What finer opportunity to develop an essay on an issue dear to her heart? Besides, had not Rousseau himself been launched on his career by competing successfully for a literary prize offered by a provincial academy, that of Dijon? Feverishly, Manon composed an essay, which has been preserved and which possesses undeniable qualities as a thoughtful and literary piece.[23] She sent it in, along with far better-known participants like Bernardin de Saint-Pierre, another Rousseau disciple whose main title to fame is his prose idyll, *Paul et Virginie.* Manon defended women's right to education but, at the same time, pointed up the need for general reform, without which the idea of bettering one sex through the influence of the other remained a purely academic exercise. For some reason, the Academy, perhaps unable to make up its mind, decided not to confer any first prize that year. Manon nevertheless had the consolation of learning that her anonymous contribution had received high praise in the jury's report. But if the young girl was more disappointed than she cared to admit in her letters to Sophie Cannet, to whom she described the whole episode in humorous and light terms, she could find some measure of comfort in the thought that Bernardin de Saint-Pierre, who had a name in the world of letters and was one of the select few admitted in the small circle of Rousseau's friends at this time, had not been more successful than she, an obscure female who had not even dared sign her essay.

The revelation of romantic love through *La Nouvelle Héloïse* produced a rather unexpected effect on Mlle Phlipon. Whereas other women of her generation found in Rousseau's novel a stirring and wholly acceptable justification of love untrammeled by social conventions and, like a Mme de Staël, henceforth felt free to break customs and even the vows of matrimony in their passionate pursuit of passion, Manon resolved, more firmly than ever, to beware of unreasoned attachments. Mingling the lesson drawn from Rousseau with a more conventional approach to such matters, she deified love, to be sure, but vowed to steer clear of the dangerous enchantments afforded by one's surrender to emotion.[24] Like Julie, the heroine of *La Nouvelle Héloïse,* she opted in favor of the kind of security one can obtain through a state that is free from emotional agitation, but unlike Julie, even when she would fall desperately in love with a young man not unlike Saint-Preux, she would continue to resist the intoxication of love and stubbornly cling to a vanishing ideal of self-control. No wonder that Mme Roland would end in a moral impasse from which the only way out was a heroic death.

There is no doubt that Rousseau's influence reinforced Manon's distrust of others and predilection for solitude. Feeling that her sensibility and inexperience of the world had made her a natural prey of unscrupulous rakes, she became ever more mistrustful of men while loving abstract Man. Proud aloofness and uncompromising frankness would be the result of this fear and insecurity. To be a brilliant, knowing hostess could not count among her achievements. Rather, her qualities of outspokenness would be considered as refreshing by men no longer attracted by the niceties of salon life. The Revolution, moreover, gave birth to a new type of salon whose Spartan simplicity would bear little resemblance to the genteel refinements of the salons of the Old Régime. It is a mark of the times that Mme Roland, introverted and painfully ill at ease before all those who were not her intimate friends, should succeed such supremely wellbred and polished hostesses as Mme de Tencin, Mme de Lambert, and Mme du Deffand. Even Mme Roland's literary style directly attests to Rousseau's influence. It combines those ample, descriptive developments that immediately bring to mind the more lyrical passages of *La Nouvelle Héloïse* with concrete, down-to-earth, and bourgeois touches for which this novel is equally famous.

While Rousseau's more personal works depicted a way of feeling which corresponded strikingly with Manon Phlipon's own frame of mind, his political treatises illuminated her ideas concerning social institutions. Not only could she find in the *Social Contract* an eloquent justification for her sense of injury as a commoner deprived of all opportunities reserved for the wealthy and the wellborn, but Rousseau also crystallized her notions of nationalism and wars of national liberation. Heretofore, she had had little use for war which, as she put it, increases the prestige of kings but adds to the misery of the people. In this connection, it might be pointed out that there was little popular nationalism under the Old Régime. The enlisted ranks of armies were filled with mercenaries and professional soldiers, who formed a class apart and were looked upon with undis-

guised hostility by the peasants and population at large. Wars between governments, or between monarchies, were fought for power,
prestige, or calculated interests, not for ideological principles.[25]
    There was one war, however, in which Mlle Phlipon was to take
a passionate interest. From the outset of the War of Independence
of the American colony, Manon sensed its import: here was no longer
a war between kings, but the revolution of a whole people fighting
for their liberty. Like many a compatriot imbued with the liberal
principles of Montesquieu and the Encyclopedists, she was quick in
denouncing the British colonial system and in upholding the justness
of the American cause.[26] As a disciple of Rousseau, moreover, she
sincerely believed in the notion of the "noble savage" and harbored
a romantic nostalgia for far-off places and exotic climes. All her life
she would entertain a highly idealized image of the early settlers, of
an unspoiled mode of living, and of the solid, simple virtues that
could be found in these frontier communities. As the product of a city
surfeited with the refinements and constrictions of civilization,
Manon Phlipon looked longingly upon primitive man, eagerly endorsing Rousseau's urgent denunciation of urbanity and luxury.
    Anxiously she plied visitors with questions about the latest news
from America. When, in September of 1777, she learned that the
Americans had suffered considerable and repeated losses at the
hands of the British, she became worried: "The enthusiasm for
liberty has not reached everyone; many rich people still remain
faithful to the mother country: this factor, added to the lack of
discipline among the troops, might give the advantage to the
English." [27] In October of the same year, however, she felt more
sanguine about the Americans' chances for success:

I think that the advantage the English have because of their excellent
discipline, in comparison with the American troops, is compensated by
the dangers of their position, which are due to their food shortage and
difficulty in getting new recruits. Washington does not fight, and he
rightly avoids doing so whenever possible; he temporizes like Fabius;
his aim is to exhaust and ruin the English through famine and fatigue.
I agree with you on the importance of this revolution; I look upon it
with keen interest, and I wish for the advent of liberty in America as

a just revenge against the many violations of natural law which have occurred in a continent that is presently unhappy, even though there is no reason why it should be so.[28]

Sophie shared her friend's enthusiasm for the American cause and repeatedly pressed her for the latest news, since Manon had the advantage of living in the capital. But Mlle Phlipon led such a retired existence that she had to admit to Sophie: "I am not up-to-date as far as the happenings in America are concerned, even though I judge them highly significant. I see so few people, and among those so few that are well-informed, that my Paris is not much better than the provinces." [29]

Manon Phlipon's sympathies for the rebellious colony, and subsequently for the new commonwealth of America, continued unabated through the years. If anything, the successful establishment of a republic intensified this interest, transforming it into something of a political symbol of democracy in action. Like other French intellectuals with a liberal turn of mind, she would come to look upon the United States of America as a promised land, as the embodiment of every enlightened principle set forth by Montesquieu and Rousseau. As for the problem of Negro slavery, the generation of Mme Roland, though aware of the iniquities of an institution that violated the very principles advocated by the founding fathers of the American Republic, were hopeful that this practice would be eradicated through the efforts of the progressive elements in the young nation. Many an action supported by Mme Roland after 1789, such as her preference for a federal system over the highly centralized one favored by the Jacobins, can be fully comprehended only in the light of her desire to follow the example set by the American revolutionaries and her ingenuous belief that this was sufficient guarantee of success in France. Mme Roland was not alone in this disregard for specific geographic, economic, and political conditions which can account for the effective application of federalism in one nation and its unfeasibility in another. With most of the Girondins, she shared the tragically naïve conviction that, in order to succeed, a revolution only has to follow a given pattern. Instead of taking into account the rapidly shifting and evolving character of the French Revolution, Mme Roland and her friends would end by losing all sense of reality by erecting a doctrinaire, abstract, and vague ideal state entirely based on their youthful enthusiasms and readings.

Yet these dreamers were sometimes capable of uncanny insights into the future. In an essay written in the mid-seventies and entitled *A Political Reverie,* Mlle Phlipon surveyed the French social scene, pointing out the disparity between the hungry, miserable masses and the privileged few, deploring the absence of a representational government, and underscoring the fact that the *Parlements* in France had become little more than courts of justice in the service of the blindest form of conservatism.[30] Obviously thinking of Rousseau's *Social Contract,* of his principle that a just order must express the general will with each citizen participating in the governing of the sovereign state, she indignantly denounced a society in which the government and the people constitute two separate bodies. Also remembering Rousseau's point that in a state where the government and the will of the people no longer coincide, the latter have the right, nay, the duty, to overthrow the system, she broodingly drew a somber picture of existing conditions in contemporary France: "Oppressed subjects do not offer without grumbling their labor, sweat, and efforts. They are not willing to purchase their livelihood twice over by paying high prices for their food, after having already earned it through hard work and the disbursement of high taxes." [31] Under such hardships, public opinion, she felt, could be repressed only by force, and this in turn would eventually lead to open rebellion. And she concluded her essay with a prediction that more daringly forecasts the French Revolution and the downfall of the monarchy than anything to be found in the writings of Montesquieu, Diderot, Voltaire, or Rousseau himself:

Odious spies and fearful informers have extended their degrading sway over the close of the last reign; these horrors seem to be alleviated, but since want has cried: "I am hungry!" troops are marched from one end of the kingdom to the other, and make it appear like a plain bristling with bayonets. Here then is established the reign of terror; this is the resource of a despotic government. Did it ever produce any good? Alas! It can only nourish animosity, lead to despair, and bury every virtue. . . . If this system lasts, if the high cost of living continues, and if the people go on suffering, *there will be either a violent crisis which may overthrow the throne and give us another form of government,* or there will be a state of lethargy similar to death.[32]

Only nineteen years after this was written, Louis XVI had indeed a revolution on his hands!

PART II

Courtship and Marriage

SIX

The Romance
of Manon Phlipon

IN THE ANCIENT, WINDING Rouen street which bore the name of rue aux Ours there lived a large, happy family: Pierre Lefebvre-Malortie, his wife Marie-Anne, and their eight children. M. Malortie combined the functions of procurer of the salt supply for Rouen and of treasurer of the Cathedral of Notre-Dame in that city. He was an important member of the Rouen community and, as such, knew scholars, administrators, clergymen, and various notables of the town bourgeoisie.[1] The Malorties were a hospitable couple and in their pleasant salon social gatherings took place at regular intervals. These soirées, however, were of a serious, erudite nature, and they well reflected the intellectualism and spirit of inquiry characteristic of the Age of Enlightenment, a spirit that had even penetrated provincial circles. As the Malortie children grew, they became acquainted with the ideas of Montesquieu, Voltaire, and Rousseau and took an increasingly active part in the learned discussions carried on by their elders. One of the girls in particular, Marie-Madeleine, coupled a quick, vivacious mind with an attractive, gracious personality. With her knowledge of modern as well as ancient literatures and her winning manner she easily came, when she reached her twenties, to dominate the salon where the erudite of Rouen liked to shine.

It is therefore hardly surprising that when, in 1761, the twenty-seven-year-old Jean-Marie Roland de la Platière, a serious-minded and ambitious apprentice inspector of manufactures, made his appearance at one of the Malortie gatherings he should have been immediately drawn to the scholarly young hostess. Without having the appearance of an Apollo, Roland was just the right type for Mlle Malortie. Tall, with regular features and an earnest expression, he had dignity and character, and the austerity of his face was somewhat tempered by a fine, sensitive mouth and a pleasant, albeit infrequent, smile. Roland detested the banal gossip which was the fare of many salons and welcomed an opportunity of debating significant issues that would show to advantage his solid fund of knowledge and varied intellectual interests.

The young man hailed from an old Beaujolais family belonging to the nobility of the robe. He did not, however, possess any personal means, since the family patrimony had been much reduced through poor investments and unwise speculations. Large broods of children had further depleted the once extensive land holdings of the Rolands until they now mainly consisted of a family house at Villefranche-sur-Saône, near Lyons, and a small country estate, known as Le Clos de la Platière, in the commune of Theizé, eleven miles from Villefranche. The Roland family, moreover, had neglected to obtain an official patent of nobility and was therefore denied all the privileges attendant to that rank.

As the youngest of five sons, Roland at the age of twenty had been left without any financial resources. Not wishing to follow the example of his brothers, who had all joined religious orders, he had determined, in 1754, to leave his home town of Villefranche and travel to the port of Nantes, with the hope of earning enough money to sail for America and settle there. He did not even have the means to go by coach from Villefranche to Nantes, but that did not deter the independent, energetic young man from carrying out his project. Tall, lean Roland was an excellent walker who had made numerous hikes through the Beaujolais countryside. Setting out on his long journey, and traveling mainly on foot, he eventually reached Nantes after having crossed the breadth of France. But there his weakened condition led to a severe illness which forced him to renounce his plans for emigration to the colonies. Instead, he proceeded to Rouen, where a cousin who was inspector of manufactures, M. Godinot, helped him find a position in this branch of the French administrative system. Thanks to his relative, Roland received excellent training and was assigned to the Rouen district in August of 1754.[2] Intelligent and extremely industrious, Roland soon drew the attention of the liberal-minded Finance and Commerce Minister Trudaine, who highly approved of the young administrator's technical papers on improved methods of weaving and dyeing wool and cotton in France. Thus recognized by his superiors, Roland could look forward to a brilliant future as an industrial expert and administrator. In these early stages of the industrial revolution, it was enlightened men like Roland who laid the groundwork for French economic growth which would reach its fruition in the nineteenth century. For, in contrast to most officials of his time who turned their administrative posts into sinecures, Roland took his duties most seriously and familiarized himself over the years with every aspect of industry and commerce, not only in France but in foreign countries as well. He engaged in extensive research on dyeing and bleaching techniques and urged his superiors to adopt some of the methods used in England. His interests, however, were not solely in trade, and his views on political economy and the great problems of government coincided with those of the *philosophes*. At the same time, he assiduously studied advanced mathematics, chemistry, anatomy, and natural history.

A deep kinship was soon established between Roland and his new circle of friends, and since they all shared a veneration for the Ancients, they decided to adopt the names of famous Greeks. Roland, because of his interest in political and moral questions, was called Thalès, in honor of the Greek philosopher, mathematician, and statesman. Cousin-Despréaux, another regular visitor to the Malortie salon and one of those elegantly erudite men of letters so common in the eighteenth century, acquired the august name of Plato. He was to become Roland's best friend and collaborator on a *History of Greece*, a publication that had very little success. As for the charming Mlle Malortie, she was baptized Cléobuline, after the poetess and philosopher of Lindos who had gained renown for her beauty and intellect. Thalès and Cléobuline became engaged and formed enthusiastic plans for their future together. But since the apprentice inspector did not yet feel in a position to assume the responsibility of a family, and Cléobuline was dowryless, both decided to await philosophically more propitious circumstances. Roland fervently hoped to be promoted to the rank of full inspector of manufactures of Rouen, and he redoubled his efforts, preparing several more memoirs on the manufacture and trade of textiles in the Rouen district. The expected results, however, failed to materialize. While Trudaine was most generous in his commendations and assured Roland of his personal esteem and friendship, on January 4, 1764, he nominated him to the disappointing post of under inspector at Clermont, four miles from the southern town of Lodève, in the Languedoc province. Probably in order to allay his protégé's ruffled feelings, Trudaine wrote him that this was a temporary post, "while waiting for a better opportunity." [3] Poor Roland had no choice but to accept this enforced exile and to bid his beloved a tender and tearful adieu.

For two years Roland vegetated in Clermont-de-Lodève (today Clermont-L'Hérault). Industry in this region languished, and commerce was completely haphazard and riddled with abuses. Roland immediately set out to establish some order in this backward and poverty stricken province. As a result, overwork caused a grave illness which brought him near death. In April of 1765, while he was slowly recovering, he received encouraging news from Trudaine, and, in July 1766, he was promoted to the rank of full inspector of the important northern province of Picardy.[4] But, alas, this meant that he would have to settle in Amiens and continue to be separated from his Rouen friends. Probably Roland had expected to be nominated inspector of Normandy and was disappointed by this promotion. That he was somewhat disgruntled is made clear by a gentle letter of reproval from Trudaine advising the young administrator not to feel sorry for himself, since he was now in charge of the third largest manufacturing province in the kingdom.[5]

During all these years of separation, Cléobuline remained faithful to her absent fiancé, but with time his feelings for her seem to have dimmed. He was sent on economic and industrial missions to various parts of France and Europe and enjoyed these journeys which enabled him to observe different peoples and customs. He took voluminous notes and recorded his impressions and observations in his diaries, evidently with the intention of publishing travel journals. This literary genre was highly popular in the eighteenth century, and accounts of voyages of all kinds enjoyed great favor with the reading public. No doubt, Roland wished to make a name for himself and he spiced his technical remarks with comments on mores, politics, and religion. As an informed and widely cultured traveler, Roland was eminently qualified to make a distinguished contribution to the travel literature of his age. But he unfortunately lacked a literary sense, his style was generally stiff and verbose, and it was not until he would meet Manon Phlipon that, with her capable collaboration, he managed to prune his manuscripts to a readable form.

Roland was now a man of importance and of significant responsibilities. In the course of his travels he had other love affairs, of which he makes no secret in his writings, and in Amiens pretty damsels and wealthy widows showed keen interest in him. He had, moreover, become very friendly with the Cannet family. The atmosphere in the Cannet salon was very different from that of the Malortie circle in Rouen. Here a purely social tone prevailed and there were hardly any intellectual discussions to stimulate the scholarly Roland. Nevertheless, he seemed to enjoy the company of the Cannet sisters, and particularly that of the elder, Henriette.

Why this apparent change in heart? One can only conjecture over the reasons for Roland's gradual estrangement from the serious-minded Cléobuline. To engage in a highly literary and lofty romance was one thing, but to take the young lady as his wife was quite another. Now that he could reason objectively about this matter far from Cléobuline's charming person, he probably felt no urgent need to make up his mind, preferring procrastination to a final commitment. Roland, moreover, was diffident and cautious by nature; the thought of making as irrevocable a decision as contracting wedding vows must have caused many a sleepless night. It is almost certain, however, that Cléobuline's mediocre financial situation had little to do with this hesitation, since it was Roland's strongly held principle that he would marry the woman he loved, irrespective of her social or financial position, a principle he would faithfully bear out, as his eventual marriage with the penniless Manon Phlipon was to prove. What also seems probable is that, even while still in Rouen, Roland may have noticed the progress of a debilitating illness, probably consumption, of which Mlle Malortie was the quiet and stoical victim. Whatever the cause of her wasting, in July 1773, she felt that she was nearing the final hour, and she begged her parents to summon Roland to her deathbed. A belated wave of affection, and also probably remorse, overwhelmed Roland at the sight of the expiring but still lucid, calm, and ever loving Cléobuline. After the sad burial ceremonies, he composed a funereal lamentation in the form of a prose poem in the tradition of the Greek threnody, wherein he gave expression to his desolation and extolled the virtues of the deceased.

Through the years Roland was to maintain bonds of friendship and affection with the Malortie family, whose many members eventually dispersed or died, leaving only two unmarried daughters in the old Rouen house. The Malortie sisters were to reappear on the scene during the Terror, after Roland's proscription. By unhesitatingly offering Roland a safe shelter, the by then elderly spinsters would put their own lives in jeopardy, a gesture which amply testifies to a devoted and enduring relationship.[6]

As inspector of Picardy, Roland once more displayed tireless zeal. During the eighteen years that he was to remain in charge of the industry of that province, he mastered every problem and followed modern, experimental methods, although these involved him in some unpleasant controversies with greedy manufacturers and timorous associates. Imbued with the liberal economic doctrines of the Encyclopedists, Roland fought tooth and nail for complete freedom of industry and trade, bringing out into the open manufacturing processes whenever he could wring these jealously guarded secrets from their inventors. It was his strong belief that everyone should benefit from improved industrial methods, and he took infinite pains to keep up with new inventions and pass these on to every master craftsman. This inevitably led to prolonged and bitter clashes with importers and manufactureres who wished to preserve the secret of these inventions in order to further their private interests and maintain the monopoly over certain industries. Roland saw in the continued practice of secrecy a threat to French industry in general, since large quantities of English cloths were imported, causing dangerous competition and widespread unemployment among French weavers and dyers. Roland was especially eager to learn the techniques of weaving, bleaching, dyeing, and printing cotton as practiced in England. As a matter of fact, no aspect of manufacturing left him indifferent; whether it involved the making of linen, paper, lace, velvet, ribbons, ironware, pottery, or the preparing of peat as fuel.

Such unflagging activity and wide-ranging interests could not fail to be invaluable to the nascent French industry. Roland was therefore encouraged by his superiors to travel widely and accumulate information that could be put to practical use. The inspector's personal punctiliousness and enlightened views had nevertheless made his work unusually difficult and ungrateful. It is hardly surprising that, as a result of repeated unpleasantness with the more reactionary elements of the manufacturing trade, Roland's serious and unbending character should have become morose and irritable. He had always been fiercely independent and outspoken. Now he tended to be dogmatic and haughty, but Trudaine was willing to disregard such personal traits, for he had the highest esteem for the man and the civil servant. Roland's industrial monographs eventually earned him the title of corresponding member of the Academy of Science in Paris, as well as that of member of a number of provincial academies so active in the eighteenth century,[7] and even several foreign societies devoted to science and progress bestowed membership and honorary titles on the diligent and forward-looking inspector. Such flattering recognition from the most exalted circles of learning was an immense source of satisfaction for Roland and consoled him for the frustrating incomprehension or outright hostility he so often met in the world of industry, commerce, and political officialdom in France.

While living and working in Amiens, Roland made frequent and prolonged stays in Paris. It is in the course of one of these trips that he became acquainted with Mlle Phlipon. In January 1776, when Roland, already slightly balding and with severe, finely chiseled features, made his first appearance in M. Phlipon's shop, duly equipped with a letter of introduction from the Cannet sisters, and struck up an elevated, philosophical discussion with the young lady of whom he had heard wonders from Sophie, Manon was greatly impressed and even a little intimidated. It seemed to her that perhaps she had not shown herself to best advantage, and this worried her, as she confessed in a letter to Sophie.[8] She had stammered somewhat and, as she suffered at the time from a very bad cold, she did not express her ideas with her customary facility. Moreover, she happened to be wearing a plain, white camisole, a housecoat reserved for days when she expected no visitors, and a bonnet hid her hair. In front of this tall, austere visitor who was called the *philosophe* by Sophie's circle, was Manon's senior by twenty years, held an important administrative post, and spoke with an assurance bordering on pedantry, she suddenly felt shy, awkward, and yet anxious to make a good impression. That Roland's opinions were trenchant and his manner rather abrupt did not displease her—far from it. This was all the more the case since, only a few months before meeting Roland, she had looked with some favor on a young man, Pahin de la Blancherie, who had proved to have had more promise than substance, a fact that had served to confirm Manon's theories concerning the unreliability of young suitors.[9] La Blancherie had seemed to have conceived a passionate attachment for Manon, but it had turned out that this penniless would-be writer had lost all interest as soon as it had become evident to him that Mlle Phlipon was not endowed with a substantial dowry. She had moreover met him in the Luxembourg and Tuileries Gardens dressed like a coxcomb complete with plumed hat and parading with gay young coquettes.[10] Manon, who had allowed herself to be moved by La Blancherie's flattering attentions and compliments, soon realized her error and vowed that she would trust only serious-minded, mature men.

Nothing in Roland's appearance or manner reminded one of the more worldly, stylish Frenchmen of the eighteenth century. Rather, this lean, slightly stoop-shouldered figure was more reminiscent of some New England Puritan. His manner of dress was starkly simple and totally devoid of the customary frills, and no powdered wig hid his thinning hair. His bearing was dignified but stiff and lacking in gracefulness. He spoke in clear, polished tones, but his voice had none of those inflections that can make a young girl's heart beat faster. His longish face had undeniable distinction, with the high, intelligent forehead and regular, sharp features, but it was generally set in a stern expression. His lips rarely softened in a smile, and his complexion was sallowed by hard work and a faulty liver. Altogether a striking, if unworldly, figure of a man. But Manon, who had recently learned that infatuation with an attractive, flashy youth generally brings only humiliation and disappointment, welcomed Roland's brusqueness of manner and Rousseau-like outspokenness. In this sober, middle-aged scholar she saw the promise of those solid, reliable qualities that could bring happiness and security to one who, like her, valued intellect and wisdom. She was willing to look beyond surface attractions and, unconsciously perhaps, was modeling her husband image on the elderly, staid, and philosophic M. de Wolmar, the spouse of the romantic Julie d'Etange, Rousseau's heroine of *La Nouvelle Héloïse*. Perhaps Roland's age, experience, and authoritative manner also pleased Manon because they seemed to indicate qualities which her own father so sorely lacked. After all these years of inner struggle and painful conflict with the spendthrift and erratic Phlipon, she craved a sense of order and stability which only marriage with a respectable man like Roland could offer her.

As for Roland, he must have found Manon enchanting, for he kept returning to the engraver's shop on the Quai de l'Horloge in order

to pursue endless discussions with the twenty-four-year-old *savante*.[11]
All the topics of the day, all the philosophical themes dear to the
heart of a worthy disciple of the Enlightenment, were duly passed in
review, and the merits of individual writers evaluated. After one of
those sessions Manon wrote to Sophie that she felt somewhat inade-
quate with this widely read and much-traveled visitor.[12] She listened
most intently to his travel accounts and tried, in turn, to show off
her own knowledge, but had the impression that she could not tell
him anything that he did not already know. As Roland's visits became more frequent and prolonged, Phlipon began showing signs of
suspicion and displeasure and even ended up by insisting on being
present at those meetings. He could not very well take part in the
intellectual exchange and his awkward presence much irritated and
vexed Manon, who sensed that Roland felt ill at ease before the
sullen gaze of Phlipon père. When, on March 7, she noted that
Roland had suddenly ceased his visits, she bitterly wrote to her
friend: "It seems that M. Roland has had it; I well suspected it and
cannot blame him." [13] Perhaps he had just returned to Amiens, but
it is curious that he should not have notified his young friend of his
departure. With characteristic caution, he probably did not wish
to commit himself and preferred thinking matters over from a safe
distance.

March and April of 1776 passed without any news from the
philosophe of Amiens. For a short spell, Manon seems to have turned
back to La Blancherie; he had just published a book whose manuscript he had asked her to read. It was a ponderous treatise entitled
*Extracts from the Diary of My Travels, or the History of a Young
Man for the Education of Fathers and Mothers.* As a great admirer
of Rousseau's *Emile,* Manon had at first thought that La Blancherie's
book had certain merits which reminded her of her favorite writer.
Upon rereading it, however, she was disappointed and lost all interest in La Blancherie when various reports on his philandering ways
reached her. On May 2 Roland made an unheralded appearance in
Phlipon's shop and spent two hours with Manon. His prolonged
absence caused Manon to appreciate his qualities all the more en-

thusiastically. After the visit, she immediately set out to write to Sophie, praising the solidity of Roland's judgment, the interest of his conversation, and the scope of his knowledge. Once more the visits multiplied, and this time a quality of intimacy and mutual esteem was established. Even Phlipon now seemed to recognize Roland as a man of merit and honor, for he became more discreet and, to the relief of Manon, made himself scarce during those visits. On June 24 of 1776, a grateful Manon wrote to Sophie: "I owe one more debt to your friendship, the acquaintance of M. Roland, a sensitive soul, an honest and sincere person, a combination of qualities I greatly value. He has a true and seasoned philosophy, and you probably guess that his kind suits me to perfection. In short, he seems to have the stuff that makes a solid friend, if the future sustains our relationship." [14]

On August 8, Roland set out for a trip to Italy. This was an official mission sponsored by Roland's financial supervisor Turgot, a man who belonged to the enlightened school of economics. Roland was to return to France a year later, in September of 1777. An interesting change then took place in Manon's letters to her friends; beginning in June, her references to Roland became reticent and rare. A twofold reason explains this unusual reserve on the part of one who, thus far, had made the Cannet sisters privy to all her thoughts and feelings: on the one hand, she realized that Henriette was a competitor for Roland's affection, and on the other, Roland himself, before leaving, had specifically instructed her to remain silent about their friendship.

During his last visit Roland entrusted Manon with all his manuscripts, which she hastened to read and annotate. As she was to point out in her *Memoirs*, these papers consisted of "travel accounts, reflections, projects, personal anecdotes," and they bespoke "a forceful character, an austere probity, rigorous principles, knowledge, and taste." [15] In Roland's absence, Manon whiled away her loneliness by working diligently on his writings. Fortunately, news from Roland soon distracted Manon from her melancholy thoughts, for the voyager had sent to his brother, the Prior of Cluny, a bulky package of notes he had already managed to amass with the specific instruction to transmit them to the young girl. To Henriette Cannet, who repeatedly inquired about Roland, Manon gave only vague and general information, obviously not wishing to break the promise of silence she had made to the Inspector.

Manon was thus pursuing her quiet, studious mode of existence when she allowed herself to become involved in a rather bizarre romantic relationship. M. de Sévelinges d'Espagny, tobacco supervisor of Soissons, fifty-five years of age, married and father of two grown sons, a close friend of Sainte-Lette, became interested in Manon, about whom Sainte-Lette had spoken in glowing terms and some of whose manuscripts he had even lent to Sévelinges.[16] At this time, Sévelinges had lost his wife. Soon thereafter, he came to Paris and was introduced to Manon by their common friend. She found the man to her liking and permitted him to take some of her personal essays back to Soissons. In November of 1776, Manon was in an especially lonely mood. Roland was traveling in distant places and sent her news only on rare occasions and through his brother as intermediary. And her father was causing her greater worry than ever with his perpetual insouciance and escapades. The financial situation of Phlipon had become so lamentable that Manon could not even afford a trip to Amiens to visit Sophie and Henriette. By December 1776, Roland had traveled the whole length of Italy, from Turin to Sicily and Malta, and was now on his way back to Naples and Rome, which he planned to revisit. It was at this time that a second batch of travel notes was sent to Manon, again through Roland's brother as intermediary. During this same month, however, the voyager almost perished in a furious storm between Messina and Naples, and Manon, who learned of the danger that Roland had incurred, worriedly asked the Prior for a more detailed account of this adventure.

Letters were also exchanged directly between Roland and Manon, but she heard from him infrequently and remained without any news for long stretches of time. She could not help betraying her anxiety in her correspondence with the Cannet sisters. In the hope of receiving at least some indirect information, she wrote: "You don't tell me anything about M. Roland. Has he braved another storm? Did he die on the way? I see everything in black, even the most distant objects." [17] Upon learning that he was well, she mused:

M. Roland is most fortunate to roam leisurely through Italy! . . . I am charmed to know that our voyager is in good health. It seems to me that there is a contradiction in your judgment of him: you grant him penetration and deny him finesse; one does not go without the other. What particular observation makes you speak thus? You believe he has dogmatic views (I presume that he is not entirely free of them); but on what subject? I have noted that with regard to politics and society he has the true principles which help make accurate observations. I am not far from agreeing with you on the degree of esteem one can grant him and I think that he will always greatly benefit from any comparison; his love and enthusiasm for the true, the simple, single him out. Since his return is expected in August or October, I see that we can hardly count on him before the latter month.[18]

One may wonder at this juncture why Roland remained so doggedly silent in the face of such flattering solicitude. The reason is quite simple. Roland's brother had meanwhile engaged in marital negotiations for an advantageous match which the traveler, still uncommitted to Manon, was not discouraging. Being an honorable man, he no doubt felt that he should not pursue his relationship with a young girl when he might become engaged to another. Thus, from February until September 1777, Mlle Phlipon thought herself forgotten. Her pride was hurt by Roland's prolonged silence and she bitterly regretted having given him many proofs of interest and esteem while he gave evidence of indifference.

The only person who brought her solace during this trying time was Sévelinges, who continued to write from Soissons. In her loneliness, she turned to him and engaged in a semi-intellectual semi-amorous correspondence with the widower. She sent him the discourse on women she had submitted to the Academy of Besançon, and he reciprocated with an essay on eloquence he had read before the Academy in Paris, for M. Sévelinges had literary interests, occasionally indulged in writing, and was a member of the Academy of

Soissons. Finding that her correspondent shared her tastes, Manon was beginning to consider marrying him and renouncing the ever-absent and apparently forgetful Roland. She was therefore rudely taken aback upon discovering that Sévelinges had altogether different intentions. At first he only discussed literature and philosophy, but by July 1777 he was openly inviting Manon to come and philosophize with him in Soissons, but without making any mention of marriage.[19] Once more, Manon sadly realized, she had allowed herself to be duped because of her lofty idealism and confidence in others. This last disappointment called for a rigorous and candid self-examination: "I don't know whether I must beware foremost of my heart or of my mind. Is it the first which misleads me? or is it the latter which induces me in error through a lack of judgment? It is a fact that I have never erred except by too much reasoning. Of all the things I have said and done in the different circumstances of my life, those that would have to be corrected were not the least thoughtful. If I were more scatterbrained, I would be less mortified. I would only have to moderate my impulses in order to succeed better. Instead, I must beware of myself, even when in perfect control. I must lack discernment." [20]

From February until April 1777, Roland had stayed in Rome, whence he proceeded north. By May he was in Venice and in the beginning of August had reached Turin. There he learned of the unexpected disfavor, retirement, and death of his protector Trudaine, which dashed all his hopes for a general inspectorship of commerce. Arriving at the family estate, in Villefranche-en-Beaujolais, on September 16, Roland finally decided to write to his young friend. After apologizing for his prolonged silence, he confided his sorrow at losing the guidance and protection of Trudaine, indicated that he had taken more notes, and expressed the hope of being able to submit these for her scrutiny, adding this compliment: "You speak of the Graces and Muses like one of them; you also speak of them like Plato himself." [21]

In the midst of his recent professional disappointment Roland turned his thoughts to the house on the Quai de l'Horloge, where he had spent so many pleasant hours. He must have taken his brother into his confidence, for the latter, without entirely renouncing his project for a brilliant match, decided to see for himself this remarkable young lady. After one visit he was completely conquered and became her staunchest ally. Moreover, Roland had made it clear to the Prior that financial questions would be of very little moment the day he would fall in love. That day seemed much nearer now that he felt the need for understanding, companionship, and solace.

Manon's reply to Roland was prompt, perfect in tone, and filled with expressions of cordiality and esteem.[22] But another disappointment awaited her, for this warm letter remained a month without an answer, and it was only on November 8 that she learned that Roland, probably as a result of his exhausting trip, had fallen seriously ill. While convalescing, Roland transmitted his travel diary to Manon. These voluminous notes were to become the basis of a six-volume work, *Letters from Switzerland, Italy, Sicily, and Malta, 1776–1778,* published in 1780.[23] Even though this voyage account contained many a useful and illuminating observation on manners and mores in diverse countries, it was too rambling, and sententious in style to appeal to the taste of the reading public and therefore missed the mark as a publishing success. A terser, wittier form might well have assured Roland's literary reputation, but although Manon spent countless hours attempting to recast the manuscript and brighten the writer's style, the final result of their common efforts still failed to live up to the eighteenth-century predilection for racy, urbane books.

Having recovered from a winter of illness, Roland arrived in Paris in the beginning of February and hastened to visit Manon. This time he must have completely fallen under her spell, for he immediately spoke of marriage. To Sophie Manon announced in rather cryptic terms that she found herself in the painful position of having to turn down the proposal of a most worthy man. A sense of duty, she explained, dictated this decision because of her mediocre dowry and social standing.[24] It is doubtful, however, that the cautious Roland formally asked for Manon's hand in marriage, since no one was informed of such a proposal. Roland stayed in Paris until June of 1778, busying himself with his administrative duties and personal writings.

In June he returned to his Amiens residence, and in July he took his law examination. Having successfully defended a thesis on canon and civil law at the University of Reims, he proceeded to Paris, where he spent the month of August, repairing once more to Amiens in the beginning of September. While in the capital, Roland evidently took delight in the increasingly intimate exchanges of confidences with Manon. She was often dreamy; he was always serious, and they spoke of the perpetual sorrows which sadden sensitive souls. She also obediently followed Roland's instructions concerning the Cannet sisters, from whom she was told to conceal their relationship. In a letter to Sophie dated May 7, she pretended seeing Roland most infrequently: "I receive only very rare visits from *your* M. Roland de la Platière; he seems to me one of those busy men who don't have time for everyone. You must have found it strange that, loving to making portraits as I do, I did not set out to paint his. I don't see him often enough to catch the resemblance. I suspect, though, that he would have been worthy of my brush. But so far as I am concerned, he is at such telescopic distance that I would willingly believe him still in Italy." [25] On June 9, Sophie arrived in Paris, and in the course of a promenade with Manon in the Luxembourg Garden, she told her that her family, and particularly her brother, was planning to marry Henriette with Roland. [26]

Back in Amiens since early September, Roland seemed to be overcome once more with doubts over the desirability of a marriage with Manon. Besides being extremely busy with his work, which left him little leisure time, at a safe distance from the young woman's charms he could ponder seriously his attachment for her. The fact that he thoroughly disliked Manon's father undoubtedly also complicated matters. During his entire stay in Amiens, from September until December 1778, Roland gave Manon no sign of life. Then, just before returning to Paris at the end of December, he impulsively wrote her a long, affectionate letter, wherein he endeavored to justify his silence by invoking his all-absorbing duties. It is evident that, after making heroic efforts to put Manon out of his mind, Roland had been obliged to admit defeat. In the same letter, he informed her of Henriette's depression and poor health and of her awareness that her family's marriage project had no basis in reality. This, of course, was an indirect allusion to his continued interest in Manon. Once more, Mlle Phlipon, valiantly setting her resentments aside, acknowledged this long delayed letter in the most friendly manner and showed her willingness to accept Roland's reasons for not writing earlier. Thus, from the moment Roland returned to Paris, the relationship resumed its course and, in February 1779, he was again speaking of marriage. Chastened by experience, Manon invoked his previous semi-engagement to Henriette Cannet, and it was decided that the latter would be informed gradually of this situation and that in the meantime they would keep their own plans secret. It is also likely that, at this time, the proud Manon, fully realizing the implications of her inferior social and financial position, determined to test Roland's intentions and to assure herself that he would not one day regret a hasty decision. She wanted him to accept her on her own terms and with the full realization that such a match would not discredit his name. In her letters to the Cannet sisters, she continued to feign indifference toward M. Roland, a strategy she loathed but which was imposed upon her by her diffident admirer.

In January 1779, Roland had moved into the Hôtel de Rome, located in the rue de la Licorne, on the Ile de la Cité and in the immediate vicinity of Manon's home. In February, Mignonne, the elderly maid who had been in the employ of the Phlipon family all her life, caught a bad case of pneumonia. Manon had more than her share of work and worry during the frantic days of crisis. When Mignonne recovered, thanks to the devoted care of the young woman, Manon decided, with the approval of her grandparents, that it was high time to make her father give an account of her tiny inheritance, since he was in the process of squandering every sou in his possession. On March 17 she was to reach the majority age of twenty-five, and this entitled her to the right of demanding a reckoning. Furthermore, Phlipon had a young mistress for whom he showed great attachment and whom he might well decide to marry, thereby cheating Manon

out of her meager dowry. And a penniless young woman under the
Old Régime was in a most unenviable position. Beset by all these
difficulties, Manon more than ever found some measure of comfort
in reading and meditation and in the stillness and solitude of her
tiny study. To Roland she confided:

The silence of darkness resembles that of the countryside; it leads to
concentration, confers on the passions a grave accent, regenerates the
mind, gathers the sensations, provokes lofty thoughts and feelings, and
finally produces enthusiasm, that plenitude of sentiments which purifies
the numerous affections which are the delights of life. I feel less sad
as soon as I am free to be so. The veil of the night soothes and consoles
me; this is what I need in the absence of friendship. In the calm of
solitude and reflection I reconcile myself with my fellow human beings. The study I make of them in society tires and embitters me. . . .
My heart is no longer oppressed, as you have noticed; but it still con-
serves something somber and fiery which would lead to disgust with
the efforts of reason alone. . . . However, my courage is not extin-
guished; life is not unbearable in my eyes.[27]

By the beginning of 1779, Manon's letters to Roland, for she
continued to write to him even though he lived only a few streets
away, had acquired a more tender, intimate character. The joys and
anxieties she used to share with her Amiens friends she now revealed to him. Having taught herself Italian, she used that language
to express her more personal feelings. Knowing Roland's admiration
for Greece, its art, culture, and customs, she frequently spoke of
them in admiring terms:

I don't know whether you communicate your preferences to me or
whether the same inclinations draw our souls together, rendering them
sensitive to similar subjects, but your Greeks appeal to me. One notes
in them, from their very beginnings, those happy seeds of grandeur,
nobility and agreeableness which developed successively in their laws,
deeds, genius, and productions. How evident are their active spirit and
powerful imagination even in the century of the siege of Troy! A mild
and cheerful religion, simplicity of manners, a lofty courage, exercises
which develop a love of glory as well as the aptitudes of the body, all
these distinguish the nation which soon was to furnish in all fields models
for posterity.[28]

The early months of 1779 thus passed in tranquil intimacy between Roland and his scholarly young friend. Many an evening
was spent in reading together or in animated discussions. Roland's
lodgment at the Hôtel de Rome facilitated numerous visits, and by
the end of March 1779 the relationship had acquired a definitely
amorous character. Roland was now deeply in love with the engraver's daughter. What had so far been a mild romance was about to
enter a more passionate stage.

In April 1779, Manon suddenly left Paris for Vincennes, where
she took refuge in the house of her favorite uncle, the canon Bimon.[29]
At least from this proper distance she could settle her dispute with
her father and also reflect more objectively on Roland's declarations
of love, which were becoming increasingly more impetuous. Since
her own feelings for Roland were more affectionate than passionate,
she looked with some bewilderment and concern upon his ardent
advances. As a sensible girl, moreover, she had vowed that she would
grant her favors only to the man willing to lead her to the altar.
Now that Roland had gone so far as to snatch from her a furtive
kiss, to which she would later refer to as "questo primo dolcissimo
bacio," [30] she was determined to let him go no farther. From the
quietude of her uncle's rectory she wrote Roland letters which expressed the troubled state of her heart. Evidently she was reluctant
to exchange a serene and comforting friendship for a more stormy
and demanding relationship. Indeed, it was not the austere quad-
ragenarian who could awaken the dormant senses of this very wise
virgin. Long ago she had so carefully repressed all thoughts concerning sex that Roland's abrupt and timid show of affection took
her completely by surprise. Her previous sentimental disappoint-
ments with La Blancherie and Sévelinges and the lack of esteem
men in general had for unmarried girls in her position had further
intensified an already natural high degree of suspiciousness. Poor
Roland was therefore quite taken aback by the plaintive reproaches
Manon directed at him from Vincennes: "It seems to me that true
friendship is not so ardent in its manifestations. It is mild, natural,
and without complications. I failed to recognize it and I became

fearful. Why try to provoke agitation and worry in my simple soul? Let me keep my peace of mind so that I can continue loving you always, always." [31]

The tone of the letters exchanged during this frantic month of April indicates that our lovers were totally at cross purposes. In this semi-tragic comedy of errors, neither of the participants suspected his partner's true frame of mind, for each saw in the other only what he was seeking: Manon a reassuring, protective father image, Roland the tender and loving sweetheart that an austere existence devoted to study and work had so far not granted him. The upright administrator, moreover, felt wounded in his pride by Manon's suspicions and reservations. In his letters he endeavored to explain that if he had shown himself to have been too enterprising, it was due, most naturally, to the powerful emotions provoked by her charming person, but that he would rather die than offend her in any way. He reminded her that he had always revealed his feelings unreservedly to her, and he hinted that he had probably committed the error of engaging himself completely in his love before she was ready to do the same. It is apparent that Roland could not fathom Manon's confused state of mind. He only succeeded in aggravating her agitation by writing: "I do not pretend that you reckon my happiness for something; I will be content not to trouble yours: and if, too affected by a sentiment which oppresses me, I must no longer see you, I shall endeavor to forestall the fatal instant when you see fit to make this order." [32]

In their correspondence, both Roland and Manon expressed themselves in a highly rhetorical and frequently pedantic style, and, as true disciples of Rousseau, constantly protested their lofty moral principles while dwelling with a good measure of complacency on the delicacy of their feelings. On and on they wrote, for their complicated emotions seemed to induce veritable outbursts of writing fever. Emulating Rousseau's combination of sentimentality and didacticism in *La Nouvelle Héloïse,* Manon blended incandescent passages with little sermons in which she assumed the poise and priggishness of a schoolmistress. Her alternating moods of passion and virtuousness, cheerfulness and gloom nonplussed poor Roland and placed him even more in her power. For just as the age of chivalry had had its established code of love, the era of Rousseau also acquired its formulas and special language. A natural literary facility reinforced by constant reading gave Manon, in this respect at least, a distinct advantage over the inspector.

In this strategy of love it was Manon who proved the stronger and who eventually gained the upper hand. Being less taken in than Roland, she could calculate her moves with greater clear-mindedness and astuteness. On April 22, 1779, Roland surrendered, but not without a proper show of sentiments and high-sounding words. His final declaration of love had a martial, almost defiant, ring: "I have but one heart, which is no longer free to offer. It is sincere and excessively sensitive: it loves you; that is all I am worth; and I am content to be worth just that. I don't know what revenge I have taken nor what you could reproach me for. You have conquered: admit it; your torments have been short-lived, and I am unhappy without having assuredly anything to repent of. Well, my friend, be happy, enjoy the resources with which both nature and art have provided you. It is from you that I am to know whether I am the obstacle to your happiness. Farewell." [33] To this act of submission Manon replied with a detailed autobiographical essay. Marriage, she proudly explained, meant for her total dedication to a worthy man, not a convenient pass into society. At the same time, she alluded to the other suitors who had already courted her and confessed that one man, M. de La Blancherie, had briefly held her affections, but that she had soon realized that he was not the right man for her after all. She also reminded him of the financial reversals of her family and of her own determination to elect spinsterhood rather than marriage with a man who might one day come to feel ashamed of her. Neither would she enter into a family that was not capable of appreciating her for her own worth. "Sir," she concluded, "I can be the victim of sentiments, but I shall never be the sport of anyone!" [34]

Manon returned home from Vincennes to find Mignonne, the

aging family maid, once more gravely ill. Despite the most devoted
care, Manon was unable to save the old woman, who passed away
in her arms. In the meantime, Roland had pressed her for a clear-
cut answer to his declarations of love, and it was an emotionally and
physically exhausted Manon who declared herself vanquished. The
only reason why she had been so proud and unyielding, she now
wrote, was because of the insecurity of her position and her awareness of the problems it entailed. Henceforth, she would have no
other concern than his happiness. It was Roland's turn to triumph
and he joyfully greeted this unexpected show of humility: "You are
mine, you have given your word, and it is irrevocable. Yes, my friend,
my sweet and faithful friend, I needed this *yes* . . . and I am in a
mood to ask you to confirm it a hundred times." [35]

The crisis was over. Roland and Manon now felt secure in their
mutual love and devotion. Pride had been conquered on both sides,
and there remained to be lifted the exterior obstacles that could
prevent marriage. Those were still numerous, however. First Manon
had to extricate herself from the embarrassing correspondence with
Sévelinges and explain this relationship to Roland, for it was her
principle that her future husband was entitled to a full account of
her sentimental life.[36] Then too, she had to announce her engagement to her father, and this in the most tactful terms, since he was
in an especially resentful mood over her request for her share of the
small patrimony. Roland and Phlipon, moreover, had always disliked
each other, and Manon feared a new explosion of ill temper on the
part of her volatile father and difficult lover. Finally, Roland expected violent objections from his family in Beaujolais. Marriage
with a practically penniless engraver's daughter could only be considered a gross misalliance by the provincial and stodgy Rolands, who
prided themselves on their venerable ancestry and rights to nobility.
Our lovers therefore determined to proceed with prudence and discre-
tion and the circumspect Roland continued to demand absolute
secrecy over their engagement even with Sophie and Henriette Cannet. The inspector had to return to Amiens, and only his letters
sustained and cheered Manon. She was nevertheless growing restive

and anxious, for Roland still insisted that she remain silent over their plans. Finally, on May 31, he permitted her to inform Phlipon of her engagement, insisting nevertheless that the name of her fiancé not be revealed. Phlipon being a quick-tempered man, Roland indicated that this was the best way to avoid unpleasant scenes between father and daughter.[37] Manon followed Roland's instructions to the letter, but it did not take much ingenuity on Phlipon's part to guess the identity of this mysterious fiancé. Moved by his daughter's eagerness to patch things up between them, the engraver expressed approval of her choice, and even went so far as to voice esteem for the Amiens administrator. Manon was transported with joy and gratitude, and a scene which had begun in a painfully constrained manner ended in an apotheosis of kisses and tears worthy of Greuze's melodramatic brush. After this, Manon experienced a sense of relief and, for the first time in a long while, knew peace of mind. She had acted boldly and of her own accord by confirming the identity of her lover, but things had worked out for the best, and Roland himself did not seem too displeased over the outcome of this crucial confrontation. Yet Roland failed to follow suit and did not take a single step to inform either his own family in Beaujolais or Manon's father of the impending marriage. He did, however, secure a lodging for his prospective bride and himself in Amiens and spoke at length of other practical arrangements he was making for their married life.

Manon, who had always prided herself on her open nature, did not know what to make of Roland's tendency toward overcautiousness. Since her father had taken the news much better than had been expected, she saw no reason for further concealment and hoped that Roland would take similar action with his family. But she was not counting with the bachelor's moodiness, fears, and excessive sensibilities. When she confided her worries to him, he chided her, sometimes none too gently: "I should have so wished to see you with a more tranquil soul, a more contented heart, a gentler disposition. I tell you, my dearest, most emphatically: I understand your adverse circumstances; I consider them only annoyances to be overcome and I love you enough to count them for little, but it is your chagrins, which you cannot define because they are not founded on anything, that are a source of torment for me." [38]

To these scolding letters Manon at first replied in apologetic terms, humbly acknowledging her excessive impressionability. To pacify her lover and soothe his outbursts of ill-humor, she promised to become more reasonable, but her letters were beginning to betray her disappointment and growing anxiety at Roland's endless procrastinations. To make matters worse, Phlipon, quite understandably, was wondering at Roland's failure to ask him for his daughter's hand in marriage. Finding such prolonged silence rather strange, if not offensive, Phlipon determined to take the matter in his own hands and wrote the inspector a blunt letter demanding a full explanation. Roland, as might be expected, took rather badly Phlipon's ill-timed initiative. Irritated by the engraver's clumsy attempt to force his hand, he peevishly complained to Manon. Recriminations soon became mutual and a tone of bitterness and acrimony was rapidly introduced in the ensuing letters. A worsening situation was hardly helped by the fact that Phlipon, whose suspicions had increased with Roland's uncooperativeness, now insisted that, before he give his consent to the marriage, he be allowed to read the entire correspondence between the lovers. A distracted Manon endeavored to explain to a furious Roland that her father, despite certain faults, was far from dishonorable or wicked and that his present attitude, vexing though it might be, was the consequence of limited, but well-meaning intentions. She recommended a conciliatory manner as the only way to mend an otherwise hopelessly complicated situation. The best solution, she wrote, was for Roland to come to Paris and have a face to face explanation with her father.[39]

As he was wont to do whenever he could not make up his mind, Roland took refuge in silence. Receiving no answer to her letters summoning him to Paris, and finding herself at her wits' end, Manon decided to take a dramatic step. In her most majestic prose, she gave him back his freedom and his word. While congratulating herself on her refusal to compromise with "virtue," she could not help making the bitter remark to Roland that a craftier, if less candid, woman might well have succeeded where she had failed. Having missed her last chance at "happiness," she gloomily wrote, she was now led to envisage suicide as an honorable way out of an unbearable existence.[40] To speak of suicide in moments of distress or even melancholy (but without converting words into action) had become quite a fashionable pose among the preromantics, and Manon must have sensed that it might have a salutary effect on Roland. She was not mistaken. Roland was alarmed, and he finally wrote, this time in gentler terms, assuring her of his undying affection and solemnly urging her not to resort to any desperate measure. But still he would not give in to her request that he come to Paris.

Finally, Manon hit upon a solution which, though less drastic than suicide, would signify retirement from the world. She would bury herself in a convent, not as a nun since she had lost the faith, but as a lay boarder. And what better place could be selected than the Convent of the Ladies of the Congregation where she had already spent a year? Perhaps there she could regain a measure of that peace of mind she so desperately needed. On November 7, 1779, Manon settled in a modest cell where she planned to live in the strictest simplicity. Informed of this move, Roland hastened to write a long, doleful letter, to which she replied in these terms: "My soul is withered, closed; I don't even condescend to hate life. I no longer feel anything. I am finally separated from my father, removed from my family, relegated under a foreign roof, which probably is my last refuge." [41]

Roland found himself in the throes of powerful and contradictory emotions which hardly left him the clear-mindedness necessary to prepare for the publication of his *Letters from Italy* or to discharge his numerous administrative duties. His letters to Manon, for the estranged lovers continued to correspond diligently, resounded with sorrowful complaints about his inability to make any headway in his work and were filled with long, lugubrious lamentations. Manon, for her part, assumed an attitude of serene, melancholy resignation and sisterly concern. Roland still refused to assume the responsibility of their broken engagement and could not bring himself to take a decisive step. He had, moreover, developed such an acute dislike for Manon's father that the very thought of the man made his blood boil. But to all of Roland's doleful recriminations, Manon replied in soothing, lofty tones. In a forgiving mood, she also asked his pardon for her past rashness, begging him to attribute it to the very acuteness of feeling she entertained for him. She also presented a touching picture of her daily routine in the convent, sensing no doubt that this would move him more than words of reproach or direct appeals: "I retire and rise early; I devote my mornings to study, my afternoons to needlework and the evenings to music. I go out twice a week, on Mondays and Saturdays, to visit my father and family. I see very few people, and this at the grating of the convent parlor. Sometimes several days go by without my speaking to anyone except my friend Sister Sainte-Agatha, who devotes a half-hour to me every evening. I take walks in the garden despite the bad weather. . . . I like to dream and my taste for solitude is becoming a veritable passion." [42]

On January 9, 1780, Roland was in the capital and on his way to the convent. When he saw Manon, pale and more desirable than ever behind the parlor grating, he was completely overcome. Tears streaming down his face, he swore to marry her forthwith. An emotional reconciliation took place and, at long last, Manon was allowed to lift the secrecy which had heretofore surrounded her affair with Roland. She had triumphed and the prize was well worth the struggle. It is in her most rhetorical style and with a sense of exultation that she hastened to inform Sophie of the happy news, tactfully alluding to the vows of secrecy that had bound her in order to justify her prolonged silence about her relationship with Roland:

I see a new horizon, happiness is smiling upon me, and my position is changing. Deeply moved, but without being intoxicated, I contemplate my destiny with eyes at once peaceful and brimming with tears. Touching and multiple duties are going to fill my heart and my every instant. I am no longer this isolated being deploring her uselessness. Austere resignation, proud courage, which sustain strong souls through misfortune, will be replaced by the pure and modest enjoyments of the heart. As the cherished wife of a man I respect and love, I shall find my felicity in the inexpressible charm of contributing to his happiness. In short, I am marrying M. Roland. The contract is signed, the announcements will be made Sunday (January 30), and before Lent I am his.[43]

In several pages of her *Memoirs*, Mme Roland was to depict her courtship and marriage in a detached, at times humorous manner which contrasts interestingly with the letters of that period.[44] In 1780, Manon had no difficulty convincing herself that she truly loved the man she was marrying. Did he not have, after all, wide experience of the world, vast learning, and an irreproachable morality? To be sure, to win him had necessitated a long, exhausting battle on her part. But if there was any bitterness left in the young woman's heart, she seems to have repressed it, for the taste of this new-found sense of security was so sweet as to be easily confused with that of happiness. Alas, what Manon felt for Roland was not passionate love, but rather that reasoned sentiment which Stendhal would aptly call *un amour de tête*, because the mind, rather than the heart, plays the major role. Thirteen years later, Mme Roland was to learn, at her own expense, the immense difference between the two.

SEVEN

Retreat into Domesticity

In her *Memoirs*, Mme Roland states with typical bluntness that, despite a naturally sensuous temperament, she found "the events of the wedding night equally surprising and disagreeable." [1] To be sure, a secluded and scholarly girlhood and a romantic, bookish idea of love had ill-prepared her for the realities of marriage. But by her own admission, Mme Roland was a full-blooded, lusciously developed young woman, and there is no doubt that she would have overcome her maidenly modesty with greater ease had she been physically attracted to Roland. Like many a sensible bride of pre-Freudian days, however, she did not take this disappointment too tragically, at least at the time. Numerous and absorbing tasks lay ahead and she threw all her energies into these, for was not marriage a serious association in which the woman is entrusted with the responsibility of securing happiness for two persons? The thought that her own share of happiness was being sacrificed in the process of organizing her existence around Roland's well-being did not yet occur to Mme Roland. With characteristic enthusiasm she set about to further the career of the estimable author and administrator she had married, spending countless hours polishing his literary style and sparing him many an ungrateful chore.

Immediately after their marriage, the Rolands settled in a furnished room of the Hôtel de Lyon, rue Saint-Jacques, on the Left Bank. Even though Roland's office was in Amiens, various duties detained him in the capital for the first eight months of his married life. Since the couple's financial means were far from plentiful, Manon did the cooking, shopping, and cleaning herself. Moreover, Roland's health, which was badly strained from constant overwork, necessitated devoted care and a special diet. At first, the young bride seems to have been awed by her husband's technical writings, but she quickly familiarized herself with his work and before long, she had mastered the arduous arts of the secretary, copyist, editor, researcher, proofreader, and even coauthor, all rolled into one! Roland was especially busy at this time, for he was in the process of preparing for publication a number of monographs on different industrial processes as well as his bulky manuscript on his trip to Italy. In addition, he pursued his unrelenting struggle to reform the old restrictions on trade, manufacture, and employment. In the large-scale manufacturing and cloth centers, the medieval guild regulations still prohibited the free movement of artisans from place to place and the unhampered hiring of workers, and the bulk of ordinary manufacturing continued to be carried out by tiny units of masters, journeymen, and apprentices under an antiquated system.

To his delight, Roland discovered that his bride had not only a much more readable style than his own, but that her judgment was sound, and that she had a remarkable ability to bring order and elegance to his untidy manuscripts. She could master the most complex aspects of a manufacturing or technical problem almost effortlessly and present it in a clear, lucid form. Indeed Roland soon grew to depend more and more on his wife's assistance and advice. In addition, the spirit of humility in which she approached his voluminous papers was most flattering to his sensitive ego. As for Mme Roland, if she vaguely sensed that married life did not quite correspond with the exalted notion of it she had entertained as a young girl, she nevertheless was genuinely pleased to make herself so useful to a man for whom she had great respect and affection. Her vigorous health and quick intelligence enabled her to cope with the manifold demands of her new existence without too much stress. And not to neglect the romantic side of her marriage, she would sometimes sing for Roland while accompanying herself on her guitar.[2] Neither were her beloved authors forgotten, but she had to develop a method of cooking while reading at the same time. She does not tell, however, whether this unusual manner of preparing meals gave entirely satisfactory results.[3] At any rate, Roland must have been delighted with married life, for his irascible temperament seems to have mellowed somewhat, and his generally pessimistic views gave way to a more cheerful outlook. He solemnly announced to one of his colleagues that he had found happiness at last. It is doubtful that Manon felt equally elated, but she had entered marriage with her eyes open and was therefore quite satisfied with her lot and determined to make the most of it. The sole diversion in Manon's busy schedule as housewife and literary assistant was a series of lectures in natural history and botany she undertook to attend at the Jardin du Roi, today known as the Jardin des Plantes. With her contemporaries she shared a keen interest in the natural sciences, and she derived much profit and enjoyment from the stimulating conferences and demonstrations conducted by Jussieu, the famed botanist, and Daubenton, the brilliant naturalist and collaborator of Buffon.

Through her husband, Mme Roland met scientists and men of letters, some of whom were to become lifelong friends. Lalande, the well-known astronomer, was a frequent visitor to the Roland household, for he was the inspector's collaborator on some articles on leather crafts. At the Jardin des Plantes, she made the acquaintance of the engaging, cultured, and sensitive Louis Bosc d'Antic, a young botanist. Bosc earned his living as an official in the post office, but his true love was natural science, and his favorite pastime was to roam the woods and fields to collect specimens of plant life. This work had gained him membership to the Academy of Sciences and a certain measure of public recognition. Bosc was quickly won over by Mme Roland and, through her, also became friendly with the inspector. Through the years, he was to remain a devoted and ever helpful adviser and confidant. Even after they left Paris, the Rolands kept up an active correspondence with the young man, whose loyalty and readiness to oblige were boundless. No doubt, Bosc's affection for Mme Roland was tinged with amorous feelings, but he was careful to remain within the bounds of the respectful, platonic admirer. It was only when she would come upon the dark days of the Terror that Manon was to discover the full extent of this shy intellectual's courage and friendship.[4]

Another person whom Mme Roland met at this time and who was to play a rather important role in her life was François Lanthenas, a business man with a keen interest in languages and anatomy. Roland had already made his acquaintance while traveling in Italy. Now they met again in the Hôtel de Lyon, where the young man was also staying. By 1780, Lanthenas had given up the world of affairs and determined to become a physician. Indolent by nature, however, he engaged in his medical training in dilettantish fashion, and it seemed as though he would remain a student forever. Only after several years did he manage to complete the thesis that finally earned him his medical degree.[5] Somehow the exuberant, energetic Manon and the melancholy, irresolute Lanthenas felt drawn toward each other. She gave him various affectionate nicknames, "il fratello" ("little brother" in Italian), "faithful Achates" (after the loyal friend and companion of Aeneas), or "the bachelor." Lanthenas, for his part, called Manon "little sister" or "sorella." He seems to have found his niche in the shadow of the earnest, industrious couple, and they, in turn, accepted him like a younger brother who needed their protection and love. For many years to come, he would remain an obedient satellite in the Roland orbit, and like Bosc, he nourished a secret, hopeless passion for the inspector's virtuous wife. Circumstances, however, were to prove his friendship of a less reliable nature than that of Bosc. It is indeed curious that a person with Mme Roland's critical acumen should have bestowed so much affection upon the weak-willed Lanthenas. But like all those who are not free from an urge to dominate others, she was flattered by his adoring admiration and derived satisfaction from the ascendancy she had over him.

Mme Roland was so absorbed with her new duties and friendships that her heretofore voluminous correspondence with the Cannet sisters rapidly fell to a trickle. Even though she assured Sophie of her undying devotion, one notes a change in the six letters to Amiens written during the year 1780.[6] No longer did Manon relate all the details of her everyday life or give a full account of her thoughts and emotions. She was now a married woman with important claims on her time, and that she viewed her new position with utmost seriousness is indicated by the emphatic way in which she rhapsodizes about it to her girlhood friends. Even though Sophie and Henriette had been hurt by Manon's secrecy over her courtship with Roland, they had graciously forgiven her. But the charm of the old intimacy was broken. The jealously possessive Roland, moreover, had insisted that Manon keep her distance with the Cannet sisters, and she obediently complied with this demand. Only much later, when writing her *Memoirs*, would she question Roland's wisdom in cutting off ties that had meant so much to her.[7] For the time being, however, she was totally engrossed in her new tasks, and her nature was such that, once she deemed something worthy of her efforts, she would become oblivious to the rest of the world.

The months of this first year of marriage flew by rapidly, as Manon busied herself with her household work and collaboration on Roland's writings. The year 1780, however, was marked by an important event for her. In September, Roland took his bride to Lyons and Villefranche to have her meet his family. The couple left Paris on September 1, but the weather, delightful at first, soon became unbearably hot, especially for the voyagers cramped in a coach. Happily, in Chalon-sur-Saône, the uncomfortable carriage was exchanged for a boat, and Manon was able to survey the Saône river, its picturesque banks and the rich Beaujolais countryside. Never before, she reported in a letter to Sophie, had she seen such beautiful and fertile land.[8]

The Rolands spent several days sightseeing in Lyons before proceeding to Villefranche. Manon liked the bustling city and its handsome piers on the Rhône river. Villefranche, on the other hand, was a quiet, dignified town. Not very far from the main church stood the two-storied Roland house, a large sixteenth-century building with elegant ironwork, a garden stretching down to the city walls, a courtyard—in the middle of which stood a beautifully decorated well—and an exterior stairway dating back to the time of Henri IV. Paneling in the style of Louis XIV decorated the spacious dining room. Roland's mother, a sprightly and imperious eighty-one-year-old dowager, and two of her five sons lived in that house. All of Roland's four brothers, of whom he was the youngest, were men of the cloth, and of these only Pierre had met Manon. The oldest, Dominique, was canon of the parish church of Villefranche and lived with his mother and a brother, Laurent.

Manon was well received, and to Sophie she gave a glowing account of her in-laws.[9] At first, the Rolands had not been too happy to learn that the only marriageable member of the family had selected a shopkeeper's daughter as his wife. But if they still had some reservations about this match, they nonetheless endeavored to make the bride feel welcome. As for her, who had always known the solitude of an only child, she was delighted to acquire "brothers," as she told Sophie.[10] In her desire to please the Rolands, especially the eldest brother of her husband, Canon Dominique, she did not spare herself. The Parisian bluestocking and the provincial priest took a ready liking for one another. Canon Dominique was charmed by Manon's lively intelligence and quick wit, and she, in turn, found his gracious manner and cultured conversation most pleasing. It was Dominique who held the title to the family property, including the country house of Le Clos de la Platière, situated about eleven miles from Villefranche. After a while, the couple sought rest and privacy in the retreat of this rustic manor house, which overlooked the picturesque Saône valley. "The old estate is rather isolated but pleasant," Manon wrote to Sophie. "The country is mountainous and almost entirely covered with vineyards; there are some woods on the heights; the landscape is varied, the sky beautiful, the air healthy, the evenings delicious. We roam in the fields; the wine-harvest is in full swing. I don't know how it happens, but I realize that to be happy is an occupation which consumes every available moment and leaves none for anything else." [11] After a two-month stay in Beaujolais, the Rolands were back in the capital, wearied by the trip but filled with pleasant memories.

It was also during this first year of marriage that Roland signed an agreement with Panckoucke, the enterprising publisher who had taken over the new, revised edition of Diderot's *Encyclopedia*. The contract entrusted Roland with the writing of articles on manufactures, industrial arts, and trades, which were to be published in two volumes. As there was a growing need for such reference works, Roland was soon commissioned to begin a third tome. The three volumes of Roland's *Dictionary of Manufactures, Arts, and Trades,* which constitute an integral part of the *Methodical Encyclopedia,* appeared successively in 1784, 1785, and 1790. [12] Like everything written by Roland, the *Dictionary of Manufactures* reveals qualities and faults typical of the author: a wealth of information, but overburdened with unnecessary details and digressions and at times rendered unattractive by an argumentative, carping manner and an ungraceful style. Despite its faults, however, the *Dictionary of Manufactures* made an invaluable contribution to the dissemination of knowledge. It was an important and worthy accomplishment, yet it failed to receive the recognition it deserved, partly because it was lost in the huge and chaotic *Methodical Encyclopedia* which, when eventually completed in 1832, counted over two hundred volumes, and partly because public interest, which had been aroused by the great *Encyclopedia* of Diderot and D'Alembert, was beginning to wane in the 1780s and by 1790, the year when Roland brought out his third volume, was completely absorbed by the momentous events of the Revolution. In addition, too many imitations, editions, and adaptations of the original *Encyclopedia* were competing on the market, and increasingly troubled times hampered the sales of these costly reference works.

The extensive research and literary skill that had to go into the preparation of the *Dictionary of Manufactures* made Manon's collaboration more imperative than ever. Thus, for many years to come she was burdened with a type of work which she pursued with meritorious diligence but which was alien to her own interests and under which she often chafed. Henceforth, much of her time was taken up with mastering the methods of tanning leather, dyeing wool, weaving cloth, preparing soaps and oils, and processing peat for fuel. In addition to his articles for the *Encyclopedia,* the indefatigable Roland had also decided to bring out a series of monographs on a variety of subjects, from the manufacturing and printing of cottons to aquatic botany. And, as it had quickly become a pattern, Manon had a direct hand in the documenting, writing, and proof-reading of every essay.

Ambitious Roland persistently sought official recognition for his tireless scientific activity, and before long he was admitted to a score of academies, both urban and provincial. Even prior to 1789, Roland could boast of being an associate member of the Academy of Villefranche, an adjunct associate of the Academy of Rouen, a correspondent of the Paris Academy of Science and of the Montpellier Royal Society of Science. The Academies of Dijon, Marseilles, Bordeaux, and Lyons gave him similar distinctions, and even foreign cities like Bern, Turin, Bologna, and Rome elected him to their learned societies. Academies played a prominent role in the intellectual life of eighteenth-century Europe, and Roland's membership in so many of them was immensely flattering to his ego. But in order to advance her husband's career, Manon had to neglect, to her chagrin, her beloved Plutarch, Montaigne, and Rousseau and bury herself in forbidding treatises on the manufacturing of practically every product in existence.

Shortly before his marriage, Roland had also undertaken to publish his *Letters from Italy,* and to that effect had made arrangements for its printing in Dieppe. But endless complications slowed up the process. Everything had to be read and approved not only by the king's censor—a normal procedure for all publications under the Old Régime—but also by the Office of Foreign Affairs, since the book purported to deal with a foreign country. To Roland's indignation, whole passages were struck out by inept and fearful officials, thus breaking the continuity of the text and sometimes even distorting its meaning. Roland's liberal views must have alarmed the authorities, for they insisted that the edition appear anonymously, bear the fictitious indication that it was being printed in Amsterdam, and be expedited from Dieppe via Neuchâtel, the small Prussian enclave amid Swiss cantons! [13] So many snags retarded the printing of the work that Roland, always undiplomatic in his dealings with others, quarreled with his publishers. Manon finally decided to go to Dieppe herself to take matters in her own hands. With her usual energy and know-how, she set out to reestablish harmony between the author and his publishers and to prevent the possibility of a pirated edition, a common occurrence in the eighteenth century. She also did her utmost to speed up the incredibly slow and inefficient censoring process, but despite all her efforts, it was not before the end of 1781 that the volumes were finally allowed to be sold. And then, Roland still had to incur the expense of shipping the entire edition from Dieppe to Neuchâtel and then back to France. Such was the logic of the all-powerful censor under the Old Régime. Indeed, a man with Roland's emancipated opinions and advanced philosophy had to consider himself lucky not to see his book burned on the steps of the Paris Parlement by the official executioner and himself carted off to the Bastille.

To the author's keen disappointment, the *Letters from Italy* met with a generally critical reception from the press and with total indifference on the part of the public. Despite undeniable faults of composition, this work did not deserve such a harsh fate. It contains many an illuminating comment on the history, industry, and arts of contemporary Italy, and it also testifies to Roland's breadth of knowledge and diversified experience. Jules Michelet, in his *History of the French Revolution*, rightly speaks of it in highly favorable terms: "This book, although written in an uneven and sometimes obscure style, is nevertheless the most instructive travel account of Italy of all those written in the eighteenth century. . . . The author judges religious Italy and especially Rome from the viewpoint of the *philosophes,* but often with a restraint and fairness too rarely evidenced by them, and which one is surprised to find in this stern observer." [14]

While Manon handled publication problems in Dieppe and paid her round of visits to Roland's friends in Rouen, her husband was busy preparing their house in Amiens. His letters were full of solicitude for her health, for she was expecting to give birth the following October. With touching awkwardness, the generally gruff Roland endeavored to express tender concern for his wife and kept her informed of the progress he was making in preparing their future abode: "I am arranging your room the best I can; I cannot tell you how much I want you to be comfortable in your quarters. The idea of seeing you well settled and happy weighs singularly on my mind." [15] As for Manon, she affectionately reassured Roland about her health and kept him up-to-date on her proceedings with the Dieppe publishers. At the end of February, when she could accomplish no more, Roland fetched her himself, the Amiens home having been made ready for the arrival of its new mistress.

The city of Amiens, ancient capital of the province of Picardy, was an important textile and manufacturing center. A typical northern town, it had an active industry and commerce, but also retained several features of a venerable past. Its magnificent Notre-Dame Cathedral, one of the largest and finest examples of Gothic architecture, and many of its winding streets reminded one of its medieval origins. As it turned out, the house Roland had rented and set up for his wife was a large, drafty, uncomfortable, and rather gloomy structure situated in the quasi-deserted rue du Collège. It adjoined the old Saint-Denis cloister whose grounds served as a cemetery. The rear windows directly faced the churchyard, and every morning from her room Manon could watch the gravediggers at work: "I never go into my dressing room without seeing them digging or filling a pit," she remarked in one of her letters.[16] She tried to be philosophical about it and joked: "People die like flies around here!" [17]

Because of its location and unhealthy humidity, the house had not been inhabited for years; for these reasons Roland had been able to rent it at a very reasonable price. The building had a courtyard, a stable where Roland kept the horse on which he made his rounds, and a garden where Manon liked to putter and where, after much effort, she was rewarded with flowers, vegetables, and even a vine.

With all the energy and skill at her command, she set about making her new home more cheerful and habitable. From the Amiens concert hall she managed to borrow a harpsichord, for her love of music was stronger than ever. Books, engravings, and a few antiques also added an air of distinction to the rooms, but during the cold months Manon shivered in the large drafty house, which was impossible to heat properly. While sleet, snow, and rain beat down on Amiens, covering the city with a veil of gloom, Manon, bundled up in several layers of winter clothes, was filled with melancholy thoughts as she waited for the birth of her child and watched from her window the gravediggers going about their dreary task. Roland was away much of the time on his tours of inspection. During his absence she wrote him long, endearing letters, giving detailed accounts of her daily activities and begging him to avoid overworking. Sometimes she added little caressing messages in Italian.[18]

Roland, who had lived and worked in Amiens for nearly fifteen years before his marriage, had a fairly wide circle of friends and associates in that city. But, as might be expected, Manon cherished her privacy, and this all the more since she considered rather insipid the provincial society of civil servants, merchants, and would-be intellectuals. If she missed the companionship that Henriette and especially Sophie could have provided during those long, solitary days when Roland was away on inspection, she did not show it in her letters to him: "In your absence, solitude and work are the only things I enjoy. All these faces are meaningless to me and make me impatient; I would much rather kill caterpillars in my garden than exchange trifles in society." [19] Through the natural science course she had attended in the Jardin du Roi, and especially through Bosc's influence, she had developed a veritable passion for botanizing. During the four years she was to live in Amiens she would mount and classify an impressive herbarium of plants typical of the Picardy region. Undoubtedly, Rousseau's own love of plant life also had something to do with Manon's taste for botany. On Sundays, she dutifully went to the nearby Collegiate Church, even though she remained a confirmed deist. If she nevertheless attended mass, each time returning home with her feet numb from the stone pavement on which worshippers had to remain standing, it was mainly "for the edification of the neighbors," as she put it.[20] A small-town inhabitant, she maintained, ought not to make himself conspicuous by openly flaunting unorthodox opinions.

On October 4, 1781, Mme Roland gave birth to a girl, who was given the euphonious but rather unusual name of Eudora. As soon as she recovered from her delivery, the new mother wrote a letter to Roland's elder brother, Canon Dominique, humorously begging forgiveness for not having brought forth a boy who would have perpetuated the family name.[21] As a worthy disciple of Rousseau, Mme Roland would not dream of entrusting her child to a wet nurse. In defiance of existing social customs and her doctor's orders, she breast-fed the baby and stubbornly followed Rousseau's famous program. To her immense chagrin, she fell ill, lost her milk, and the infant began wasting away for lack of proper nourishment. Yet, her determination won out; with the help of the *Encyclopedia* and against the advice of everyone, she concocted a special diet for herself, regained her wholesome embonpoint, and Eudora thrived and grew big and fat. At this turn of events, the young mother's pride knew no bounds. She threw herself into her new tasks with fierce determination. At a time when infant mortality was extremely high, Manon lived in constant dread of losing Eudora. Poets and philosophers were temporarily relegated to the back shelves of the library while medical dictionaries and the *Encyclopedia* were constantly consulted. The slightest sign of a possible ailment in the infant, a sneeze, an imperfect digestion, sent the frantic mother scurrying to the *Encyclopedia* for such articles as "Children," "Children's Diseases," and "Nursing." [22] But while some of her ideas were excellent, others gave less successful results. As a firm believer in nature, she nursed the infant, not according to a regular schedule, but allowed it to gorge itself with milk to its heart's content. To her dismay, she found that Eudora was a little glutton who never tired of suckling and howled endlessly as soon as she was replaced in her crib.[23] Poor Manon no longer had a minute to herself and was at her wits' end, for like many a young mother, she could not bear to hear the infant scream itself hoarse. Mme Roland began having some doubts about the theory of the natural goodness of man: "I have concluded," she wrote Roland, "that the fable of Eve is not so stupid and that gluttony is truly an original sin. You philosophers, who do not believe this, who tell us that all the vices originate in society through the development of the passions and the clash of interests, tell me why this six-week-old child, whose imagination is not yet awakened, whose peaceful senses should have no other master than need, is already overstepping its limits." [24]

Roland continued to be away most of the time. During his absences, Manon described in loving detail the daily progress accomplished by Eudora. It was all very touching and a little absurd: the bluestocking was turning into a real mother hen. This, of course, could not last forever since Roland's manuscripts claimed attention. A reliable maid, Marie-Marguerite Fleury, was found. Manon declared herself highly pleased with the services of husky, good-natured "Fleury," as she called the new servant and learned to entrust Eudora to her part of the day. Efficient Fleury turned out to be one of those passionately faithful servants whose loyalty to their mistresses remains as absolute in times of stress as in prosperity. She was to remain in the employ of the Roland family all her life. Other domestics, especially cooks, came and went, but Fleury stayed on, eventually becoming Manon's personal maid and companion, and a strong bond of affection and mutual respect developed between the two women.[25]

The first four years of Manon's married life passed in uneventful domesticity, and Manon's interest in politics waned under the pressure of more immediate matters of concern. To Bosc, who from Paris kept her informed of the latest news, she quipped: "I no longer dabble in politics." [26] When in 1781, an excited neighbor paid a special visit to tell her all about the decisive Franco-American victory in Yorktown over the British general Cornwallis, she listened politely but later wrote to her husband that she could not conceive "the interest that a private person may have in these affairs of kings who are not fighting for us." [27] A surprising remark indeed, to say the least, from one who earlier followed with anxiety the events in America and who, after 1789, was to live and breathe politics! However, this mood was not to last. By 1787, Manon was again immersed in matters of public concern and had regained her enthusiastic admiration for the newly founded American Republic. As a general principle, Mme Roland was opposed to war, reflecting in this, as in many other beliefs, the pacifistic, humanitarian, and cosmopolitan views of the *philosophes*. To the Cannet sisters she had written: "Our modern histories do not offer revolutions in which entire nations rise to fight for freedom and the public good. We see only subjects killing one another for the sake of princes. They are, as says Raynal, chained slaves fighting for the entertainment of their masters." [28] At Amiens, she tended to regard the American Revolution as a war between the French and English governments and not as a war of liberation of a proud young nation.

Because Roland was too involved in his economic research and professional quarrels to engage in epistolary debates on philosophy or literature, Manon turned to good, reliable Bosc, who was willing enough to cross pens with her, but who did not constitute a very challenging adversary. One such epistolary discussion concerned the respective qualities of the sexes, and Bosc, expecting his adversary to champion the cause of feminism, launched the debate by claiming the biological superiority of the male. It was with some surprise that he read Manon's reply, dated July 29, 1783, in which she did not dispute his point, but added some qualifying thoughts on the subject:

You were not mistaken about the claims of your sex. . . . But even then you have not endangered your position, for I do not intend to challenge it. You have been careless in your method of attack, that is all. For what are the deference and consideration your sex shows toward mine if not the regard the powerful have for the weak, which they honor and protect at the same time? When you speak like masters, you immediately make one think that you can be resisted, and go even further than that, your strength notwithstanding (Achilles was not totally invulnerable). Do you pay us homage? It is like Alexander treating his female prisoners as though they were queens, even though they remain aware of their dependence. Perhaps only in this respect does our civilization follow nature; the laws keep us constantly under your thumb, and usage grants us in society all the small honors. In action we count for naught; in appearance we are everything.

Do not imagine, therefore, that I delude myself about what we can demand or expect. I believe, I would not say more than any woman, but as much as any man, in the superiority of your sex in every respect. In the first place, you have strength, and everything that goes with it results from it: courage, perseverance, wide horizons and great talents. It is up to you to make the laws in politics as it is to make the discoveries in science. Govern the world, change the surface of the globe, be proud, terrible, clever, and learned. You are all that without our help, and through all that you are bound to be our masters. But without us you would not be virtuous, loving, loved, or happy. Keep therefore all your glory and authority. As for us, we have and wish no other supremacy than that over your morals, no other rule than that over your hearts. I shall claim nothing beyond that. It often angers me to see women disputing privileges which ill befit them. And even the name of author, whatever the circumstances may be, strikes me as ridiculous when applied to them. No matter what their facility may be in some respects, they should never show their learning or talents in public.[29]

In subscribing to the theory of male superiority and in condemning feminism, Manon was being consistent with herself, for she had often set forth this view. In this she was following, uncritically and perhaps unwittingly, Rousseau's own brand of antifeminism. Rigid and unswerving in this belief, she was convinced that a woman's purpose in life was to bring happiness to her spouse, and that those who sought personal achievement did so at the cost of their most sacred trust. Curiously enough, only when it was too late to change the course of her life would she become aware, and this only dimly so, of the discrepancy between her theories and some of her strongest aspirations. For the time being, however, it was probably her unconscious hope that by adhering scrupulously to time-honored conventions she might achieve happiness, or at least inner peace.

In this respect, Mme Roland was at the opposite pole of a Mme de Staël, who sighed for peace of mind and domestic happiness, yet could not resist the urge to publish her writings and make a name for herself. Of a much more introvert nature than Necker's daughter, Mme Roland was quite willing to make her husband the sole beneficiary of her literary and intellectual endowments. She could not realize while writing her letter to Bosc that her rigidly antifeminist position would one day backfire and that, to a large extent against her own wishes, she would eventually find herself in the limelight. For like Mme de Staël's, hers was a nature that needed a broader stage than that provided by family and friends. By rashly passing judgment on those women of mettle who dared defy the conventions attached to their sex, she was making matters more difficult for herself by creating a conflict between her avowed principles and her emotional needs.

EIGHT

A Mission to Paris

IN 1784, ROLAND DECIDED to claim a patent of nobility, which would automatically grant him many important privileges as well as the offiical right to use the *de* before his surname, Roland de la Platière.[1] After all, his family tree could be traced to the sixteenth century, and the Rolands were among the most respected members of Beaujolais society. More importantly, Roland was nearing the age of retirement and felt that his many years of public service entitled him to this recognition. Such proceedings, we should point out, were by no means unusual in the eighteenth century. To accuse Roland of undemocratic leanings because he took this step in pre-Revolutionary France, as some French historians have done, is to fail to recognize the political realities of the Old Régime and the fact that an official title of nobility conferred numerous financial and social advantages. To be able to add the nobiliary particle was a common enough ambition in a society where rank and birth meant everything, and personal accomplishment very little. Even such great liberals as Voltaire, whom Diderot was always careful to call M. de Voltaire, and the brilliant playwright and political intriguer Beaumarchais ennobled their names at the first opportunity.

Owing to Roland's gruffish countenance and his unpopularity with the authorities, it was decided that Manon would have a better chance of success if she went to Paris and deployed all her wit and diplomacy with influential officials. Leaving Eudora and Roland in Amiens, she set out for the capital on March 18, 1784.[2] She was accompanied by Fleury and had provided herself with several copies of her husband's publications and genealogy. Once more she settled in the Hôtel de Lyon, where she had spent her honeymoon. There she found Lanthenas, who was eager to interrupt his medical studies to accompany her on the endless rounds of visits. Bosc, too, graciously neglected the post office and botany for her sake.³ With these two gay companions Manon regained all the youthful high spirits of more carefree days. It was good to be in Paris again, and to come and go as one pleased. Manon's mission was rather delicate, and required both time and patience. She visited her husband's superiors, generously distributed copies of his recently published *Letters from Italy,* summoned all her eloquence to sing his praises, and made several trips to Versailles where one inevitably ended up in any kind of favor seeking.

As a young girl Mme Roland had been extremely critical of Versailles. Now she approached it in a spirit of amused tolerance and played her game of soliciting with assurance and even some relish. She held long interviews with wives of important personages, behaved with appropriate deference, and took advantage of her stay to revisit the palace and its gardens. Since a great deal would depend on the impression she produced, she paid more attention than was her custom to her appearance. For the first time in her life, she absorbed herself in questions of fashion, selecting her dress materials and hats with the care of a coquette. And to make full use of her time, she learned to carry on her correspondence while her hair was being arranged in elaborate coiffures.⁴ All these efforts seemed to produce the desired results: men welcomed her warmly and appeared to listen to her with interest. Unhappily, her charm and eloquence did not suffice to offset the ill feelings most intendants of commerce had for Roland, and without their recommendation her mission was doomed to failure. One, the influential Tolozan, even went so far as to tell her bluntly that her husband was too proud and independent, and had moreover acquired the reputation for being an overweening pedant and an insubordinate administrator. Rising to Roland's defense, yet careful not to lose her sang-froid, Manon shrewdly turned these harsh criticisms to advantage by retorting that

such vague and unfair accusations only proved that Roland's superiors must resent his industry and uncompromising love of truth.
As for his independent turn of mind and lack of submissiveness,
they clearly indicated one thing: he was cut out to lead and not to
be led. In short, Manon had a ready answer for every objection. Her
interviewers were quick to sense that they would never have the last
word with this determined woman. They therefore let her have her
say, showered her with compliments, and made nebulous promises
while assuring her of their wholehearted moral support.

In her letters to Roland, Manon made full reports of her discussions; she even repeated, somewhat mischievously, a few of the
disagreeable things she had been told about him.[5] Yet she did not
give up. Going from one intendant to the next, she hoped to reach
eventually Calonne himself, Roland's highest superior and the Con-
troller General of Finances. Finally, however, she had to face the
inescapable fact that, between Paris and Versailles, she was being
given the run-around. Fares and incidentals were beginning to mount
up and entire days passed in waiting in antechambers or in listening
politely to long-winded speeches by conceited bureaucrats. She was
tempted to go to Calonne and present her case directly to him, without any further ado. Such a blunt approach appealed to her, but
she feared that it might do more harm than good. Calonne had just
been appointed and was eager to please everyone at this time, especially his immediate subordinates, the intendants of commerce, who
were unfortunately ill-disposed toward Roland. She resolved, therefore, to pursue the more prudent course.

Getting into the spirit of the game of intrigue, Manon resorted
to subterfuge to impress Roland's superiors with the urgency of her
case. When she was asked why she took all this trouble to seek a
title of nobility, as she had only a daughter, she slyly implied that
an heir might well be expected within a few months. "This makes
my case more touching; they watch me walk and I laugh in my
sleeve. I do not go so far, though, as to tell an outright lie," she
reported to Roland.[6] She also wrote that she had the makings of a
first-rate intriguer and that, given a house in Paris and the necessary

financial means, she could accomplish anything through string-pulling.[7] All this boasting, however, was to cheer up lonely Roland. On the whole, while she enjoyed her stay in her native city, she was beginning to despair of the outcome of her mission.

To distract Manon, her friends took her to a series of lectures on electricity, the newest discovery and the fad of Paris at the moment. It was believed that electricity could be used for curing all manner of ailments; a professor of obstetrics at the Faculty of Medicine, Alphonse Leroy, lectured on this fascinating subject.[8] Lanthenas, an enthusiastic disciple of mesmerism and physiognomy, also introduced his friend to the mysteries of hypnosis, and Bosc lent her Lavater's treatise on personality study through facial characteristics. Mme Roland was intrigued but still a bit skeptical. She found Lavater's descriptions highly interesting, but doubted that they were based upon truly scientific principles.[9] For relaxation she reread Richardson's *Clarissa* in the French translation; after a full day of soliciting she was too exhausted to struggle with the complexities of the English language.[10] Bosc and Lanthenas helped Manon forget the vicissitudes of the French bureaucratic hierarchy and the obstacles that lay in the path of ennoblement. At first, she hardly budged from her hotel room in the evening, but gradually she started going out to attend plays, operas, and ballets. On April 27, 1784, a sensational event brought the theatrical season out of a period of doldrums. Beaumarchais' *Marriage of Figaro*, condemned several times, yet performed for the court at Versailles, was given its Paris première. It immediately enjoyed a political *succès de scandale* and caused, as Manon reported to her husband, "a great crush." [11] Not being especially fond of the theater, she made no special effort to see the play herself and relied on secondhand comments. More conscientious when it came to music and ballet, Manon made it a point to attend *Les Danaïdes*, an immensely successful opera by Antonio Salieri, an Italian composer who was a friend of Haydn and later to become the teacher of Beethoven, Schubert, and Liszt.[12] It was at this performance that she heard the renowned singer Sainte-Huberti and saw the incomparable Guimard dance.

One evening was also spent at a variety show, where a parody of Grétry's opera, *La Caravane du Caire,* made her laugh heartily.[13] At a concert, she had something of a shock when she recognized, sitting in the adjoining loge, Pahin de La Blancherie, the man with whom she had at one time been infatuated. He had turned into a literary and music critic and an art promoter of some sorts. More vain looking than ever, he gazed at the audience with superior airs and either did not, or pretended not to, notice the woman to whom he had sworn eternal love. Manon thought little enough of this unexpected encounter to relate it, in humorous terms, to her husband.[14] With the exception of Beaumarchais, there were hardly any controversies over the theater in Paris that year, a rather unusual situation for a city where the latest plays were invariably the subject of passionate discussions and even acrimonious quarrels.[15] The musical world, on the other hand, was in a state of effervescence. Gluck seemed temporarily downgraded, and the merits of other composers were heatedly debated.

Early in 1784, air travel by balloon had just made its appearance; everyone was excitedly talking about the next projected trip by the physicist, Jacques Charles, which was scheduled to take place during the Easter holidays. In 1783, the Montgolfier brothers had invented and sent up the first practical balloon, a large linen bag inflated with hot air. The same year, Jacques Charles, filling a balloon with hydrogen gas, had made an ascent of almost two miles. Now he was to repeat the experiment. From the Jardin du Roi, Manon and her two friends witnessed the historic flight; to Roland she described the thrill of watching the elaborately decorated balloon, carrying the daring aeronaut, climb steadily and disappear in the horizon.[16] These were man's first attempts to travel through air, a feat dreamed about since early classical times and causing wild enthusiasm in France and much of Europe.

As a wife who took her husband's interests very much to heart, Manon was not content chasing after a title of nobility. Between errands and official visits, she also managed to see Panckoucke, the editor of the *Methodical Encyclopedia* for whom Roland was preparing his *Dictionary of Manufactures*. What is more, she badgered the printers, corrected proof sheets, and inspected the plates that were to illustrate the text, consulting with such a renowned engraver as Michel Audran. Soon, Roland was receiving a steady stream of proofs and detailed reports on the printers' progress. Manon also tried, but in vain, to stimulate the sales of the *Letters from Italy*. All this activity did not prevent her from fulfilling some personal duties. One afternoon was spent at the Convent of the Congregation, where she learned from Sister Saint-Agatha that Phlipon had paid a visit only a week before and had bitterly complained about his daughter's prolonged silence.[17] Manon was willing enough to let bygones be bygones, but in this, as in many other matters, was not free to act as she saw fit. Roland had given her strict orders to stay away from her father. One might have wished for less vindictiveness; but while avoiding all personal rapprochement, he did not abandon the improvident old man to his fate. Through Bosc and Lanthenas, he settled Phlipon's debts, paid his back rent, and also enabled him to retire from his unsuccessful business by providing for a pension. During her two-month stay in Paris, however, Mme Roland, heeding her husband's instructions, not once crossed the threshold of her former home on the Quai de l'Horloge. Grandmother Phlipon, with whom she had lived after leaving the convent, had recently died in her eighty-ninth year. But good uncle Bimont was as alive and cheerful as ever, and he excitedly greeted his niece in his little Vincennes cottage.[18]

As the spring weather grew milder, Lanthenas and Bosc took Manon on several outings. They went for strolls in the Bois de Boulogne, botanizing to their hearts' content. In the Jardin du Roi, they could combine pleasure with intellectual stimulation, since public lectures continued to be given there. They walked to the Palais-Royal to inspect the Duke of Orléans' famous collection of paintings.[19] At Chaillot, they viewed a fire engine, a new invention that was drawing curious crowds.[20] In nearby Charenton, they were shown the latest spinning and weaving machines, and Manon dutifully sent her husband a sample of the cotton that these turned out;

and since Roland was also interested in sheep, she made a trip to the village of Alfort, where the naturalist Daubenton was attempting to acclimatize a herd of Spanish merinos.[21]

Both Bosc and Lanthenas were striving to give Manon the best time of her life. When Bosc heard her say that she missed her harpsichord, he hastened to have a pianoforte installed in her hotel room.[22] The two young men paid her respectful yet flattering court. It was a pleasant feeling to know that, even though she was married, a mother, and had reached her thirtieth birthday, she could still be attractive to men. Roland, however, began fretting and took in bad part the familiar and jesting tone Bosc assumed in his letters to him. With characteristic lack of humor, he sent a rather disagreeable missive to the young man, who in turn good-naturedly scolded the jealous husband: "What the devil are you trying to quarrel about? We are only teasing you. But this does not mean that we feel less sorry about your loneliness. And yesterday, when your better half told me the approximate date of her departure, I thought more of your reunion than of her leaving which, despite my busy schedule, will certainly leave a very considerable void in my life." [23] Such concern for Roland's feelings had the desired effect of mollifying his temper; he replied in a more playful spirit: "You are absolutely right and one must be fair. But where is one to find this woman you are debauching? Every day I hear of new pranks, and if you are not the author, at least you take part in them. What have you to say for yourself? . . . Tell me seriously, though. Are you determined to keep my Manon much longer? Do you know that I am beginning to weary of so long an absence and, if it is not soon cut short, I shall end up getting angry?" [24]

In her own letters to Roland, Manon soothed her dispirited husband by repeating how much she missed him and Eudora and how eager she was to return home. But it would be a shame, she patiently explained, to abandon her mission just as things seemed to be coming to a head. She therefore pleaded for a little more time and showered her letters with liberal doses of expressions of tenderness and concern: "Above all else, dearest, tell me about your health. I

almost feel like scolding you when you don't write a word about it.
Do you regularly apply poultices? What is magnetism doing for you?
Do you digest? Do you sleep? Are you yellow or is your complexion
good? How do you feel? Please speak in detail and at length on all
these points." [25] Roland continued to suffer from a bad liver and a
case of ulcers, and his wife was eager to have him try the new "mag-
netic treatment." [26] She also constantly inquired about little Eudora.
The remembrance of her daughter's childish voice once brought her
to the verge of tears: "I am nothing but a mother," she wrote Roland,
"with all the weaknesses of mothers." [27] With good Fleury, who was
totally miserable and lost in the big city and did not dare to go to
the street corner by herself, Manon could chat at length about
her little girl. The two women were much amused to learn of Eudora's latest prank. Right under her father's nose, while he was
writing away, she had managed to cut into strips his best garters, a
destructive accomplishment that had been carried out in such a quiet
manner that Roland had suspected nothing until the damage was
done. [28]

Waxing philosophical, Manon spoke of the futility of worldly
honors and the fickleness of Dame Fortune: "It seems to me that
we are as happy as we can be, with our little plot of land where we
will be able to rest our heads, bidding goodbye to all the vanities.
Be healthy, my friend, and may heaven keep and preserve our Eudora. I wish for nothing more on earth. I kiss you and her *affettuosis-
simamente*." [29] The fact that, after two months of doorknocking, Manon was hardly more advanced in her mission than on the day she
had left Amiens must have contributed to this mood of world-weariness. In the meantime, Roland had become positively neurotic and
was plaintively clamoring for her swift return. In an unexpected
way, however, Mme Roland's stay in Paris was to prove of great
importance to the inspector's career.

During one of her innumerable visits, she overheard that the
General Inspectorship of Lyons might become vacant through an
administrative reshuffling. Immediately realizing that this might be
her golden opportunity, since the Lyons post was of greater conse-

quence than the one at Amiens and also more desirable because of
its location near the family house at Villefranche and the small
Roland estate of Le Clos, she applied for it, then ran back to the
hotel to inform Roland of this turn of events.[30] In order not to
ruffle his masculine pride she explained that there had been no time
to consult him before staking her claim to the position; someone else
might have got wind of the opening and seized it while she was
waiting for her husband's approval. By now, however, loneliness
had made Roland submissive. He gave his blessing and added that
he subscribed in advance to anything she would judge suitable, so
long as it would speed up her homecoming.[31]

Lo and behold; whereas claiming a patent of nobility had been
a tiresome and frustrating business, Roland's transfer to Lyons was
approved without a hitch. Within three days the petition was granted
and confirmed. Mme Roland, moreover, had not forgotten a thing,
driving a hard bargain for salary, gratuity, and retirement benefits.
M. Tolozan, who had once spoken so harshly to her, now seemed
to be under her spell and promised that Roland's emoluments would
be equal to those of the highest-paid provincial inspector.[32] It was
a personal triumph for Manon, and one for which her husband felt
humbly grateful. At first, apprehensive over his reaction to this
sudden change in his situation, she was much relieved to receive
generous praise for her successful efforts and to detect, in his letters
to her, a new note of confidence in and respect for her capabilities:
"For us, my dearest," she gaily wrote him, "it is definitely Le Clos,
greenery, Eudora, delightful peace, our mutual devotion. We shall
have all that and I don't give a hoot for the rest." [33]

All this frantic activity had left its mark on the once plump
Manon: "I feel active and vigorous, but have become as skinny as
a cuckoo," she jested, adding: "It does not show because of my round
face. On the whole I feel rather well, though I need a rest badly." [34]
Nervous exhaustion finally got the better of her; an alarmed Roland
rushed off to Paris to fetch his ailing wife and bring her back to
the nest. The parting with Bosc and Lanthenas was not without tears,
especially on the part of sentimental Bosc.[35] Before repairing to

Amiens, the couple decided to make a pilgrimage to Ermenonville, where Rousseau had died in 1778 and had been laid to rest. Fervent disciple of Jean-Jacques that she was, Mme Roland felt deeply moved by the sight of the famous Isle of Poplars, in the lake of Ermenonville.[36] The castle, lake, and isle proper were picturesque enough and had an appropriately melancholy aura, but Manon was rather disappointed by the gardens landscaped in an artificial imitation of the English style. The valley, woods, and marshes, moreover, she found gloomy and depressing. To Bosc she wrote that, if Jean-Jacques had not made this place famous by his presence, she doubted whether anyone would ever have made a detour to visit it. Upon being shown the writer's room, which remained as it was when he had lived and worked there, she reached the conclusion that he had indeed been poorly lodged: "He is better off now than he ever was in his lifetime. This world was unworthy of him," she philosophized.[37]

By June 7, 1784, Manon was back in Amiens. Little Eudora no longer recognized her and howled with fright when her mother made a move to lift and embrace the child. This proved a shock to Mme Roland's maternal feelings. "I can't think about it without a terrible heaviness in my heart," she confided to Bosc, "and though Eudora has resumed her tender ways with me, I no longer dare have faith in her caresses." [38] There was much work to be done during this month of June. Preparations for the moving to Lyons had to be completed, proofs of the *Dictionary of Manufactures* kept coming in and needed careful correction, and a number of officials in Paris had to be thanked in writing for Roland's advantageous transfer. Moreover, the inspector had impulsively decided, probably as a reward for his wife's successful efforts, to take her on a one-month trip to England before settling in Lyons.

NINE

A Journey to England

WHEN, ON JULY 1, 1784, the Rolands left Amiens for Boulogne, the first lap of their journey, Manon saw the fulfillment of a long-cherished dream. Like so many of her contemporaries who had become imbued with the tenets of the Enlightenment, she was a rabid Anglophile. In her admiration for England and all things English, she had taught herself to read the language and had steeped herself in the history, literature, and philosophic thought of that nation. Despite neoclassical prejudices that still prevailed in French literary circles, she was one of the first to venerate Shakespeare; she ranked Richardson above all other novelists, including her beloved Rousseau, and had a keen appreciation for the poetry of Young, Thomson, and Gray. Indeed, in the presence of a beautiful natural setting, she could think of nothing more fitting than Thomson's *Seasons*, large portions of which she had committed to memory. Nor were Newton, Locke, and Hume mere names to this earnest student of philosophy for whom Descartes' vortices and animal spirits and Leibniz's monads held no secret. But, above all, she had a particularly keen interest in British political institutions and in the development of constitutional monarchy and had spent many hours poring over treatises on English history, from the Magna Carta to the Revolution of 1688. As a Parisian with a lower middle-class background, who had oftentimes smarted at the arrogance of the French nobles, she looked upon the English system, with its constitutional monarchy and parliamentary traditions, as a model which France would do well to imitate if she was to achieve an enlightened social system of her own. Through Montesquieu's *Spirit of the Laws* and Voltaire's *Letters on the English Nation,* she had familiarized herself with the traditions and customs of the one nation which, despite certain imperfections, offered a greater measure of political freedom, religious tolerance, and judicial equity than France had ever done. And the *philosophes* had taught her that no human happiness is possible without political guarantees of the individual's natural rights and without a fair distribution of power. Indeed, few people were as thoroughly prepared as Manon for a trip to the abode of Shakespeare, Locke, and the *habeas corpus.* England, for this disciple of the Encyclopedists, was not only a mighty nation endowed with great intellectual and political traditions, but embodied as well an ideal, a way of life that prized individual merit and genius.

At Boulogne the Rolands boarded a two-cabin boat. The weather was balmy and the sea perfectly serene. Mme Roland, moved by the spectacle, fell into a typically preromantic mood: "The beauty of the sky, the smoothness of the water, the vast expanse of both, presented a sight at once impressive and pleasing. Led to meditation, we feel ourselves drawn into a delightful reverie; the ripples of the waves attract our gaze and keep, in a manner, our reflections suspended, impressing upon our mind a certain melancholy from which we should not wish to be distracted." [1] After a smooth crossing, which lasted ten hours, a swift voyage for that time, the boat docked at Dover.

Once in England, Mme Roland set out to investigate every aspect of English life which was to fall within her reach. Her travel diary, crammed with observations of all kinds, reveals that very little escaped her inquisitive and tireless scrutiny: comments range from a comparison between French and English livestock to an account of the current parliamentary debate between brilliant young Pitt and his opponent Fox over the East India Company. In addition to having qualities of directness and immediacy, this lively and informal journal, which its author dedicated to her daughter without any intention of publication, is interspersed with a number of remarks serving to point up the political and economic shortcomings of contemporary France. With a feminine concern for concrete and practical details of everyday life, she set down specific features that one would seek in vain in the more general reports of such famous French visitors to England as the Abbé Prévost, Montesquieu, and Voltaire. In his *Letters on the English Nation,* Voltaire had been chiefly concerned with religious, political, and literary topics. Mme Roland's range of observation emphasizes customs more fully than Voltaire's. To be sure, her essay is less original and no longer reflects Voltaire's provocative, revolutionary intention. By 1784, it had, after all, become quite fashionable, in French enlightened circles, to admire and copy everything English. In the meantime, Rousseau, penetrated with the ideas of another Swiss writer, Béat Louis de Muralt, who had published his influential *Letters on the English and the French* as early as 1725, made his own contribution to French interest in England and to a conception of the English as brave, generous, proud, freedom-loving, and reasonable through his fictional character Lord Edouard Bomston in *La Nouvelle Héloïse,* a novel that had made an extraordinary and lasting impression on Mme Roland and her generation.

To French eyes Britain in the third quarter of the eighteenth century presented an exciting blend of privilege and liberty, elegance and easy informality, tradition and reform. As Mme Roland surveyed from her coach placid countrysides and prosperous, bustling towns, she sensed the presence of a powerful nation of tough, confident, resourceful individualists. While journeying from Dover to London by stagecoach, she singled out for praise the well-kept roads, where "there is not a rut to be seen." [2] The trim cottages, surrounded by sleek lawns and tidy gardens, the clean, comfortable inns and public carriages, all these were outward signs that testified to the industriousness, ingenuity, and well-being of a creative people. Everywhere the useful had been tastefully blended with the pleasant and, in comparison with these fine, flourishing cities and villages, she thought the French provinces sadly neglected: "It is evident that man, whatever he may be, is here reckoned something and that a handful of rich do not constitute a whole nation." [3]

On the road to London, the Rolands stopped briefly at Canterbury and approvingly commented upon the tidiness and unobtrusive dignity evident in the humblest homes and tradesmen's shops. "The English who travel in France must, by comparison, think us terribly filthy," was Mme Roland's sharp comment.[4] As for the famous cathedral, the stark austerity of its interior greatly impressed her. Accustomed as she was to the richly adorned Catholic churches, she welcomed this simplicity, which she found in keeping with the spirit that should pervade places of worship: "No image, no statue obscure the simple and sublime idea of the First Cause; two books on the altar are all its ornaments." [5] As a Catholic who had renounced orthodoxy in favor of Rousseau's sentimental brand of deism with pietistic overtones, Mme Roland was favorably disposed toward Protestantism.

Upon leaving Canterbury, the Rolands drove through the open, fertile country of Kent and enjoyed its magnificent vistas, softened by a thin haze. Now and then alighting from the carriage in order to linger upon the stately prospects of large hamlets and country seats bounded by the Thames, the traveling party reached the towns of Chatham and Rochester. The port of Chatham teemed with vessels and frigates, ready for service. The Rolands had themselves rowed about in a rented dinghy, but were not allowed to board any of His Majesty's ships. What she saw prompted Mme Roland's remark that nothing demonstrates England's wealth and power so vigorously as her crowded ports. On the right bank of the Thames, the crisscross pattern made by the masts of ships at anchor, the barracks and docks, and the sailors attending to their tasks formed a lively picture—one that contrasted sharply with the quietness and pastoral character of the left shore. After landing, the couple took a leisurely walk alongside the river and came upon a Scottish regiment in kilts, a sight that delighted them. Before reaching London, Manon made several observations on the English countryside: crops were more abundant than in France; cemeteries were simple but well-kept,

and even the graves of those too poor to afford tombstones were
carefully arranged and covered with turf; stone pavements were laid
out in front of village houses for the convenience of foot passen-
gers; both town and country women went out bareheaded and almost
all had "an easy and lively air, and appeared neat and modest." [6]

At last Georgian mansions and myriad houses announced the approaching capital, and St. Paul's great dome rose majestically in the
distance. After taking up quarters at the house of a Frenchman,
where they were offered room and board "at three shillings a day
for the apartment and two shillings a head for each meal," [7] the
Rolands were free to inspect the city's sights to their hearts' content.[8] Like a huge magnet, London attracted about one-tenth of England's rapidly growing population. Its teeming harbor was crowded
with riches from the high seas, nearly all its houses appeared to
have been built with a view to convenience and comfort, and along
its cobblestone streets vendors hawked their wares and shopkeepers
did a brisk business. In all fashionable places, in theaters and pleasure
gardens, the nobility found itself jostled by the rich middle class.
London, at once the seat of Parliament and a throne of high finance
from which ruled the prosperous merchant princes, mirrored an ex-
panding, prosperous nation. Commercial traffic was dense over
London Bridge and on the Thames, and the air was thick with
smoke which, together with the fogs, surrounded the city in a perpetual haze. "One has to go to St. Paul's at sunrise to get a clear view
of London," noted Mme Roland.[9] Here indeed was an aggressive
metropolis full of contrasts and diversified spectacles, which our visitors explored with their usual thoroughness. Mme Roland was impressed with the numerous squares and gardens. Strolling through
the Strand, she admired its shops, all provided with glass windows, a
novelty not yet much seen in Paris:

Broad pavements of flagstones run along before the houses and afford
people on foot the facility of walking without being in fear of the carriages. Everything showy and brilliant that jewelry, fashions, cloths, and
the arts can offer, as well as cutlery and a thousand consumer goods, is
placed to advantage in the shops, behind beautiful glass panes that

protect them from every inconvenience. Even fruit, pastry, fish, and butcher's meat are set out with this luxury of cleanliness; the climate no doubt and the smoke of the pit-coal make this necessary.[10]

A visit to the Houses of Parliament enabled Mme Roland to witness the much admired English system in action. St. Paul's Cathedral caused her to say, with typical eighteenth-century disregard for the great Gothic churches, that "in France we have nothing that can be compared to it." [11] Whitehall immediately evoked the fate of Charles I, for he was beheaded just outside the palace. St. James's Park, with its extensive but formal walks and well-kept lawns, pleased her without answering to her romantic notion of English gardens. St. James's Palace, on the other hand, provoked reflections on the simple mode of living of George III and Queen Charlotte. No doubt Mme Roland had in mind Marie-Antoinette and her profligate ways when she spoke of Queen Charlotte's devotion to home and family:

It is in this palace or at Windsor that the queen, entirely employed in her family, spends her life, which might in many respects be compared to that of the princesses of the heroic times of which Homer makes mention. The queen does not possess a handsome face, but she has the look of a sensible woman, and is so in reality. As a result, she is generally esteemed and loved. She sees little company, displays her dignity only on occasions of ceremony and gives no other entertainments than two balls a year, on the anniversary of the king's birth and of her own. These balls finish at midnight: some minuets are danced, as well as a few country dances; in other respects, no supper, no show, no expense.[12]

The Royal Exchange and Bank of England afforded Mme Roland an idea of the economic workings of a powerful and wealthy nation; Guildhall, where a court of law was held before the Lord Mayor himself, and where were heard litigations arising within the city, vividly illustrated judicial procedures she had learned to appreciate through Montesquieu and Voltaire. She even saw the Lord Mayor proceeding to Guildhall in great pomp: "Six fine horses drew his coach, which is very large and extremely ornate, like the state carriages of the king of France." [13]

An excursion on the Thames revealed sweeping panoramic views of the English capital. The imposing spectacle of ships of all nations bringing to London their commodities and riches, the bustle on the docks, the massive Tower of London looming over the waters, the "sixty-four guns leveled on the quay, giving its entrance a respectable appearance," [14] and the endless rows of workshops, storehouses, and shipyards succeeding one another from London to Greenwich, made her sense, more forcefully than anywhere else in the city, the vital rhythms of a nation proud and vigorous.

An afternoon was devoted to visiting two hospitals for invalid soldiers and sailors, one in Chelsea and the other in Greenwich. Forgetting the Hôtel des Invalides, Mme Roland hastened to point out that her own country had no such magnificent and well-run establishments built entirely for the welfare of its defenders: "We have some fine things in France, but all done by the princes at the expense of their subjects and arbitrarily imposed; while ignored in their provinces the people weep over a good of which they partake only through the sweat of their brow and the depth of their misery." [15] A visit to the Tower of London was also *de rigueur*. There the Rolands were shown huge arsenals of weapons, including instruments of war and torture captured from the Spaniards by Elizabeth, wax effigies of the kings of England clad in armor and mounted on horseback, and the place where Edward V had been confined and put to death by Richard III.

Not without pride, Mme Roland recorded that her husband was received at the house of Sir Joseph Banks, who had accompanied Captain James Cook on his celebrated voyage around the world and who had served as President of the Royal Society. The members of this distinguished group had assembled especially to welcome, as Mme Roland put it, "the enlightened and industrious author with whose works they were acquainted." [16] And addressing herself directly to Eudora, to whom she had dedicated this journal, she added this little moral: "Your father thus received that reward so flattering to a man who, by his own efforts, has devoted himself to the public good and can find countrymen among all nations." [17] Neither could the Rolands, with their keen interest in the arts and sciences, fail to inspect the various collections housed in the British

Museum. Winckelmann had recently aroused general curiosity about antiquity and classic art, and Mme Roland noted the "very considerable" number of finely preserved archeological finds, from mummies to such household items as vases. She also singled out for praise "the cabinet of natural history, particularly rich in mineralogy, and the very extensive library." [18] Animals, she pointed out, had been classified according to Linnaeus' method and "could not be more conveniently arranged." [19] In this connection, it might be pointed out that the British Museum, in the eighteenth century, was located in a palace that had formerly belonged to the Duke of Montague. It was only in 1845 that Montague House was pulled down and the present building erected.[20]

Sunday in London, Mme Roland observed with some amused puzzlement, was far more rigidly observed than in Paris: shops and public places were shut, and games of all sorts strictly prohibited. The people congregated mainly in the churches and streets. "It should not be imagined, however," Mme Roland tells us, "that the crowds are as great in the churches as in the streets, for the inhabitants walk more than they pray." [21] Entering a church during service, Mme Roland was struck, once more, by the simplicity of the interior, as well as by the fact that prayers were said in English rather than in Latin. St. James's Park, too, was well worth a visit on a Sunday afternoon and evening, for its principal walks were filled with strollers. Women wore gowns of fine muslin and richly beribboned hats while men favored plain cloth coats, white waistcoats, and black shoes. Despite her tendency to admire everything English, Mme Roland had to admit that, in the realm of ladies' fashions at least, the French remained unexcelled: "Except for a very small number, one cannot find among them an elegance and good taste anything like ours." [22] English women nevertheless possessed a romantic appeal, due primarily to their winning modesty and serious demeanor, which Mme Roland found lacking in her compatriots: "The women, who are well-educated and well-read, but who make no display of their knowledge, have a maidenly and compelling look. Their fair complexion and gentle, melancholy expres-

sion inspire an interest of a very different nature from the sensations aroused by our smart figures and sprightly airs; these entice
while the others soften: a man would be tempted to amuse himself
with the one, and to love the other. . . ." [23] English women, she
further observed, generally led a very domestic life and spent a great
deal of time with their children. Neither did the greater separation
of the sexes escape Mme Roland's notice: morality was thereby
enhanced, and the happiness of family life secured. The typically
British institution of men's clubs, already quite prevalent towards the
close of the eighteenth century, furnished the subject of a detailed
and favorable description:

The men form among themselves what are called *clubs*. There are some
of lords, some of porters, some of men of science, and some of lawyers;
the Royal Society has its club, and so on. When the men have dispatched
their private business, they repair to the club; there they read the public
papers. First they converse on politics; this is the subject of most general interest, the affairs of the state being also those of everyone. They
then talk over matters which more particularly concern the persons
belonging to the club. The women therefore remain most of the time
alone; they visit each other, hardly gamble, take walks and are not diverted
from the management of their family; the house and children are their
department and to these they confine themselves.[24]

In her highly successful novel *Corinne* (1807), Mme de Staël,
a far bolder feminist than Mme Roland, was to depict English society in a much dimmer light, precisely because of the many restrictions it imposed upon women and the sedentary existence it forced
them to lead. The heroine of the novel, a young woman with superior
talents and an uncommon dose of natural energy, in other words
an alter ego of Mme de Staël herself, felt painfully stifled as long
as she had to remain in London. Mme Roland, on the contrary, had
only words of praise for the virtues of domesticity and modesty
evidenced by English ladies and, faithful disciple of Rousseau that
she was, commended the fact that the fair sex in England, unlike
that in France, exercised practically no influence over political and
intellectual matters—a curious attitude on the part of one whose own
behavior after 1789 would blatantly contradict those antifeminist notions inherited from Rousseau.

As a mother who had spent much time pondering the educational theories set forth in the *Emile*, Manon also had a great deal to say about English children and the treatment accorded them by their elders. On the whole, they impressed her as being less restricted than their French counterparts. They were dressed for comfort and had unpowdered hair: "Freedom and cleanliness are the two laws of their early age." [25] Mme Roland found them utterly charming with their fair complexion, flowing long hair, and unhampered countenances. As an example of the greater freedom enjoyed by English children, she told how, at the house of a duke where she had been invited, they were not scolded when they breached some rule of etiquette such as placing their elbows on the table at dinner: "No attention is paid to these trifles; it is well-known that at some future time, the child will observe that no one acts in this way and will correct himself from a desire to do well." [26] In short, children in England were granted the prerogatives of their age, without any undue insistence that they behave like miniature grownups. As a result, they glowed with well-being, and one sensed in them "something free, easy and bold in motion and behavior, which is imprinted forever and which blends happily with the pride and independence of man." [27] Pains were moreover taken to instruct boys and girls in the laws of their country, in a correct understanding of their language, and in the importance of moral and patriotic virtues. Boys were sent to public schools and universities, but girls rarely left their mother and were presented to society much later than in France.

One evening the Rolands went to the theater in the Haymarket. Manon, who was accustomed to the stately dignity of the French classical tradition, expressed some surprise at the many "liberties taken with the dialogue and even in the action." [28] The theater in the Haymarket, she observed, corresponded more or less to the French *Comédie Italienne*. The music, both simple and harmonious, pleased her; yet she had to admit that "never with us are there seen exchanged on the stage kisses so lascivious." [29] The opera and great theaters, closed at this time of the year, showed hardly more refinement, she was told. This greater laxity she attributed to the fact that the British theater, more than the French, appealed to popular taste and that "people of a certain rank very seldom frequent these public places, going there only when the best plays are performed." [30]

Since the Rolands held that it would not be seeing a nation to neglect those places of entertainment where the lower classes assemble, they also went to Sadler's Wells which, in the eighteenth century, was London's counterpart of the famed Nicolet variety show on the outer boulevards of Paris. Here they could watch little comic operas, dog acts, rope dancers, and tumblers. Mme Roland found the acting indifferent, but was charmed by the music and by the lively songs. The spectators laughed and expressed their mirth with "singular energy and frankness," [31] and she sought in vain, in this boisterous yet good-natured merriment, the melancholy and splenetic tendencies for which Englishmen were reputed on the Continent. In many ways, she enjoyed these plebeian gatherings more fully than the proper and formal Ranelagh Gardens, the rendezvous of fashionable society. Here people behaved with decorum, but one could not see any of those colorful, expressive types common among the less respectable crowds. Vauxhall Gardens, like Sadler's Wells, had been established as a place of amusement under the Restoration. The oldest public resort in London, Vauxhall was less aristocratic than Ranelagh, yet not so noisy as Sadler's Wells. The visitors spent several pleasant hours there. The grounds, within easy reach of the capital, were spacious and admirably illuminated: trees planted in groves and with lights concealed in their foliage lined the walks; there were cascades and even an obelisk; covered galleries, supported by slim, elegant pillars, led into a large hall where concerts were frequently given; and in case of rain, strollers could withdraw to a rotunda, preceded by a salon, where fine paintings were on permanent exhibition.

Herself an ardent music lover, Mme Roland was pleased to note the Londoners' fondness for concerts. At Vauxhall, as well as in several other places of public entertainment, she heard music, "both vocal and instrumental, and always organs." [32] Even though nearly all music was in the Italian style, the words were invariably English. The effect, however, did not displease her, and she attributed it to "the pliancy and facility with which this language bends to the music; more accented than ours, having a more distinct prosody, perhaps it is better adapted to it." [33] It is evident that Mme Roland's sympathies, like those of the *philosophes,* lay with Italian music, for she states that, by adopting that style of composing, the English, "not having a claim to a music of their own," [34] have by this been the gainers. Music, she also pointed out, was not only a greatly cultivated art in England, but composers were accorded special honors as well. Handel, who had a monument in Westminster Abbey, was the object of as much veneration as a king or noted statesman: "About a month ago, the anniversary of his funeral was celebrated with the greatest splendor: the number of performers assembled for this purpose at Westminster was six hundred. The court and all the notables of the city were present." [35] This was another example of the enlightened attitude of the English toward individual greatness and achievement.

It should be obvious by now that Mme Roland, following in the footsteps of noted French predecessors, saw in England only what confirmed her preconceived notions about this country. As a result, she tended, quite unconsciously, to close her eyes to the less attractive sides of English society. Yet she was too perceptive an observer to remain wholly impervious to certain discordant elements. Beneath the surface prosperity, she could not help but sense, albeit dimly, the existence of the poverty stricken underprivileged. To be sure, she did not stay long enough to dwell upon the discrepancy between the working hours and low wages, and overcrowded tenements, which were the lot of so many Londoners. She nevertheless felt compelled to point out that prostitution and thievery were rampant in the streets of the British capital, and that the city was infested with pickpockets, robbers, and burglars, and, especially after dark, presented innumerable dangers: "A person must take care of his pockets and look about him when he happens to be in the streets in the evening. Prosperous Londoners leaving town for the summer expect their homes to be broken into and therefore take their valuables with them, and frequently travelers carry what is called the robbers' purse in the event of a highway attack." [36]

Having once been made to witness a public execution by the wheel and stake in her native city of Paris, an experience that had filled her with horror,[37] Mme Roland gives the impression of having found comparatively less inhumane the method of capital punishment employed in England. Malefactors and thieves, many of them women and children, were hung in batches of ten or more, and the movable bottom of their scaffold, combined with the weight of the condemned, terminated their suffering with relative speed. When executions took place at Tyburn, relations and friends of the wretches could claim their bodies and even "strive to restore them to life." [38] It seems that sometimes the hangman had not done his job with maximum efficiency, and Mme Roland assures us that she herself "saw a beggar who was thus saved from death." [39] Every few weeks a required number of men, women, and children, guilty for the most part of only minor offenses, were dragged to Tyburn or led to a scaffold conveniently erected in front of Newgate prison, in order to meet their end at the hangman's noose. At times, too, a robber was caught in the act. An outraged mob then handled him so roughly that he was left dead or very nearly so.

The Rolands tried to visit Newgate, but were admitted no farther than the entrance hall, where they caught sight of a dreadful apparatus of chains, handcuffs, weights, and irons with which prisoners were fettered. No doubt, the visitors' request must have surprised the gaolers, who found a pretext to get rid of these embarrassing tourists: "The keeper, a man of colossal stature, told us that he would not let us enter because there were some prisoners who were not in irons and might do us mischief: he offered to admit us at an hour when they would be more closely confined and he able to escort us in person. I had seen enough of this terrible place not to wish to return there." [40]

In an age when punishments were commonly out of all proportion to the crime committed, it is perhaps curious to find Mme Roland, always one to stress humanity and justice in her letters and essays, remaining silent about imprisonment for debt and failing to censure practices which allowed unfortunate offenders to be treated as dangerous criminals. Nor does she raise her voice in protest against capital punishment for petty misdemeanors. Nothing, perhaps, indicates more clearly her desire to depict England in a favorable light. She could not repress her indignation, however, when told that "in London old harridans make a trade of kidnapping little girls and selling them to houses of ill fame." [41] What puzzled her just as much was the brutality with which not only thieves but also women suspected of prostitution were treated by the people of London. All these contradictory faces of a great city left her in a pensive mood. In a manner reminiscent of Rousseau she mused: "What a diversified spectacle is presented by a city harboring so much wealth and so much luxury, and where prevail laws so wise, passions so fierce, and so many sources of crime and virtue." [42]

Like many another French visitor, Mme Roland had the opportunity of discovering the charm of English country life and the romantic beauty of informal gardens surrounding estates at once comfortable and elegant. Strolling through the tree-lined alleys of Kensington, she was enchanted by the vistas, the picturesque disorder, which bespoke nature, "free, noble, and beautiful." [43] Winding paths led to large, green lawns and running streams. "How awkwardly and ridiculously we have copied the English gardens, with our little ruins, which have the appearance of doll-houses, and our affectation of gloominess, that assemblage of parts and monuments only fit to be laughed at!" she scornfully exclaimed.[44] Undaunted by a spell of poor weather, the Rolands made several excursions to country homes near London. One such outing took them to the mansion of the Duke of Devonshire at Chatsworth. They also visited Kew, a country seat belonging to the king, remarkable for its admirable grounds and botanical garden (which Mme Roland, incorrigible Anglophile that she was, immediately deemed superior to the Jardin du Roi of Buffon fame), and for its tall pagoda, from which the horizon extended as far as Windsor Castle. Neither did they overlook Richmond, still another royal residence, and at Hampton they stopped at Garrick's villa in order to pay their respects to the widow of the famous actor (Garrick had died in 1779). The house had a lawn bordered by weeping willows and the garden extended to the very edge of the River Thames. In the middle stood a circular temple with an Ionic peristyle dedicated to Shakespeare, before whose statue the visitors paused reverently.

It is a well-known fact that the English nobles and prosperous merchants prided themselves on their country estates. Here they spent much of their time, sparing no expense in adorning the rooms with Chippendale and Sheraton furniture and with paintings by Gainsborough, Romney, and Sir Joshua Reynolds, not to mention the countless art treasures purchased on the Continent. These splendid mansions and their magnificent grounds reflected a way of life, well-ordered and confident. The excursions undertaken to some of these estates afforded the Rolands a revealing glimpse into country life in eighteenth-century England.

Before departing from Britain, the Rolands were introduced to a few Frenchmen permanently settled there, among whom was Linguet, an exiled political writer and journalist who had caused a sensation with his *Memoirs on the Bastille,* a place of which he had had firsthand knowledge.[45] They also met Morande, a notorious penman and adventurer who had made a name for himself by publishing a scandal sheet about the French court and who, in 1774, had managed to obtain a fat pension from the Crown thanks to a daring *coup de maître.* He had threatened Mme du Barry with the impending publication of a sensational four-volume work devoted to her less than respectable career. Fearing the consequences of such a book, Louis XV had entrusted the playwright Beaumarchais, always resourceful in such delicate matters, with the negotiations between the blackmailer and the royal mistress. Beaumarchais carried off his mission with singular success, but returned to Paris just in time to learn that the king was dying of smallpox and thus never received the expected reward. Mme Roland was highly amused by rakish Morande, for he cut a colorful figure and showed no little pride in his achievements.[46]

After a twenty-seven-day visit, the couple left London on July 27, 1784, accompanied by pouring rain, thunder, and lightning, but sustained by a wealth of pleasant and instructive memories. For the last time, Mme Roland let her eyes wander over the English country-side, which struck her as beautiful, even though "terrestrial paradise would have appeared gloomy in such bad weather." [47] The last meal on British soil was taken at a Dover inn, in the company of some Frenchmen, whom our travelers found typical in that they endlessly "complained of all the customs which are not their own, seeming to value nothing but their own conceit." [48] Here indeed was a picture of Frenchmen abroad, vain and overcritical, that was by no means unique in the eighteenth century: already in 1725, Béat de Muralt, in his *Letters on the English and the French,* had sternly criticized French pride, and his allegations were to be echoed and amplified from Rousseau to Mme de Staël.

Mme Roland repaired to Amiens more convinced than ever in her high esteem for a land which, in her eyes, eminently symbolized those political and social attributes she yearned to see implanted in France. Until the outbreak of the French Revolution would suddenly bring within the realm of possibilities hitherto unhoped for reforms, England, with its easygoing acceptance of strong individuality, to-gether with Rousseau's idealized Switzerland and Benjamin Frank-lin's young and rugged United States of America, would figure in the minds of those who, like Mme Roland, chafed at the restrictions of the Old Régime, as a place of human promise and fulfillment, favored by a happy conjunction of history and circumstance.

TEN

Rustic Interlude

ROLAND'S TRANSFER TO LYONS brought him so close to the family home at Villefranche-sur-Saône that the couple could economize on rent by living part of the year with Roland's mother and his older brother. Summers and autumns would be spent at the family's small country estate, Le Clos de la Platière.[1] For two of the winter months the Rolands meant to settle in a small Lyons flat to facilitate the inspector's work. Madame Roland departed from the large, somber house at Amiens with no special regret. All their personal belongings piled in a carriage, the Rolands reached Villefranche after a rather long, wearisome trip. The house where Mme Roland was to spend many months between 1784 and 1789 still stands, according to the latest report, on the Grand-rue, at the corner of the small rue Sainte-Claire. Even though its exterior was quite ordinary, it boasted a fine staircase and, on the second floor, a spacious dining room with wooden paneling.[2]

Before long, Mme Roland came to the realization that life in Villefranche was hardly more exciting than in Amiens. At first, Mme Roland *mère* showed appreciation for the help and company of her capable daughter-in-law. She herself was too advanced in years to be an effective house mistress.[3] Soon, however, her unpleasant disposition caused even the resourceful and patient Manon to be oftentimes at her wits' end. It turned out that the eighty-five-year-old woman was as meddlesome and ill-tempered as she was pious. Eating, gossiping, gambling at cards, and quarreling were her favorite pastimes. Roland himself had to admit that his mother prolonged her existence only for the pleasure of scolding and making those around her miserable. She went to church every day, took Holy Communion often, and performed her religious duties scrupulously. Roland noted jokingly that his mother was at her worst when she had just returned from Mass.[4]

During her husband's frequent and sometimes prolonged absences, Mme Roland kept him informed of her daily activities in affectionate and detailed letters. A subject of special concern to her was the fact that Roland traveled on horseback, and sometimes on foot, in all kinds of weather, and through lonely roads haunted by thieves and hungry wolves, with a servant as his sole companion. Roland continued to drive himself hard, and this in spite of his fragile health and increasing age. Overwork occasioned many an ailment and hardly improved his naturally bilious disposition. Because of his fiercely independent nature, he neglected those social amenities that could ingratiate him with his superiors. His wife, who thought of everything that could help his career, sent him frequent, and tactfully worded, reminders to call on a newly appointed administrator or to address a courtesy note to an influential official.

Mme Roland's insatiable curiosity about every rumor emanating from Paris shows how sorely she missed, without admitting it, the pace and excitement of city life. Was it true, she would ask, that Beaumarchais had been jailed at Saint-Lazare for assaulting an official who had condemned his *Marriage of Figaro*? If so, he will most probably manage to get himself freed before long and, in his clever way, take a resounding revenge for this humiliation.[5] When it was reported that the British had captured a French ship and refused to return Pondicherry to France, she wondered whether this would lead to another war and roundly denounced such "private" conflicts between kings as scourges to the peoples of the world, a remark worthy of the pacifist views of the *philosophes*.[6] And what does the public think, she also inquired, of the new three-volume treatise on high finance by Necker, slyly adding that sensible people would recognize it as yet one more public testimony to the minister's foolishness and self-adulation, emitted in pompous, inflated phrases.[7]

Mme Roland harbored no liking for Necker and, after 1789, when his brilliant daughter Germaine achieved notoriety in her own right, expressed her disapproval for the lady's tumultuous love life and political agitation by hardly ever mentioning her name. Neither did Mme de Staël refer to Mme Roland in her voluminous correspondence and in her writings devoted to the Revolution. Between the self-taught daughter of a modest Paris shopkeeper and the carefully nurtured offspring of the Swiss financier and his bluestocking wife there seems to have been, aside from a certain feminine rivalry, a good deal of natural hostility, even though both women shared many ideals and beliefs as well as a common veneration for Rousseau.[8]

With a measure of disappointment, Mme Roland came to the realization that her daughter's temperament was very unlike her own. After repeated and fruitless attempts at correcting Eudora's character and inculcating in her a love of learning, her mother had to resign herself to the fact that nature had not fitted the child for studious pursuits. Eudora Roland was hardly a new version of Manon Phlipon, but rather a charming if quite ordinary little girl who preferred her toys to reading instructive books.[9] With resignation, Mme Roland renounced her ambitious educational projects. In a letter to Roland, she nevertheless pointed out that Rousseau had somewhat missed the mark when he had Julie depend entirely on personal attention to cure children of bad habits. It had been her experience with Eudora that the more one pets and threatens them, the more inured they become to this constant supervision. Children, she had found out, ought to learn self-reliance early in life, and no amount of constraint could change their basic nature.[10]

Two months of the year, ordinarily in the late summer and early fall, were spent at Le Clos, the small family estate situated in the Beaujolais hills. In 1787, Roland's older brother Dominique gave the house over to the couple. Thereafter, it was here that Mme Roland spent the greatest part of the year. If life at Villefranche was not altogether satisfactory, in the country retreat of Le Clos one could find all the ingredients of Rousseauistic happiness: the constant spectacle of nature, a simple yet healthy setting free of all

the fetters of urban civilization, and a good deal of solitude that could
be devoted to reading and gardening. Her pleasure enhanced by the
lyrical descriptions of country life in *La Nouvelle Héloïse,* she set
about her activities, readily taking part in the life of the neighboring
villagers and farmers, kindly, simple folks whose ways she described
with sympathy and genuine understanding to Bosc, and whose
company she far preferred to that of the stuffy bourgeois of Villefranche. Like Julie Wolmar, she thoroughly enjoyed her role as the
spiritual guide and counsel of the peasants in the district. That these
would come to her in order to confide their sorrows and problems and
to seek advice and help deeply touched her, and she cared for them
with true devotion and solicitude. Bosc found himself constantly
plied with queries on remedies for various ailments and on antidotes
for possible vipers' bites.

Everywhere she turned, Mme Roland found the most abject
poverty and was amazed that in her own land the rural population
was more destitute than the remote primitives with whom she had
commiserated when reading descriptions of them: "Nothing but
poverty! Sometimes one is surprised or touched by accounts of the
difficult existence of distant peoples, without reflecting that our own
peasants are, for the most part, a hundred times more miserable than
the Caribs, Greenlanders, or Hottentots." [11] Visiting the shabby
hovels overcrowded with emaciated, sick human beings, she realized
that, of all the French population, the peasantry was the most unfortunate and neglected. They lived in total ignorance, were treated
as work animals, and yet carried the main burden of seignorial dues
and governmental taxes. She saw farmers suffering from a variety
of diseases, and yet continue their labor until they died without ever
consulting a doctor because they could not afford the expense. Some
even welcomed death as a deliverance, and most accepted it with
equanimity. The winter months were especially hard on the peasantry, and Manon observed with dismay the dreadful effects of cold
and famine. When it became known in the district that Mme Roland
had some knowledge of medicine and that she personally cared for
the sick, she was much sought after by the farmers. The gratitude

and confidence shown in return for her services stimulated her zeal
to such a point that Roland became alarmed and feared for his wife's
health. In more troublesome times, when the walls of the Terror
would close in on her, leaving her no alternative but to turn her
gaze inwards and back in time for comfort, she was to derive much
satisfaction from the memory of those who had traveled from distant
hamlets to ask her to the bedside of a relative in the knowledge that
one did not solicit the mistress of Le Clos in vain.[12]

Not everything in the life of the villagers was gloomy, however.
The wine harvest was celebrated by joyous gatherings of farmers.
Ever mindful of Rousseau's recommendations that chatelaines take
a part in these rustic festivities, Manon discovered, not without pride,
that she had lost none of her youthful zest and energy when, after
having danced lively rigadoons until midnight, she retired feeling
that she could have continued until dawn. Having to grow her own
vegetables and supervise the work in the fields and vineyards in the
absence of Roland increased Manon's already considerable knowledge
of plant life and agriculture. She also learned to make pies and prepare jams and tackled with seriousness the art of drying fruit. To
direct the operations on washday, to mend the linen, to see that
the hens and rabbits were properly fed, to make sure that nothing
went wrong during the wine harvest, all these tasks, and many
others, Manon accomplished with her usual aplomb. But if she was
kept occupied much of the time, she also enjoyed more leisure than
at Villefranche. A copious picnic lunch washed down with good
Beaujolais wine, an afternoon nap in the grass, a long walk in the
woods or meadows, an occasional hour stolen from Roland's manuscript to read fiction or poetry, these were some of the simple yet
refreshing distractions she enjoyed recounting in her letters to Bosc.
For the first time she became aware of nature, not through books,
but in a direct, intimate way and felt close to the soil of France.

The countryside around Le Clos undoubtedly had something to
do with this heightened appreciation of the beauties of nature. The
little village of Theizé nestled on a slope, amid vineyards and a
spectacular landscape. The snow-capped peaks of the Alps were

faintly perceptible in the distant background, while the heavily wooded hills of Beaujolais bordered the Saône valley. To be sure, the abrupt panorama was more impressive than cheerful. Nature here assumed a rough and rugged quality, which could at times become forbidding, as during the long winter months, but its austere grandeur did not displease Manon. Medieval châteaux, old Romanesque churches, hamlets in terra cotta, and fortified walls dotted the landscape. Le Clos itself, shut in by high walls, stood at the end of a winding country road. It was a simple one-storied structure with whitewashed walls, a red-tiled roof, and two small pavilions at either side. The courtyard, with its ancient well, was surrounded by barns. There was an English garden, and a stone terrace faced the breathtaking view of the Beaujolais hills. As the eye wandered over this ocean of verdure, it encountered the bluish peaks of the Dauphiné Mountains and, on a clear day, the snowy crest of the Mont Blanc.

The years spent at Le Clos unquestionably represent the most serene time in Mme Roland's life. She would have been quite content to live out the rest of her existence in this quiet retreat, working at the side of the conscientious inspector, helping the neighboring farmers, educating Eudora, and reading in her spare time, had not the Revolution summoned Roland to Paris and jolted his wife out of this comfortable and secure routine. Temporarily at least, Mme Roland's restless nature seems to have been subdued by the simplicity and calm that surrounded her. For the first time, she allowed herself to drift pleasantly, without too much self-questioning. Uneventful days were marked only by seasonal activities and family occasions, days that imperceptibly stretched into months and years and that appeared to promise to continue uninterrupted until both she and Roland would reach old age. This prospect seemed agreeable enough; occasional visits from a few devoted friends, but especially good books would enliven the pattern, and for Bosc she drew an engaging and humorous picture of herself as an old lady, reading Rousseau aloud to a doddering Roland.[13] Musing over such thoughts while knitting at the fireside and listening to the wind howl outside during the long winter evenings, she had to admit that fate had been kind to her.

In the frozen countryside she knew that men and women, lacking shelter and sustenance, were dying of cold and misery. While the snow fell silently on Le Clos, a log crackled cheerfully in the hearth and the clock ticked away time. Eudora was playing at Manon's side, and Roland, seated at his desk, was working away on his *Dictionary of Manufactures*. What more, thought Mme Roland, could one expect of this troubled world? Happiness, if there be such a thing, was to be found only in that *aurea mediocritas* already praised by Horace. To lead an honorable and useful existence, far from the artificial values and empty din of city life, to nurture one's love of literature and philosophy, but without any personal ambition, to help those in need and contribute to the happiness of one's family, were not these pursuits worthy of a disciple of Rousseau? As late as 1788, she confided in one of her letters: "Yes, I feel that I shall spend all my life in the country, in contentment and peace of heart, and particularly in this part of the country." [14] Circumstance, however, would decree otherwise. As in Amiens and Villefranche, Mme Roland attended religious services regularly. But since she had to climb a steep mountain in order to get to the church of Theizé, a donkey was placed at her disposal. In a letter to Roland she drew with much merriment a picture of herself, in her Sunday best, proceeding to Mass perched atop her slightly ludicrous and frequently recalcitrant mount.[15]

In the middle of July 1787, the Rolands set out for Switzerland, taking along six-year-old Eudora. They were to visit the principal sites and cities, especially those made famous by Rousseau, and return to Le Clos by August 15. As an admirer of the republican form of government, Mme Roland was eager to see for herself what Switzerland was like. Moreover, her favorite writer was born in Geneva and proudly signed his works, Rousseau, Citizen of Geneva. Voltaire, too, had elected to live there when he had had to leave Frederick's court under humiliating circumstances only to find the doors of France locked for him. In Switzerland he had finally achieved a relative sense of security and from there had flooded Europe with his tales, essays, and pamphlets directed against intolerance and fanaticism. Upon her return, Manon set down her impressions and observations, and these afford one an excellent idea of how such a journey could be effectuated at the end of the eighteenth century; and they also reveal the changing attitudes toward nature.[16]

Until the middle of the eighteenth century, French travelers like Montesquieu who had visited the Alps had found mountains only objects of horror and disparagement. For the classical mind, mountains were ugly accidents which marred the harmonious face of nature. But as an exclusive preference for the tame, man-made landscapes with geometric patterns slowly gave way to an appreciation for the wilder aspects of nature, the Alps became a subject of admiration and esthetic pleasure. It fell to Rousseau in particular to popularize in France an awareness of the poetry that can be found in such awesome natural features as towering summits, overhanging rocks, steep gorges, thundering torrents, and dark forests.[17] By the time Mme Roland undertook a tour of Switzerland, a number of voyagers had already made the literary pilgrimage to Geneva, Vevey, and Clarens in order to recapture the spirit that had inspired Rousseau's *Nouvelle Héloïse*. Thus Mme Roland's itinerary, in addition to retracing the stages of a journey that was to grow in popularity with the passing of time, increases our understanding of the cult of Rousseau between the publication of his famous novel in 1761 and the outbreak of the French Revolution.

Geneva somewhat disappointed Mme Roland. She thought its attempts to emulate Paris (by 1787 it boasted a theater and an opera, both mediocre, according to our traveler) self-conscious and its atmosphere at once too commercial and narrowly provincial. From Rousseau she had inherited the notion that luxury and commerce can only weaken civic virtue in a republic. She was surprised and disappointed to find so little evidence of austerity in Geneva. What had also contributed to a relative decline in the moral fiber of the Genevans since the times of Rousseau and Voltaire, she speculated, was the abortive bourgeois revolution of 1782 that had been crushed by the aristocrats, with the help of France. Speculating about the future of Geneva, she accurately prophesied that some neighboring government would take advantage of this situation. It was France, in effect, which annexed Geneva in March 1798. It also vexed her not to be able to find anywhere in the city a monument in honor of Rousseau, its most illustrious son.[18]

While enumerating the wonders of the Swiss landscape, Mme Roland was well aware of the feelings and thoughts that mountains ought to evoke in a true nature lover. Her descriptions, consequently, exhibit all those images that were to become the stock-in-trade of the Romantics. The neatness of Swiss inns and dwellings, the simple yet hospitable manners of the inhabitants, the modest wholesomeness of Swiss women, the thriving agriculture of the country, all these things reminded Mme Roland of England. Again she had occasion to note, approvingly, the dignified austerity of Protestant temples and to contrast these with the ornate interiors of Catholic churches. To this she added that Swiss ministers preached about ethics and practical questions of morality, while French priests expound more often questions of dogma. Following Montesquieu's example, she was also led to speculate on the relationship between the character of a nation and its physical environment. To the presence of mountains, whose snow-crest outlines were visible almost everywhere she went, she attributed the serious, introspective temper of the Swiss.[19]

Bern, with its air of calm opulence, its fine buildings, attractive streets decorated by colorful water fountains, and picturesque setting, greatly appealed to the Rolands. True, the city was governed by an absolute aristocracy, and the barriers separating the nobility from the people were very strict. But the officials, from all evidence, governed with prudence and wisdom, and as a result prosperity seemed fairly widespread, although the Bernese seemed more concerned with politics and commerce than with literature and the arts. Lucerne, on the other hand, in spite of its beautiful location, struck Mme Roland as dull and uninspiring.[20] This she attributed to a greater despotism on the part of the nobles, which stifled all individual initiative and creativity. For Zurich she had only the highest praise.[21] The city proper was not especially attractive, but it bustled with activity and was ruled by a just and fair administration. Any respectable citizen, whether he be of noble birth or a mere bourgeois, could be elected to office. The right of citizenship, however, was restricted to a fifth of the Zurich population, and it was not extended to newcomers. While in Zurich, the Rolands visited Johann Kaspar Lavater, the Swiss theological writer whose work on physiognomy, the art of judging character from facial features, had first come to Mme Roland's attention in 1784.[22] The pastor turned out to be a very gracious host and even drew a charming picture in silhouette of the couple and Eudora in typical, informal attitudes. After her return to France, Mme Roland was to keep up a fairly active correspondence with Lavater, a man whose strong personality, simplicity of manners, and Rousseauistic religious fervor made a far greater impression on her than had his ponderous treatise.[23]

After leaving Zurich, the Rolands crossed the Rhine at Schaffhausen, where they were shown the imposing cataract that the river forms at this spot. Listening to the deafening noise of the rushing, falling waters, Mme Roland dwelled on the feeling of near terror that such sites evoke in the spectator, but added that nature serene and orderly could also stir powerful sentiments, albeit of a different order.[24] Basel was the last Swiss city the Rolands saw before reaching French territory. Villages and farms in her native country were sparse and miserable in comparison with those she had just had occasion to visit, commented Mme Roland, and it was evident that here peasants had been reduced to "the most pitiable condition of the human species." [25]

In February of what was to become a historic year, 1789, Mme Roland accompanied her husband to Lyons. After a particularly rigorous winter, spent in the isolation of Le Clos, it was a welcome change to attend plays and concerts and meet with intellectuals and writers belonging to the Lyons academy, of which, it will be recalled, Roland was also a member. One favorite subject of discussion in these cultured circles was the idea of a universal language that would help break down national barriers and promote peace. With the help of his wife, Roland had written an essay on this topic and submitted it to the academy.[26] Contrary to most Frenchmen, who considered their own language best qualified for international use, the Rolands chose English. In March of 1789, Mme Roland took pen in hand to defend this point of view against the challenge of another member of the academy. Her long letter is an interesting document attesting not only to the ever growing Anglomania among disciples of the *philosophes,* but also to a change of mood that distinctly presages the open revolt against neoclassicism in France.[27]

The counterattack was launched by the statement that "the English are the most imaginative and sensitive people in Europe, their novels are the most fascinating and varied, and if their theater is not the most polished, it is perhaps the most compelling." [28] In addition, the relations of the British with the United States of America, the advantages of their laws and traditions and of their commerce "will spread in all parts of the world the need to learn their language." [29] To be sure, it was not an easy tongue for a Frenchman to master, but its riches largely compensated for the effort. It could boast not only philosophers like Locke and Newton, and "sublime" poets like Milton, but also the incomparable Shakespeare: "How is it that you have never attempted to know Shakespeare, for whom after centuries, and in spite of our much vaunted perfections, the English are still so enthusiastic? How is it that you have not had the curiosity to find out the reasons for the admiration, the enchantment, the enthusiasm of such an enlightened nation for an author who takes it into his head to overlook the three unities, to cause many people to die on the stage, to mingle pictures of ordinary life with the most noble actions, precisely as they are in nature, and to have no other master, no other law than nature and his own genius?" [30] In a century when French taste was still conditioned by the classical rules and by the exigencies of propriety and delicacy, it took courage and boldness to place the Bard above all other dramatists, especially those of the French classical and neoclassical school. As an added argument, Mme Roland invited her correspondent to compare powerful characters like Hamlet and Othello with Voltaire's pale imitations, to study Shakespeare's women, "so delicately drawn, his tender Cordelia, his in-

genuous Desdemona, his unfortunate Ophelia," and to try to conceive how the same man was able to unite so much grace with so
much force and to evoke terror as well as the sweetest emotions:
"Call his works monstrous, if you wish, but you will reread them
twenty times." [31]

Leaving the Elizabethan theater, Mme Roland went on to extol
neoclassical poetry and Restoration drama, from Dryden to Pope
and Congreve. She then passed in review the novel in England
and France, concluding that Richardson and Fielding were the undisputed masters in this genre: "You will mention Rousseau's *Julie*
[*La Nouvelle Héloïse*], and I shall answer you that I reread it every
year. But I venture to say that, in spite of all my respect and love
for that one among our writers to whom I give my preference, it is
not as a novel that *Julie* is admirable. This work is delightful through
beauties that are extraneous, so to speak, to its nature. Besides, Rousseau himself was the first to recognize Richardson as his master." [32]

While still in Lyons, Roland fell dangerously ill in June of 1789.
It was when ministering to her convalescent husband that Mme
Roland learned of the storming of the Bastille and other exciting
happenings that were taking place in Paris. Through the months of
July and August, she was too busy with the still ailing Roland to
write at length to her friends in Paris, but the urgent tone of her
letters, her anxious questions, and pertinent observations show that
the import of the recent events had not escaped her.[33] Eventually
Roland felt strong enough to undertake the trip back to Le Clos.
In vain Manon tried to recapture the charm of her tranquil retreat.
The magic that a place can offer us will work only if it is in con-
formity with our mood. After July 14, 1789, the spell of Le Clos was
broken for Mme Roland. What had pleased her before she now
found painful to bear, and she yearned to flee from these woods and
fields where she had spent many a carefree, dream-filled hour in
order to be once more in the midst of the noisy Paris crowds, where
the future of France was being shaped.

PART III

Passion
and Politics

ELEVEN

1789
and Soaring Hopes

DURING HIS MANY YEARS of public service, Roland had obtained disappointingly little recognition and reward for his efforts on behalf of progress and enlightenment. He was justifiably proud of his contribution to technical know-how and to the administration of the Lyons district, the second most highly industrialized area in his country. Yet, time and again he had seen the best positions go to undeserving, incompetent but influential aristocrats. He had fought many, but losing, battles for scientific and technical liberalization of commerce and industry and for putting the most recent inventions at the disposal of every shop in order to stimulate creative competition and general well-being. He wished for an entire freedom of investigation and enterprise, and had not feared to engage in heated controversies over the current secrecy of manufacturing processes. No wonder he had come to view the contemporary social system with a jaundiced eye and, like his wife, unhesitatingly espoused the principles of the revolutionaries.

It would nevertheless be an injustice to represent the Rolands' growing detestation of the Old Régime and all it symbolized as guided solely by narrow personal resentments. Each had independently, through reading and study and often in open opposition to their immediate environment, worked out a concept of life and society that was directly molded by the ideals of the *philosophes*: civil equality and religious toleration, the dignity of the individual and his liberation from oppressing institutions, the right to earthly happiness and well-being, together with the freedom of intellectual investigation. Each stemming from different sectors of the bourgeoisie, Manon from a near-working class family and her husband from near-nobility, had readily identified with a set of beliefs that fired the entire Third Estate into action against the representatives of entrenched privilege. In this the bourgeoisie, it should not be forgotten, was joined by the enlightened members of the aristocracy itself, for an entire generation, from Lafayette to Robespierre, had read the same works. The books that young Manon Phlipon had so avidly devoured in her father's shop were also those that had shaped the minds of Mirabeau, Brissot, and Danton, to name only a few of the future leaders of the Revolution. Sons and daughters of great nobles and of petty bourgeois alike had been imbibing the same spirit and were all in favor of political innovation. Even some courtiers were affected by the Enlightenment and viewed reforms with favor because they bore old, deep-seated grudges against an absolute monarchy that had stripped them of their ancestral rights. Many members of the highest nobility had lost faith not only in the king but also in the church and therefore welcomed rebellion against despotism and fanaticism. Living at Versailles, where they had been reduced to the role of parasitic courtiers, they envied the English lords who were allowed to play a significant part in politics. Mirabeau, Lafayette, Larochefoucauld-Liancourt, Lally-Tollendal, Clermont-Tonnerre, and, of course, the Duke of Orléans, cousin of Louis XVI, were some of the striking figures among these liberal-minded nobles. And Condorcet himself, one of the last surviving representatives of the Enlightenment, was a marquis.

But if the Revolution did not arise solely among the oppressed, if forward-looking aristocrats identified themselves with the cause of the Third Estate, it was the younger generation of the bourgeois that felt the kind of solidarity that results from firsthand humiliations. Mme Roland and others of similar background were stirred by more than abstract theories, and the works they studied only confirmed beliefs born from personal experience. Mme Roland would never forget being relegated to the servants' quarters after accepting an invitation to the mansion of a rich *fermier général*. Neither would she ever overlook the open condescension with which her grandmother had been treated by a lady of rank.[1] Such memories would be recounted in detail in her autobiography, and not even the prospect of the guillotine was to efface their bitter sting. Far from being appeased, her resentments had grown in the course of her married life to Roland, for she had seen how industry, diligence, skill, and devotion to public welfare were ignored by a system that recognized only prerogatives of birth or unscrupulous opportunism. As a woman who prized above all character and intellect, moreover, she felt particular scorn for the scatterbrained Marie-Antoinette and the weak-willed Louis XVI.

Upon learning that, on July 15, 1789, the king had pledged his allegiance to the National Assembly, she was overtaken by fears and suspicions: "Before one can believe in the sincerity of the promise to agree to what the Assembly shall do, it is necessary to forget everything that has passed. The king should have started by sending away all the foreign troops." [2] And giving vent to her disappointment with what she considered softness and naïveté on the part of the revolutionaries, she exclaimed: "We are closer than ever to the most dreadful enslavement if we let ourselves be blinded by misguided trust. . . . The salvation of twenty million men is involved. All is lost if care is not taken." [3]

Before the taking of the Bastille, Mme Roland had been too concerned over her husband's poor health to become emotionally aroused over the dispute between Necker and Calonne or the struggle between Brienne and the Parlements. As she had done in the past, she sided with the Parlements and regarded their recall as desirable. And she regretted that the Estates General had to be organized according to the forms of 1614. But the event-packed days of July suddenly revealed to her the full extent of what was happening. In her letter of July 26 to Bosc, a new language appears, sharp, blunt, virile: "No, you are not free; no one is yet. Public confidence is betrayed, letters are intercepted. You complain of my silence, I write you by every post. It is true that I no longer write of our personal affairs: where is the traitor who today has other affairs than those of the nation? It is true that I have written you more vigorously than you have acted; if you are not careful, you will have made nothing but a vain gesture. . . . You are only children; your enthusiasm is a flash in the pan; and if the National Assembly does not put two crowned heads on trial or if some fearless Decius does not strike them down, you are all done for." [4]

Mme Roland's political theories were rarely, if ever, influenced by practical considerations and by the necessity for compromise. And since her dislike for absolute monarchy was intense, and had been fortified even further by her contempt for the undecided Louis XVI and his light-hearted queen, she did not hesitate, from the very outset of the Revolution, to state repeatedly her conviction that the primary condition for success was to do away with the monarchy. Her fear that the royal family and its supporters would betray the revolutionaries, or that these would be softened into accepting a compromise solution, goaded her into using strong, even violent language in order to awaken others to the danger of keeping a hostile court amidst the nascent republic.

A constant stream of letters, full of exhortations and admonitions, flowed from Le Clos to her Paris friends. Some of her missives having strangely disappeared in the mail, she angrily summoned the culprits: "If this letter does not reach you, let the cowards who read it blush with shame upon learning that these words were written by a woman, and let them tremble to think that she can fire a hundred men who will in turn fire a million others." [5] Or she would end on a ringing call to arms: "Let France awaken and come to life! Let man recapture his rights, let justice commence its reign, and from one end of the kingdom to the other let one universal cry be heard—*Long live the people and death to the tyrants!*" [6]

From the moment Mme Roland learned of the Revolution, her epistolary style underwent a significant change. Gone were the charming vignettes in the tradition of Mme de Sévigné. All personal feelings, all private activities were now relegated to the background in favor of the national events that were making history. To read Mme Roland's correspondence from July 1789 on is to witness the French Revolution as reflected by a passionately interested witness who was also destined to become an important participant. She was so involved in these events that the indifference or hostility of the provinces threw her into fits of vehement rage. With alacrity she kept warning her friends in Paris to beware of the reactionary tendencies of the smaller cities, which she knew only too well. What also contributed to her agitation was the fact that news from the capital trickled down slowly, and often in distorted fashion, to her village of Theizé.

It was not long before the revolutionary sympathies of the Rolands became known to their conservative acquaintances and family. But disagreeable scenes did not discourage Mme Roland from preaching the new gospel to all those with whom she came in contact. Her brother-in-law in particular, Canon Dominique, with whom she had spent many an hour reading and discussing Rousseau, was bewildered and outraged by her inflammatory speeches. Soon they were no longer on speaking terms. Angrily Mme Roland wrote: "My brother-in-law is more bigoted, despotic, fanatical, and stubborn than any priest you have ever listened to." [7] As she had never had much sympathy for the rich Lyons merchant group and for the provincial upper bourgeoisie, she welcomed the opportunity to denounce openly their narrow selfishness, social ambitions, and pretensions, and greedy love of money and property.

At a time when the most fearless revolutionaries only sought to establish a constitutional monarchy patterned after the English system, Mme Roland's friends in Paris, not to mention her Lyons acquaintances, must have thought her quite out of her mind to propound radical measures against the royal family. Events, however, were to bear out her misgivings, and it is interesting that only three years later, when repeated internal crises and war with Europe had brought France to the edge of disaster, would a group of men be sufficiently determined and bold to bring about a new revolution and a true republican form of government. But by then, a number of factors, both political and personal, will have considerably cooled Mme Roland's revolutionary zeal.

For the time being, however, she trembled lest the Revolution fail through the overconfidence and conciliatory spirit of its makers. This fear, together with her knowledge of history, made of her one of the first to advocate methods of intimidation and repression against all suspicious elements. A revolution, she sensed, cannot be won through a spirit of universal fraternity and cooperation, through public ceremonies, no matter how grandiose and inspiring, and through patriotic speeches. Louis XVI, moreover, was not the type of man who would ever relinquish any of his powers willingly or accept sincerely principles that violated his own beliefs. He was too ordinary a mortal, and one too influenced by his wife and uncompromising entourage, to heed reason and forgo prerogatives which he considered as God-given. From the start, Mme Roland suspected him of conniving with the foreign powers and French counterrevolutionaries, even while outwardly cooperating with the new government. She therefore held that so long as the king and his court would be allowed to operate freely, the Revolution would be in grave jeopardy. Only a strong government and general preparedness could stave off betrayal from within and attack from without. If Mme Roland was ideologically and historically right, her radical viewpoint totally ignored political realities. Whatever may be said about the difficulties which derived from maintaining a king and so many conservatives in the new government, in 1789 the public temper in France was definitely not ready for a republic, and the revolutionaries themselves were not sufficiently organized to pave the way for the kind of social system Mme Roland so persistently advocated.

In the spring of 1787, the Rolands had become acquainted through correspondence with Brissot de Warwille, a lawyer and versatile writer who shared their liberal views[8] Born like Manon in 1754, he was of middle-class origin and hailed from Chartres, but had made a name for himself through his pamphlets and books. In his many activities, he was served by an admirable memory and an inventive mind. Rarely at a loss for ideas, projects, and schemes, he was never-theless an idealist who, in 1781, had entered a strong plea for penal reform in a book, *Theory of Criminal Laws,* largely influenced by Montesquieu and Beccaria. In 1787, he published another work, this time in collaboration with Clavière, a Genevan banker. This book demonstrated the usefulness of the American Revolution for France and recommended closer political, cultural, and commercial ties between the two countries. The work, entitled *Considerations on the Relative Situation of France and the United States,* was well received in America and, when Brissot visited the new republic in 1788—a journey for which he was admirably prepared—he was able to have interviews with noted men like Washington, John Adams, Madison, Hamilton, and others. He had an excellent knowledge of English and, as might well be expected from one who had long been an active sympathizer of the American republic and who had founded a Gallo-American society, he came back more enthusiastic than ever about the political principles and policy of the new state.[9] Upon his return to France, Brissot published an account of his journey in which he described life in the new republic in the most glowing terms. As a friend of the oppressed and firm believer in racial equality, Brissot immediately established in Paris the abolitionist *Society of the Friends of the Negroes,* whose immediate aim was the elimination of slave trading and the progressive emancipation of all slaves both in America and in the French colonies.

While working on his book on America, Brissot had discovered the writings of Roland and, much impressed with the inspector's courageous views, had quoted liberally from the *Letters from Italy* and given long extracts from the *Dictionary of Manufactures.* Recognizing Roland's sane logic and strong reasoning, as well as his keen perception of existing social evils, he excused his literary shortcomings by attributing them to a desire to go to the heart of important problems without regard for embellishments. Roland's harshness in style was regarded as the effect of an energetic and virile soul. Men like Roland, he told his readers, were extremely valuable and deserved to be encouraged and respected, instead of being relegated to obscurity. At the same time, Brissot wrote a friendly letter to Roland, expressing his high regard.[10] The inspector, who was not used to such generous praise and whose published works had caused him only endless worry as well as difficulty with his superiors, felt genuinely moved by this flattering token of esteem and respect from a man he had never met personally. For the first time in his laborious career he tasted the sweetness of critical acclaim.

Henceforth, long, cordial letters were frequently exchanged between the Rolands and their new friend. After his return from America, Brissot conceived the idea of founding a newspaper, for he had realized the importance of spreading the new ideas through a popular organ. He was naturally on the lookout for qualified and liberal-minded writers, and it occurred to him that the Rolands would make excellent Lyons correspondents. The *Patriote français* was announced as early as March 16, 1789. It was to be a journal uncensored and free from all political influence. The official censor was none too pleased with the first issue and, deeming it too subversive, forbade further publication of the journal. Shortly thereafter, however, the Bastille fell and Brissot was now able to follow his bold, original plan.

Lengthy extracts from Mme Roland's correspondence with Brissot appeared frequently in the paper in the form of newsletters.[11] It was with keen pleasure that Manon read her published pieces, but if her *amour-propre* was flattered, she staunchly remained consistent with her principles, insisting on remaining incognito. Constant epistolary contact and journalistic collaboration reinforced Mme Roland's friendship for Brissot. Her letters to him became informal, uninhibited, and affectionate. The Revolution would bring Brissot even closer to his new friends.

Because of his extensive traveling, international relations, vast energy, and likeable personality, Brissot was to become one of the active leaders of the revolutionaries. He was, moreover, the first of all French revolutionary journalists, and one well equipped with the makings of a successful promoter. The Revolution would provide him with a stage worthy of his many talents. With insouciant aplomb Brissot would promote governments and wars and, until the triumph of Robespierre, was to remain one of the most influential men in France.

In Lyons, the Rolands made the acquaintance of another person to whom they immediately felt drawn by a strong bond of sympathy. Luc-Antoine Champagneux, a lawyer of liberal views, was an ardent admirer of the Enlightenment.[12] He had, moreover, known Rousseau personally and, in 1768, as mayor of the town of Bourgoin in the Dauphiné, had played host to the philosopher, accompanying him on botanizing excursions, and even serving as witness at Jean-Jacques' belated marriage to Thérèse Levasseur.[13] It was at the beginning of the Revolution that the cordial relationship between the Rolands and Champagneux evolved into a close and lifelong friendship. Before long, Champagneux emerged as one of the revolutionary leaders of the Lyons municipality. He shared with the Rolands a common enthusiasm for the new order of things and Manon, to whom he confided his project for a daily newspaper, the *Courrier de Lyon*, gave him her wholehearted support and encouragement. She did even more. Aware of the immense possibilities that political journalism enjoyed in shaping public opinion, she became a regular, albeit anonymous, contributor to the paper.[14]

One of her articles, a stirring account of the May 30, 1790, *Champ de la Fédération*, a patriotic and revolutionary celebration on the banks of the Rhône in which sixty thousand uniformed national guards and two hundred thousand spectators took part, caused something of a sensation in Lyons. And an impressive, inspiring spectacle it had been! The elaborate ceremonies had lasted from dawn to dusk. An artificial rock, fifty feet high, had been built for the occasion. On its summit stood a colossal statue of Liberty with pike and Phrygian cap, and at her feet had been erected an "altar to the Motherland." Inside the rock a "temple of concord" could be seen. Multicolored banners fluttered in the wind; drums and trumpets were flourished; High Mass was sung; and the sixty thousand guards pronounced the civic oath in a mighty chorus that echoed on the shores of the river. It was through such mass celebrations, both theatrical and symbolic, that the French nation communed and saluted the dawn of a new day.

Mme Roland's description of the pageantry and high color of the fete was found to be so exciting that, according to Champagneux, some sixty thousand copies of the issue were sold, as every federate wished to take home a memento of this great occasion.[15] Other patriotic newspapers, including Camille Desmoulins' *Révolutions de France et de Brabant,* reproduced the article in full.[16] Watching with the happy crowd the deployment of brightly dressed troops and their impeccable formation, Mme Roland experienced unforgettable jubilation, and her article was popular because it aptly expressed thoughts and feelings shared by all patriots alike. A joyful dream had filled the participants and spectators with the same emotions: France was at the threshold of a new, more promising era and would become the first European abode of justice and civil equality. Industry and commerce would thrive in such a state, and its people would be friendly and peace-loving.

A patriotic exaltation, verging on religious fervor, swept over France during those early days of the Revolution. Momentous reforms were heralded, not in an atmosphere of terror and disorder, but amid a widespread feeling of euphoria and good will. In the capital, as well as in the provinces, great gatherings solemnly swore allegiance to the new order of things and renounced the ancient privileges. These successive *Fêtes de la Fédération,* at once civil and military, confirmed the nationhood of France and abolished the separate statehood of such provinces as Brittany, Burgundy, Provence, and Dauphiné. The celebrations culminated in the Paris Federation on July 14, 1790, the first anniversary of the fall of the Bastille. The ceremony took place in the Champ-de-Mars, in the presence of the royal family, deputies from all over France, and five hundred thousand cheering spectators. After hearing Mass and a *Te Deum,* the deputies pronounced the oath of allegiance to the nation, the law, and the crown—a truly "sublime" spectacle from all contemporary accounts.

Mass demonstrations appealing to the feelings and combining pageantry, symbolism, and high theatricality became the order of the day. Torchlight parades, grandiose spectacles, triumphant and colorful corteges, punctuated with rousing speeches and enlivened with military marches and fireworks, brought the ardor of the people to fever pitch and whipped up a sense of national purpose. Spectators, with shining eyes and smiling faces, fraternized in the streets; strangers embraced and shed tears of happiness over the triumph of the Revolution; class distinctions were temporarily forgotten in the joyous excitement. Artisans and soldiers joined elegant ladies in dancing the gay farandole. The streets teemed with lively crowds boisterously celebrating the new-found dignity of the individual and abolition of the hateful privileges. Bailly, president of the National Assembly, and the deputies were noisily feted, covered with acclamations and benedictions, and called the fathers of the nation. This mood of brotherhood and good will even extended to the royal family. On October 6, 1789, when Louis XVI and his queen, having been removed from Versailles and brought back to Paris, appeared at the Paris town hall, a deafening roar of loyalty and dedication greeted them from the huge crowd amassed on the square and neighboring streets.

This wave of enthusiasm had already been heralded by a moral climate fostered through the plays, novels, and paintings of an entire generation of writers and artists. The works of Rousseau, the sentimental dramas of Diderot and Mercier, and to a lesser extent the tragedies of Voltaire, the melodramatic compositions of Greuze, all these and a host of other literary and artistic productions aimed at extolling the man of feeling and compassion who prized above all personal and civic virtue. Admiring anecdotes circulated about the spontaneous outbursts of sensibility exhibited by famous men of letters. Even the most satirical and witty of writers, Voltaire himself, had prided himself on his tender heart and wept freely whenever he felt moved by a touching scene or a generous thought.

No one was more subject to the appeal of the emotions than Mme Roland. Yet she was made uneasy by the general mood of optimism and confidence. Repeatedly, she cautioned her friends against the many dangers that still threatened the Revolution. There was not only the king, who had every reason to betray the trust that the people were so generously placing in him, but the French character as well, which tended to be too lighthearted, too easily won over by a theatrical flourish or a gracious gesture, like the appearance of the royal family and Lafayette on the balcony of the Versailles palace on the morning of October 6. And would not other European nations, still dominated by absolute autocracy, band together to crush the Revolution and reestablish the Old Régime? This was no time, she wrote time and again, to relax one's readiness and indulge in continuous celebrations. In and out of France, conservatives were establishing contact with counterrevolutionaries and foreign powers were massing on the frontiers. Vigilance, a sharp control of all court activities, a tight organization of the new government, these should be the immediate concerns of the French at a time of national crisis and peril.

Surveying the situation in the Lyons district, she reported to Brissot: "Our provinces are much fuller than the capital with the clamors of the aristocrats. Not that there are more nobles here, but inequality of class is more marked in the provinces, more harshly felt, more fanatically defended. . . . 'Religion is lost, the State is broken up, we live in an anarchy, there is no longer any obedience,' these are their favorite expressions, and it is with such incendiary phrases that they try to have the people be disloyal to a Revolution that places all men on the same level. In small cities, pride and vanity create more distance between the professions than there ever was in Paris between a bourgeois and a titled aristocrat." [17] She deplored the ignorance of the peasants and satirized the petty administrators, small-time financiers, and insignificant councilors who, in their fear of losing their offices and prerogatives, raged more furiously against what they called the populace than princes and courtiers. No class of people, she pointedly added, nursed greater pretensions and were more attached to their selfish interests than these provincial conservatives and royalists.[18]

In early October, Mme Roland was deeply saddened to learn of the death of her favorite uncle, Canon Bimont. Other difficulties continued to beset her, for Roland was having a great deal of trouble recovering from his illness. Repeated bleedings had caused painful sores on his legs, and he was in such a state of weakness that he hardly could move. And to make matters worse, terrible storms and hail were ruining the vineyards, fields, and orchards. The country looked desolate, and Mme Roland had to fight against a feeling of depression. Setting all personal sentiments and worries aside, however, she valiantly determined to concern herself only with the fate of France. To Bosc she wrote on October 6, 1789: "All grief ceases, all sorrow is suspended, all private business sinks into insignificance. Despotism has been unmasked; the nation is under way; let men of good will rally and let their close union strike terror in the hearts of the wicked!" [19] And to Brissot she confided that had Roland been a few years younger, he would have settled in America with her. But, she cheerfully added, "We regret less this promised land now that we have hopes of our own. The Revolution, imperfect though it may be, has changed the face of France." [20] Even at this early stage of the Revolution Mme Roland already felt mistrust for such moderates as Lafayette, Mirabeau, and Necker. The latter she continued to regard as a vain, narrow-minded bookkeeper.[21] Neither did she trust the general and the fiery orator for their willingness to deal with the court and their eagerness to save the monarchy.[22]

In June of 1790, Mme Roland entered into a correspondence with Henri Bancal des Issarts, a lawyer from Clermont-Ferrand who was four years her senior and who had given up his profession for politics.[23] Even though she did not know him personally, she had heard much of him through Bosc, Lanthenas, and Brissot, who were his friends. Like Brissot, Bancal was enterprising and needed a broad sphere of activity, and with Bosc he shared a keen appreciation of nature and of natural history. On Sundays, both men would leave Paris and roam in the Montmorency forest in search of plant specimens. In the course of one of these outings, Bancal, who had more financial means than his friend, purchased the small, almost abandoned church property of Sainte-Radegonde, which he graciously put at the disposal of Bosc. It was this isolated retreat which would one day serve as an asylum during the dark period of the Terror. Together with Brissot and Lanthenas, Bancal feverishly engaged in writing pamphlets and brochures which were meant to pave the way for the New Order. He was also a regular contributor, with Lanthenas and Mme Roland, to Brissot's *Patriote français*. He moreover belonged to a number of liberal clubs such as Brissot's *Society of the Friends of the Negroes* and the *Society of the Friends of the Constitution,* which was to become better known later under the name of the Club of the Jacobins. As one of the more active deputies to the National Assembly, he endeavored to spread the new gospel among the inhabitants of southern France. During these early, promising days of the Revolution, Bancal and his friends did much to further the cause of republicanism.

In addition to their enthusiasm for the Revolution and their veneration for Jean-Jacques Rousseau, Bancal, Champagneux, Bosc, Lanthenas, Brissot, and the Rolands now shared a common project. It was to buy one of the large ecclesiastical properties set up for sale by the revolutionary government and to found a communal association. As worthy disciples of Rousseau, they dreamed of living in the midst of the beauties of nature and of working together toward the regeneration of France while combining the useful arts, such as agriculture, with more intellectual pursuits.[24] It is indeed a mark of the utopian turn of mind of these men that each eagerly seized upon this scheme and saw in it the realization of Rousseau's ideal. Not the least carried away by the prospect was Manon, who already pictured herself leading a joyful and active existence among intelligent companions and in a setting worthy of *La Nouvelle Héloïse.*

When she learned that Bancal had arrived in Clermont-Ferrand, where he was organizing revolutionary societies, she urged him to visit her household either in Lyons or at Le Clos. Bancal was also traveling extensively through that part of the country looking for an advantageous buy for the future association of philosopher-farmers. Nothing came of this beautiful project, but in the early part of July 1790 Bancal was able to accept Mme Roland's invitation. Having been elected representative of the Clermont district to the first Paris Federation of July 14, he stopped off at Lyons on his way to the capital. He accompanied the Rolands to Le Clos, and even though he could stay there only one day, this first contact broke the ice. Thereafter a warm relationship was established between Bancal and the couple. Manon took an immediate liking to Bancal and included him among her regular correspondents.

In Lyons the situation was becoming increasingly more alarming, for the aristocracy and conservative bourgeoisie were powerful there, and the municipal body was overwhelmingly antirevolutionary.[25] This made Roland's position very difficult; official authorities, knowing his revolutionary sympathies, showed open hostility. At the end of July, popular riots broke out as a result of the municipality's reluctance to abolish the excessive *octroi* duties which stifled industry and caused widespread unemployment. And because of Roland's well-known republican views and long-standing opposition to the *octroi*, which lowered considerably Lyons' place in the competitive market of cloths and silks, he was now being accused by his enemies of having fomented the disturbances. He hastened to answer these charges in Champagneux's *Courrier de Lyon*.[26] Mme Roland herself was not spared by those who wanted to repress the popular movement in Lyons and intimidate its supporters. Both the inspector and his wife were regarded as dangerous agitators by the reactionaries of the Lyons district, but, as Manon wrote to Bancal, this campaign of vilification did not frighten her and she hardly missed her neighbors' tiresome visits.[27] What worried her more was the fact that troops had been brought in to pacify the city. She feared that a counterrevolutionary and court-inspired plot was being hatched. On August 4, she even left the peaceful retreat of Le Clos and rode into town on horseback to see for herself what the situation was like.[28]

Manon's letters of that period—to Brissot, Lanthenas, and especially to Bancal—give a vivid picture of the political role of Lyons and the Beaujolais during this first, critical phase of the Revolution. The powerful influence that the aristocracy, mercantile bourgeoisie, and clergy continued to exert was disheartening to partisans of reform. Lyons, Mme Roland wrote to her friends, was a hotbed of counterrevolutionary activity, and the National Assembly seemed insufficiently aware of the danger this important city presented to the future of France. It was the weak link in the chain and had to be watched carefully. Repeatedly she urged Bancal to warn the Assembly and instruct it to distribute propaganda leaflets in the provinces and to take the proper measures against a reactionary uprising. Together with her husband she consistently supported the most democratic elements of the municipality and justified the protest actions of the people. Even Brissot received a sharp rebuke from her when an article published in his *Patriote français* showed a lack of sympathy for the artisans of Lyons.[29]

By August 30, 1790, when Bancal arrived at Le Clos for a more leisurely visit with the Rolands, the situation in the Lyons vicinity had somewhat quieted down. Political cares were temporarily pushed into the background as Bancal and his hosts gave themselves over to the delights of rambling in the fields and woods, playing shuttlecock, chatting with the neighboring peasants, and discussing plans for the future. That summer was especially torrid and rainy, but time was spent pleasantly in the cool dining room during the spells of heat and, when the weather allowed, on the terrace overlooking the valley. From the nearby fields came the familiar sound of the threshing of wheat. In her light muslin dress and large straw hat Manon looked radiant, and she was as agile and vivacious as a young girl.

This time, Bancal prolonged his visit until the beginning of October. His five-week stay in the company of Manon and in a setting that brought out her most appealing qualities had colored his attachment for her with romantic overtones. A noticeable change in his manner as well as a quickly whispered confession during a tête-à-tête revealed to Manon her friend's dangerously tender feelings. With customary self-possession, she proceeded to discourage her admirer's amorous but respectful advances. But all the while, she felt strangely moved and, for the first time in many years, became aware that disquieting emotions were encroaching on her inner tranquillity. But what she experienced was a sentimental, rather than truly passionate, attraction. She therefore did not find it overly difficult to control her own feelings and bring her guest to reason in a firm but tactful manner.

Roland, true to his role as unsuspecting husband, never guessed that a discreet romance was unfolding under his roof. As the long summer turned into autumn and the day of Bancal's departure neared, Manon was overtaken by a mood of melancholy. Who knew when, if ever, they would be able to share such pleasant, carefree days again? When the moment of separation came, on October 2, Manon accompanied her friend through the fields part of the way. Around them, yellowing and russet-colored leaves were falling; the countryside was ablaze with autumnal golden and purple hues. In silence the voyager took leave of his hostess and mounted his horse. Slowly Manon made her way back to the house, which stood alone amid the fields that lay barren after the harvest.

A few days later, Manon wrote a letter to Bancal in Paris, unbeknown to Roland. She had never done this before. But she still was oppressed by the strong emotions she had just experienced, and what she had to tell her friend was of a highly private nature: "I take up the pen without knowing or being able to judge what I am going to set down. My mind is filled with a thousand thoughts, which I would probably find easier to express were they accompanied by less tumultuous feelings. Why are my eyes dimmed with tears that keep falling unceasingly? My will is unshaken, my heart is pure, and yet I am not at peace!" [30] But reverting to a more objective tone, Manon sensibly concluded her letter with warm wishes for Bancal's future success in politics and for personal happiness and fulfillment.

Subsequent letters from Manon to Bancal did not contain the slightest reference to romantic sentiments; they resumed a more orthodox friendliness and brimmed once more with vigorous observations and lengthy comments on current affairs and "the public good." In November of 1790, Bancal set out for a trip to the British Isles. Why this voyage at a time when men like him were urgently needed at home? First, his political hopes had been disappointed, for he had failed to be elected to a significant post either in Paris or in Clermont. Then too, Brissot had so convincingly underscored the importance of a favorable reception to the French Revolution in England that his friend decided to survey the situation there for himself and establish contact with as many liberals as possible. Edmund Burke's *Reflections on the Revolution in France* had just been published, making a strong impact on British public opinion. Finally, bearing in mind the complexity of human motivations, one should perhaps also add that Bancal's involvement with Mme Roland, and his realization that it was a hopeless thing, probably had something to do with his decision to leave France on an unofficial goodwill mission. He stayed on in England until June of 1791, and distance in time and place seemed indeed to have helped him get over his infatuation. He nevertheless continued to correspond regularly with Mme Roland, turning to her for advice and counsel in politics and even in matters of the heart, for it was not too long before other women attracted his interest.

In November of 1790, the Rolands left Le Clos to spend the winter months in Lyons, where the situation for the "patriots," as sympathizers with the Revolution were commonly called, had improved and the influence of the counterrevolutionaries weakened. This time, Roland's well-known views resulted in an appointment as a municipal officer of the Lyons Council. Nine-year-old Eudora was entrusted to the nuns of the Convent of the Visitation in Villefranche so as to permit Mme Roland to devote all her energies to the new, demanding tasks lying ahead. Perhaps she unconsciously welcomed this opportunity to let others take over the absorbing duty of educating a child who had shown so little intellectual promise. Setting aside her favorite poets, Mme Roland braced herself for the political arena by rereading, whenever she had some free moments, Tacitus, Rousseau's *Social Contract,* and Mrs. Macaulay, an English historian with liberal views.

If the political climate had become more favorable to the revolutionaries in Lyons, the economic situation, on the other hand, was almost desperate. The vital manufacturing and trading centers were practically at a standstill and thousands of workers joined the ranks of the unemployed as a result of the disastrous effect of the *octroi* duties and the staggering municipal debt incurred before the Revolution. To calm the anxious inhabitants by demanding the recall of the regiments sent after the uprisings of July was not sufficient. It was imperative to expose the critical situation to the Constituent Assembly and obtain financial relief by persuading the government to take over the debt, which amounted to the formidable sum of thirty-nine million francs. The municipality did not know how to pay these arrears—which were in great part due to the royal needs —and was of the opinion that the Assembly should declare the debt a national one. Only then could the Lyons industries be revived and given new impetus.

No one was better qualified than Roland to unravel the financial maze inherited from the Old Régime and aggravated by the recent happenings. On February 1, 1791, he was therefore appointed by the municipality, together with François Bret, another Lyons official, to the delicate and difficult mission of presenting the case to the Assembly and negotiating a loan of three million francs to cover the most immediate needs of Lyons. Roland's more conservative colleagues probably also saw in this appointment a good way of removing from the scene, at least temporarily, an embarrassingly strict man whose unbending character and untiring zeal sometimes made life difficult for them.

Mme Roland greeted the news of her husband's mission with delight, for she was to accompany him to Paris. It had been more than six years since she had seen her native city, and she was growing increasingly impatient to leave the provinces and be in the center of things. Having entrusted Eudora to the Villefranche nuns, the couple set out for the capital, where they arrived on February 20, 1791. As the stagecoach made its entrance into Paris, Manon eagerly surveyed the familiar landmarks and noticed that the streets were full of animation. People were everywhere, discussing the posters and patriotic signs covering the walls. Fashion had turned revolutionary and patriotic: women favored brightly colored or completely white dresses with light shawls gracefully draped over their bodices. Liberty hats, constitution jewelry, and ribbons of all shades were the rage. Men, on the other hand, no longer powdered their hair, and many wore large cockades on their hats to show their allegiance to the New Order. And on almost every street corner a gathering discussed the events of the day or read intently the latest posters.

The Rolands settled down in a furnished flat on the second floor of the Hôtel Britannique, which was situated in the rue Guénégaud, on the Left Bank, only a stone's throw from the Pont-Neuf, where Manon had spent her youth.[31] Bosc, as obliging as ever, had prepared this lodging according to Manon's specifications. She had indicated her preference for the Faubourg Saint-Germain, since this district was conveniently located without being as expensive as the Tuileries area. The street, moreover, had to be clean and accessible, so that "a citizeness who knows how to use her legs can go out without wading in the mud." [32]

Versailles was no longer the royal residence, since the people of Paris had brought the king back to the Tuileries palace, where they could keep a watchful eye on him. The Constituent Assembly, too, had moved to Paris and held its meetings in the former royal riding school on the north side of the Tuileries Gardens. And the pleasure-seeking Paris of the Old Régime was no more. A popular meeting center was under the graceful arcades of Palais-Royal, the residence of the Duke of Orléans. Palais-Royal was now the forum of Paris. Men mounted on chairs and harangued little circles of onlookers. Orators, hawkers, newscriers, and idlers constantly thronged the garden, forming an ever changing, colorful procession. Here Camille Desmoulins, journalist and pamphleteer, had by his oratory contributed to the popular unrest that had eventually led to the fall of the Bastille, and here too every political rumor and activity had its origin. Nearby was the Jacobin Club, known from its premises in the old Jacobin monastery (the Parisian name for the Dominican order), in the rue Saint-Honoré. It was in this building that deputies and private citizens alike would meet to discuss the questions before the Constituent Assembly. Young Robespierre held forth almost every evening, steadily developing his oratorical ability and exerting a growing influence. On the Left Bank, more radical societies, such as the Cordeliers Club, were thrown open to students, artisans, and shopkeepers. Here Danton thundered against the government to the delight of his audience of malcontents. As for the workers whose poverty and shabby clothes excluded them from the clubs or cafés, they could turn to Marat, the "friend of the people," who expounded their rights and vented his hatred against all in power.

Everywhere Mme Roland went, she could see groups of varying sizes discussing, arguing excitedly and sometimes in angry tones and with emphatic gestures. In the evening, the cafés and restaurants were packed, and this despite the rising cost of food and drink. The jammed theaters frequently became the scene of violent quarrels between royalists and "patriots." Marie-Joseph Chénier, the brother of the poet, was the playwright of the day with his national dramas in which political themes had replaced the traditional subjects of classical tragedy and comedy. Art exhibits in the *Salon* also extolled the revolutionary ideal, clothed in the noble dress of Roman antiquity. David dominated the artistic scene as the undisputed master, while Fragonard, the former protégé of Mme du Barry and poetic painter of frivolous scenes in the rococo style, and even Greuze, the once popular virtuoso of moralizing genre compositions, tried to elude starvation by specializing in portraits of revolutionaries. For the public wanted nothing that could remind it of the Old Régime, and even the theater and the arts had to reflect the new spirit in an austere, virile style.

Paris had taken charge of the Revolution; its citizens competed for seats in the public galleries of the Assembly, noisily demonstrating their approval or dissent, thus exerting the pressure of public opinion on governmental authorities. The Parisian crowds, conscious of their newly won power, were in a jocular mood.[33] The city was now the heart of the Revolution, a world within a nation, and it felt confident that it had the right to dictate not only literature and art, but also to govern the rest of France.

TWELVE

A Revolutionary Salon

BEFORE PLUNGING INTO POLITICS, Manon had to fulfill a few private obligations, such as paying the good sisters of the Convent of the Congregation a visit. Of her own family there were few surviving relations; her father had died in the winter of 1788.[1] In order better to acquaint herself with the workings of the revolutionary government, she hastened to attend the sessions of the Constituent Assembly.[2] The hall itself consisted of six tiers of seats disposed in an ellipse around a central arena. The president's table was on a stage on the south side of the rink. Opposite him were the bar and tribune, from which deputies made their speeches. At each end, galleries for the public and boxes for distinguished visitors had been built. The Assembly deliberations were immensely popular in these early days. The din of the chatting deputies and spectators frequently prevented speakers from being heard, despite the huge bell that the president occasionally sounded to obtain silence. But when a well-known orator like Mirabeau addressed the Assembly, the hush which fell over the audience was interrupted only for enthusiastic ovations. To the left of the seats representing the most radical wing of the revolutionaries were especially noticeable handsome Pétion, fiery Buzot, and solemn Robespierre. Over the conservative right towered Mirabeau, famed for his oratorical ability as well as for his dissoluteness and venality. In the center could be seen liberal nobles like Clermont-Tonnerre and Liancourt and progressive priests like the Abbé Grégoire.

On the whole, Mme Roland was disappointed by what she saw at the Assembly.[3] But then one must bear in mind that her critical faculties were highly developed and that reality frequently failed to live up to her expectations. Idealistic and impervious to the necessities and limitations of practical politics, she became irritated with procrastinations and compromises. With the enthusiasm of the newcomer, she fully expected all the deputies to be equally dedicated to the public weal. But by February of 1791, revolutionary fervor had cooled, and the Assembly had settled down to the difficult business of making representative government work for the first time in France and of completing the Constitution. Factional pressures were heavy, parliamentarian procedures were in their infancy, and disorder often prevailed. Mme Roland was appalled by the near anarchy that ruled among the deputies and especially by the influence that the conservatives and reactionaries combined continued to wield in the government. Liberals, on the other hand, she found discouragingly isolated and disorganized.[4]

What also displeased her was the atmosphere in the Assembly, which at times verged on the frivolous, and the tendency of the speakers to make a play for the gallery.[5] None of the members who sat on the right side of the hemicycle impressed her, not even Mirabeau, despite his powerful appearance and rhetorical genius. His readiness to defend the royalist cause and to uphold the idea of an absolute veto for the king made her view him in a very harsh light. Subsequent events were to bring her around to a more favorable opinion of a statesman capable of steering a middle course in dangerous times of upheaval and turmoil.[6] Mme Roland's judgment of the Assembly was unduly severe, and her evaluation of the leading figures of the day, especially of those with moderate or conservative tendencies, unfair and frequently scathing. There is no doubt that the pragmatic art and complex dynamics of politics completely escaped her. And since she had expected something more heroic and grandiose, or at least more orderly and coherent, she was frightened lest the reactionaries take advantage of the situation and organize a coup. Here as in Lyons she was obsessed with the dread of a royalist plot. Eyeing each deputy suspiciously, she was quick to note his foibles. Mme Roland lacked the shrewdness, the realism, and the sense of timing without which one can be a political theorist but never an effective statesman. That so many revolutionaries still seemed to believe in the practicability of a constitutional monarchy shocked her. As an impulsive, introspective disciple of Rousseau, she tended to be intransigent and could never gloss over the defects of those to whom had been entrusted the fate of the Revolution.

This is perhaps the reason why the deliberations of the Jacobins, which she also attended, gave her far greater cause for satisfaction than did the sessions of the Constituent Assembly. Here at least, she could listen to speeches by outright republicans who sought to limit the powers of the king and to pressure the Assembly into serving the true ideals of the Revolution. The hall in which the Jacobins met was outfitted nearly in the same style as the National Assembly. The tribune from which members spoke was opposite that in which sat the president. There was a table for the clerks, and galleries for the audience had been provided. When the debate became overly turbulent, ushers walked around the hall ordering, or rather pleading for, some silence.

Soon Mme Roland took a special interest in the group of militant young "patriots" who sat on the left of the president in the Assembly and who were also active in the Jacobin Club. These men, particularly Pétion, Buzot, and Robespierre, she would soon get to know personally through Brissot. Watching the three "incorruptibles," as she was fond of calling them—a term that was later to be associated with Robespierre alone—struggle valiantly in order to put into effect the most advanced reforms, she felt less depressed over the chances of the Revolution and came to the conclusion that the Right, after all, did not remain unchallenged at the Assembly. But the true "patriots" constituted a minority in comparison with the reactionary forces, and it saddened her to see them overwhelmed time and again by their more numerous opponents.[7]

As for the friends with whom she had been corresponding before her arrival in Paris, Bosc was unchanged, as quietly devoted and tender-hearted as ever, a tireless worker for the good cause, but a bit of a dreamer. Lanthenas, too, had his heart in the right place, but continued to be indolent and not particularly reliable. Bancal was in England, and Champagneux in Lyons. It was Brissot who introduced the Rolands to a number of men, some of whom were to become their close associates and friends.[8] Brissot had naturally hastened to pay his respects to the Rolands. Referring to this encounter, Mme Roland writes in her *Memoirs*: "There is nothing more amusing than the first meeting of people who are acquainted through correspondence without knowing one another's faces." [9] Brissot's simplicity of manner and straightforwardness appealed to Manon. But she was less pleased with his lighthearted insouciance and lack of dignity which, she felt, hardly befitted a writer and political figure.[10]

Brissot was very active in the political world. He knew practically everyone, and the men he brought to the Rolands' salon at the Hôtel Britannique, almost all still in their thirties, shared a common dedication to the republican principles. As the apartment was conveniently located in the center of the city, it soon became an informal gathering place four times a week. Brissot and his friends would drop in on the Rolands between the close of the Assembly meetings around four and the opening of the Jacobin Club at six. Here those who constituted the radical Left could exchange ideas, review the state of affairs at the Assembly, and discuss proposals for future measures. These reunions, however, had nothing of the concerted, backdoor caucuses at which questions of policy are decided. Parties as such did not yet exist at this early date, though later events were to cause the deputies to fall naturally into fairly coherent groups. Rather, these meetings enabled men who had similar views on a number of issues to discuss the happenings and speeches of the day in the relaxed atmosphere of a salon and in the presence of an attentive, intelligent woman.[11]

There was Brissot himself, friendly, warm, outgoing, dressed in the plain fashion of an English Quaker. There was tall, good-looking, invariably cheerful Jérôme Pétion, who was to become the mayor of Paris and, for a while, the idol of its people. Later, Mme Roland would come to the realization that Pétion was a rather weak-willed man, one moreover who tended to be overly trustful and who was too eager to please.[12] There was enthusiastic, sensitive Buzot, who would one day awaken Mme Roland's slumbering heart. The thirty-three-year-old Robespierre also attended these gatherings, albeit irregularly. He usually sat in a corner of the salon, silently listening to the animated discussions. At the time he still retained a slight trace of a provincial accent, and he did not as yet possess the easy polish of his more urbane colleagues. But his reticent manner intrigued Mme Roland, while his aptitude for hard work and the dogged way in which he fought for the most liberal reforms greatly impressed her. Watching with sympathetic interest this slightly built, impeccably dressed young man with pale, sharp features, Mme Roland could hardly suspect the power he would one day wield.[13] Brissot also brought along Clavière, a finance expert from Geneva, who struck his hostess as a rather dry and colorless person but able and diligent and, what was more unusual for a man of his profession, scrupulously honest. There were other visitors as well, but it was in the trio Buzot, Pétion, and Robespierre that Mme Roland placed her hopes for the future of the Revolution. For the time being, these men, so divergent in temperament, worked together, and their hostess sang their praises while charitably overlooking those personal idiosyncrasies which, pitiless observer that she was, she had detected in each.

As a hostess Mme Roland did not care to display the social graces and amenities so highly prized under the Old Régime. Affected civilities and gallant chitchat were things of the past. Manon's was a decidedly political salon with a Spartan flavor. She officiated with tact and, what was even more appreciated, in silence. Unlike Mme de Staël, she did not crave to be the center of attraction at all times. A woman's place, she continued to hold, was definitely in the background. In her *Memoirs* she tells us that she never allowed herself to utter a word until the meetings were over.[14] Deliberately seating herself outside the circle of men, she quietly did needlework or wrote letters while the debates went on. To be sure, she occasionally had to bite her lips to keep from commenting upon what was being said, notwithstanding how unreasonable it appeared to her.[15] Such training was helpful in developing self-discipline and, if the Montagnards would later make much of Mme Roland's presence at the gatherings in her salon, several contemporaries, not all sympathetic to the Girondists, have confirmed in their own *Memoirs* her claim that she refrained from taking a direct part in the discussions of her friends.[16] It goes without saying, however, that such an attempt at self-effacement did not prevent her from exerting a certain influence on the men who regularly met in her salon. Ironically enough, of the men who obtained her most unqualified praise, it was Robespierre who was almost invariably singled out for special plaudits.

In the exciting atmosphere of revolutionary Paris, Manon's wholesome good looks blossomed. She had always thrived on effort and activity, and to her admirers she presented a picture of full-blown womanhood enlivened by girlish vivaciousness. She wore plain dresses either in white muslin or with those brightly colored stripes made popular since 1789. A large kerchief of white linen was usually draped over her shoulders, and her décolletés were prim, as behooves a woman of virtue and modesty. Only one uncharacteristic portrait, that by Heinsius now at the museum of the Versailles palace, shows her in a more provocative, low-cut gown. Such a coquettish outfit, together with the languorous pose, must have been a concession to the artist and to the eighteenth-century genre of salon portraiture. As a rule, Mme Roland paid scant attention to adornment and elegance, although her frocks were always in good taste. A contemporary, Etienne Dumont, noted that "her simple attire in no way detracted from her charm." [17] Her long brown hair was now allowed to fall casually on her shoulders; short bangs and ringlets framed her face, which was brightened by lustrous eyes and a ready smile. With her swift step and plump but lithe figure, she looked younger than her thirty-six years. Roland, on the other hand, appeared older than fifty-six, for hard work, a poor stomach, and a bilious disposition had aged him prematurely. Next to the radiant Manon he could easily be taken for her father.[18]

As the winter changed into the spring of 1791, the course of public affairs, to Mme Roland's intense irritation, slowed down to a standstill. The new legislation embodying the ideals of 1789 was being disrupted by royalist and counterrevolutionary forces. The general enthusiasm that had marked the early days of the Revolution was slowly giving way to doubt and, in some quarters, even to disillusionment. Mme Roland's marriage to a member of the provincial bourgeoisie had not made her forget her early association with the Parisian artisan class. Her faith in the *menu peuple* of her native city is evidenced by her stated belief that "the good people only need support to find the right way" and that the revolutionary principles "will always spread more effectively among the people than among shopkeepers and those who set themselves up as persons of consequence and who, without being more enlightened, consider themselves above the populace." [19] That in 1791 she sided with the most democratic causes is also demonstrated by her strong protest against the legal distinction that was being established between *active* and *passive* citizens, that is between taxpayers and those too poor to pay taxes. On April 28, 1791, she intently listened to members of the Assembly debate the question. When a bill was voted which would admit to the National Guard only active citizens she immediately set about to oppose it both in Brissot's *Patriote français* and in her private correspondence.[20] That Pétion, Robespierre, and Buzot, who had boldly and eloquently spoken up against this law, had been drowned out by a clamorous and hostile majority in the Assembly was disheartening:

When Dubois, d'André, Rabaut have insidiously repeated that only beggars would not be active citizens, how is it that someone did not point out that in all cities with large industrial plants, there are vast numbers of workers who, because of industrial crises and manufacturers' competition, find themselves temporarily unemployed, unable to pay their taxes, even forced to resort to public relief? Thus in Lyons alone, more than twenty-five thousand souls were reduced to misery during the terrible winter of 1789. These workers are nevertheless useful and good citizens, honest family men, very devoted to the Constitution, intent on maintaining it; and they will not have the right to be armed? And the arbitrary authority of the municipalities will be able to reject them? [21]

All through the spring of 1791, Mme Roland's letters reflect disappointment over the lack of cohesion of the liberal forces in the Constituent Assembly. Roland's mission, moreover, was meeting with discouragingly little success. When a "small victory" was won over the monarchists with regard to the king's power of veto, she sounded a more cheerful note. On the whole, however, she was in a restless, fretful mood: "I no longer go to the Assembly because it makes me sick, nor to the theater, which is far too frivolous for my taste in such grave circumstances. If I did not have relatives and friends who give me duties to fulfill, I would isolate myself in order not to be made to witness so many selfish interests and passions whose perpetual clash weakens the public spirit." [22] She was beginning to look forward to the coming elections in the hope that more dedicated young men would be sent to the Assembly, "—incorruptible" republicans like Robespierre, Buzot, and Pétion, who were waiting for an opportunity to make their move, an opportunity that would soon present itself with the king's flight to Varennes.

At this time, Mme Roland thought, felt, and wrote in a manner reminiscent of the early Romans, or rather what the revolutionaries regarded as such. She recognized only the civic virtues; the all too human failings of those around her filled her with righteous indignation. Her letters were replete with such expressions as "patriotism," "freedom," "courage," "the public weal,"—all terms which, for Mme Roland and other fervent republicans, embodied the new democratic ideal. It irked her, therefore, to see so many deputies preoccupied with petty, self-seeking aims. Such behavior, to her mind, was tantamount to outright treason.

When, in the morning of June 21, 1791, she learned that the royal family had taken flight, she manifested little surprise.[23] This action,

after all, bore out her long-held conviction that the king had only
waited for an opportunity to betray the Revolution and join the
enemy. Gathered in Pétion's house on that historic day, the Rolands,
Buzot, Brissot, and Pétion maintained that the king's flight spelled
the doom of the monarchy and, in an elated frame of mind, discussed the means of preparing public opinion for a republic.[24] Before long they were all carried away by enthusiasm and speaking at
once. France would at last have an "ideal," "virtuous" republic,
modeled on Sparta, Rome, and the United States of America. But
Mme Roland noted that Robespierre, who was also present, did not
share in the general rejoicing. He silently watched the others rhap-
sodize, then abruptly interrupted to ask in a sharp voice what manner of thing this "virtuous republic" would be. This unexpected
intervention, and the ironical look that went with it, had a sobering
effect and made everyone feel uneasy and a little foolish. The incident is related in Mme Roland's *Memoirs* and is completely in
character with the participants.[25] As one who, by that time, must
have had a pretty well-defined notion of what constituted a "virtuous republic" and who, before long, would not hesitate to impose
it on the nation at a high cost in lives, Robespierre must have looked
upon these hot-headed and optimistic young men with secret contempt.

Mme Roland also observed that, while her friends rejoiced over
the king's flight, seeing in it a solution to the irksome monarchical
problem, Robespierre was in a somber mood: "I found him that
afternoon at Pétion's house, saying in a tone of alarm that the royal
family would never have taken this step unless they had in Paris a
body of supporters ready to organize a Saint-Barthélemy type massacre of patriots and that he did not expect to outlive the day." [26]
Other contemporary testimony confirms the basic veracity of this
statement, although it was written at a time when Robespierre had
become one of Mme Roland's bitterest enemies. His fears, moreover,
were not merely the manifestations of morbid suspiciousness. Cautious, diffident Robespierre was better aware than his fellow revolutionaries of the grave dangers that threatened France. His warning

soon spread to other radicals, and, on the night of June 21, the Cordeliers even sent a guard to protect the "apostle of liberty."

Mme Roland and her friends had greeted Louis XVI's flight joyfully in the belief that, as she puts it, it had rid the government of a "pest." [27] His arrest and forced return spread gloom among her group. Now royalist intrigues would begin anew and the issue of the king's fate would be a source of major dissensions. Robespierre, on the other hand, appeared relieved: as long as he had expected the king to reach the Prussians, he had envisaged an invasion of France accompanied by reprisals against the patriots. As the confusion subsided somewhat, Mme Roland became frankly alarmed. Would Louis XVI be restored to the throne without as much as a trial? Such a prospect enraged her. Now was the time, she felt, to declare the republic and show the French people that a king is not necessary for the effective functioning of a governmental machine. She pleaded with all the eloquence at her command, even though at that time the Assembly and the Jacobins themselves balked at such a radical measure. Mme Roland pleaded well indeed, but she was pleading in the desert, for only the extremist Cordeliers and such men as Robespierre, Condorcet, Brissot, and Thomas Paine dared then speak out openly against the monarchy. She nevertheless persisted in her views. In a letter to Bancal she wrote: "To put the king back on the throne is an ineptitude, an absurdity if not an outright abomination; to declare him mentally unfit is to be obliged, according to the constitution, to name a regent; to name a regent would not only confirm the defects of the constitution at a time when these should and can be corrected, but also open the way to civil war. . . . The best, most righteous measure would be to try him, but they are incapable of adopting such action." [28] For her the best solution, under the circumstances, was to suspend and guard the king, to name a temporary president, and to continue legislating without royal consent. [29]

But few shared such a bold stand. The Jacobin Club, which comprised at the time many believers in a constitutional monarchy, was split on the issue. In her June 22 letter to Bancal, Mme Roland had

had only high praise for Robespierre's resoluteness in the face of general indecision: "Robespierre mounted the tribune. He had the courage to express, with his customary energy, what I have just outlined in this letter. One could sense that he was depressed by the slackness of the Assembly, by the corruption of many of its members, and that he had to unburden his heart before a once illustrious society." [30] It is one of the ironies of history that, for a long time, Mme Roland should have been in greater agreement with her future enemy than with most members of her own circle of friends.

When the Assembly, on July 16, decreed the temporary suspension of the king, to be followed by his reinstatement as soon as he had signed the Constitution, all action in favor of deposition became illegal. On July 17, a Sunday, demonstrators gathered in the huge open space of the Champ-de-Mars in order to sign a petition calling for the king's abdication. Bailly, Mayor of Paris, along with Lafayette, sent a detachment of National Guards who dispersed the crowd, leaving some fifty dead.[31] The Rolands, true to their staunch republicanism, were present at the demonstration. It was on this occasion that they made the acquaintance of another Jacobin, the painter David.[32]

The first thought of the Rolands during this crisis was to protect against the reactionary coalition those who had expressed themselves in favor of a trial, for a wave of repression and terror followed the Champ-de-Mars massacre. Fear and suspicion were in the air. To Bancal Mme Roland wrote that public opinion and freedom of the press were being ruthlessly suppressed and that "the machinery of war is set up everywhere against a defenseless people." [33] Leaders of the popular clubs were arrested or went into hiding, and the more radical journals were suspended.[34] Mme Roland worried over the fate of Robespierre, for who had been more outspoken against the monarchy? [35] It was rumored that he would be put on trial and, at the same time, that he ran the risk of assassination. As the Jacobin Club, of which he was a leading force, had agreed to join the radical Cordeliers in petitioning against the king, it was threatened with extinction, since the more conservative members seceded in order to unite with the rightist Feuillants.[36] Robespierre, owing to a last-minute withdrawal, escaped outright proscription, but once again he felt directly threatened. Together with her husband, Mme Roland hurried over to his lodging in the quiet Marais district to offer him a safe shelter until things would calm down. But he had already taken a room in the home of Maurice Duplay, a carpenter who lived on the rue Saint-Honoré, within easy reach of the Club and the Assembly. Two years later, while languishing in prison, Mme Roland would look back with understandable bitterness to the circumstances of this episode.[37] It was one of those peculiar twists of fate that she should have done her best to save a man who, when power came to him, would have no compunction about removing her from the scene. But in July 1791, Mme Roland saw in Robespierre a hero and martyr of liberty, and therefore worthy of all her support and assistance.

Ideologically, and even temperamentally, Robespierre and Mme Roland had much in common. Both hated the monarchy, advocated strong measures against it, and were highly suspicious of the royalists, aristocrats, and even moderates in the Assembly. Such men as Mirabeau, Lafayette, and Dumouriez aroused their hostility because of their lukewarm republicanism and willingness to compromise with the court. Both were fastidious and had a passion for work. Both were deists, but deists of a sentimental, Rousseauistic kind, who shared with Rousseau the belief that an official state religion is beneficial to morality and social order.[38] Atheism they rejected as an aristocratic attitude, for it did not take into account the effect it would have on the illiterate. As one who had long lived in daily contact with Paris artisans, Mme Roland was well aware that the Revolution could not be political alone, that it had to adopt social and economic reforms as well. To be sure, the practical means of achieving necessary reforms escaped her, but in this she was no different from most eighteenth-century revolutionaries. The French historian Albert Mathiez contrasts Robespierre's interest in the welfare of the people with the Girondist indifference toward socioeconomic problems.[39] This distinction may be true of such Girondists as Vergniaud, but it hardly applies to Mme Roland, friend of the Girondists that she was to become.

Yet, while championing the rights of the common man, Mme Roland remained keenly conscious that centuries of oppression and ignorance did not make him particularly fit for representative government. If, like Rousseau and Robespierre, she credited the people with common sense and good will and held that the interests of the government should coincide with those of the majority, that the voice of the government, in other words, should represent popular will, she was deeply concerned by the ease with which clever demagogues can dupe the people by flattery. A strong constitution was therefore urgently needed in order to safeguard the rights of the citizens. But the success of the Revolution would be insured only through widespread education. In the meantime, though, much could be accomplished through a well-organized popular press that would enlighten the public on its new civic responsibilities. Hence the enthusiasm with which Mme Roland threw herself into journalism. In her attitude toward the church, she remained consistently faithful to the anticlericalism of the *philosophes.* That meant a wholehearted approval of the confiscation of church property and of the measures against those priests who refused to swear allegiance to the Revolution—the refractory or non-juring priests.

On all these matters, her views coincided remarkably with those of Robespierre. No wonder, then, that she should have been pleased to see the growing influence he was wielding among true liberals. Buzot, too, shared the same convictions, but at this time he was not yet giving the full measure of his talent. His participation in the deliberations of the Assembly and the Jacobin Club was more sporadic than that of tireless, single-minded Robespierre. To be goaded into action, proud, romantic Buzot needed a great passion. That day had not yet come, and in the meantime he served the right cause, but in an undistinguished manner. Handsome Pétion was well-meaning enough, but childlike and prodigiously vain. As for Brissot, Mme Roland was beginning to note his lack of foresight and political acumen, facile optimism, and simplistic belief that all men were as good-natured and well-intentioned as he. It was therefore in cold but energetic young Robespierre, the ex-lawyer from Arras, that Mme Roland placed her hopes at this juncture. True, Robespierre the man had little appeal for her, but she was quite willing to overlook some unsympathetic personal traits, since he clearly appeared to be destined for great things.

Composing her *Memoirs* two short but eventful years later, Mme Roland was to recall, with a pang of bitterness, the high esteem she had once held for Robespierre. Had he not, more vigorously than Brissot, Pétion, and Buzot, supported the idea of a republic in the face of mounting opposition? This is how, in her prison cell, she was to justify her former admiration for Robespierre:

At that time, Robespierre had for me all the earmarks of an honest man; and because of his principles I forgave his tiresome way of speaking. I had, however, noticed that he was always reserved in our meetings, listening to the opinions of all and seldom giving his own. I have been told that the next day he was the first to mount the tribune and set forth the arguments that, the evening before, he had heard from his friends. When he was sometimes gently reproved for this conduct, he would get off with a quip, and this ruse was forgiven as the effect of that burning *amour-propre* which truly tormented him. Persuaded then that Robespierre was a passionate defender of liberty, I tended to attribute his faults to an excess of zeal. That kind of reserve which seems to indicate either the fear of being seen through, or the suspicion of a man who can find no reason in his own bosom to trust others, and which characterized Robespierre, puzzled me, but I mistook it for modesty. Thus it is that through a favorable bias we transform the most ominous signs into indications of the best qualities. Never did the smile of confidence rest on his lips. . . . His talents, as an orator, were unremarkable. His voice was ordinary and his speeches could be quite tiresome. But he upheld principles with fire and doggedness, and there was courage in continuing to do so at a time when the defenders of the people had been extraordinarily reduced in number. The court detested and calumniated them: to support them was therefore the duty of a patriot. I esteemed Robespierre on this account and told him as much. And though he was not very assiduous at my little gatherings, he occasionally had dinner at our house.[40]

Mme Roland's reservations about Robespierre's oratorical ability are not unfounded. Admirers and detractors alike have pointed out his rather high-pitched voice, his provincialisms, and his tendency to drone on interminably. And yet, it is only in her *Memoirs* that Mme Roland mentions Robespierre's defects as a speaker. In her earlier letters she invariably calls attention to the energy and sincerity of his verbal interventions at the Assembly. There is no doubt, however, that other speakers, especially among those who were later to become known as Girondists, had more appealing personalities and possessed greater facility, but none had Robespierre's persistence, tenaciousness, and capacity for hard work. It was not only wariness that kept Robespierre from being a regular habitué in Mme Roland's salon. His daily attendance at the Assembly and the Jacobin Club, preparation of speeches, writing of letters, and organization of the Parisian revolutionary forces left little time for visits. And the Duplay family with whom he now lived provided a simple, congenial atmosphere that fulfilled all his social needs.

In April of 1791, Thomas Paine was introduced to Mme Roland by Brissot. Soon he was a familiar figure in her salon. Recently debarked from England, he was eager to meet French revolutionaries and to take an active part in events. His knowledge of French was limited, though, for if he could understand the language, he was unable to speak it. This handicap, however, could not prevent him from throwing himself into the thick of the fray. His *Rights of Man*, in which he had defended the French Revolution against the attacks of Edmund Burke, as well as his open criticisms of English institutions had led to his prosecution in Britain, but endeared him to liberals like Mme Roland.[41] Together with Brissot and Condorcet, Paine formed a society and published a journal, *Le Républicain*.[42] A prospectus of the paper, posted by Paine on July 1, 1791, proclaimed that by taking flight the king had freed the nation from all allegiance to him. Such premature radicalism frightened many members of the Assembly, deepened the rift between the partisans of a constitutional monarchy and outright republicans, and failed to appeal to the people at large.

In her *Memoirs* Mme Roland traces a portrait of Paine which takes into account the shortcomings as well as the outstanding talents of the famous pamphleteer: "Declared a French citizen as one of those celebrated foreigners whom our nation was, quite naturally, eager to adopt, he was known by writings which had been useful in the American Revolution and which might have contributed to producing one in England." [43] But while she admired his impetuous frankness, the boldness of his ideas, the originality of his style, and the striking truths he did not hesitate to express even in the midst of hostile listeners, she nevertheless thought him more fit to sow the seeds of popular action than to lay the foundation of a solid government. In short, she deemed him a capable political theorist, a gifted journalist, and a molder of popular opinion more than a legislator: "Paine throws light upon a revolution better than he contributes in making a constitution. He can uphold those great principles in a manner that strikes the eye and can obtain the applause of a club or excite the enthusiasm of a tavern." [44] But for cool discussion in a committee, for the regular and sustained efforts necessary in the legislative process, he was not temperamentally suited, according to Mme Roland—a judgment that has been ratified by historians and biographers alike.

The tone of Mme Roland's letters in July of 1791 betrays weariness. Intrigues, fear, and a powerful reactionary faction loomed heavily over the uneasy Assembly, and Roland's negotiations for Lyons were still in a deep morass. In this state of affairs, Paris was becoming increasingly less inspiring. With the coming of the summer months, moreover, Mme Roland was beginning to yearn for the quietude and beauty of the Beaujolais countryside: "I need to see my trees again after watching so many fools and scoundrels." [45] Manon also longed to see Eudora. Continuous excitement and anxiety finally got the better of Mme Roland's robust constitution. She fell ill during the latter half of August 1791, then abruptly decided to return to Le Clos. Roland's mission was nearing its end anyway, since the state had finally agreed to take over thirty-three million of the Lyons debt, leaving only six million to the city's responsibility.[46] Besides, work had to be done at Le Clos and the wine harvest supervised. Manon left Paris the evening of September 3, arriving in Villefranche five days later. Roland joined her at the end of that month.

As soon as Manon had settled at Le Clos, where she now expected to live out the rest of her days, she penned a long fan letter to Robespierre in her most majestic style:

In the midst of this capital, which is a hotbed of so many passions and where your patriotism has called you to a career at once arduous and honorable, you will not receive, Sir, without some interest, I hope, a letter sent from a remote corner of the provinces and authored by one who is motivated only by a feeling of esteem and pleasure at communicating with men worthy of respect. Even if I had followed the course of the Revolution and the proceedings of the legislative body solely through the newspapers, I would have distinguished the small number of courageous men who always remain faithful to principles, and, among these men, the one whose energy has not ceased to oppose the greatest resistance to the claims and schemes of despotism and intrigue.[47]

She then interjected a more personal note, one that betrays her present mood of lassitude and melancholy:

In this city I have taken a course in observation the depressing result of which is similar to that of almost any study of mankind: that is that the majority of men are infinitely contemptible and that this is the fault of our social institutions; that one should work for the good of the species in the same manner as the Deity, for the satisfaction of being creative, of being true to oneself, of fulfilling one's destiny and earning self-esteem, but without expecting either gratitude or justice from individuals; and finally that the few elevated souls capable of great things are scattered on the surface of the globe and commanded by circumstances, and are therefore almost never able to unite and act in harmony.[48]

She also gave Robespierre a detailed account of the situation in the Lyons district, where she had met many self-styled patriots, "who like the Revolution because it has destroyed what was above them, but who understand nothing about the theory of free government and who do not even suspect this sublime sentiment that makes us see brethren in our fellow men." [49]

As for the ordinary folk, they were imbued with the right principles, she informed Robespierre, but she also pointed out that they were all too easily duped and misled: "I have found here, as in Paris, that the people are deceived by their ignorance or by the doings of their enemies; they have a small knowledge of or judge badly the state of things. Everywhere the masses are good; they have a just will, because their interest is that of all of us, but they are seduced or blinded." [50] As an example of the ease with which the people could be turned against their own defenders, she told Robespierre that a rumor had been circulated by Roland's political enemies in Lyons that he had been arrested as a counterrevolutionary and, as a result, that the farmers and peasants of the village of Theizé had at first greeted her with shouts of *"Les aristocrates à la lanterne!"* [51] The letter ended with generous praise for Robespierre's past performances and with warm wishes for continued success in his political career:

You have contributed much, Sir, toward the propagation of democratic principles. It is therefore inspiring, and indeed reassuring, to be able to render you this homage at a time when so many don't yet know what career they are destined to. You have a great one before you, and the stage upon which you stand will demand much fortitude. From my remote retreat I shall learn with joy of your accomplishments and I shall call for the triumph of justice through your efforts.[52]

It is not known whether Robespierre acknowledged this flattering letter. The French historian Gérard Walter, whose partiality for Robespierre and hostility for the Girondists are well known, has accused Mme Roland of showering these compliments on Robespierre with ulterior motives in mind.[53] But Mme Roland could hardly hope to gain anything from gratifying Robespierre's vanity, since her husband had determined to retire from politics and spend his remaining years in Le Clos. Did she hope to attract Robespierre's attention to Roland's civic virtue and thereby obtain a post for her husband in the Lyons area? Not likely, for Robespierre's influence, although on the rise, was still confined to the Jacobins and their sympathizers. Besides, nothing was more foreign to Mme Roland's

nature than a calculated, premeditated gesture. She lacked the cun-
ning of the intrigante; more than once she was to alienate the goodwill of influential men through her blunt straightforwardness. Had
she wished to push her husband back on the Lyons political scene,
she would have flattered conservatives, who were then more powerful in that area than men like Robespierre. As a matter of fact, she
knew very well that her husband did not have a chance in the Lyons
legislature. His uncompromising republicanism had so incensed the
rightists that these were attempting to arouse the people against him
by attributing his absence to counterrevolutionary activities! It was
undoubtedly on an impulse that Mme Roland wrote to Robespierre,
out of a need to communicate with a man she then sincerely admired. Did she ever tell him that during the wave of repression
following the Champ-de-Mars massacre she had rushed over to his
lodging in the Marais to offer him a safe hideout, only to learn that
he had just moved to the rue Saint-Honoré? Probably not; she was
too proud to court gratitude.

Her stay in revolutionary Paris had enabled Mme Roland to observe how men act in times of crisis, and what she had seen made
her more fatalistic, less hopeful about man's ability to improve himself. How fallible and weak even the most remarkable individuals
could be! What irrational, destructive tendencies lurked behind the
best-intentioned human acts! While holding fast to the concept of
an ordered, purposeful universe ruled by a benevolent God, she now
took a less sanguine view of human nature and the possibility of
its regeneration through more equitable laws. She nevertheless clung
to the ideal of virtue, but for virtue's sake, with little confidence in
an earthly reward for one's toils and sacrifices.

This melancholy mood can be explained in part by the anticlimax
brought about by Mme Roland's return to the provinces at a time
when momentous events continued to take place in the capital. She
believed Roland's retirement to be permanent and contemplated
with little cheerfulness a future of rural mediocrity and domesticity.
Looking around her, she was more aware than during all the previous years of the forlorn isolation of Le Clos and the forbidding

quality of the surrounding countryside. She noted, too, how barren and uncomfortable the house was and felt overwhelmed by a sense of despair at the thought of spending the rest of her life here.

On September 27, 1791, a decree abolished the inspectorships of manufactures, depriving Roland of his badly needed retirement pension.[54] His personal means were so limited, and the revenue from the sale of his books had been so meager, that he now had to find another source of income. In addition, he realized that there was no political future for him in a district where the conservative elements had prevented his election to the Legislative Assembly. His absence from Lyons at the crucial time of the elections, moreover, had killed any chance he might have had as a candidate. By November 30, the couple had reached the decision that they would return to Paris in order to take the necessary steps to obtain a pension for Roland or to find a new position by renewing contact with other revolutionaries.[55] By December 15, the Rolands were back in Paris and had once more settled at the Hôtel Britannique, but since the future was uncertain, they had decided to be thrifty and moved to more modest quarters on the fourth floor. Their stay in Le Clos had lasted only three months.

THIRTEEN

Uneasy Triumph

ON SEPTEMBER 30, 1791, THE KING signed the constitution and the Constituent Assembly was dissolved. The new Legislative Assembly convened on October 1. By the time the Rolands returned to Paris, many changes had taken place in the capital. The Legislative Assembly had to be composed of new men, since the members of the Constituent Assembly, following Robespierre's motion, had excluded themselves from election to the new body. The party distribution reflected the rapid leftward movement of the Revolution. The old Right had all but disappeared, giving way to the moderate members of the Jacobins who had joined the Feuillants. These were constitutional monarchists, but the radical Cordeliers called them counterrevolutionaries. In the center sat the so-called independent deputies, who in fact were uncommitted because they were undecided. To the left were those who would later be known as Girondists, for Vergniaud, Guadet, and Gensonné, all deputies from Bordeaux, in the Department of the Gironde, were prominent among them.

The men who had frequented the salon of the Rolands all held positions of power now. Brissot had been elected deputy from Paris to the Assembly and headed the diplomatic committee; Pétion was mayor of the capital; Robespierre was public prosecutor and leader of the party of the extreme Left. At the Jacobin Club, moreover, he now played a major role. Buzot had returned to Evreux, his native city, in order to accept an appointment as a criminal judge there. The Rolands were somewhat isolated.[1] Their friends, all very involved with their new responsibilities, called more rarely. Pétion, and especially his wife, had become so grand with their status that Mme Roland, trying to renew an old friendship by paying Mme Pétion a visit, was given the cold shoulder. Such unrepublican display of vanity dismayed Manon. She resumed her scholarly habits while her husband busied himself with the third volume of his *Dictionary of Manufactures* and with a report of his past services so as to obtain a retirement pension. He again spoke of retiring to Le Clos, this time permanently. Men who only the previous year had eagerly sought her company and advice neglected or even ignored her now. The mood of melancholy to which she had been prey at Le Clos returned; her usual vitality seemed to ebb away; her cheeks lost their bloom and, something most unusual with her, she complained of loss of energy and of ill health.

The Rolands did not retire altogether from political activities, however. Bosc, one of the most active members of the Jacobin Club, got Roland to serve as secretary of the correspondence committee.[2] And since epistolary writing had always been one of Manon's favorite occupations, she eagerly shared her husband's work. And convinced as she was that molding public opinion played a vital role, she put all her literary skill into answering the numerous letters sent to the Club from the provincial departments, just as she had applied herself in her journalistic reports. The fourth-floor furnished flat of the Hôtel Britannique being a rather uncomfortable place in which to live and work, Roland rented a small apartment on the third floor of a house on the rue de la Harpe, also on the Left Bank. A six-year lease was signed; summers would be spent at Le Clos, winters in Paris. Manon stole time from her work to prepare and decorate her new dwelling, which the couple planned to occupy in early April. The furniture was simple but tasteful. A concession to luxury, or rather to Mme Roland's love of music, was made by the purchase of an expensive Erard pianoforte.

Before the Rolands had a chance to occupy their new apartment and to settle down to an industrious but uneventful routine, removed from the limelight of revolutionary politics, unexpected developments abruptly projected them to an unhoped-for place of eminence. In the evening of the twenty-first, Brissot called on Mme Roland when she was alone and informed her of the probability of Roland's nomination to the Ministry of the Interior. Manon laughed and enjoined Brissot to stop teasing. She was assured that no jest was meant, that Roland was being seriously considered for this important post because of his background and experience, the liberal opinions he had fearlessly expressed even under the Old Régime, and his personal integrity and character. Mme Roland was asked to sound out her husband and to transmit his opinion on the following day. When he returned home that night, Roland was as astonished as his wife at this news.[3] It may safely be surmised that Mme Roland did not discourage her husband from accepting the nomination. While the more diffident Roland weighed the pros and cons of this position in his mind, Manon assuaged his fears by reminding him of his high qualifications and by drawing a glowing picture of all the contributions he could now make to the public weal. After a night of sleepless excitement, they indicated Roland's willingness to serve his country.

Mme Roland was transported by this belated but glorious recognition of her husband's services and merits. That his position would be precarious and fraught with dangers in these times of crisis and sudden changes did not mar her joy, so irresistible are the attractions of power, even to one who prided herself on practicing Montaigne's detachment from worldly things. To be sure, she realized that Roland's new, demanding duties would tax his strength and abilities to the utmost; yet she felt confident that he would discharge them to his credit and to the benefit of the nation. And would she not stand by his side, ever ready to share the burden and the responsibilities? The *aurea mediocritas*—the notion that happiness can be found only in obscurity—by which she had lived for so many years, seemed totally forgotten in the present flush of exhilaration. On March 23, at eleven in the evening, Dumouriez, the Minister of Foreign Affairs, called on the Rolands on his way to the Council, bearing orders from the king confirming officially Roland's nomination.[4]

It is most likely that Roland's personal qualifications were not the sole reason for his selection as Minister of the Interior by the Brissot group. In calling Roland, a competent but totally unknown administrator to this high post, Brissot and his friends knew that they would have in the ministry a man through whom they would be able to further their cause, a reliable and faithful sentinel of their ideas. They also knew how influential Mme Roland was with her husband and they correctly calculated that she could be useful to their purpose. And indeed Mme Roland was filled with gratitude to Brissot for having recommended her husband for the post. And if the thought occurred to her, as it must have since she had always been an avid student of history, that things might at times be difficult and even dangerous for public figures in times of upheaval, she quickly pushed it aside and gave herself over to the sweetness of this new-found sense of power and importance.

What circumstances had so suddenly brought Roland to the attention of the Brissot group? A ministerial crisis had broken out in March as a result of the king's vetoes of the decrees against émigrés and non-juring priests. Brissot led the movement to discredit the existing constitutional ministry, composed of Feuillants. To quiet growing suspicions and unrest, and to satisfy the so-called patriots, the king appointed Dumouriez, a general who enjoyed great popularity with Brissot and his friends, to the Office of Foreign Affairs, leaving the formation of the rest of the executive council in the hands of the new minister. Brissot was naturally consulted on the most suitable candidates for ministerial posts. Meanwhile, Dumouriez paid a visit to the Jacobin Club and, in order to win over the extreme Left, donned the red cap and embraced Robespierre. Nevertheless, neither Robespierre himself nor any member of the Mountain were offered posts in the new ministry. In her *Memoirs*, Mme Roland attempts to justify, but not too successfully, the absence of men she had heretofore so warmly admired from the ministry by stating that it was vital to elevate men of ability as well as of respectable character and to keep away the more "hot-headed Jacobins" whose extravagance would justify the complaints of the court and bring discredit to the "patriots." [5] A curious reasoning indeed on the part of one who had so far been a "hot-headed" revolutionary herself and whose main worry had been that patriots, turning luke-warm, would fail to offer a staunch resistance to the schemes of the reactionaries! In other words, the group that now came to power with the Rolands, and that was to become known as "Brissotins" or "Girondists," fluctuated between the Feuillants and Constitutional-ists who wanted to maintain a constitutional monarchy and the Jacobins who opposed the monarchy, the 1791 Constitution, and war with Europe. Brissot and his group also were suspicious of the extreme republicanism of the Cordeliers, the vehement spokesmen of the populace of the Paris faubourgs.

Brissot and his friends, gathered in the elegant salon of Mme Dodun, a wealthy bourgeoise who lived on the fashionable Place Vendôme, had not found it easy to select men leaning to the left, but not the extreme left, who would not be too offensive to the king.[6] The field of possible choices had been further limited by a law eliminating members of the Assembly from executive posts and by the youth and lack of experience of many possible candidates. Finally, someone, probably Lanthenas, suggested Roland's name, and all present wondered why they had not thought of him before: he was unquestionably an upright, respectable person to whose appoint-ment the king would find it difficult to present serious objections and whose civic devotion could not be attacked by the Jacobins.[7] That Roland's prissy character would not facilitate relations with the king, on the one hand, and with the cabinet members, on the other, did not seem to trouble his supporters. Only one person present at the gathering, a woman by the name of Sophie Grandchamp, who knew the Roland couple intimately enough to question the suitabil-ity of the appointment on this basis, took the liberty of informing Lanthenas that she, personally, did not think her friends fitted to lead an administration in such stormy times because of their limited knowledge of either the court or men in general. Mme Grandchamp's comment, although ungenerous from a friend, had an element of truth.[8] But apparently her objection was overruled.

Having overcome her misgivings, Sophie Grandchamp hastened

to the Rolands to offer her congratulations. She found the couple still in bed, pale and exhausted after a sleepless night. Everyone burst into tears of excitement; kisses and promises of everlasting loyalty were exchanged. This emotional little scene, described by Mme Grandchamp in her own *Memoirs,* could easily fit into a typical eighteenth-century *comédie bourgeoise:* the apotheosis of the devoted civil servant and of his virtuous wife witnessed by a faithful friend of the family.[9] Sophie finally went out to run several errands for the Rolands. When she returned in the evening, she found a transformed Manon: "I thought I was dreaming when I entered the salon. My friend, who had seemed that morning on the point of death, had recovered her freshness and charm. She was surrounded by a number of people who were showering her with compliments. Roland took his share in these civilities and seemed quite satisfied. I threw myself into an armchair near the fireplace, and there observed the new personalities: the room was crowded with ministers, chiefs of state and the principal deputies. Two lackeys, standing outside the door, opened one or two panels for the visitors, depending on their rank." [10] No doubt a touch of envy enters into this vivid but somewhat malicious account of the Rolands' first day as important personages. But then, human nature, no matter how perfected, is never inured to the titillations of satisfied vanity.

On March 31, the new Minister of the Interior and his wife moved from their modest lodging in the Hôtel Britannique to the imposing, lavishly furnished mansion that the renowned Le Vau had built for the Count de Lionne and that had housed the fashionable Minister Calonne as well as Mme Necker in her heyday as a *salonnière.*[11] A magnificent marble staircase led to a huge salon with crystal lusters, large Venetian mirrors, ormolu inlaying, veneer paneling, and a life-size painting of Louis XIV crowned by Victory. That night, Mme Roland slept, for the first time in her life, under a canopy of ostrich feathers surrounded by mythological gods and goddesses voluptuously prancing about on the frescoed walls and ceilings.

Too many burning issues, however, needed attention to allow

Mme Roland to be overwhelmed by her new surroundings. She let it be known that she would not distribute political favors or make introductions, and immediately set about organizing her schedule with the same regard for work she had while still an ordinary citizen. Her fondness for privacy could not be altered by circumstance. Nevertheless, twice a week, on Mondays and Fridays, there were guests for dinner; one evening was reserved for Roland's colleagues as well as some deputies, the other for the heads of the different departments of the ministry and a mixed company of people connected with political affairs. On these occasions, the table was served in a simple style and little time was spent over the meal. After dinner, the guests talked for a while in the salon. By nine o'clock, everyone had taken his leave.[12]

Mme Roland also remained faithful to the custom of abstaining from political discussions. But since friends and colleagues tended to call on the Minister at his home rather than in his office, matters of state were frequently brought up in his wife's presence. Under the pretext of leaving messages for the absent Roland, associates also got into the habit of calling on Manon and presenting their case to her, for they were well aware that she would be consulted anyway. In her *Memoirs,* Mme Roland tries to repudiate the accusation that she was actually running the ministry by pointing out that, being almost always home and enjoying her husband's fullest confidence, it happened quite naturally that she found herself "in the midst of things without intrigue or vain curiosity." [13] But she hardly had to intrigue in order to impose her views. In the intimacy of a select group her opinions carried increasing weight. Everyone knew, and Brissot, Buzot, and Pétion better than anyone, that Roland was a conscientious, dedicated administrator, but that without his wife's imagination, conviction, boldness, and literary know-how, he could be rated barely higher than a superior clerk.

Roland's first appearance in the Tuileries palace, where the king now resided, created something of an uproar. True to his ideal of puritanical simplicity, he made his entrance wearing his usual black suit. He had scorned the elaborate court attire, symbol of a bygone age of servility and vain extravagance. Courtiers and lackeys, however, stared disapprovingly at this tall, gaunt figure of a man, with a simple round hat covering his long, thinning hair, and shoes tied with ordinary strings. Roland looked more like a rustic Quaker than a French minister calling on his king. The master of ceremonies stepped up to General Dumouriez, who accompanied Roland, and indicated the cause of his consternation: "Sir, there are no buckles on his shoes!" With mock chagrin, Dumouriez replied: "Sir, all is lost!" [14] As a minister, Roland continued to be as careless about his appearance as he had been as a provincial inspector of manufactures. He could be seen in the streets on foot, dressed in his eternal black suit and coat, which were threadbare at the elbows, with woollen stockings and round black hat. His gruff, rigid manner, too, remained unchanged: he spoke in authoritarian, abrupt tones, never condescending to be pleasing or amiable.

In Dumouriez Mme Roland soon detected an opportunist, and his courtly manners and brilliant wit only strengthened her suspicion that he was untrustworthy. The courtier-soldier spoke with ease and charm of the king's sincere determination to support the constitution, and seemed to make light of everything except his own interest and glory. In her *Memoirs*, Mme Roland presents a vivid and, on the whole, accurate picture of a man who was later to defect from the revolutionary army and pass over to the Austrians: "Dumouriez is active, vigilant, witty, and brave, equally talented for war and for intrigue. Possessed of great military ability, he was the only man in France, even in the opinion of jealous colleagues, capable of commanding a large army properly. An adroit courtier, he was better fitted by his shifty disposition and dissoluteness to serve under the old court than under the new government." [15]

During the first few weeks of Roland's ministry, Louis XVI behaved with the appearance of utmost cooperation and goodwill. The Brissotins, greatly encouraged by this auspicious beginning, were in a confident, optimistic mood. For her part, however, Mme Roland still found it unlikely that an absolute monarch should be willing to relinquish much of his power in such a gracious manner.

Only a man above the ordinary could be sufficiently farsighted to disregard personal considerations and rise to such an unusual situation. Unfortunately, Louis XVI was a quite ordinary man, one who would have been in his place as a private citizen but whose limited abilities made it impossible for him to comprehend, let alone sympathize with, the aims and ideals of the patriots. Thus Manon warned her husband and friends not to trust appearances and to consider the king as a dangerous foe, all the more dangerous because he pretended to work with them when in actuality he was marking time and waiting only for an opportunity to bring about their downfall. But flushed by success, none of the Brissotin group took heed of this advice.[16]

With her penetrating understanding of human nature, Mme Roland saw the king for what he was: neither a brutish imbecile, as his enemies made him out to be, nor the kindly man of sensibility, as his supporters liked to represent him. She rather detected in him a common, mediocre being, whom nature had actually destined for a much less exalted position, but whom a courtly education and training had provided with certain advantages. She also credited him with a good memory and diligent habits. On the other hand, she deplored his weakness of character and his narrowness of mind. If he had been born two centuries earlier, and had his wife been a more reasonable woman, he would have made no more noise in the world than so many other princes who came and went without doing much good or harm. But raised to the throne amidst the profligacy of Louis XV's court, and surrounded by a corrupt aristocracy, he was led even further astray by a woman who combined Austrian arrogance with youthful insouciance.[17] If Mme Roland mistrusted Louis XVI, she frankly hated Marie-Antoinette, as only one woman can hate another, with fierce vindictiveness.

It was not long, either, before she realized that the council meetings attended by the king were spent, more often than not, on idle, petty matters. Such was the king's turn of mind that he would almost invariably steer his ministers away from deliberations on basic issues of domestic and foreign policy. At the end of three or four hours, the meetings would break up without anything substantive having been accomplished. "But this is pitiful!" she could not help crying out upon Roland's return and after listening to his account of the proceedings. "You are all in a good mood because you haven't encountered opposition and because you are treated with courtesy. I am afraid you are being duped," and she bitterly added that these hours passed in inconsequential chatter constituted an irretrievable loss at a time when swift-moving events needed constant attention and vigilance.[18] When Roland and his colleagues, in order to reassure her, pointed out that the king was too sensible a man not to realize that his own interest coincided with that of the new government, she reminded them of his flight to Varennes.[19]

The Assembly having voted funds to Roland for the propagation of writings useful to the cause of the Revolution, Manon persuaded her husband to finance a newspaper in poster form. It was entitled La Sentinelle and, in order to reach as wide a public as possible, it was printed in bold type in three columns, on large pink or gray posters, and distributed twice a week.[20] The man selected for the important position as editor of the newspaper was Jean-Baptiste Louvet, a writer and journalist who had made a certain name for himself before the Revolution by publishing a mildly scandalous and highly successful adventure novel, Les Amours du Chevalier de Faublas.[21] An active and ubiquitous man, Louvet saw in the Revolution an opportunity to give free play to his literary and journalistic talents. As early as 1789 he had published brochures in favor of the Revolution and, in 1791, had worked with Brissot, Lanthenas, Bosc, and Roland on the correspondence committee of the Jacobin Club. At that time, he shared Mme Roland's admiration for Robespierre.

A slightly built, blue-eyed young man with thinning blond hair and a bohemian nonchalance of dress, Louvet made an unimpressive appearance. But his features were intelligent and animated, and he combined Old Régime politesse with revolutionary fervor. His literary style, too, retained a great deal of the charm and brilliance characteristic of the light novels of the eighteenth century. For that reason, perhaps, it was not best fitted for revolutionary journalism, which required an inflammatory type of rhetoric capable of appealing to the man of the street.

The first major issue that was to pit Robespierre against Brissot, and eventually to rend the revolutionary forces into two mortally hostile camps, involved the advisability of declaring war against the other European nations. Brissot and his friends favored war, perhaps in the hope of rallying popular support. From this it must not be supposed, however, that they were militaristic or bellicose by nature. Their outlook, after all, had mainly been shaped by the *philosophes*, themselves outspoken pacifists. A treatise by the Abbé de Saint-Pierre, *Project for Perpetual Peace*, which proposed to outlaw war by a league of European nations pledged to support one another against any member-state proving aggressive, had been amply commented upon by Voltaire and rewritten by Rousseau. Like Montesquieu and the other Encyclopedists, the Girondists regarded war as an inhuman tradition fostered by power-hungry despots. But in this as in many other respects, they had no firm, consistent stand, and allowed political circumstances to take precedence over principles.

It must nevertheless be recognized that the whole of Europe resounded with violent denunciations of the French Revolution, the least of which was not Burke's thunderous *Reflections*. The revolutionaries felt encircled by a wall of ever growing threats from counterrevolutionary quarters and hostile nations. Great Britain, Prussia, Austria, and Russia all expressed sympathy for the French émigrés and openly proclaimed their support of the French monarchy. What is more, in their Declaration of Pillnitz of August 27, 1791, Emperor Leopold II, Marie-Antoinette's brother, and King Frederick William II of Prussia proclaimed their readiness to restore Louis XVI to his position of power so as to consolidate the monarchical form of government everywhere. This, together with the agitation of the émigrés in European courts, the counterrevolutionary movements in France itself, and the secret negotiations of Marie-Antoinette with the knowledge and approval of Louis XVI, led the Girondists to advocate a preventive war.

They were mistaken, however, in counting on a few brilliant campaigns leading to a rapid victory and to the rallying of the French people behind their party. Fired by a missionary zeal to liberate the other nations of Europe, they confidently expected peoples to rise against their kings and feudal lords at the first signal given by France. Few dared to denounce the idea of war, for to do so was tantamount to being a traitor, and only one opposed it with all the eloquence and energy at his command. This was Robespierre, who repeatedly stressed that a military conflict might easily play into the hands of the king and his supporters. For the time being, however, the war party won the day. Robespierre was practically isolated. Dumouriez, moreover, as a professional soldier who welcomed an opportunity for personal advancement, lent all his support to Brissot's campaign. On April 20, 1792, the king presented a declaration of war on Austria to the Legislative Assembly. It was approved almost unanimously.[22]

As a disciple of the *philosophes*, Mme Roland herself had espoused the pacifist ideal because, as she had written Bosc in 1784, "I regard these quarrels between kings as scourges for the people." [23] But in 1792, her attitude, under the influence of her Girondist friends, underwent a marked change. No longer was it a question, she thought, of a private dispute between autocrats, but of a crusade undertaken by a free people to liberate the captive nations of Europe. Had not the American revolutionaries triumphed despite apparently overwhelming odds against them? The enthusiasm, the courage of every good French citizen would be so stirred as to insure success, as had been the case in the newly established United States. All one needed to win was faith in the Revolution and its leaders. Such was the well-meaning but rather naïve reasoning at the basis of Mme Roland's support of the Girondist aggressive foreign policy. Interestingly, in her *Memoirs* the only comment she makes on this vital issue is that "it had become necessary to declare war," and that this measure had been the subject of lively debates.[24] By the summer of 1793, when she was writing her autobiography, she had evidently lost much of her crusading fervor. Modern historians tend toward the view that Louis XVI was in agreement with the Girondists' bellicose policy, for he saw in it a chance for his return to full power.[25] Mme Roland, on the other hand, probably in order to justify her friends, states that the king long delayed approving the opening of hostilities, and finally yielded with "great reluctance" and under the pressure of the overwhelming majority of the Assembly.[26] Since she was not one to resort to lies, even for the sake of loyalty, we must surmise that she endorsed this belief in good faith.

It was in this spring of 1792 that Robespierre, already suspicious of the Brissotin ministry and further alienated by a war campaign he deemed rash and dangerous, stopped frequenting Mme Roland's salon altogether. Dismayed by Robespierre's scathing attacks against men she considered her friends, she summoned him, with characteristic directness, to pay her a visit in order to explain his absence from her gatherings and his reasons for opposing the war issue. It is obvious, from the tone of her April 25, 1792, letter to Robespierre, that she earnestly was seeking to hear his side of the dispute, that she was hurt by his disdainful silence, and that she still held him in high esteem.[27] She therefore exhorted him to practice tolerance and stop treating good patriots who differed from him on certain policy matters as though they were enemies of the state. Was it fair, she asked heatedly, to arouse public opinion against those who happened not to see eye to eye with him? Robespierre chose to ignore this appeal and left the letter unanswered. More than Mme Roland herself, it was no doubt her entourage that he disliked and mistrusted. After this, the paths of these two ardent disciples of Rousseau were to follow widely divergent courses to end, however, in the ugly shadow of the same guillotine.

One thing is quite clear from Mme Roland's comments on the quarrel between Brissot and Robespierre. Her friends committed the fatal error of underestimating the reticent, unsmiling young deputy from Arras. From the height of their success and popularity they treated him with slightly patronizing benevolence. For her part, however, Manon had always shown deference to Robespierre. Four days after her husband's appointment as Minister of the Interior, on March 27, 1792, she had hastened to assure him of her continued friendship and admiration: "I am staying at the Hôtel Britannique, at least for a while; you will find me there habitually at dinner time. . . . I hope only to be able to make some contribution to the common weal with the help of enlightened, devoted, and wise patriots. You are for me at the head of this class. Please come soon; I am eager to see you and reiterate these sentiments, which nothing could alter." [28] Robespierre had accepted the invitation.[29] But the picture had now been totally altered by the alliance of the Brissotin ministry with Dumouriez and by its dealings with the king. How could one explain such things to a woman who, as a personal friend and close political associate of Brissot, was bound to side with a faction to which her husband owed his present position of eminence? She was part of a government from which he and his Jacobin colleagues had been deliberately excluded. A man not to be moved by personal considerations, Robespierre set upon a course from which nothing would sway him. He had one immeasurable advantage over the overconfident Girondists: all his impulses, passions, and habits had been subordinated to a single goal: the successful application of his doctrine. He allowed himself no human weaknesses, no rest from his labors; his speeches were minutely detailed, impeccably thought out, irrefutable in their logic. The veiled threat, the insidious hint, often more potent than direct accusation, were among his favorite weapons.

Understandably, Mme Roland took Robespierre's aloofness toward her as a personal affront, and henceforth viewed him with increasing acrimony. Even though she also became more and more aware of her friends' shortcomings as statesmen, she was convinced of their honesty and devotion to the nation. After her final appeal to Robespierre, in the spring of 1792, had fallen on apparently deaf ears, the die was cast; Mme Roland's fate became inextricably bound with that of the Girondists. As an observer more than a direct participant, she could not fathom why Robespierre, long a friend of Brissot, had suddenly turned into his bitterest critic. Such a radical change of heart she could only ascribe to envy and, probably because her own political views matched so closely those of Robespierre, she tended to minimize, both in her correspondence and in her later *Memoirs,* the real differences that estranged a leader of the Montagnards from the Brissot faction. Consistently, emphasis is placed upon personal, rather than ideological, motives in her comments on the Brissot-Robespierre rift. "Robespierre, who was fiery, jealous, hungry for popularity, envious of the success of others, domineering by nature," she writes in her *Memoirs,* "decided to become the leader of the party that opposed the declaration of war." [30] She furthermore asserts that Robespierre never forgave Brissot his political victory and that every ensuing defeat, every "inevitable misfortune" was capitalized on and laid at the door of the war party.[31] This policy, she tells us, became a refined system of calumny, carefully planned and doggedly followed. But of the dubious wisdom of declaring war against the whole of Europe—at a time when France was being torn by inner difficulties—the danger of defeat, the added sufferings and hardships for the people, and the fact that the king must have greeted war with secret joy, not a word is said. Rather, Robespierre's campaign against Brissot and his ministry is interpreted solely in the light of petty jealousy and private rivalry. Brissot's own ineffectiveness is excused on the basis of his good-natured character: while Robespierre swore to ruin the man who had once been his associate and friend and tirelessly worked for his undoing, Brissot, with his trustful temperament, continued to believe in his adversary's uprightness and in the good sense of the voting citizens.[32]

One personal trait strongly reflected on Mme Roland's politics. She found it difficult to admire and almost impossible to forgive. Once she had detected flaws in a person's character, her judgment was swift and irrevocable. In few instances do we see her revising an earlier opinion or admitting that she had been wrong. At the same time, however, it should be remembered that her psychological insights were frequently uncanny and that personal friendship and loyalty rarely interfered with a penetrating evaluation of the merits and defects of the actors who took part in that great drama of the Revolution.

In this respect, the case of Vergniaud, probably the most eloquent and talented of the Girondists, should be mentioned. While recognizing Vergniaud's extraordinary rhetorical powers, Mme Roland scored his indolence, skepticism, and Epicurean ways: "I do not like Vergniaud; I find in him the philosopher's egotism. Disdainful of men, because he knows them well, he does not trouble himself about them." [33] Such an attitude, excusable in a private citizen, was disastrous in a representative of the people. To be sure, intellectual and personal qualities made of Vergniaud the most colorful member of the Girondist group. If any of these men carried in him the spark of genius, it was certainly he. Brissot was a versatile publicist and resourceful promoter but a poor orator; Roland, austere "virtue" incarnate, was a tireless but unimaginative administrator; Condorcet, the philosopher of the group, lacked decisiveness as a man of action. Vergniaud was the poet and artist; he could create magic with words and possessed great depth of feeling.[34] But persistent diligence and a passionate sense of commitment were not his strong points. He frequented Mme Roland's salon irregularly and never belonged to her inner circle of friends and admirers. He seems to have preferred the less austere salon of the wealthy Mme Dodun, wife of an East India Company official.[35] That, at a critical time, he should neglect politics and desert everyone in order to be in the company of a pretty actress, Mlle Candeille, was a further cause for Mme Roland's stern censure. His lukewarm republicanism, for he thundered against the king, yet was willing to negotiate with him, infuriated her. After his famous July 3, 1792, speech, in which he summoned Louis XVI to come to terms with the revolutionaries, she wrote to Bancal: "If you see Vergniaud at Mme Dodun's, don't hesitate to tell him that he will have to work hard to rehabilitate himself in the public opinion, if he is still interested in this as an honest man, which I doubt." [36] The bitterness of this reproach leveled at one of the most gifted Girondists was motivated by the fact that she suspected Vergniaud, and rightly so, of still supporting a constitutional monarchy and of placing too much trust in Louis XVI. But it was with such cutting statements that she could offend friends and foes alike.

In Paris, meanwhile, the economic situation was growing alarm-

ingly worse, and the Girondists continued to hesitate as to the attitude
they should adopt toward popular outbreaks. In order to establish a
strong hold over the capital and to intimidate the king, the Girondists voted three decrees on May 27 and 29, and on June 8, 1792: to
dissolve the constitutional guards of the king, to deport refractory or
non-juring priests, and to establish an armed camp of twenty thousand provincial National Guards under the walls of Paris to protect
the city from possible attack either by the Austrians or by Lafayette's
army—perhaps, also, to prevent any Jacobin insurrection.

On June 10, Roland addressed a letter, actually written by his
wife, to Louis XVI, severely reprimanding him for opposing his veto
on the decrees penalizing refractory priests and creating the camp
of federal troops.[37] As a republican, Mme Roland had been deeply
hostile to the king from the start. For the sake of her husband and
friends, however, who were now at the helm of the state, she had
been willing to still her qualms. She was prepared to tolerate a
monarch so long as he humbly recognized that he was no more than
a servant of the people and subject to dismissal if proved unsatis-
factory. But as she watched the king insidiously undermine the work
of the cabinet, her suspicions and restlessness grew and her fury
mounted against him for so tenaciously clinging to outdated notions
of absolute power. Such purblindness, she estimated, jeopardized
not only his own position, about which she could not care less, but
the future of the Revolution by unleashing the forces of anarchy and
mass rebellion. These reasons determined her to give a lesson in practical politics to the recalcitrant monarch. That he might not be altogether sympathetic to this talking down could hardly deter her
from her set purpose.

The resulting letter is indeed an extraordinary document.[38] In a
simple yet dignified style, reminiscent of the famous letter of admon-
ishment that Fénelon had addressed to Louis XIV at the end of the
preceding century, Mme Roland undertook to appeal to Louis XVI's
better instincts and to awaken him to his duties. But unlike the
seventeenth-century churchman and writer, she was not content
with a lecture on statesmanship. This time it was not a disgruntled

subject respectfully begging an absolute monarch to come to more
reasonable ways; it was, rather, a free and proud citizen defiantly
challenging a disobedient servant of the sovereign people and un-
abashedly mixing advice with veiled threats. Realizing that Louis
XVI would most likely find her message improper, if not downright
impertinent, Mme Roland pointedly remarked that "the austere
language of truth is rarely welcomed by the throne." [39] That, however, did not prevent her from giving the king a masterful lesson in
history and in the meaning of the French Revolution:

Sire,
The present plight of France cannot long endure. The violence of
the crisis has reached its highest degree; it must terminate in a crisis
that ought to interest your Majesty as much as it concerns the whole
nation.
Honored by your confidence [she was now speaking for Roland], and
placed in a position which compels me to speak the truth, I make so
bold as to withhold nothing from you; it is an obligation you yourself
have imposed upon me.
The French have adopted a Constitution; there are those who are
dissatisfied and rebellious because of it. The overwhelming majority of
the nation, however, wishes to uphold it, has sworn to defend it with
its blood and has even joyfully accepted war as a means of securing it.[40]

She then proceeded to lecture Louis XVI on his duties as a constitutional monarch:

Your Majesty enjoyed great privileges which you believed were the
rights of royalty. Brought up on the idea of preserving them, you could
not witness their suppression with pleasure. These sentiments, natural
enough in the human heart, must have entered into the calculations of
the enemies of the Revolution. They have therefore counted on secret
approval until such times as open patronage would be permitted. This
situation could not be ignored by the nation, and mistrust resulted
from it. Your Majesty has thus been faced with two alternatives: either
yielding to your early habits, to your private preferences, or making
the sacrifices dictated by wisdom and demanded by necessity, consequently, either fostering the rebels and alarming the nation, or pacify-
ing the nation by uniting with it. Everything runs its course, and this
uncertainty must end soon.[41]

What followed was a stern warning that "the Declaration of Rights has become a political gospel and the French Constitution a religion for which the people are ready to die" and an ominous warning that "when the law has not been sufficiently vigorous to meet the situation, the citizens have taken matters in their own hands." [42] Then, becoming more exalted, she proceeded to enlighten the sovereign on the meaning of patriotism: "Motherland is not just a word which the imagination takes pleasure in embellishing. It is a being to whom one makes sacrifices, to whom one grows more attached every day through the cares it imposes, who has been created by great efforts, who grows in the midst of anxiety, and who is loved as much for what it costs as for what it promises." [43] Jules Michelet, the famed nineteenth-century historian, was so impressed by this passage that he termed it "sublime" and quoted it in his *History of the French Revolution.*[44]

Further delay in sanctioning the decrees proscribing non-juring priests and in establishing a camp of twenty thousand soldiers from the provinces could be fatal, she sternly admonished: "Fermentation in all the parts of the nation is extreme; it will explode in a terrible manner." [45] Only rapid and effective action on the part of the king could reestablish confidence and forestall disaster. And probably referring to the radical elements among the revolutionaries that were becoming increasingly more vocal, she painted a grim picture of the dire consequences if the present state of confusion was allowed to continue: "Should terror spread throughout Paris, and discord and stupor strike its outskirts, then the whole of France would rise in indignation and, throwing herself into the horrors of civil war, would deploy that somber energy, mother of virtue and crime, always fatal to those who have provoked it." [46] And, indeed, nothing could be more accurate than this dark prediction, for exactly two months after this letter was written, Paris found itself once more in the throes of a revolution, this one of a much more violent nature than that of 1789; one, moreover, that paved the way for the Reign of Terror.

Had the king heeded Mme Roland's blunt remonstrances, he might well have escaped his tragic fate. But Louis XVI, in a fit of anger, closed the last door that could have led to a compromise between the revolutionaries and the monarchy. On June 13, he wrote a curt note to Roland, relieving him henceforth of his office:

You will kindly, Sir, surrender the portfolio of the department of the Interior which I had entrusted to you to M. Mourgues, whom I have put in charge of the Ministry.

Louis.[47]

It was not long before the whole Girondist cabinet fell. Mme Roland's letter had cost her husband his ministry, but had given her a resounding moral victory. She greeted Roland's dismissal with relief, for ever since his appointment she had felt uneasy, fearing that he was being used by the Royalists. At least now Roland had redeemed himself as a republican. Her letter, moreover, was read before an enthusiastic Assembly and a vote of confidence in the dismissed ministers immediately agreed upon by the Girondist-dominated legislative body, which also ordered the publication of the by now famous document.[48] With the exception of the Royalists and the Constitutionalists, who held that Roland should not have made public a message destined to the king alone, the ex-Minister was widely applauded for his courage and forthrightness.

Having moved to the modest apartment on the rue de la Harpe that Roland had leased before his appointment, Mme Roland showed little sign of missing the stately suites of the Hôtel de l'Intérieur. As for her Girondist friends, elated over their increased popularity following the fall of their cabinet, they set about organizing a campaign of intimidation and general uprising, so as to force the king to reinstate the ministers he had dismissed. This course of action, however, was eventually to have disastrous consequences for them.

With the invasion of the Tuileries Palace on June 20, 1792, and the riots ending with the revolution of August 10, which put an end to the monarchical constitution, the more radical elements took the initiative. While the Girondists agitated noisily and defied the royal veto by bringing to Paris the Federal Volunteers of the South, the famed Marseillais troops, Robespierre, behind the scenes, was busy establishing contact with the leaders of the insurrectionary forces

and providing them with a specific program calling for the election
of a National Convention based on universal suffrage to replace the
present Legislative Assembly. In her *Memoirs,* Mme Roland maintains that the events of August 10 took her completely by surprise.[49]
She is no doubt making this statement in good faith. But it was
nevertheless in her salon, with her approval and perhaps even at
her suggestion, that the Marseillais soldiers were called to Paris.[50]
The Rolands became friendly with Charles Barbaroux, a fiery and
handsome young man of twenty-five who had recently arrived in
Paris as the leader of a Marseilles delegation, and were won over by
his enthusiasm and his repeated assurances that the South could be
counted on to save the Revolution.[51] Barbaroux trained the famous
battalion of Marseillais that was to contribute to the overthrow of
Louis XVI and to the unleashing of the popular forces in Paris.

Curiously enough, the Rolands and their friends simultaneously
planned the insurrection of Paris by federal soldiers, so as to restore
the "patriot" ministers to power, and talked of defending France
from beyond the Loire river should the capital fall to the allied
armies. With the help of a map, ebullient Barbaroux even demonstrated how the South could utilize its natural resources and frontiers
and become the last haven of liberty.[52] This idea of retreating to the
South, leaving Paris to the enemy, although not envisaged seriously
by the Girondists, according to Mme Roland, was nevertheless
brought up again when the military position of the French worsened.
It would become an effective weapon in the hands of the Montagnards and the Paris deputation in their campaign to discredit the
Girondists and show them up as defeatists and traitors. After August
10, the Girondists felt by-passed and made desperate efforts to hold
back the movement they had made possible. Until then, Mme Roland
had created in her mind a romantic, exalted concept of the Revolution embellished with noble heroism and patriotic dedication. Her
enthusiasm began to wane, however, when the triumph of the popular insurrectionary forces brought to the fore leaders of a quite different temperament than the Girondists.

FOURTEEN

The Gathering Storm

AFTER THE AUGUST 10 UPRISING and the suspension of the king, Roland and other men friendly to the Girondists were recalled to their ministries.[1] Danton, nominated as Minister of Justice, was the only outsider. With his stentorian voice, overwhelming oratory, and forceful personality, Danton soon came to dominate the scene. Roland found himself overshadowed by the new idol of the Paris people, for his dry, carefully prepared reports could not compete with the fire of Danton's magnificent improvisations. No greater disparity between two men could indeed exist: Roland, solemn, unbending, colorless as a personality; and Danton, coarsely jovial, with a fascinatingly ugly physique and an overflowing animal vitality. The Minister of Justice tried to win over to his side the Minister of the Interior, but to no avail: Roland's puritanical instincts were outraged by Danton's moral laxity and by his huge and unaccounted expenses.

The physical and moral contrast between the two ministers struck an English witness of the French Revolution, John Moore. His own characterization of these profoundly different men is so apt as to be worth quoting from:

Roland is not supposed to possess all the energy of character that belongs to Danton; in many other respects they differ. Roland is believed to be a thorough republican: Danton, it is thought, does not lay much stress on the form of government, and would have no objection to monarchy, provided the monarch were a creature of his own. . . . Roland and Danton were often in opposition with each other when joined in the same administration. Roland struggled with all his might against the usurpations of the General Council of the Commune of Paris after the tenth of August: Danton favored and abetted them. . . . In external appearance and manner, those two men differ as in all the rest; Roland is about sixty years of age, tall, thin, of a mild countenance and pale complexion. His dress every time I have seen him has been the same, a drab-coloured suit lined with green silk, his gray hair hanging loose. Danton is not so tall, but much broader than Roland; his form is coarse, and uncommonly robust: Roland's manner is unassuming and modest—that of Danton fierce and boisterous.[2]

In the early months of her husband's second ministry, Mme Roland had numerous occasions to see and speak with Danton. She took an immediate and intense dislike for this powerful man whose face was ravaged by pockmarks and whose mouth was distorted by a gash made by a wild bull. His whole countenance breathed confidence and tranquil audacity: his booming voice, his boisterous laughter, his bold, deep-set eyes made her recoil in instinctive, unreasoned fear. Even though his popularity was now reaching its zenith and, with Robespierre and Marat, wielded growing power over the Convention, he attempted to effectuate a rapprochement with the Girondist party and even tried to win Mme Roland's good graces. "Danton hardly let a day pass without coming to our house," she writes in her *Memoirs*. "Sometimes he did so while on his way to the council . . . or else he would call on his return, usually accompanied by Fabre d'Eglantine [the revolutionary poet]. At other times, he would invite himself to dine with us, on days when I was not receiving company, so that he might discuss some business with Roland."[3] But even though Mme Roland assured herself that appearances were not trustworthy, she could not bring herself to associate the image of a goodly man with this amazing, tortured face: "I have never seen anything express so perfectly the violence of brutal passions and the most astonishing audacity half-veiled behind a jovial air, an affectation of frankness and a sort of good-naturedness."[4] One can see that, at first, Mme Roland's hostility for Danton was more emotional than political. Next to this rough-hewn and forceful figure of a man, the elderly, thin Roland must have appeared puny and the refined Girondists must have paled into insignificance. While the Girondists theorized about the Revolution in polished phrases, Danton seemed the living incarnation of popular insurrection. His was a vital, natural force, similar to an erupting volcano, and his earthiness, which hypnotized the Commune, deeply unsettled Mme Roland.

She had other, more serious, reasons for doubting Danton's good faith. She had heard of his amazing extravagance, and for people as fastidiously honest as the Rolands the heavy suspicion of venality and extortion which surrounded Danton's ministry was overwhelmingly distasteful. In her *Memoirs*, Mme Roland reports the following dialogue as she aired her suspicions of Danton to her Girondist friends:

—What a shame that the ministry should be spoiled by such a man! Where on earth did you find him?
—What can we do, he is at the head of a party of barkers. If he wasn't made part of the machinery, he would turn against it, and, besides, he has served the Revolution and can be useful to it.
—I doubt it, and your policy strikes me as detestable. . . . It is better to have one's enemy on the outside than within. Besides, a man who seeks only his private advantage will always be the enemy of the public good.
—This is no reason. People like him need a position and means. Flatter their *amour-propre*, satisfy their ambition and they are your creatures. Besides, Danton has wit and can discuss things pleasantly. He will work out for the best.
—I wish it and don't want to prejudge him because I don't know him. But since you are my good friends, let me tell you frankly that in politics you reason like little boys.[5]

At this remark, the Girondists burst out into hearty laughter and Mme Roland politely joined them, her fears temporarily allayed.

In the course of his visits, Danton talked to Mme Roland of the need to unite the parties so as to expel the invaders from the motherland. In cool silence she listened to his entreaties and, as she observed, she sensed that she, too, was being carefully studied by her visitor. She therefore controlled her reactions in order not to betray her feelings and thoughts. One remark by Fabre, however, almost destroyed her composure, nearly bringing about one of her typical outbursts. At the end of August, as the allied armies were making alarming progress in the province of Champagne and extreme measures were being contemplated by the Executive Council, Fabre said, as if to test her: "The only solution is to tighten governmental power in the Executive Council and to invest its president with dictatorial powers; it's the only way to obtain the necessary rapidity of action for the salvation of France." [6] Mme Roland bit her lips violently but remained silent. Finally, sensing her unshakable hostility, Danton spaced his visits and, before long, stopped them altogether. After that, their relation deteriorated rapidly. The Rolands made no secret of their suspicions, and Danton countered by siding with Robespierre and Marat. Thus Mme Roland's impetuousness, inflexibility, and her personal antipathy for Danton contributed to the estrangement of a potentially powerful ally.

Later, Mme Roland justified her haughty attitude toward Danton by accusing him of an alliance with the court, with the Duke of Orléans, and with various complicities and huge extortions. Historians have marshaled impressive evidence which has indeed borne out these accusations.[7] Moreover, she laid the responsibility for the September massacres at his door, and the anecdote she relates to underscore the man's cynicism cannot be overlooked. Roland had appointed a certain Grandpré, a man of integrity and compassion as Mme Roland was to discover for herself when she would unexpectedly come under his jurisdiction, to the post of supervisor of prisons. When the September massacres began, Grandpré rushed to the Ministry of the Interior to report the bloody goings on. The ministers, being in council, were then unavailable. At the end of the session, Danton was the first to leave the chamber, and Grandpré approached him and began relating the happenings. He was rudely interrupted by the Minister of Justice who, his eyes bulging with fury, roared: "I don't give a damn for the prisoners! Who cares what happens to them. Let them fend for themselves!" [8] And indeed, at a time when the advancing armies of Prussia and Austria were threatening Paris, Danton was not the only one who felt that the massacres represented popular justice, the sacred will of the nation.

Mme Roland, however, maintains in her autobiography that Danton not only sanctioned the slaughter, but actually planned it and even arranged that some of the prisoners be declared innocent so as to give the gruesome proceedings an appearance of popular judgment. In order to contrast Danton's lack of conscience with Roland's humanity, she makes much of the letter her husband addressed to the Assembly on September 3, 1792, publicly denouncing the Commune for the massacres.[9] That the Rolands were personally shocked by the atrocities is undeniable. But it still remains that the Minister of the Interior failed to take swift, effective steps to stop the bloodshed. Whether out of ignorance of the events, which is unlikely, or tacit complicity, which is hardly in keeping with Roland's upright character, or sheer helplessness, which is most probable, the reprisals were allowed to go on. In his public letter, Roland was as moved by a desire to exonerate himself from all blame and by personal resentment against the capital and the Commune as by true indignation at the atrocities. His letter fell short of an outright condemnation. Like his Girondist friends, he hedged and was unable to adopt a clear-cut stand.

By shifting the responsibility to the capital as a whole, by indirectly threatening it with separation from the rest of the nation, and by not recognizing that the overwhelming majority of Parisians had nothing to do with these crimes, Roland failed to strike at those directly responsible for the bloody deeds and only succeeded in fanning the growing ill-feeling and resentment of the Parisian people against him and the Girondist deputies. Behind the mitigated protest, however, made at a time when most were paralyzed with fear and shock, an undertone of sincere revulsion is apparent. The impact of these events, together with the realization of his own impotence, had a frightful impact on Roland's mind and health. He worked without letup; he hardly ate and slept, and his already sallow complexion now turned alarmingly yellow. But he was struggling against the mounting tide of Jacobin popularity, and his many proclamations and circulars were largely ignored by his enemies and failed to rally his friends.

On Sunday, September 2, 1792, at around five in the afternoon, as elsewhere in the city the prison massacres were getting under way, Mme Roland heard a tumult outside the Hôtel de l'Intérieur. About two hundred men had encircled the house, vociferously demanding to see the Minister and clamoring for arms. Roland had gone out and the mob was in an ugly mood. But his wife did not lose her head. She invited in ten of the men, calmly informed them that the Minister had no arms in his house and advised them to present their request to the Ministry of War. They replied that they came from there, shouted insults, and insisted on seeing Roland: "I am sorry that he is out," she told them. "You can search the house from top to bottom, and you will see that he is not in and that there are no arms here. Go back to the Ministry of War, or to the Commune, and make your complaints there. And if you wish to speak to Roland, go to the Ministry of the Navy where the whole Council is gathered." [10] They finally retreated; from her balcony Mme Roland saw fierce-looking ruffians in shirt-sleeves, wildly brandishing gleaming sabers and declaiming against the "betrayal" of the ministers.

Such incidents were not made to reassure the Rolands. They quickly became convinced that every effort was being made to intimidate and paralyze them. Still more ominous events were to follow. In her *Memoirs*, Mme Roland speaks of the threat of assassination that constantly hung over her husband and friends during this period of crisis and extreme tension. That the Rolands feared for their lives at this time was not just the result of overwork and hysteria. In a speech delivered at the Commune on September 4, while the massacres were still going on, Robespierre denounced Brissot and Roland without naming them, but at the same time making unmistakably clear whom he meant, as conspirators and agents of the Duke of Brunswick, commander of the Prussian and Austrian armies. The Vigilance Committee even went so far as to issue warrants for the arrest of Roland, Brissot, and other prominent Girondists. But Danton, either recoiling before what might have been a premature move against a fellow minister, or still hoping for a reconciliation with the Girondists, had the warrant withdrawn.[11]

Did Robespierre actually count on the massacres to rid him of dangerous rivals while these were helpless prisoners? Even historians who tend to be his apologists have not been able to discount this sinister intention. Mme Roland, for her part, had no doubt as to Robespierre's plans: "We are under the hatchet of Robespierre and Marat," she wrote to Bancal on September 5, "They have set up a *chambre ardente*. They maintain a small army, paid for either by money they found at the Tuileries or by funds provided by Danton, who is the hidden leader of the gang." [12] Danton's intervention on behalf of her husband, far from reassuring her, only confirmed her strong suspicion that he was biding his time and waiting for a better opportunity.

The legislative elections, which coincided with the massacres, ended with a resounding victory for the Mountain, and the influential Paris deputation was found to be represented exclusively by candidates of the Commune. Robespierre, Danton, and Marat were elected. Danton gave up his Ministry of Justice, since it was legally incompatible with a legislative seat. The Girondists still held a numerical majority, but many of them came from the provinces and had very little understanding of the recent developments. They were a heterogeneous group, and each prided himself on his independence of judgment and will. The Robespierrists on the other hand, highly conscious of being a minority in the country at large, organized the power of Paris along rigorous lines. As a result, Roland's faction, though prepared to fight, could not muster the necessary support from the undecided provincial deputies.

The National Convention held its first meeting on September 21, 1792. Significantly, the Girondists, who had constituted the Left in the Legislative Assembly, now sat with the Right. Even though the Convention was still dominated by the middle-class representatives of the provinces, in Paris itself the Commune had triumphed and, owing to the fact that the seat of government was located in the capital, it would constantly be under the pressure of the radical Left, better known as the Mountain from the position it occupied on the high tiers of the Assembly Hall. Between the Gironde and the Mountain there extended a third, uncommitted group, the Plain, so called because it occupied the lower benches. This faction, also mockingly referred to as the Swamp,[13] generally waited for a clear outcome before casting its vote.

Thus far, Mme Roland and the Girondists had not hesitated to appeal to popular insurrection in order to intimidate the Right. Now they made an about-face and began to defend law and order with the same ardor with which they had agitated for violence. The terroristic means and inflammatory propaganda resorted to by the Mountain had left them by the wayside. The September massacres in particular had convinced them that the Commune encouraged, indeed planned, such acts of mass murder. Even though the number of men directly involved was not large, Paris had witnessed these horrifying scenes and done nothing to prevent or stop them: "All Paris looked on—all Paris was accursed in my eyes," writes Mme Roland in her autobiography. "And I can no longer entertain hopes of seeing liberty established among cowards who could be indifferent to the last outrages against nature and humanity and contemplate coolly enormities which the courage of fifty armed men could easily have forestalled." [14] In this somber frame of mind, she turned once more to the example of the American Revolution and praised the wisdom of a Washington who had removed Congress from Philadelphia so as to protect the seat of government against the pressure and action of the populace. Such a decision, she wrote to Bancal on September 2, 1792, was not carried out because of fear, and the Girondists would be well advised to advocate the removal of the Assembly to Blois, on the Loire river.[15]

As the party of the Mountain, which relied primarily on Paris and the Commune, began gaining initiative and popularity to the detriment of the Girondists, Brissot, the Rolands, Thomas Paine, and their friends saw in a federal system, based on that of the United States, the only way to right the political balance between the capital and the provinces. As representatives of the educated middle class of the provinces, most of the Girondists had a natural suspicion of the Paris Commune and of the Parisian working class. In this respect, Mme Roland's own attitude underwent a significant change. As a native

Parisian, she had looked upon the city as the natural leader and champion of the Revolution and had repeatedly decried the reactionary tendencies of Lyons and its surroundings. Under the influence of her friends she came to hate the "dictatorship" of Paris and demanded that a departmental guard protect the Convention and the Executive Council from the Commune. Naturally enough, Roland echoed these demands in motions presented to the Convention. Only one year earlier Mme Roland, in a letter to Roland, had violently castigated the provinces and their blind conservatism; it was in those provinces that she now placed her trust. More and more, the Girondists, basing themselves on the preference that Montesquieu and Rousseau had shown for a federal system, as well as on the concrete example of the United States, leaned toward the decentralization of power and toward greater local authority as a means of checking the overwhelming preponderance of Paris. As a result, it was not too difficult for the Jacobins to equate federalism with the theory of provincial rights, divided authority, and counterrevolution. And since the alarm of impending invasion and civil war had been sounded, federalism, or even a tendency toward it, came to be viewed popularly as treasonable.

With the growing success of the Paris municipality, Mme Roland's erstwhile sympathetic concern for the well-being of the illiterate masses turned into an increasing suspicion that they were very much like children who, through flattery and clever manipulation, could be swayed in any direction. She now spoke bitterly of revolutionaries like Danton who mixed with the rabble, adopted their manners, and spoke their language so as to please the radical *sans-culottes*. When Danton, Robespierre, and Marat joined with the Paris Commune, identifying their cause with that of the masses, she promptly drew the conclusion that popular tyranny would ensue and denounced it as being as nefarious as royal absolutism. The prospect of a dictatorship of the Commune was as hateful in her eyes as the unlimited monarchy of the Old Régime. Frantically she urged her friends to rally the provincial deputies behind their cause and to oppose a common front to the increasing threat of Parisian domination. In her

agitated state of mind, it did not occur to her that such action, instead of saving the Revolution, could well wreck it irremediably.
Most of the Montagnards, too, came from bourgeois origins, and
Robespierre shared Mme Roland's dislike for vulgarity and sloven-
liness. But the Jacobins' well-timed insistence on direct social and
economic reform, universal manhood suffrage, and general education
won them the enthusiastic backing of the Paris Commune and of
the working class. It was Mme Roland's fatal mistake to believe that
the Jacobins represented only the ragged mobs of Paris while the
Girondists were the spokesmen of the whole people of France.

In their personal dealings, the Rolands committed the tactical
error of inviting to their house only friends and sympathizers. On
Mondays and Fridays, a select group numbering about fifteen partook
of a frugal dinner with the Minister and his wife. The most frequent
visitors were Brissot, Pétion, Barbaroux, Bancal, Louvet, Lanthenas,
and Buzot, who had returned to Paris as a deputy to the Convention.
Condorcet and Vergniaud were less regular guests. If sometimes men
of different opinions found themselves invited, they immediately
became aware of the preference shown those who were in accord
with the Rolands. Such favoritism, it goes without saying, resulted
in the prompt withdrawal from these gatherings of all those save the
most docile disciples. The Montagnards would not fail to exploit
this situation by conspicuously holding their own meetings in the
broad daylight and public glare of the Jacobin Club and by accusing
the Girondists in general and the Rolands and their immediate
friends in particular of conspiratorial activities.

Mme Roland tried her best to defend herself against Jacobin
charges that she held elaborate banquets at which she cast an evil
spell on men: "I gave a dinner only twice a week: once to my husband's colleagues, with a few deputies; the other to a mixed company composed either of deputies and head clerks or of such other
persons as took a part in politics or were concerned with affairs of
state. Neatness and taste presided at my table, but profusion and
luxurious ornaments were equally unknown. Everyone was at ease
and spent little time over the meal because I served only one course

and did myself the honors of the table. . . . Such were the repasts which popular orators at the tribune of the Jacobins have converted into sumptuous entertainments where, like another Circe, I corrupted all those who had the misfortune of being present." [16]

With every passing day, the Rolands felt more keenly the helplessness of the Executive Council in the face of the Jacobins' persistent attacks. Upon learning that her husband had been elected as a representative of the Somme to the Convention, Manon, who had come to the conclusion that he could better serve his country as a deputy, urged him to resign from his ministry, the two functions being incompatible according to the law.[17] Friends like Brissot and Buzot, on the other hand, viewed such a resignation as a public calamity, since there would be no one left in the executive branch of the government to oppose Danton and Robespierre.

On September 29, 1792, therefore, Buzot introduced in the Convention a motion "inviting citizen Roland to continue serving the Republic in the position he has so far occupied and, if necessary, to choose, through devotion to the motherland, the ministerial portfolio over the seat of deputy." [18] Hearing this, Danton rose from the upper tiers occupied by the Mountain and thundered with a voice that resounded through the entire hall: "No one is more fair to Roland than I, but I suggest that if you invite him to be Minister, you should also extend the invitation to Mme Roland, for everyone knows that he was not alone in his department! As for me, I was alone in mine." [19] A loud burst of laughter from the Jacobins, mixed with furious protests from the Girondists, greeted this malicious and ungentlemanly remark. The incident was of course reported to Manon; it only heightened her intense dislike for Danton.

But the Gironde succeeded in convincing Roland to remain at his post. On October 1, he published a letter in the *Moniteur* making his decision official and stating that, inspired by the confidence shown him, he would not be deterred by the responsibilities and dangers of the ministry.[20] And his vanity was not a little flattered when a crowd of deputies and citizens actually came to his house to entreat him to retain the ministry. Mme Roland, too, was pleased at seeing her husband's services considered indispensable. Yet she could not help fearing for his safety and already undermined health, so rudely strained by constant overwork and worry.

On October 18, Roland submitted a detailed account of the expenses of his ministry.[21] In his comments he indirectly but clearly challenged Danton to do the same. This placed the ex-Minister of Justice in an embarrassing position; his finances were hopelessly entangled and in his reply to the Convention he satisfied no one. The Roland faction, it goes without saying, made much of Danton's weak spot. He, in turn, countered by relating a conversation he had had with Roland in early September, after the fall of Longwy, in which the Minister of the Interior had mentioned the desirability of setting up the government south of the Loire. Such a thought, at a time when Longwy had just fallen and when the road to the capital seemed open to the advancing Prussians and Austrians, could well have been expressed, especially in view of the fact that Mme Roland herself speaks of similar discussions with Barbaroux. But Danton's accusation was no doubt meant to cast a shadow on Roland's patriotism. It must nonetheless be conceded that the Girondists were not overly eager to defend a city where their influence had waned in favor of their mortal enemies. In the South they expected to encounter far less resistance in carrying out the will of the "true" revolutionaries. Danton, for his part, had of course no intention of giving up the capital, where he and his ally the Commune were everything, for the provinces, where his influence would be nil. Hence his eloquent speeches and untiring efforts on behalf of the city during those dark September days when all seemed lost. Whatever his motives, there is no doubt that Danton succeeded in firing the patriotism of Frenchmen and in instilling in his fellow countrymen the will to fight, and die if need be, for the defense of Paris. No wonder he emerged as the savior of the capital and of France while Roland and his friends, who had initially favored this war, played a rather pallid role during the moments of crisis. The great victories of Valmy and Jemappes would only delay the consequences of this defeatist policy.

Danton's popularity eclipsed even that of Robespierre during those tense September days when the enemy seemed at the gateway of Paris, and the city was in the grips of hysteria and panic. "Danton directs everything," wrote Mme Roland to Bancal on September 9, "Robespierre is his puppet, and Marat holds his torch and dagger." [22] Since the idea of compromise between "virtue" and "crime" was unthinkable for the Roland group, it found itself isolated, not only from the moderate deputies, most of whom belonged to the passive, obedient middle group, the Plain, but also from several influential Girondists. Brissot himself hesitated to support a direct attack against the Mountain that could fail or backfire. Vergniaud did not oppose the idea of dealing with Danton. Hence Mme Roland's deep resentment against a man she regarded as a remarkable orator but ineffectual statesman. Condorcet, for his part, kept himself aloof from what he at the time considered no more than personal squabbles, an attitude which would earn him Mme Roland's everlasting contempt and some of the most searing comments in her *Memoirs*. Even after misfortune and persecution had caused all the victims of the Terror to draw closer together, Mme Roland would find herself unable to forgive such otherwise brilliant men for failing to sense the danger while there was still time. In the Jacobin Club itself the debates were growing increasingly more tumultuous and disorderly. On October 12, Brissot was excluded for having dared to denounce the Commune; on October 29 it was Louvet's turn to have his name struck off the rolls. From that time onwards, the other Girondists gave up attending the gatherings and left the society they had helped to found to their opponents. Robespierre, Danton, and Marat were now the undisputed masters of the famous revolutionary club.

The three deputies to the Convention who worked most closely with the Rolands and enjoyed their greatest confidence were Buzot, Barbaroux, and Louvet. Zealous and fearless critics of the Mountain though they were, they lacked a concerted plan of action. Louvet's paper, *La Sentinelle,* was used less as an organ against counterrevolutionaries than as an antidote to Marat's *Ami du Peuple* and Hébert's *Père Duchesne*. But Louvet's witty, sophisticated style was hardly a match for the studied vulgarity and ferociousness of Marat and Hébert. Louvet, perhaps even more than the other knights-errant of the Rolands, had a quixotic temperament and committed the rash imprudence of attacking all his formidable adversaries simultaneously, thereby destroying none but merely contributing to unite them. The art of invective, moreover, was not his strong point; his charges produced much of an uproar but few if any concrete results.

The signal for a frontal attack on the Mountain was given by Roland himself on October 29. In his report to the Convention he proceeded to indict the Commune for usurpation of power and acts of terrorism. Then he read a letter addressed to the vice-president of the Criminal Tribunal, which warned of the possible recurrence of the September massacres and directly accused Robespierre of aiming at a dictatorship.[23] This dramatic denunciation produced a violent commotion and placed the ex-lawyer from Arras in a difficult position. In the midst of the confusion and tumult Robespierre demanded to be given the opportunity to justify himself against Roland's "calumnies." Ascending the tribune, he ignored several interruptions from the floor and spoke, as usual, at length and in a lofty manner. He concluded with a challenge: "There is not one man here who would dare accuse me to my face by spelling out positive facts against me; there is not one who would dare mount this tribune." "I," shouted someone from the end of the hall, "I ask to be given the floor in order to accuse Robespierre!" In the hush that ensued, a slight, pale-complexioned young man was seen rapidly approaching the rostrum. He stopped directly before the speaker and repeated "Robespierre, I accuse you!" in a clear, ringing voice. It was Louvet, Mme Roland's trusted spokesman.[24]

Having in turn gained access to the rostrum, Louvet launched into a long diatribe against Robespierre, ending with the demand that he be impeached. Louvet's speech, passionate and at times persuasive, made a strong impression on the deputies.[25] Sensing this, Robespierre asked for a week's time to prepare his reply. It was granted. Hearing of her friend's bold intervention, Mme Roland deemed it worthy of Cato's famous speeches and Cicero's orations against Catiline.[26] Unfortunately for the Girondists, Louvet, despite his obvious sincerity and good will, was no Cato or Cicero. He did not possess the vituperative genius, towering personality, and impressive delivery necessary to make a public accusation effective. His reputation as the author of a light, bawdy novel also made it hard for many to take him seriously. As soon as he had mounted the tribune, a number of deputies had broken into a smile, remembering that the salacious adventures of the fictional Faublas were reputed to be largely autobiographical. To be sure, since 1789 Louvet had reformed, but the fact remained that he was not among the most respected or influential Girondists, and it is rather ironical that it befell him to confront the austere, puritanical Robespierre. Louvet had also remained too vague and general in his allegations, and if he was warmly applauded, not a single Girondist rose to support him. This disappointing reaction greatly irritated Mme Roland. From that day on, she lost whatever little faith she still had in the Convention. That the deputies did not rise to their feet shouting "Robespierre must be arrested! He is a public enemy!" was the cause of much wonder and bitterness on the part of the Roland faction of the Girondists.

In the final analysis, Louvet's peroration achieved nothing save to provide Robespierre with a magnificent opportunity to play the martyr, a role in which he excelled. And when, on November 5, his turn to speak came, he handled his defense with consummate mastery, taking up and refuting one by one Louvet's charges, indeed turning them to his own advantage.[27] It soon became clear to the deputies that Louvet had bitten off more than he could chew. From this verbal duel Robespierre emerged the victor and, more than ever, the idol and prophet of the Jacobin Club. As for the Girondists, their disunity had caused them to pass up another opportunity to humble, if not to crush, one of the leading spirits of the Commune. Robespierre, for his part, did not fail to capitalize on his latest triumph. From now on, he would intensify his campaign to isolate and discredit the Girondists.

That such otherwise brilliant men as Vergniaud and Condorcet had chosen not to associate themselves with Louvet's onslaught only reinforced Mme Roland's grave doubts concerning their political acumen and personal courage. Condorcet's aloofness in particular disappointed her bitterly. Was he not, after all, the last surviving representative of the Encyclopedists, a man with whom Roland had had dealings as far back as 1781? They had occasion to correspond when Roland, seeking recognition from the Academy of Science for his monographs on industrial arts and crafts, approached Condorcet, then secretary of the Academy. It was Condorcet's signature which approved the publication of Roland's essays. In 1781, at a dinner given by Panckoucke, the publisher of the new *Encyclopedia*, the two men had finally met in person, an acquaintanceship that was to be renewed in July of 1791, during the crisis precipitated by the king's flight to Varennes. Yet, despite intellectual and political affinities, truly friendly relations were never established between the Rolands and the philosopher turned revolutionary. Like Vergniaud, Condorcet seems to have favored the more worldly salon of Mme Dodun over the austere gatherings of Mme Roland. But what especially brought the wrath of the Minister's wife upon Condorcet's head was his sympathetic attitude toward the Paris Commune and Jacobin radicalism, and his unwillingness to become involved in the quarrel between the Roland faction and the Mountain. There is no doubt, however, that the aloofness of such moderates as Condorcet and Vergniaud weakened the effect of the offensive of Roland, Barbaroux, Buzot, and Louvet. It was not until the Jacobins showed marked hostility against the constitutional proposals made by Condorcet that he finally severed himself from them and joined the Girondists. By that time he had earned himself Mme Roland's contempt for his inaction. Later, Condorcet was to experience the hardships of proscription, and the tragic and mysterious circumstances of his death are well known. Of all this Mme Roland would remain ignorant and thus, until the end, she was to harbor ill-feelings toward the profoundest intellect of her party, making this harsh statement in her *Memoirs*: "I must say a word or two about Condorcet, whose mind will always soar to the most sublime truths, but whose character will never rise above the level of fear. . . . The timidity which characterizes him, and which he shows to the world in his face and attitude, is not only a defect in his temperament; it is inherent to his soul, and all his intelligence cannot overcome it. Thus it was that after having established a principle or demonstrated a truth, he voted in the Assembly contrariwise when he should have stood up in the presence of these thundering rostrums, armed with invective and sowing threats." [28]

For a while, the Girondists continued to enjoy the prestige that had sprung from Dumouriez's smashing victory at Valmy on September 20, to be followed by another at Jemappes on November 6. Having repulsed Brunswick's veteran army, Dumouriez proceeded north to attack the Austrian Netherlands. Before setting out, however, he returned to Paris, ostensibly to discuss the situation with the government, but in reality to see where the political wind was blowing. Because of Dumouriez's military success at Valmy, Roland thought it best to mend their differences and make an effort at party unity. True, Dumouriez could still be suspected of royalist sympathies, but one does not snub a victorious general. Dumouriez was duly invited to dine at the Hôtel de l'Intérieur. "When he entered the room," writes Mme Roland, "he seemed somewhat embarrassed and offered me a beautiful bouquet he held in his hand with an air of awkwardness unusual in a man of so much self-assurance." [29] Dumouriez's uneasiness is not difficult to understand: he knew the Minister's wife well enough to realize that in her he had one of his most intransigent critics. And indeed, although Manon accepted the gracious offering with a smile and a well-turned compliment, she made it plain in the course of the evening that she still entertained doubts about the hero of the hour. After the meal, Dumouriez expressed the wish to go to the opera, probably to show himself to the adoring Parisians. Mme Roland was asked, in the presence of the general, whether she too planned to attend that performance. Her answer was evasive, for she had no desire to make a public appearance with Dumouriez. She went later, but precipitously retired when she noticed that the ministerial box was occupied by Danton, who was

moreover engaged in a lively conversation with the general.[30] Several
months after Dumouriez's return to Belgium, Mme Roland was not
overly surprised to learn that he had gone over to the enemy. She had
always suspected that he would fight for the republic only as long as
it worked out to his personal advantage. The Convention had humiliated him by sending commissaries to the front and had also sown
fears in his mind with its radical decrees, thereby convincing him
that he was better off casting his lot with the Prussians and Austrians. Whatever his motives, he turned out to be the evil genius of
the Girondists, and the damage caused by his defection in March
1793 was irreparable.[31]

In the midst of growing difficulties, Mme Roland enjoyed a moment of personal satisfaction when she was asked to pen an important
document for the Executive Council on November 23, 1792. It was
an official letter to Pope Pius VI, demanding the release of two young
French artists who had been arbitrarily arrested by the pontifical
authorities as sympathizers of the revolutionary regime.[32] As was her
custom, Manon violated all diplomatic rules and conventions. She
spoke her mind openly to the supreme and sovereign Pontiff of
Christendom and freely vented her resentment against the church
and its antirevolutionary policy. As a deist and opponent of organized
religion, she took special delight in authoring a rebuke to one whom
she curtly addressed as "Prince-Bishop of Rome" and whom she did
not hesitate to lecture on church history as well as on religious tolerance and liberalism.

"Free Frenchmen," she wrote in the name of the French Republic, "children of the arts, whose stay in Rome sustains and develops the tastes and talents that are her pride, are presently being
unjustly persecuted by your order. Torn from their work in an arbitrary fashion, locked up in a forbidding prison, held up to the public
as criminals, even though no tribunal has revealed their crime, when
they are guilty of nothing but their respect for the rights of humanity
and love of motherland, they are the victims of despotism and superstition combined." [33] After proclaiming that the days of the Inquisition were over, she warned the pope that a new era, ruled by reason
and justice, had been ushered in by the French Revolution and that

only through the practice of "those evangelical principles which breathe the purest democracy, the tenderest humanity, the most perfect equality, and which Christ's successors have harbored solely in order to augment a domination which today is falling into decay," could he hope to maintain his authority over the church.[34] Like her letter to Louis XVI, her message of defiance to the pope was dashed off in one sitting, in Manon's little study which Marat, in his journalistic onslaughts against the Minister's wife, never failed to call a boudoir.[35]

While the king's fate was being debated, the Jacobins kept pressing for swift action against the deposed monarch while the Girondists, in a significant reversal of tactics, showed less enthusiasm for radical measures. As a result, they were accused of dilatory maneuvers and hidden royalist sympathies. The Minister of the Interior was a favorite target of the Jacobin press: it was repeatedly insinuated that he had engaged in secret correspondence with Narbonne and other émigrés in London and even that he had established contact with the Prussians. He was, moreover, accused of "corrupting public opinion" in the provincial departments by subsidizing journalists through misappropriation of public funds and finally that his proposal to establish a departmental guard in Paris only masked the intent of carrying out a counterrevolution. Roland's strenuous denials and his monthly financial accounts seem to have been largely ineffectual in the face of these damaging charges. Roland worked harder than ever, but he lacked the shrewdness of his adversaries, and if his intentions were honorable, his judgment did not always serve him well. A good case in point is the hasty and imprudent way in which he handled the notorious iron safe affair.

On November 20, Gamain, the king's locksmith, revealed to Heurtier, architect and inspector of National Buildings, the existence of a cache in a panel of the Tuileries palace. The locksmith had made it for Louis XVI. Heurtier reported the matter to his chief, Roland. The latter, together with the architect and locksmith, hastened to the designated place and, without calling official witnesses, collected and rapidly looked over the secret documents. Realizing their explosive nature, he brought them to the National Convention for a public examination. But by failing to consult the commissaries especially assigned to the Tuileries, Roland ruffled the feelings of his immediate subordinates and, what was much more serious, exposed himself to the charge, immediately leveled by the Mountain, that he had deliberately avoided summoning official witnesses so as to abstract those papers that incriminated his Girondist friends. The fact that the documents sealed Louis XVI's doom by revealing his dealings with the enemy and simultaneously implicated several members of the Legislative Assembly made the accusation against Roland all the more potent. The Minister protested that he had acted in good faith and insisted that he had been under no obligation to call further witnesses since he already had two in the persons of the architect and the locksmith, both good patriots and honest citizens. An investigation ensued, which ostensibly cleared Roland. The whole affair had raised such an uproar that it further harmed the waning prestige and popularity of the Minister of the Interior.[36]

After the discovery of the safe which, among other incriminating papers, contained the king's secret correspondence with Austria, demands for a trial could no longer be stayed. The Girondists feared, however, that the condemnation of the king would essentially mean a Jacobin victory and the opportunity for the Paris Commune to seize power. Some of the men closest to the Minister and his wife now favored postponement of the trial. For the Girondists the question had become less one of eliminating the king than of preventing Robespierre from seizing power. Thus, after formal charges of treason had been made against Louis XVI and the trial was under way in January 1793, Buzot launched a Girondist move to delay the final verdict in order to associate the whole country with the decision through a plebiscite of the provincial departments. This was clearly a political move, since the Girondists saw in an immediate verdict a triumph for the Jacobins as well as their own isolation from all moderate elements. The Jacobins, for their part, wished to avoid appealing to the departments, where royalist feelings still ran very high.

Once more, the strategy of the Girondists was doomed to failure because of disunity. When their motion for postponement was defeated and the decisive votes counted on January 17, nearly all the leaders—Vergniaud, Guadet, Gensonné, Louvet, Brissot, Buzot, Barbaroux, Pétion—cast their vote for the death penalty.[37] Had they opted for death out of conviction or out of fear of being accused of royalism? Whatever their motives, and here one should refrain from generalizing since their political philosophy was far from uniform, their ill-timed and unsuccessful delaying tactics cast a shadow of suspicion over their devotion to the republican cause. The condemnation and execution of the king, coupled with Dumouriez's defection and a series of reversals at the front, proved the nemesis of the Girondists. Patriotic ardor, which had been whipped to a fever pitch, as well as general acute anxiety and economic distress had made Mme Roland's friends easy targets of inflammatory speeches and articles.

All along, Manon had been deeply aware of the shortcomings of the Girondists and had endeavored to fire them with a common purpose. She had only managed to instigate some untimely and largely ineffectual interventions at the Convention and to bring upon herself the hatred of the Jacobins. And as a woman she was particularly vulnerable to denunciations and satire. No insult, no matter how gross or obscene, no innuendo, no matter how sly, was spared to destroy her influence and belittle her party by picturing the latter as wholly dominated by a petticoat—a peculiarly damaging form of ridicule for the Gallic mind! The Girondists found themselves trapped: from the outside, implacable hatred in the form of relentless attacks from the Mountain, accompanied by the barely hidden hostility from the Royalists who had been bitterly shocked by the Girondist last-minute but decisive support of Louis XVI's condemnation; and within the party, confusion and indecisiveness in the face of the bewilderingly rapid unfolding of events over which all control had been lost.

For these liberal-minded, idealistic men who had thrown their energy and hope into this collective venture, who had indefatigably toiled for the revolutionary cause, this was indeed a rude awakening. Popular support was withdrawn from them because they had lacked leadership and organization, as well as the ability to gauge popular opinion and needs. In many ways, these well-intentioned but rash young revolutionaries had been their own worst enemies. Had they not, at the height of their popularity and while they enjoyed a large majority in the Assembly as well as the power to force the king to appoint a ministry of their own choosing, indulged in drawing up laws and proclamations, challenging the whole of Europe and provoking violence and unrest? They were now reaping the bitter fruits of a foolhardy, overoptimistic belief in quick, easy solutions.

It was with a heavy heart and somber forebodings that Mme Roland faced an uneasy future during the bleak winter that ushered in the year 1793. Louis XVI was guillotined on January 21; food riots were breaking out, and the country remained with no working government to check the inner unrest and to conduct the war; the Gironde and the Mountain continued to be locked in a deadly struggle.[38] Looking back on the preceding tumultuous months, Manon began to realize that her own enthusiastic fervor and political inexperience had contributed to the confusion now reigning in the Girondist camp. Like her friends, she had impetuously agitated for a radical policy whose implications she had not grasped and whose end results she had not foreseen. Now that her eyes had been opened, it was too late. The Mountain had gained the upper hand, and the Revolution, propelled in an irreversible course, left no room for those who did not share Robespierre's brand of republicanism.

FIFTEEN

Love and Ideology

MME ROLAND'S RELATIONS WITH MEN had always been of an eminently cautious nature. As a young girl, she had so trained her sensibility that she had acquired absolute control over her impulses. Spontaneous and unreasoned amorous feelings for a man who did not also deserve her full admiration belonged to a domain from which she had carefully shied away. Like the heroines of the French classical theater, especially of Corneille's dramas, she was incapable of indulging a penchant without proper consideration for self-esteem.

Just when she first began to feel an attraction for the young deputy François-Léonard Buzot, however, is not known, though it is likely that it was after his return from Evreux, during those feverish months following the August 10 uprising, when the Girondists, particularly the Roland group, worked frantically to stem the tide of Jacobin popularity and influence. Like Manon, Buzot had been nurtured on Plutarch and Rousseau. Already in the Constituent Assembly, he had drawn attention because of his eloquence and youthful, romantic appeal. True, he had none of Brissot's engaging gaiety, Barbaroux's ebullience, or Vergniaud's brilliance, and he was no wit. But his serious demeanor, touched with a becoming wistfulness and melancholy, bespoke a passionate soul. In many ways he was similar to Robespierre. He had fine features, a rather pale complexion, and a generally pensive expression. Rather than for the rough arena of revolutionary politics, nature seemed to have destined him for the quiet, peaceful existence of a country squire, for he was an introvert at heart and liked nothing better than solitary meditation in the midst of the beauties of nature. Like Robespierre, too, he harbored a

predilection for neatness and propriety and scorned political compromise and moral laxity.

Hailing as he did from Normandy, he had started out as a lawyer
in his native town of Evreux. He came to Paris as one of the deputies to the Estates General, and in this capacity he aided in preparing
the petition the Third Estate of his district submitted to that body. As
a follower of the *philosophes* and impassioned admirer of Rousseau,
he became totally committed to the Revolution and readily identified
himself with the most ardently republican elements of the Constituent Assembly, with such men as Robespierre by whose side he
fought for common goals during this early period. He was introduced to the Rolands by Brissot, at a time when the couple, freshly
arrived from Beaujolais, still lived at the Hôtel Britannique.[1]

In those days Mme Roland seems to have entertained only cordial
feelings for the dedicated young deputy and his wife. Upon her return to Le Clos in September of 1791, she had written them several
friendly letters and continued to correspond from Paris, although
irregularly, during the year Buzot served as President of the Criminal
Court of Evreux. Following Buzot's election to the Convention, in
September 1792, Mme Roland was brought into daily contact and
collaboration with a man who unreservedly admired her intelligence
and charm, and this all the more so since his own wife, thirteen
years his senior and moreover homely and dull, was hardly equipped
to compete with the brilliant wife of the Minister of the Interior.
Their mutual feelings of respect and friendship had not diminished
during the year's separation, thanks to their epistolary exchanges, for
both possessed that mixture of passion and prudence that feeds on
absence.[2] Each regarded love as too serious a business to enter such
a relationship precipitously. Political matters, moreover, were summoning all their energies, retarding the moment when they would
yield to the sentiments that were drawing them slowly but irresist-
ibly together.

It must have been early in October 1792, after the prison massacres and first onslaught of vituperation against Roland had left
Manon in a state of shock and confusion, that she turned to Buzot

as the sole remaining deputy still worthy of her implicit trust. There were still other staunch friends, but none could buoy her spirits and restore her will to go on like Buzot, probably because none had stirred her emotions so deeply as the reflective deputy from Evreux. For one who, like Manon, was possessed of a romantic imagination, Buzot must have been endowed with the irresistible aura of such fictional heroes as Mme de Lafayette's Prince de Nemours and Rousseau's Saint-Preux rolled into one. And like the heroes of the novels on which Mme Roland's fancy had fed, Buzot combined physical attractiveness with that delicacy of manner that is a token of a tender nature, which is capable of great depth of feeling and loyalty. Unwittingly, Manon patterned her own behavior upon the virtuous but loving Princesse de Clèves, the highborn lady whom the Prince de Nemours had sought in vain to possess, and the less rigorous if equally passionate Julie de Wolmar. Thus two novels, the classical *Princesse de Clèves* and the preromantic *Nouvelle Héloïse*, furnished Mme Roland with a model that one could aspire to emulate in such an exquisitely agonizing situation: she would remain as reproachless and inflexible as the princess who perpetually flees from Nemours for fear of yielding to him, but the intensity of her feelings would match that of the more human Julie.

In the thirty-eighth year of her life, while a national upheaval reverberated throughout Europe and sent crowned heads reeling, Mme Roland encountered true passion for the first time. Her love for Roland, full of conviction though it had been, could hardly be regarded as something more than an *amour de tête*, an attachment contrived by a willful girl embittered by marriage conventions that had callously by-passed her because of her lack of status and wealth. Roland had appeared to her in the reassuring guise of a benevolent, world-wise father figure. For the aging husband, whose spirits had been frayed and body weakened by the formidable impact of revolutionary politics, she retained abiding respect and tenderness mingled with compassion. Many years ago she had thought him superior to her in purpose and character. Now she knew better. Moreover, his authoritarian, unbending ways had let some understandable resent-

ments well up within her. Yet to leave him in favor of the younger
man was unthinkable, especially at this critical juncture when enemies were howling at him from all sides.

Mme Roland was faced with an extraordinarily painful, indeed an
impossible dilemma. And since hers was a bold, energetic nature
that loathed secretive situations, she resorted to a drastic solution the
likes of which, at least in her time, are to be found only in fiction.
Caught up between a respected elderly husband and an adored
young lover, both the Princesse de Clèves in the novel of that name
and Julie de Wolmar in *La Nouvelle Héloïse* had determined to
confess to their own husbands. With her usual directness, Manon did
the same thing.[3] It is not too difficult to imagine the scene of the
confession: the stunned stupor of Roland, the initial self-possessed
calm of his wife soon replaced by a growing agitation as she was
requested to reveal the identity of the man who had succeeded in
alienating her affections. This she stubbornly refused to do, insisting
that this point was of no consequence in view of the fact that she
was sacrificing her love for the sake of her marriage. That Roland
obviously failed to appreciate her selflessness left her in a state of
utter bewilderment. On the contrary, Manon's rash confession, while
solving nothing, dealt a cruel blow to Roland's masculine pride and
only served to arouse his jealous fury. She had been too wrapped up
in her own turbulent emotions to fathom the effect of such a blunt
revelation on the overwrought Minister of the Interior. He was shat-
tered, and the will to continue the fight that had thus far sustained
his taut nerves, now deserted him altogether. For a man with his
amour-propre and possessiveness, this was an intolerable situation.

As for Buzot, like a drowning man he multiplied his delaying
tactics prior to the king's trial in the hope of checking Robespierre's
triumphant advance. But to no avail, for despite Mme Roland's admiration, Buzot was not made of the same stuff as Robespierre. His
Memoirs, written during his proscription, are replete with recriminations and self-righteous indignation; they form an undeniably interesting historical document without the insight and literary originality of a Mme Roland, or the bold political vision of a Robes-

pierre. To be fair to him, however, it should be added that these *Memoirs* were written under the most adverse circumstances.[4] In person and in the political arena he must have evidenced qualities not apparent in his written work. As for his speeches, generally judged severely by historians, they possess a lofty, if rather vague, rhetoric which no doubt had strong appeal for a sympathetic listener like Mme Roland.[5] Sensitive and kind-hearted, he also exerted a certain ascendancy over the more impetuous Barbaroux and Louvet, both of whom became his close friends.

To Mme Roland Buzot confided his hopes and fears, and his attitude of humble adoration was immensely flattering to a woman who thought that she had passed the age for love. He combined the polish of the Old Régime with the virtues of a republican citizen. At long last, Manon felt loved as she deserved to be, an exhilarating feeling she treasured all the more because she fully realized how hopeless it was. For years she had lived with a man who had accepted her self-effacement and unrecognized collaboration as his normal due. With the callousness of this new-found love, she conveniently forgot that if someone was to blame for the relationship she had established with her husband, it was only herself. Had she not always eagerly volunteered to engage in all the ungrateful work preparatory to Roland's articles, lectures, and books? Had she not conceived marriage as a one-way proposition where the responsibility for the happiness of two beings rested entirely on the shoulders of the wife? [6] Imbued with these theories, she had never bothered questioning their validity in the light of reality or of her own needs and aspirations. Now, in the wake of the emotional turmoil aroused in her by the Revolution, she found herself facing the shambles of her long, patient effort toward an ordered self. Had she been an ordinary woman, she might have humbly recognized the falsehood of her principles and obeyed her instincts. Mme Roland was too stubborn to admit personal defeat. Rather than contradict all the moral values by which she had thus far lived, she would sacrifice herself and her lover on the altar of virtue. But to keep her self-respect she would have to pay a frightful price.

A rather unexpected result of Mme Roland's romantic involvement with Buzot was the fierce jealousy it aroused in the heretofore gentle and submissive Lanthenas. With the acute perspicacity of an unrequited lover, Lanthenas had immediately sensed that Manon's interest in Buzot was of a different nature from her friendship for men like Bosc or even Bancal. So long as no one had been singled out by the Minister's wife, Lanthenas had accepted without protest his platonic role as the little "brother." In the meantime, he had become Roland's amanuensis with no official title, as well as the errand boy of the Girondists. His good will was touching, but his inefficiency disrupted everything. This mild, indolent man exploded when he realized that Buzot was supplanting him and all others in the heart of Mme Roland and that she, upon whom he had long looked as a paragon of virtue, to be adored from afar, was just like ordinary women, susceptible to amorous feelings that were not necessarily legitimate. He threw himself into the role of the spurned lover and, in this as in all his other endeavors, he was eminently unsuccessful and pathetic. He made no effort to hide his jealousy, sending letters filled with crude reproaches to Mme Roland, embarrassing her with violent scenes, and threatening to reveal all to her husband, a rather incongruous menace in view of the fact that she had already done just that. Characteristically, while quarreling with Manon he did not think it unbecoming to continue living as a permanent guest in the Hôtel de l'Intérieur.[7] As the rift between Girondists and Jacobins deepened, Lanthenas began drifting over to the side of the Mountain. His perpetual vacillations, however, earned him the scorn of both sides. With the uncharitable severity she reserved for those who had fallen from her esteem, Mme Roland writes of him in her *Memoirs*: "He became less than nothing and made himself despised by all."[8] Jealousy and weakness of character, rather than political conviction, turned an old friend into an enemy. But no one, not even the ferocious Marat who considered Lanthenas a simpleton, took the trouble to attack him. Almost alone he survived the storm, a lost and forgotten man feebly preaching for unity and writing utopian treatises which, as one colleague put it, were fit for the moon.[9]

Added to her inner conflict, Mme Roland was beginning to feel the physical and emotional exhaustion brought about by two years of unending turmoil. A general weariness, a yearning for everlasting, forgetful sleep overwhelmed her, and the revolution now left her curiously detached and indifferent. In her last letter to this unreliable friend, during that gloomy December month of 1792, she wrote:

I have too much courage to have the need of showing it, and I have too little respect for life to go out of my way in order to keep or lose it. Indeed, I find life so toilsome for people of good will that I would not be disappointed to see the end of it; I would perhaps even contemplate death with a kind of delight. I know men well enough not to expect any justice from them; besides, I don't need it; my conscience takes the place of everything else. To be sure, the outcome of the Revolution is not very clear, and what people call *the parties* will be judged by posterity; but I am convinced that it will grant my husband the recognition that is due him, and I have the foreboding that we will pay this with our lives.[10]

Disillusionment made her fatalistic. She had tried her best; now come what may, she was ready, her interest in politics all but lost, but determined to meet her fate with dignity and steadfastness.

In the meantime, the Rolands continued to live under the same roof; they took their meals together and shared their evenings. But whether they spoke to each other or remained silent, an abyss separated them. With each word, each look, they increased their hurt. And their private grief, together with the mounting danger surrounding them, only contributed to their estrangement. After his wife's confession, Roland had tried to match her sublimity by offering to give her back her freedom and step aside for the man she loved. This proposal was naturally turned down, and Roland did not dare to insist, for he could not imagine life without Manon. Divorce had just been sanctioned by the state, but for Mme Roland this was unthinkable in view of her husband's dependence upon her as adviser, collaborator, secretary, nurse of his fragile health, and mother of his child. Curiously enough, even though she had dealt Roland a cruel blow, she felt no guilt. She had confessed, not out of remorse, but out of pride, and perhaps out of fear that keeping her feelings secret might lead her to succumb to them. Fate, she convinced herself, owed her this one great passion, and she gave full scope to her love for Buzot while clinging to her determination to remain "virtuous." It did not occur to her, however, that infidelity of the heart can be just as damaging as outright adultery. Quite the contrary: she gloried in her emotions, and this all the more since they had been repressed for so many years. Now she could either die a violent death in the revolutionary turmoil or see the doors of old age opening before her; if the joys of life had been denied her, she had at least tasted the bliss of true love.

While Manon dealt as best she could with an impossible situation at home, the scurrilous campaign of slander directed against the Roland ministry, and where she came in for a good share of abuse, continued unabated. The Montagnards even went so far as to accuse her personally of being the moving spirit behind a royalist conspiracy and of having corresponded with Narbonne, Talleyrand, and other émigrés. She was summoned to appear before the bar of the Convention on December 7, 1792. Her obvious devotion to the Revolution, coupled with her uncanny presence of mind and dignified but feminine demeanor, stirred the enthusiasm and gallantry of the deputies. Her eloquent yet restrained defense was followed by a rousing ovation. Not only was she cleared of the charges against her, but the members also rose to their feet and accorded her the honors of the meeting.[11]

It was an exhilarating victory after months of anguish. But flattering though this homage had been, it could hardly turn the tide. Undaunted, Marat grimly pursued his violent attacks against the Minister's wife in his vitriolic but highly popular sheet, _L'Ami du Peuple_. There was something about Marat, in addition to the fact that he was a political adversary, that terrified Mme Roland. If she had a respectful hatred for the icy and correct Robespierre and a natural hostility for the sensual and coarse Danton, she invariably spoke of Marat as though he were some kind of amphibious monster.[12] And indeed, this isolated, sickly man, who had hidden in the Paris sewers during the wave of repression following the Champ-de-Mars incident and had as a result contracted a disease of the skin which he tried to alleviate with constant baths, had an unkempt appearance and rough ways that repulsed even his allies. But his corrosive prose, which spared few people, had become a force behind the scene with which even Robespierre and Danton had to reckon. What had brought down Marat's wrath on the heads of the Rolands was not only the Minister's staunch opposition to the Commune and its radical measures, but reasons of a more personal nature. After the August 10 revolution, Marat had his men carry off four presses from the royal printing office, claiming that he needed them to replace those that had previously been confiscated. Roland was outraged by what he considered a highly irregular procedure, and he denounced it with his usual alacrity. And to make matters worse, he refused to allocate the requisite sum of money for the publication of a bulky manuscript by Marat without the prior approval of the Council. This was enough to provoke the anger of one who, as the "friend of the people," held his works above such petty scrutiny. He soon became convinced that Roland had deliberately sabotaged his efforts on behalf of the Revolution.[13] Tirelessly, he harped on the theme that it was not M. Roland, but rather Mme Roland, who actually ran the Ministry of the Interior. She was a siren who distributed her favors to her most submissive adorers. Indulging in the coarsest allusions, he compared her to sundry disreputable or unpopular women, from Lucrezia Borgia to such notorious female poisoners as Brinvilliers and Voisin and, to make matters complete, to the hated Marie-Antoinette herself.

Revolutionary journalists, in order to show their democratic sympathies, deliberately cultivated a style rich in profanity and vulgarity. Against such specialists of gutter language Mme Roland was helpless. She took refuge in a dignified silence. On Christmas eve, she was in a somber mood as she sat down to write to General Servan, the Girondist ex-Minister of War now commanding the Pyrenean army: "The sleuthhound Marat has been unleashed; he is after me and has not lost my trail for a moment. Pamphlets against me have multiplied and I doubt whether more dreadful things have been published against Marie-Antoinette, to whom I am likened." [14]

Gallantly, Louvet in *La Sentinelle* tried his best to parry the enemy's verbal blows; his shafts were as effective as arrows against heavy artillery.

A mood of exasperation and near hysteria overtook Mme Roland in the last months of 1792 and spring of 1793. She was not alone in experiencing a growing sense of doom. France was threatened by invasion from without and civil war from within; half of Europe was besieging her and, to make matters even more desperate, the provinces of the south and west were rising against the capital. As Paris fell in the grip of fear, mob rule became rampant; many were those, especially among the Girondists and moderates, who forecast another September massacre more dreadful than the first. Marat's posters now boldly denounced the Convention and the Executive Council, and Mme Roland correctly predicted that both institutions would soon be assaulted. With nightmarish rapidity the days succeeded one another; Manon hardly ever stopped writing and her husband's activity reached fever pitch. Both felt their lives imperiled as they noticed suspicious-looking *sans-culottes* lurking around their house at night and as a deluge of letters threatening assassination rained on their desk. Friends warned the couple not to sleep home. One evening, Mme Roland was on the point of giving in and, so as not to be recognized by the armed prowlers, started to disguise herself as a country girl. She had just put on a plain bonnet when she suddenly flung it to the other end of the room in a fit of anger: "I am ashamed," she cried, "to have to act like this. No, I shall neither disguise myself nor leave this place. If they wish to murder me, they can do it in my own house." [15] No one ventured to contradict her.

Fear of death, she had come to realize, could be worse than death itself. But if she had little concern for her own life, she was worried for her daughter's. She therefore took measures for Eudora's care and education in the event that the little girl would lose her parents. An official document signed by the couple and dated December 25, 1792, entrusted the child to her governess, Mlle Mignot, who would take her to Le Clos and assume all necessary authority. For eight years the governess would share the means of her pupil and, after-wards, would receive a generous annuity while enjoying complete independence. It must have been with heavy hearts that the Rolands added these words to the deed: "We rely with confidence on Mlle Mignot's affection, care, and enlightened kindness." [16] The fact that Mlle Mignot was to prove unworthy of such trust by testifying against her masters during the Reign of Terror adds a note of irony to this statement.[17] Mme Roland also wrote to her husband's brother, the kindly Canon Dominique, asking him to look after both Eudora and Mlle Mignot.[18]

To take flight and emigrate, as so many had done before her who had at first staked their hopes on the Revolution, was unthinkable for a woman of Manon's character and principles. On January 15, 1793, she addressed an affectionate letter to Lavater, the Swiss pastor and physiognomist. Recalling that already distant year of 1787, when she had spent many delightful hours with the scholar and his family in Zurich, she tried to give her correspondent a picture of the violence and chaos that now surrounded her:

The threatening circumstances under which we live do not leave me a moment's respite. Always in the eye of the storm, always in the shadow of the popular hatchet, we walk in the glint of lightning, and if we did not possess that peace of conscience that resists everything, we might very well be weary of life. But with a little strength of mind, one becomes accustomed to facing the most painful thoughts, and courage becomes only a matter of habit. . . . I send you my portrait and reiterate the eternal affection I have conceived for you. My husband joins me in embracing you; he pursues his career like the honest man he is; proscription hangs over our heads, but one must go on rowing, reach port if it is possible, and prove worthy even of ostracism if that is to be the reward for virtue.[19]

Robespierre, by now more convinced than ever that Roland stood in the way of establishing the ideal republic, resorted to his favorite weapon of insinuation. On January 6, he mounted the tribune of the Convention and, amidst grumbles of protest and interruptions, proceeded to denounce the "virtuous Roland," who invariably, under the pretext of shaping the public spirit, "depraves public opinion by always directing it to his own aim, that is, by praising himself and his friends as models of virtue, while depicting the others as rascals, brigands, factionists and disorganizers." [20] And Robespierre went on to hint that the offices of the Minister of the Interior, where pamphlets proliferate, "would be subsidized by the bankers of London and Berlin, if they were not in the pay of the public treasury of France." [21] Such an allegation of treason against a man who, if anything, was probity itself, was immediately echoed in the press favorable to the Commune and found willing believers.

This last onslaught, made at a time when Roland was smarting from his wife's revelation that she loved another man, must have contributed to his decision to give up the fight and resign from the Ministry on January 22. His enemies could now rejoice. As for Mme Roland, she doubtless approved the decision, since the draft of the letter of resignation, read before the Convention on January 23, is entirely in her hand, with only a few minor corrections by Roland himself.[22] In an autobiographical fragment, which was probably part of the *Memoirs* Roland planned but never managed to write, he tells us that if, among his Girondist friends, "a single man" had dared mount the speaker's platform of the Convention to challenge openly his accusers, he would have found the will and courage to "face the greatest storms." [23] But as it was, no one, not even Louvet, Barbaroux, or Buzot, had come to his rescue.

Roland had been defeated not so much by Robespierre, Danton, and Marat as by the ineffectiveness and apathy of the moderates and the sentimental desertion of his wife. But though he desperately yearned for retirement and the seclusion of Le Clos, he was not yet ready to abandon the capital to his triumphant enemies. His honor and good name had been impugned by the Jacobin press. With dogged obstinacy he pressed for an official examination of his record and financial accounts as a minister. This desire for public justification acquired in his mind the obsessive quality of an *idée fixe*; he clung to it like a drowning man, occupying his new-found leisure in the minute preparation of his report and of repeated petitions that his case be reviewed before the Convention. Only then would he feel free to seek forgetfulness and tranquillity amid the Beaujolais countryside. But repeatedly, the Convention, either too engrossed in urgent matters of national concern or under the influence of the Mountain, delayed undertaking the much sought investigation.[24]

Once more the Rolands took up residence in their third-floor apartment on the rue de la Harpe. Once more they found themselves cut off from the mainstream of political life, practically isolated in their simply furnished sitting room, where Manon, in the eerily quiet afternoons, resumed playing on her beloved pianoforte. With the exception of a few intimates, most friends had vanished into thin air since Roland's resignation; the risk of guilt by association was, after all, not to be taken lightly. The ex-Minister's papers were seized on March 31 and, from then on, every day grew more tense and alarming.[25] It is not too difficult to imagine the heavy silence that weighed on the Rolands as the winter changed into spring, flooding the sitting room with sunshine. Manon's heart, despite the somber circumstances, was filled with the joyous wonderment of love; having been relieved of political cares and responsibilities, she could now give herself over to the new feelings that it was no longer in her power to repress. As for Roland, racked by a helpless and mute rage, he paced the apartment restlessly or feverishly dashed off letters and justificatory statements. Since his administrative conduct and expenditures had been impeccable and every spent sou could be accounted for, he hoped to confound his enemies. After his eighth petition, however, he was no nearer a public hearing than after his first.[26] Instead, the Jacobins continued to proclaim him a traitor and to clamor for his head.

By the middle of May, Mme Roland, whose health was beginning to suffer from the effects of constant strain, suddenly decided to leave for Le Clos to recover. Roland would remain in Paris pending the clearing of his ministerial conduct. Manon therefore applied for the necessary passport, but had to wait until the last week of May before her request was granted.[27] Then, at the last moment, she was unable to leave: what was called a case of "colic," the result no doubt of nervous exhaustion, forced her to take to bed.[28] Perhaps she still could not bring herself to accept defeat and separation from Buzot and somehow expected a miraculous reversal of events. When, after a week, she had sufficiently recovered to get up, it was May 31, a historical date marked by the downfall of the Girondists.[29] It was too late to flee the city or even to leave it legally: the gates had been closed, several sections of Paris were up in arms, and riots were raging in the streets. The tocsin of the Hôtel de Ville was sounding a general alarm. Mme Roland had waited too long and had thereby forfeited her last chance of escape. Now her fate was in the hands of the Montagnards who, with surprisingly little resistance, were in the process of assuming full control of the government.

The publisher Panckoucke breathlessly ran over to the Rolands' flat to warn them of the danger.[30] Manon's blood boiled when she was told that the Parisians had passively accepted Jacobin rule through what amounted to a bloodless coup. It was agreed that Roland would sleep out that night since his arrest seemed imminent. And sure enough, shortly after five that afternoon six armed men came to the house. To Roland, who had not yet managed to leave, one of the men read an order of arrest issued by the Revolutionary Committee. "I know of no law," Roland remarked icily, "which has been granted the authority you mention, and I shall not comply with this order. If you use violence, I can only resist with the strength of a man of my advanced years, but I will protest till my last breath." [31] Before such determined resistance on the part of a once distinguished citizen, the captain hesitated to resort to force. He answered civilly: "I have no order to use violence, and I will convey your reply to the Council of the Commune, but I must leave my colleagues here with you." [32]

As Mme Roland stood by witnessing this scene, it suddenly occurred to her that she ought to take advantage of this delay to denounce her husband's arbitrary arrest to the Convention and present his case publicly. Behind this reasoning lurked the hope of another personal victory, such as the one that had marked her appearance at the bar of the Convention in December. To convey this project to Roland, pen a message to be presented to the President of the

Convention, throw a black shawl over her housedress, and hail a hackney coach was a matter of minutes. Her mind functioned more clearly now than it had for weeks; at long last she would confront her enemies face to face.[33]

When the coach approached the Carrousel, she noted that the courtyard was thronged with armed men and that every entrance to the building where the Convention met was shut and guarded. Alighting from the coach, she flew through the crowd and asked the sentinels to be admitted into the hall, but to no avail. She then hit upon a clever subterfuge. "Why, citizens," she shouted in the best *sans-culotte* tradition, "in this day of salvation for our motherland, in the midst of traitors from whom we have everything to fear, you don't know of what importance may be the notes I am supposed to transmit to the President!" [34] The doors opened at once, and she found herself in the President's antechamber. She asked for a messenger. After a quarter of an hour, she caught sight of one who knew her, but he showed no special willingness to help the wife of an ex-Minister now in disgrace. He nevertheless promised to take her letter to the President. An hour elapsed; she nervously paced to and fro, and every time the door of the main hall opened, she could hear the tumult that always accompanied a stormy session. The usher reappeared at last: "Well?" she eagerly inquired. "Nothing yet. There now prevails a confusion that is difficult to describe. Petitioners at the bar are asking for the arrest of the twenty-two Girondists." It dawned on her that, under such circumstances, she would not have her opportunity to address the Convention. Her last hope was dashed to the ground. As if thinking aloud, she said: "My letter will not be read." [35]

As a last resort Mme Roland asked to speak to Vergniaud, for whom she had little personal liking but whom she still trusted for his Girondist sympathies. Again she had to wait for what seemed an eternity. At last Vergniaud appeared and confirmed what she already knew too well. In its present frame of mind, the Convention would never listen to her; it was helpless against the riot: "The Convention can do everything," she cried out in an outburst of anguish and indignation, "Most Parisians only want to know how to act; if I am admitted, I shall dare to say what you cannot express without endangering yourself. As for me, I am not afraid of anything in the world, and if I don't succeed in saving Roland, at least I will have spoken some truths which will not be useless to the Republic. Why not warn your colleagues that a show of courage can produce a great effect and will at least serve as an inspiring example?" [36] She was in such a state of agitation that she trembled, but words came easily to her, and she spoke with force and clarity. "At any rate," replied Vergniaud, "Your letter cannot be read in this chaos. Besides, a motion of six articles is going to be discussed in the next two hours, and petitioners, delegated by different sections, are waiting to be heard." "I will go home, then, to see what has happened there, but will return later. Please warn your friends." "They are absent for the most part; when they are here, they show courage, but they lack assiduousness." "That, unfortunately, is only too true." [37]

Again she took a hackney carriage, but the streets were so crowded with battalions of national guards that the horses could not get through. She jumped from the coach and proceeded on foot. No one was in the apartment; from the concierge she learned that, the guards having left Roland momentarily alone, he had managed to escape through the back door of the building. Suddenly, Mme Roland felt faint; fatigue and shock had at last overcome her. Kindly neighbors brought some wine. As soon as she recovered, she hurried to Bosc's flat, for it was located in the immediate vicinity and she hoped to find Roland there. Her supposition turned out to be correct. Hurriedly the couple talked over the situation and mapped a plan of action. The ex-Minister was bent on making his escape from the capital.[38] Manon, for her part, while approving this decision where her husband was concerned, refused to follow him and clung to her original plan of returning to the Convention to denounce the illegality of his arrest. There was no way of dissuading her from this idea, and Roland knew his wife's determined character too well to insist. Sadly, with hardly a word, they separated. They were never to see each other again.

By the time Mme Roland once more hailed a cab, the streets were deserted and dark. Her body ached with exhaustion, but sheer will power sustained her—also the wild hope that her ringing denunciation would galvanize the sluggish Girondists and the wavering center party, the Plain. Little did she suspect that the Convention had been cowed without even a token resistance, that it had passively accepted the indictment of the twenty-two most prominent Girondist deputies, and that it had been encircled by armed men and cannons from the Commune. When she reached the Place du Carrousel, the large square was empty except for the guards posted at the doors of the Tuileries palace. When she asked to be admitted, she was told that the session had been adjourned. Her astonishment and disappointment knew no bounds.[39] On a day like this, when the tocsin kept ringing incessantly, filling the air with its ominous, monotonous sound, when forty thousand men surrounded the Convention, she had expected the deputies to sit in permanent session. It was hard to believe that such a distinguished body, representing as it did the whole of France, had so easily been subjugated by the Paris Commune.

One may well wonder why, fully aware that she was of the risks involved, Mme Roland then determined to return home rather than seek concealment in the house of a friend. As she herself explains in her *Memoirs,* she had a naturally strong aversion for anything inconsistent with a straightforward course of action. To escape from injustice would have cost her greater effort than to face it squarely. Only recently, this same need to bring matters out into the open had led her to sacrifice her personal happiness. The rest seemed indeed insignificant in comparison with that initial, painful decision.

It was about midnight when she sat down at her desk to write some messages to Girondist friends. She was interrupted by the noisy irruption of a deputation from the Commune demanding to see Roland. "He is not at home," she coolly replied. "But where can he be?" asked a man in an officer's uniform. "Surely you must know his habits and can tell us when he will be back." "I don't know, and moreover nothing obliges me to answer you. Roland left while

I was at the Convention. . . . I have nothing more to say." [40] The soldiers withdrew, but a guard was left at the door of her room and one at the entrance of the house. Mme Roland had some supper brought to her, finished her letters, entrusted them to her maid Fleury, and calmly went to bed. She had been asleep for about an hour when Fleury burst into her room to inform her tearfully that "gentlemen of the Section" wished to see her. Having dressed, she went into the sitting room and there heard the expected words: "We came, Citizeness, to take you into custody and to put seals on your property." "Where is your warrant?" An order of arrest from the Revolutionary Committee of the Commune was presented, but did not specify an indictment. She was to be taken to the Abbaye prison "for questioning." [41]

For a moment she debated in her mind whether she ought to denounce, as Roland had done on the previous afternoon, the illegality of these proceedings: "I could tell you," she said, "that I know nothing of your Committee, that I will not obey its orders and that you will take me from here only by force." [42] A slight but hard-featured man, however, proceeded to read aloud a paper issued by the Council of the Commune directing the arrest of both Roland and his wife, but again without stating any charge. Nocturnal arrests had been forbidden by decree on September 20 of the previous year; the lack of any specific accusation was also irregular; and so was the authorization of the Paris municipality to seize suspects in its own name. By now, however, such legal safeguards had become meaningless. To offer resistance would have been both futile and undignified. Mme Roland therefore packed a few things while the soldiers affixed seals on every piece of furniture, including the piano-forte. By the time all formalities were completed it was seven in the morning. A new day, June 1, had begun. Going to the window for a breath of fresh air, Manon caught sight of a few passers-by hurrying to work. Everything in the quiet rue de la Harpe seemed perfectly normal and ordinary as housewives and shopkeepers prepared for another day. Mme Roland's world was coming to an end amidst what appeared to her as universal indifference.

Two rows of armed men lined the hallway, and a carriage was waiting across the street. As Mme Roland emerged from the house, a few curious bystanders assembled, and one or two women shouted: "To the guillotine!" [43] Slowly the carriage proceeded to the nearby Abbaye prison, followed by the soldiers. One of the commissioners gallantly suggested that the curtains be drawn so as to insure the prisoner some privacy. To this she retorted that innocence feared the eyes of no one. "You show more strength of character than many a man in the hands of justice," was the compliment the officer paid her. "Justice!" she could not help exclaiming. "If such a thing existed today, I would not be here." [44]

It was but a short ride from the rue de la Harpe to the gloomy prison, which had witnessed some horrifying scenes during the September massacres. The carriage and its escort rattled past the gates into the cobbled outer yard. Mme Roland was made to climb a slimy, narrow staircase and led into a tiny, dark cell. The door was closed and bolted behind her. The prisoner sat down and collected her thoughts: reviewing the events of the past, she drew from her inmost being the strength to defy the rigors of a portentous future. If her mood during these first moments of imprisonment was solemn, it was by no means, as she proudly reports in her *Memoirs*, somber: "I resolutely dedicated myself to my destiny, whatever it might be." [45]

SIXTEEN

Victory in Defeat

IN THE SPRING OF 1793 one could still entertain optimistic expectations about a trial conducted by the Revolutionary Tribunal. After all, so far only confirmed enemies of the Revolution had been guillotined; condemnations and executions on a large scale and terrorist measures had not yet gone into effect. At the time of her arrest, therefore, Mme Roland could well hope that a public trial would clear the Girondists and herself of the charge of conspiracy. To be sure, she no longer expected clemency on the part of Robespierre and the other leaders of the Mountain, but she counted on the weight of public opinion and especially on the resistance of the provinces against the supremacy of the Paris Commune. Since her incarceration, she more and more staked her hopes on a general uprising against the capital: in the letters she managed to smuggle out of her cell, she repeatedly referred to what was becoming a fervent wish. In this sense, at least, Mme Roland was indeed conspiring against the Revolution, as her enemies were accusing her of doing, for a general uprising of that nature would have spelled the end of everything that had been accomplished since 1789. The ensuing disorder and violence would have permitted counterrevolutionaries, backed by the European powers, to reestablish the Old Régime. But caught as she was in a cruel death struggle, the prisoner saw no other way of vindicating her persecuted friends and overthrowing Robespierre and the Mountain. Indeed, to her present state of mind the tyranny of the Commune was a hundred times more oppressive than absolute monarchy, for it operated under the pretense of democracy and republicanism and with far greater efficiency than the corrupt old order.

To her jailers and prison mates Mme Roland presented the serene face and unruffled demeanor of a worthy disciple of the ancient Stoics. But in her letters to Buzot she poured forth all the feelings of a passionate, romantic nature. To her persecutors she penned defiant, proud messages; to Buzot she wrote in the simple, yet elevated and deeply touching language of all star-crossed lovers. Tender words of endearment and of concern for his safety were mingled with heartening expressions of encouragement and hope. It was on June 22, almost a month after Mme Roland's arrest, that the first two letters from Buzot, who had managed to escape to Caen, in the Calvados region, were secretly brought to her by a courageous visitor.[1] She immediately dashed off a reply:

How often I read those dear letters over and over again! I press them to my heart, I cover them with kisses; I had lost all hope of hearing from you! . . . The mail is unsafe; I did not want to address anything to you through official channels, for I was certain that your name would cause the letter to be intercepted and that this would endanger you. I was proud and calm when I came here, forming wishes and still retaining some hope for the defenders of Liberty. When I learned that a decree of arrest had been made against the Twenty-Two, I cried out "My country is lost!" I was torn by the most cruel anguish until I received the comforting news of your escape. My fears were renewed by the decree of accusation that concerns you. Indeed they owed this affront to your courage! But as soon as I heard that you were in the Calvados, I recovered my peace of mind. Persist, my friend, in your efforts; on the fields of Philippi, Brutus despaired too soon of the salvation of Rome. As long as a republican draws breath, as long as he is free, let him retain his energy, he must, he can be useful. In any case, the South offers you a refuge; it will become the haven of people of good will. It is there that you must turn your gaze and direct your steps if you find that perils surround you; it is there that you must go on living, for there you will find your peers and practice your high virtues.

As for me, I know how to await peacefully the return of the reign of justice, or endure the excesses of tyranny in such a way as not to make my example useless. If I had any fear, it was that you might do something rash for my sake.[2]

She then went on to give a reassuring picture of her living conditions and of the little privileges humane guardians accorded her secretly. And Buzot having evidently urged her to try and make her escape with the help of one of her visitors, she gently but firmly turned down this suggestion. She did not wish to gain her freedom at the expense of someone else's safety; neither would she repay the kindness and trust of her guards with an act that might endanger their positions and even their lives. And finally, strange as it might seem, prison life was far from intolerable for her. She had had some of her favorite authors, Tacitus, Plutarch, Shaftesbury, and Thomson, brought to her cell, and they kept her good company:

I lead here the life I led in my study at home, in the ministry or elsewhere; there is no great difference. I would even have sent for an instrument had I not had misgivings about the ensuing hue and cry. My room is about ten feet square. Here, behind bars and bolted doors, I enjoy the freedom of my thoughts, I summon objects that are dear to me, and I am at greater peace with my conscience than my oppressors are with their power.[3]

She also informed Buzot of Eudora's stay with the kindly family of the Deputy Creuzé-Latouche and of Roland's escape to Rouen, where friends from his days as a young administrator had offered him a safe shelter. Her faithful maid Fleury, she added, was even allowed by the guards to visit her now and then and bring her things she needed:

I dare not tell you, and you are the only one in the world who could understand this, I was not greatly distressed at being arrested. They will be less angered and vengeful against R. [Roland], I said to myself. If they attempt some sort of trial, I shall be able to defend him in a manner that will enhance his reputation. I thus shall be able to acquit myself of a debt I owed him for his sorrows. Don't you see that by being alone, it is with you that I remain? It is through captivity that I sacrifice myself for my husband and keep myself for my friend, and it is to my persecutors that I am indebted for this reconciliation of duty and love; don't pity me! Others may admire my courage, they don't know my joys; you who must share them, preserve all their wonder by the constancy of your valor.[4]

In another letter to Buzot she alluded to the various plans contrived by him and Roland in order to save her. She rejected them all, not because of the multiple difficulties and dangers they presented, but because freedom would mean not happiness but exposing friends "in order to exchange chains that honor . . . for others that no one can see." [5] In plainer words, her present captivity was more bearable than life with a husband she no longer loved but from whom moral principles forbade her to break free. She also inquired about Louvet, Barbaroux, and Pétion, whom she knew to be with Buzot. Remembering the incurable optimism and lightheartedness of her friends, she surmised that Louvet was probably helpless far from Lodoïska, his beloved mistress; and Barbaroux was no doubt up to his old tricks with the hospitable ladies; as for Pétion, his natural serenity and indolence must have got the better of him by now: "I fear," she sadly concluded, "that these good people, now as before, spend their time dreaming about the public weal instead of setting themselves to the task of bringing it about." [6]

In all, there are five extant letters to Buzot that date from Mme Roland's captivity, and these did not see the light of day until 1864.[7] During the intervening decades, Mme Roland's secret lay buried with her. In November of 1863, an unidentified young man appeared in one of the bookstores lining the Quai Voltaire in Paris, bearing a package of manuscripts, among which were the *Memoirs* of Buzot, Louvet, Pétion, and observations by Barbaroux. Also included were the five love letters from Mme Roland to Buzot. The bookseller, who had an interest in the Revolutionary period, happens to have been Noël France (he had changed his name from François-Noël Thibault), the father of the writer Anatole France. Noël France purchased the lot and brought out a catalog of these papers.[8] When the famous heroine's letters were published in 1864, they caused something of a sensation. What had long been suspected, that Mme Roland had known a belated but passionate love, was at last confirmed by this extraordinary find. How these manuscripts escaped destruction and, after seventy years, found their way into the hands of the unknown young man will probably remain an unsolved mystery.[9]

By sacrificing her happiness, perhaps even her life, after placing her child in trusted hands, Mme Roland had fulfilled her obligations toward Roland and earned the right to give full play to her personal sentiments. To be sure, there were moments when the prisoner was unable to resist despair, when the walls of her cell seemed to converge upon her, and when the thought of the precarious position of all those dear to her filled her being with throbbing anxiety and an unbearable sense of helplessness. To others, however, she invariably presented a smiling, undisturbed countenance, though swollen, red eyes sometimes betrayed the inner battles that had to be sustained in order to achieve this remarkable equilibrium.[10] To keep her mind occupied and to ward off the torment of worry and incertitude, she determined to take up the pen again. In addition to a steady flow of letters and messages to friends and foes, she began working on her *Memoirs,* for it had occurred to her that the experience of one individual can have universal meaning and, if recounted with fearless sincerity, can contribute to a better understanding of the complex workings of the human heart. For a disciple of Montaigne and Rousseau, such reasoning, especially when prompted by the awareness of impending danger and peril, was a most natural thing.

Until now she had steadfastly refused to publish or even to sign her writings. The imminence of death, however, made her look forward to future generations and their corrective judgment. By presenting a boldly truthful picture of herself, she would defy the injustices and injuries she was made to suffer and would continue to live on in the memory of men and women yet to be born. Fortified by this conviction, she resolutely entitled her autobiography *Appeal to Impartial Posterity,* thereby asserting her faith in human history. Looking back on her life and on the extraordinary events that had so unexpectedly propelled her from obscurity, she found consolation and reassurance in her long held belief that individual destinies, despite the baffling contradictions and vagaries of circumstance, are ordained by a divine Providence and that the practice of high virtues is rewarded by immortality of the soul as well as by the grateful remembrance of mankind.

The riches of her stored-up memories made her relive, as in a trance, her studious, introspective adolescence and her years as a dutiful young wife. She became oblivious to her somber surroundings, to the nightmarish sights and sounds that encircled her within the prison walls, and as her pen raced across the pages, filling them with her regular, elegant handwriting, she gained confidence in her talent as a writer. Her spirits soared, and it is in a cheerful, humorous mood that she recounted many an incident that had marked her youth. "If I had been allowed to live," she confidently declared in the midst of her reminiscences, "it seems to me that I would then have had but one ambition: to record the annals of my age." [11] But time was growing short; she could not dwell on the Revolution and its protagonists, but had to content herself with fairly rapid sketches so as to be able to tell in vivid detail what she knew best: the story of her own life, from those far-off years in her father's modest engraver's shop to the brief but event-packed months in the stately, luxurious suites of the mansion she had occupied as the wife of the Minister of the Interior.

She was too profoundly committed to a political party, too passionately engaged in self-justification to make any pretense at objectivity and detachment. Yet her sharp critical faculties and devotion to truth would not permit her to conceal or dissemble for the sake of embellishment. Besides, candor and straightforwardness had been among the qualities she had most admired in the *Essais* of Montaigne and *Confessions* of Rousseau. She would prove a worthy disciple. That, as a woman, she might be less free to tell all did not deter her from revealing her inmost self. As a result, her blunt outspokenness, even on matters of a private nature, shocked some of her nineteenth-century admirers, particularly the French critic Sainte-Beuve, who could not help finding some of her revelations unladylike.[12] Today, however, Mme Roland's candid reflections on sex and marriage appear most innocuous in comparison with the unrestraint of much of the confessional literature made in part possible by the huge success of Rousseau's own autobiography. Neither could Mme Roland bring herself, for the sake of friendship or party loyalty, to minimize the errors and weaknesses of her Girondist friends. But if her frank appraisals at times lack charity, they invariably bear the stamp of a luminous, penetrating intelligence. As for her style, it had by now attained its greatest force and maturity: in turn elevated, realistic, intimate, or lyrical, it enriches the narrative with an unusual range in moods and a gallery of memorable character sketches of men both famous and unknown.

It was Mme Roland's belief, as it had been Rousseau's before her, that the essential clue to self-knowledge lies in the child within the adult. It was Jean-Jacques who prevailed upon her to unlock the door to the inner recesses of her subconscious by moving back in time to that last recapturable moment of her past, to those outwardly unimportant yet deeply portentous experiences that stamped an indelible mark on her personality. It is true that she cannot always resist the temptation of dwelling, with a certain narcissistic complacency, on her own abilities and accomplishments. But this she does with such ingenuousness that we easily forgive an occasional touch of vanity and sidelong glance in the mirror. For it is precisely this healthy egotism, this belief in the dignity and worth of the self, that kept Mme Roland from maudlin self-pity or hopelessness. At the same time, her compulsion to tell all is less morose than that of her master. When speaking of her childhood and adolescence in particular, she surrenders to moods of engaging humor and gaiety. It is only when approaching the more recent events that she assumes a sober, solemn style, for here she had an urgent message to convey, a warning against political fanaticism to the coming generations. Hers, to be sure, is a simpler nature than Rousseau's, and her autobiography does not reveal those unexpected, puzzling twists of character, those sudden, inexplicable acts which have baffled and touched many a reader of the *Confessions*. Less tortured, also less complex and profound a soul than the Citizen of Geneva, she nevertheless evidences a vast gamut of feeling and thought.

When she was not absorbed by her self-imposed tasks, Mme Roland took a lively interest in her co-inmates, generously sharing her supplementary ration with less fortunate prisoners, heartening those whose courage threatened to break under the strain, noting in her letters many an incident with pointed wit, and observing the goings-on with compassion and amusement. Not only her mind and sensibilities, but her whole being was now sharpened into a higher state of awareness and nervous concentration. Even her passion for Buzot underwent a notable change: it lost all character of frustrated exacerbation and was sublimated into a joyful acceptance of the inevitable, into a sentiment that reached beyond all hope of earthly happiness.

On the twelfth of June, she was finally summoned by two police commissioners for interrogation.[13] Among the many loaded questions put to her, she was asked whether she knew of the difficulties that had beset the Republic from the moment Roland had been appointed Minister of the Interior, and whether she was aware of a plan to arouse the provincial departments against the authority of Paris. To this she countered that as a woman she could hardly take any part in political affairs and that her only knowledge of events was through the newspapers. This, of course, was a not altogether truthful reply, and when the examiners pursued the point and insisted that she must have had more information than the average person, she observed that a woman is not expected to make special inquiries into matters that do not concern her sex. When urged to furnish names of Roland's old friends and political associates, she continued to remain evasive, declaring that her husband received a great number of men whom it would be impossible to enumerate. The interrogation turned to Roland's use of public funds for the subversion of the provinces against the capital. Such an accusation, she firmly countered, was groundless in view of the ex-Minister's well-known integrity. She added that the funds allocated to Roland for publications deemed useful to the Republic had been used most sparingly and had all been accounted for in his detailed and complete statements of expenditures. Pressed to give her opinion of the publications approved, she said that they were available for anyone to read and that it was up to the French people, for whom they had been destined, and not to her, a mere woman, to pass judgment on them. Finally, when her interrogators demanded to know Roland's present whereabouts, she replied, as one might well expect, that she neither could nor indeed would say where he had gone after leaving Paris. When roughly admonished and reminded that it was her duty to render a truthful account to justice, she responded that an accused person owes an account of himself, not of others and that, moreover, no human law obligated her to betray, in the name of justice, the most basic sentiments dictated by nature. It is obvious, from the report that has come down to us, that Mme Roland's examiners got nowhere with her and that she parried with superb self-control all their leading questions. She could congratulate herself for not having compromised any of her friends and for having shown herself worthy of their trust.

Actually, the allegations against Mme Roland amounted to little more than guilt by association and conspiracy. Since no tangible evidence of treason could be presented, her condemnation rested mainly on her activities as the wife of an ex-Minister now in proscription. Once more Jacobin newspapers were filled with oft-repeated and grossly vicious charges against her. This constituted an obvious effort to appeal to public opinion. Day after day, the sheets echoed with more strident reports of the "orgies" over which she had presided. Even in her cell she was not spared the inflammatory denunciations, for newspapers secretly reached her there and, on at least one occasion, an incensed group of Parisians gathered outside the prison shouting threats and insults.[14] With the exception of occasional visits from Sophie Grandchamp, Bosc, and Champagneux, Mme Roland was left alone with her thoughts. While continuing her *Memoirs,* she now worked on the preparation of her defense before the Revolutionary Tribunal, for she had determined to be her own advocate, and she braced herself for this supreme test of verbal skill and self-possession.

"Never but for this experience would I have thought so poorly of my species," [15] she confided in one of her darker moments. The arrest or proscription of those attractive, idealistic young men who had dedicated themselves to the betterment of the French people also evoked unhappy reflections: "O Brutus! you whose daring hand vainly freed the corrupt Romans, we have erred like you. These pure men, whose ardent souls aspired for liberty, whom philosophy had prepared for it in the calm of the study and the austerity of seclusion, these men who flattered themselves, as you did, that the overthrow of tyranny would forthwith usher in the reign of justice and peace, have been deluded; it has been the signal only for releasing the most hateful passions and most hideous vices. . . . Thus I grew indignant in the depths of my prison; but the hour of indignation is past, for it is evident that we should no longer expect anything good or be astonished at anything evil." [16] When moved by passion or self-righteous anger, Mme Roland, like her enemy Robespierre, naturally turned to figures of Roman history and used the same rhetorical devices in order to castigate the corruption and cruelty of those she looked upon as the foes of the Revolution.

On June 24, exactly twenty-four days after her imprisonment, Mme Roland was told that an official wished to speak to her. In the waiting-room a man was walking to and fro while another sat writing. Neither took notice of her arrival. After a prolonged silence, she was abruptly informed that she was free to leave the prison. Astonished, she returned to her cell, quickly packed her things, said good-by to a few co-inmates she had befriended, walked down the narrow, winding staircase and into the street. In the carriage taking her to the rue de la Harpe, she finally began realizing what had happened to her. Joyously she jumped from the coach and entered the house. She had hardly reached the staircase when two men (who had actually been shadowing her) called out from behind: "Citizeness Roland!—In the name of the law, we arrest you!" [17]

The release had been but a formality to legalize her first detention which, having been ordered by the Commune, was irregular. This time, the arrest could not be deemed unsound, for it emanated from the Committee of Public Safety. Her crime against the state was now specified: it consisted of alleged conspiracy against the Revolution and complicity with her husband and other Girondists. As Mme Roland was being led to another prison, Sainte-Pélagie, unbeknown to her, Brissot, who had just been seized outside Paris, was being brought to the Abbaye, to the very cell she had left barely an hour earlier. Less than three weeks later, the same cell, which was too small to accommodate more than a single prisoner, was to be occupied by Charlotte Corday, the young girl from Caen who assassinated Marat in his bath and who, ironically, contributed by this deed to the demise of her heroes the Girondists.[18]

To be so near freedom, only to find herself confined once again, was almost more than even the stout-hearted Manon could bear. She felt dangerously close to panic and hysteria. Once more, however, pride came to the rescue. No, she would not allow her enemies the satisfaction of breaking her spirit. She resumed rereading her favorite authors and working on her autobiography. Her transfer, however, had far from improved her lot. If the Abbaye had been no paradise, Sainte-Pélagie could give a closer idea of hell. The July heat beat mercilessly on her tiny cell. Narrow corridors and thin plaster partitions, moreover, magnified every sound, and prostitutes, murderesses, and female thieves were her immediate neighbors.[19] Next door, in a spacious cell, a group of actresses of the Comédie Française, who had been arrested because some "antipatriotic" manifestation had taken place in the audience during a performance, were having a gay time. Everything was done to make their stay in prison as pleasant as possible; they were dined and wined by the officer in charge, and shrill laughter at spicy jokes reached Mme Roland as she sat writing.[20] Neither could she avoid witnessing scenes of coarse vulgarity as the women prisoners flirted with the opposite sex through the grated windows facing the men's wing of the prison.

By an ironical coincidence, however, the director of Sainte-Pélagie, a kind-hearted man by the name of Grandpré, had been appointed by Roland himself.[21] Taking a special interest in his famous prisoner, he managed to grant her various privileges, including unlimited visits from friends. Bosc brought her flowers from the *Jardin des Plantes*, Champagneux encouraged her to continue her *Memoirs* until his own arrest deprived her of a faithful friend, and the vivacious Sophie Grandchamp tried her best to amuse her with anecdotes and gossip.[22]

Even Sister Saint-Agatha, from the now disbanded Convent of the Congregation where Mme Roland had spent a year as a young girl, paid her a few visits.[23] Still another visitor was Helena-Maria Williams, the Englishwoman befriended by Bancal, who in her own *Memoirs* covering her activities in Revolutionary France speaks with affectionate admiration of Mme Roland during her imprisonment. Her testimony, although perhaps favorably biased, is worth quoting:

Mme Roland was indeed possessed of the most distinguished talents, and a mind highly cultivated by the study of literature. I had been acquainted with her since I first came to France, and had always observed in her conversation the most ardent attachment to liberty, and the most enlarged sentiments of philanthropy: sentiments which she developed with an eloquence peculiar to herself, with a flow in power of expression which gave new graces and new energy to the French language. With these extraordinary endowments of mind she united all the warmth of a feeling heart, and all the charms of the most elegant manners. She was tall and well shaped, her air was dignified, and although more than thirty five years of age she was still handsome. Her countenance had an expression of uncommon sweetness, and her full dark eyes beamed with the brightest rays of intelligence. I visited her in the prison of St. Pélagie, where her soul, superior to circumstances, retained its accustomed serenity, and she conversed with the same animated cheerfulness in her little cell as she used to do in the hotel of the minister. She had provided herself with a few books, and I found her reading Plutarch. She told me she expected to die; and the look of placid resignation with which she spoke of it, convinced me that she was prepared to meet death with a firmness worthy of her exalted character. When I enquired after her daughter, an only child of thirteen years of age, she burst into tears; and at the overwhelming recollection of her husband and her child, the courage of the victim of liberty was lost in the feelings of the wife and the mother.[24]

In her first days of captivity at Sainte-Pélagie, Manon also received the visit of her girlhood friend from Amiens, Henriette, the elder of the Cannet sisters. Henriette, now a widow, had come expressly to Paris to see Mme Roland and to submit to her a plan she had hatched, perhaps at the instigation of anguished Roland. The two women would exchange their clothes, thereby permitting the prisoner to leave in the disguise of the visitor. Henriette's argument was that her own life was useless anyway, as she was a childless widow, while her friend still had important duties to fulfill. As can be expected, Manon would not hear of such a generous exchange. Entreaties, tears, nothing could change her mind: "But they would kill you, my dear Henriette," she patiently repeated, "your blood would fall back on me, and I would rather die a thousand deaths than be responsible for yours." [25]

The rumors from the outside world reaching Mme Roland quickly took a turn for the worse. The Girondists hidden in Normandy failed to rally the people behind their cause. Evreux was evacuated; Caen sheepishly abandoned the men to whom it had at first given refuge; Paris was totally subjugated. Charges of conspiracy with the royalist Vendée rebels and of federalism were leveled against the proscribed men. They were declared traitors to the country; their property was confiscated; their wives and children were taken into custody. Everywhere the party of the Mountain appeared triumphant. As a curtain of silence fell between Mme Roland and her proscribed friends, she increasingly thought of America as the last refuge of liberty.[26] In her fondest dreams she imagined Buzot safely reaching the shores of that distant but happy land. She urged Buzot, not knowing whether her message would ever reach him, to give up all thought of reversing the course of events and to concentrate all his efforts on making his way to the United States.[27]

It was in this frame of mind that, remembering her former esteem for Robespierre, she wrote him an ultimate appeal. A person with less pride might have attempted to mollify her persecutor by reminding him of the marks of friendship that she had so generously given him in the past and of her concern for his safety during the July 1791 repression, when she had rushed to his lodging to offer a safe shelter. She might also have drawn a heartrending picture of her present position. But, abstaining from all private considerations, she addressed Robespierre in the impersonal, austere manner of the Roman Stoics that both admired. To beg anyone for sympathy was not in Mme Roland's nature.

Robespierre, it is not to elicit your pity which is beneath me, and which would probably offend me, that I write you; it is for your enlightenment. Fortune is fickle, and so is popular favor: consider the fate of those who stirred the people, appealed to it or controlled it, from Viscellinus to Caesar, and from Hippo, the haranguer of Syracuse, to our Parisian orators. Justice and truth alone endure and console us in everything. . . . Marius and Sulla proscribed thousands of nobles, a great number of senators, countless unfortunates. Have they smothered history, which consigns their memory to execration, and have they tasted happiness? Whatever fate is reserved for me, I shall meet it in a worthy manner, or forestall it if necessary. . . . If you wish to be just and reflect on my words, my letter will not have been useless to you, and from that moment it will not have been useless to my country. In any case, Robespierre, I know this, and you cannot but know it too: whoever has been acquainted with me cannot persecute me without remorse.[28]

Upon second thought, however, Mme Roland decided not to forward her letter. Robespierre, she remembered only too vividly, was not a man to be swayed by personal appeals, no matter how dignified and eloquent. She therefore added this postscript at the bottom of the page:

The idea of this letter, the writing of it, and the project of sending it have occupied twenty-four hours; but what effect would my reflections have on a man who sacrifices colleagues whose innocence he knows well? The moment my letter serves no purpose, it is out of place; it would compromise me uselessly with a tyrant who can immolate me, but who cannot debase me.[29]

Before long she had occasion to congratulate herself for abstaining from sending her letter to Robespierre. The newspapers were filled with reports of his renewed attacks against the Girondists, and against Roland and Brissot in particular. Forgetting how quickly she had herself been ready to believe Danton personally implicated in the theft of the crown jewels, she was outraged that Robespierre should now insinuate that Roland had been responsible for the misdeed, and she interrupted her *Memoirs* to inject this bitter remark: "This Robespierre, whom I had at one time thought an honest man, what an atrocious being! How he lies to his conscience! And how he likes blood!"[30] In this belief, however, she was mistaken and simplifying Robespierre's motives. No one actually had a greater revulsion for bloodshed and physical violence than the scholarly ex-lawyer from Arras. But in his conviction that he had been entrusted with the sacred mission of carrying out Rousseau's bold political vision, that his own will coincided with that of the French people whom he was protecting from her enemies abroad and within, he was ready, like most puritanical reformers, to chastise the body that he might save the soul. That in the process he now called "enemies of the people" men and women with whom he had formerly associated did not appear to him as a personal betrayal. Of what significance for a man preoccupied with founding a republic and shaping "good patriots" was the freedom, even the life, of some individuals, compared with the future of a whole nation in the grips of an upheaval the like of which history had not yet witnessed?

July gave way to August, and outside the prison ordinary Frenchmen, despite the general uncertainty, went about their business. The theaters and cafés continued to be thronged; on Sundays, families followed the Parisian tradition of picnicking; young lovers slowly walked along the tree-shaded lanes of the public gardens or along the quays of the Seine. Some men became wealthy through the purchase of cheap national property, and resourceful manufacturers turned the Revolution to profit by selling cloth, hats, household objects, jewelry, and even playing cards decorated with patriotic emblems and inscriptions.

By the fall, Mme Roland had nearly completed her *Memoirs*. If she had, under the pressure of time, cut short some of the episodes of her life, she had nevertheless presented a vivid picture of her spiritual development, of those small yet significant events, known only to herself, which had marked her growth from childhood into young womanhood and which form the unique fabric of every human experience. Having put her affairs in order, she penned her last messages to her family and friends and even carefully pondered the advisability of committing suicide rather than waiting for an outcome that every day appeared more inevitable.[31] Buzot, whose

escape to America she had so devoutly wished, was now hiding in
the Gascony countryside and was being tracked so closely that arrest appeared imminent.[32] "As for me," she wrote, "everything is
finished. You know the malady the English call *heartbreak;* I am
hopelessly attacked by it, and I have no desire to delay its effects. . . .
I shall never recover my freedom; heaven be my witness that I would
devote it to my unfortunate husband! But I shall not have it and I
could expect worse. It is well examined, considered, and thought
out." [33]

On October 24, the trial of the Girondists began under the most
inauspicious circumstances. From the outset, the scales were heavily
weighted against the accused. Summoned as a witness, Mme Roland
changed her mind and decided that this was not the time to commit
suicide, since her testimony might be useful to her friends: "I shall
drink, since I must, the cup of bitterness to the dregs," she wrote
in a letter dated October 25.[34] Mme Roland waited in vain for endless hours; she was never called. Only hostile witnesses were finally
asked to testify, and the President of the Tribunal, as well as individual jurors, joined in the attack.[35]

Under the impact of this event, Mme Roland again turned her
thoughts to suicide. On October 27, she wrote to Bosc, asking for a
sufficient quantity of opium to cause death and setting forth her
reasons for this decision: "Consider my determination, weigh the
pros and cons, reason dispassionately, and you will realize how unworthy the *canaille* is of the spectacle on which it thrives." [36] In
her present frame of mind, she felt that to await the final *coup de
grâce* was less honorable than suicide, for it amounted to "exposing
oneself to the insolent clamors of insensitive crowds which are as
undeserving of such an example as incapable of drawing a lesson
from it." [37] Bosc, however, persuaded her to give up this resolve,
sorrowfully pointing out that she would better serve the cause of
freedom by bravely accepting martyrdom.[38] When, on October 30,
the Tribunal brought the trial against the Girondists to an abrupt
end by declaring them all guilty, Mme Roland calmly prepared for
a similar fate.

At a time of national crisis, when most Frenchmen were either Royalists or outright Jacobins, the cause of the Girondists was doomed to failure. Feared by the Royalists as dangerous radicals and called monarchists by the Paris Commune, those that had escaped arrest found support rapidly waning and few ready to face death to come to their aid. Even moderate republicans who bore a grudge against the overwhelming power of Paris and who, under normal circumstances, would have sympathized with the hounded young men, now rallied behind the existing government for the sake of national survival. France was too busy fighting counterrevolutionaries and repulsing a foreign invasion to be overly concerned with the tragic fate of the Girondists.

In her cell Mme Roland waited for her trial. Only the thought of Eudora could still arouse turbulent emotions that might threaten to disrupt her steadfastness. Learning that the child had been transferred, because of the danger involved, she anxiously asked Bosc: "My poor little one! Where is she? Please tell me, I beg of you; give me a few details, so that I can at least picture her surroundings with my mind's eye." [39] That her daughter had to conceal her identity like the offspring of criminals caused what probably was the cruelest blow to Mme Roland since her arrest. Upon finding out that the child had been placed in a boarding school run by a Mme Godefroid, she composed a letter to the schoolmistress filled with tender, maternal recommendations and pathetic expressions of gratitude.[40] Prudence dictated that a name that had by now become anathema not be affixed to the missive. So it is merely signed "Eudora's mother." It is the last letter from Mme Roland's pen that has come down to us.

Long ago, Rousseau had taught Mme Roland to believe implicitly, with her heart rather than her reason, in a benevolent Deity, in a personal Providence, and in the immortality of the individual soul. This faith now sustained her: "When I am separated from all I love, when all the evils of society strike us at once as though to punish us for having sought its betterment, I perceive beyond the boundaries of mortal life a reward for our sacrifices and a happy reunion with those dear to us. How? In what manner? I don't know; I only feel that it must be so." [41] Nearly thirty years earlier, Rousseau had proclaimed his own sentimental brand of deism in strikingly similar terms. Even Mme Roland's ultimate message to Buzot could well have been uttered by the heroine of *La Nouvelle Héloïse* as she lay on her deathbed. Julie had parted from her lover in a manner befitting one who had found her creed in the depths of her heart: "No, I am not leaving you; I shall await you. Virtue which separated us on earth will unite us in the eternal abode." [42] And the imprisoned wife of the ex-Minister, in all respects a faithful disciple of Rousseau, also repeated these words, no doubt unconsciously, in her own last reference to the man she had secretly yet so passionately loved: "And you whom I dare not name! You who will be better known one day when our common misfortunes will be pitied, you who respected the barriers of virtue in spite of an overpowering passion, will you grieve to see me precede to an abode where we shall be free to love each other, where nothing will prevent us from being united? . . . There I shall await you." [43] And she concluded her final instructions and recommendations with this thought: "Adieu. . . . No, from you alone I do not part; to leave this earth is to be near you." [44]

On October 31, the day on which the condemned Girondists were executed, Mme Roland was transferred to the Conciergerie prison, the third she had known since her arrest five months earlier. In this large, noisy, overcrowded prison, located on the banks of the Seine and with rooms dating back to the fourteenth century, men and women of all ranks and backgrounds had been thrown together and awaited trial. The Conciergerie, being part of the Palace of Justice, also housed the Revolutionary Tribunal.[45] Not far from Mme Roland's cell was the room that had just been occupied by her Girondist friends, as well as the one in which Marie-Antoinette had been detained. Most prisoners slept on foul straw, but a kindly soul provided Mme Roland with a cot.[46]

Even though her months of imprisonment had somewhat affected Manon's wholesome good looks, she continued to generate a magic that held the other prisoners spellbound. If she had lost some of her bloom and pleasing roundness, her features retained much of their customary animation. As Riouffe, a Girondist sympathizer who was at the Conciergerie at the time of Mme Roland's detention there, puts it in his *Memoirs of a Prisoner*: "Though past the prime of life, she was still a charming woman; she was tall and had an elegant figure. Her face was very expressive, but misfortunes and a long confinement had left on it traces of melancholy which tempered its natural vivacity. . . . Something more than what is generally found in the eyes of women shone in hers, which were large, black and full of softness and expression." [47] When she spoke of the Girondist deputies, Riouffe further reports, she did so with respect but without effeminate sentimentality and "even criticized them for not having adopted sufficiently strong measures." [48] The quality of her conversation in general struck him as being "serious without being cold, and she expressed herself with a purity, harmony, and cadence of which the ear could never tire." [49] Sometimes too her virile fortitude would give way to feminine tenderness. "It was easy to see that the recollection of her daughter and husband had made her shed tears," also noted Riouffe, and he marveled that an austere, "republican language" should issue forth from a charming woman "for whom the executioners were preparing the scaffold." For Mme Roland's fellow prisoners this "was one of the miracles of the Revolution" to which they had not yet grown accustomed.[50]

Count Beugnot, another prisoner who was to survive the storm and who at first viewed Mme Roland with a certain hostility, for he was of more conservative leanings than the Girondists and moreover had a natural aversion for intellectual, aggressive women, was also rapidly won over by her charm and dignity. "She did not have regularly beautiful features, but her face was very pleasant to look at," he writes in his *Memoirs*.[51] "She had a graceful figure and perfectly shaped hands. Her eyes were expressive, and even in repose her face had a noble, winning quality. One suspected that she possessed wit even before she began to speak, but no woman ever spoke with more purity, grace, and elegance. . . . To a musical voice she added gestures full of expressiveness and a glance that gained in animation as she spoke. . . . These rare gifts she combined with a wide knowledge of literature and political economy. Such was my impression of Mme Roland against whom I must admit that I had been prejudiced before knowing her." [52] Some of Mme Roland's opinions shocked Count Beugnot's royalist sympathies, as when reminded of Louis XVI's courageous death, she replied: "Very well, he was rather impressive on the scaffold, but he deserves no special credit for this; kings are trained for public performances since childhood." [53] The two prisoners had some heated political discussions, and Mme Roland defended her friends with her usual vigor and passion. Beugnot found her intolerant and unjust toward those who did not share her views, and he told her so. But despite his reservations about her political allegiances, Beugnot had only admiration for her personal qualities and was especially moved when she spoke of her family: "No one defined better than she the duties of a wife and mother and proved more eloquently that a woman knows happiness only in the accomplishment of these sacred duties. The picture of domestic life took on ravishing colors when she painted it; tears fell from her eyes whenever she mentioned her daughter and husband." [54] He further noted that she easily commanded respect from the other women prisoners, even from the coarsest streetwalkers: "As soon as she appeared in the courtyard, her presence immediately established order and good manners among these women." [55]

Twice before the trial Mme Roland underwent interrogation at the Conciergerie.[56] Both sessions, the first of which lasted three hours, duplicated the pattern of the examination held at the Abbaye prison. Lescot-Fleuriot, the substitute Public Prosecutor, directed the proceedings, which were transcribed by a clerk. Questions, Mme Roland was quick to notice, were worded in such a way as to make self-incrimination and implication of her friends almost inevitable. Her examiners were much harsher than at the Abbaye and, after a few evasive answers, they lost their temper and rudely instructed her to limit her replies to "yes" or "no" and not to attempt to show off her wit as though she were still in the ministerial mansion. Whenever she tried to elaborate on a point, she was abruptly interrupted. This was downright persecution, and she clearly sensed a determination to destroy her.[57]

Unfortunately for the accused, evidence of her secret correspondence from her prison cell with the proscribed Girondists in the Calvados had in the meantime been discovered. Lauze-Deperret, a deputy with Girondist sympathies who had served for a while as a go-between for Mme Roland and her friends, had been arrested on suspicion of conspiracy, and his papers, among which were incriminating letters from Mme Roland herself, had been seized. Deperret's arrest and his subsequent trial and execution along with the other prominent Girondists furnished Mme Roland's accusers with the only tangible material that could be used against her. These secret letters, although almost entirely personal in nature, gave the Mountain the evidence it sought. Now a relationship between Mme Roland and the anti-Parisian uprising that Buzot, Barbaroux, and Pétion were organizing in the provinces could be established and the prisoner's guilt proved. Especially humiliating to Mme Roland were those questions which insinuated that she had entertained intimate relations with some of her husband's friends.[58]

The trial before the Revolutionary Tribunal was set for November 8.[59] On that day, according to Count Beugnot and other eyewitnesses, she put on an English-style gown of white muslin held by a black velvet belt; her long hair flowed freely on her shoulders; her face struck everyone as more animated than usual, and a faint smile played on her lips. Beugnot was so moved that he rushed up to her. Remembering their political disagreements, she stopped, graciously pressed his hand and said: "Farewell, sir; let us make peace, it is time." Noticing that he was struggling to keep back his tears, she seemed touched, but said simply: "Courage." [60]

The Revolutionary Tribunal was one floor above the cells. The prisoners gained access to the courtroom through a series of narrow corridors and winding stairs. In the center of the hall stood a statue of Justice holding scales in one hand and a sword in another, with a book of laws by her side. Beneath the statue and at a long, draped table sat Dumas, the President, with the other four judges. Under them was the same man who had conducted Mme Roland's interrogations, Lescot-Fleuriot, substituting for Fouquier-Tinville, the Public Prosecutor whose bloody fame during the Terror would go down in history. The judges were dressed in black, and each wore a turned-up hat, *à la Henry IV,* adorned with three colored ostrich plumes, as well as a tricolored scarf with a large medal, sign of his position. To the right were the benches for the accused, as well as gendarmes with carbines and fixed bayonets at their sides. To the left was the jury, appointed by the Commune and obliged to express its opinion aloud and in public. The docile jurymen, numbering thirteen, sat in two rows between high windows. Clerks took notes at a side table; armed soldiers and pike bearers separated the public from the judges; a high balustrade also helped to keep the spectators in their place.

Just before the opening of the trial, Mme Roland appeared and walked over to the seat of the accused, guarded by a husky soldier with naked sword in hand. The witnesses were heard first. Beginning was Mlle Mignot, Eudora's former governess, who, despite evident efforts to please the court, could produce only vague and hearsay evidence as to the nature of the conversations that had taken place between her mistress and Roland's guests. She did manage, however, to produce the impression that an atmosphere of conspiracy had prevailed in the ministry and that news of provincial uprisings had been greeted joyfully. But she had to admit that she knew little of what was going on, since Roland and his wife never talked politics in her presence. Her testimony was of so little weight that Fouquier-Tinville, who despite his absence at the trial proper drew up the official indictment and act of condemnation, threw out the trivial charges made by the malevolent old spinster. Nevertheless, Mlle Mignot's accusations served the accusers' intention of picturing the Roland home as a hotbed of counterrevolutionary intrigue. The other members of the Roland household, however, Louis Lecocq, the butler, and Fleury, the cook and maid, remained faithful to their masters. They had to pay for their loyalty by being in turn accused of "complicity" with the Girondists, tried, and imprisoned for several months.[61]

Lescot-Fleuriot then read the official charges, which largely duplicated those leveled at Mme Roland during her interrogations: she was a schemer who had presided over many gatherings of the Girondist faction and who, even while in prison, had secretly corresponded with the proscribed men. It was now the turn of the accused to speak. This was the moment Mme Roland had been waiting for. Ever since her transfer to the Conciergerie, she had been working on her defense feverishly, drafting a text of the speech that would appeal to the conscience of jurymen and judges alike.[62] But no sooner had she begun to justify the Girondists and the Roland administration than she was abruptly interrupted by one of the judges, who sharply told her that she was abusing her right of defense by singing the praises of traitors condemned by law. Mme Roland protested and, turning toward the audience, exclaimed: "I ask you to bear witness to the injustice that is being done to me!" But the people, who had repeatedly been told by Marat and other journalists that this woman was another Marie-Antoinette, shouted her down with cries of "Long live the Republic! Down with the traitors!" [63]

The case was summed up by Dumas, one of the judges, and the jury promptly pronounced the accused guilty of being one of the accomplices, if not one of the authors, of a "horrible conspiracy against the unity and indivisibility of the Republic, and the liberty and safety of the French people." The penalty was confiscation of all property and death by the guillotine without appeal and within twenty-four hours. When told of this sentence and asked if she had anything further to say, she stated: "You judge me worthy of sharing the fate of the men you murdered. I shall try to mount the scaffold with the same courage they have shown." [64] The judgment was hardly pronounced when Fouquier-Tinville set the order of execution for the afternoon of the same day, November 8. As Mme Roland left the courtroom and walked down to the prison to have her last meal and go through the final preparations for the execution, she caught sight of fellow prisoners anxiously awaiting the outcome of the trial. Perhaps she felt something akin to a sense of relief, now that it was almost over, for Riouffe describes her as showing "a certain joyfulness in her swift steps; and as she crossed the wicket she made a playful gesture, pointing her thumb downward, to signify that she was doomed." [65]

Outside, in the prison courtyard the tumbril was already waiting for her and for a man also condemned to the guillotine; his name was Lamarche, and he had been convicted for forging and selling *assignats,* the paper money put out by the revolutionary government. Having no high ideal to sustain him, Lamarche was a broken, terror-stricken wretch. Noting this, Mme Roland expressed the wish to share her lunch with him, and she managed to make him eat and even smile once or twice with her witticisms. We owe vivid and detailed accounts of Mme Roland's last hours to her friend Sophie Grandchamp, who gleaned them from Grandpré, the prison official who had taken a special interest in the prisoner, as well as to other inmates, such as Beugnot and Riouffe, who recorded their firsthand observations in their respective *Memoirs.*[66]

After the lunch, Mme Roland was led into a small, windowless room where her hair was cut short and her hands were tied behind her back. When Lamarche emerged with his own hair shorn, she quipped: "It suits you admirably. You now have the head of an ancient Roman." [67] The prisoners were led to the yard called *Cour de Mai,* where the cart had been halted. Sanson, the head executioner, was there in person, going over the list of condemned drawn up by the Revolutionary Tribunal. A crowd of people, hostile or merely inquisitive, waited to see the day's batch. The appearance of a woman, only yesterday so influential, aroused some curiosity. A hush fell, soon broken, however, by cries of "Down with the traitors!" and "Long live the Republic!" When the distraught Lamarche stepped in front of Mme Roland in order to get into the tumbril, she gently chided him: "You are not gallant, Lamarche. A Frenchman should never forget what is due a woman." [68]

It was one of those bleak, wintry November afternoons, when the air chills the body, penetrating the spirit, and when dusk comes early. The trees were barren of leaves and the people of Paris, preoccupied with the urgent business of finding fuel and nourishment for the harsh months ahead, paid scarce attention to the tumbril and its accompanying detail of mounted gendarmes and pike bearers of the Commune slowly proceeding to the Place de la Révolution (now Place de la Concorde). There were, to be sure, the usual clusters of curious or indifferent onlookers. On the whole, however, the public had had its fill of sensational trials and public executions: Louis XVI, Marie-Antoinette, Charlotte Corday, General Custine, the Duke of Orléans and, only a few days earlier, the Girondist leaders, not to mention numerous lesser counterrevolutionaries, spies, and ordinary common-law criminals or mere suspects. That Mme Roland, the brilliant friend of the Girondists, should have to face the guillotine together with an embezzler only served to confuse public opinion. Executions had become an everyday occurrence, and the sensibilities of the people, like the wind-swept gardens of Paris in this late autumn season, had withered. The great wave of enthusiasm and hope that had swept over the nation had slowly receded, giving way to a harsh struggle for survival. There was no room left for exalted, generous sentiments; only for unwholesome curiosity and morbid thrills. Like nature, the Revolution was on the threshold of its winter.

As the procession reached the corner of the Pont-Neuf, Sophie Grandchamp strained to see her friend, for she had made a solemn promise to be at that spot. Finally she caught sight of Mme Roland: the short brown locks which had just been cut flicked about her forehead; her cheeks were flushed from the sharp wind; and she stood erect, despite the jerky motions of the heavy, springless tumbril and her arms pinned behind her back. Mme Grandchamp later recorded every detail of this final encounter: "She was fresh, calm, smiling," she writes. "Near the bridge she looked for me, and I read in her eyes the pleasure she felt at seeing me at this ultimate rendez-vous. When she passed before me, a movement of her eyes and a smile told me that she was glad to have her wish fulfilled. I controlled myself a few moments longer, but as soon as she was out of sight, I felt exhausted by the effort I had made to constrain myself, my head spun; I don't know what happened to me or how I reached my house." [69]

At the familiar sight of the Pont-Neuf and quays which had witnessed her youthful years, shadows and faces from the past, now vanished forever, must have flashed across Mme Roland's inner vision. Or perhaps she was so intent on playing her last and most demanding role with appropriate dignity that she concentrated all her will on the present, casting off any disquieting remembrance that might shake her resolve to die well. Whether, as the tumbril passed the house that had sheltered her girlish dreams and thoughts, tender and nostalgic memories surged through her mind, her appearance never betrayed it, for all eyewitness accounts underscore her imperturbable calm and the enigmatic smile that played on her lips. Having crossed the Pont-Neuf, the cart moved through the center of the capital, along the rue Saint-Honoré, past the Palais-Royal, to the west end of the Tuileries Gardens. At last the Place de la Révolution came into view. And there it loomed against a leaden sky, a tall, sharp silhouette with the blade high up, poised for action. Dusk was beginning to invade the great square, for it was after five and the days were growing short. A cordon of soldiers formed a ring around the scaffold, and the habitués, including the shrewish *tricoteuses* as well as more elegant spectators who came as they would to a play, were at their usual posts. There were also the familiar newspaper vendors and sellers of cakes and lemonade.

Beyond the instrument of death the naked trees of the Tuileries Gardens were visible. When the tumbril reached the foot of the guillotine, Mme Roland's companion, Lamarche, showed every sign of losing his composure. Noting this, Manon asked Sanson, the executioner, to shorten the poor fellow's misery by letting him go first and sparing him the sight of her own death. French etiquette, she was told, specified that ladies, in this as in other ceremonies, be given precedence. Besides, Sanson had his orders: her name was first on the order of execution. "Monsieur," she insisted with a smile, "can you refuse a lady's last request?" Sanson reluctantly gave in.[70]

When it was her turn to mount the short ladder leading to the platform, Mme Roland embraced in a glance the wide expanse of darkening sky above the crowded square and then fastened upon the statue of Liberty, a clay figure of heroic proportions designed by the painter David and erected to celebrate the first anniversary of August 10. At that moment she uttered the words that have been immortalized by history: "O Liberty, what crimes are committed in thy name!" [71] A few seconds later, she was strapped to the plank, and the relentless blade slid down with a steely crash. Manon Roland was no more.

SEVENTEEN

The Aftermath

ON JUNE 2, 1793, WHILE AN ARMY of eighty thousand blocked the approaches to the Convention and patrols searched for suspects from street to street, Roland, with the help of the ever faithful Bosc, had succeeded in passing the city barriers. He eventually found his way to Rouen, where the Malortie sisters, who had known him as a young apprentice inspector, offered him a safe refuge. There he languished, consumed by helpless rage, until the news of his wife's execution reached him November 10. On the evening of that day, he had a long talk with the two elderly women who had so generously sheltered him. They could not convince him that life was preferable to death. As night fell, Roland sat down, wrote for a few minutes, and, after slipping several sheets into his pocket, departed without a word. As a walking stick he used a cane, given him by Bosc, which, when pressed upon a hidden spring, released a dagger's blade.

Around ten at night, Roland reached the small town of Lande, about three good miles from Rouen. He went beyond the town, passed the adjoining village of Mesnil-Raoul, and, stumbling through the wind-swept and deserted country roads, reached a lane bordered with bushes. It led to one of those provincial residences somewhat pretentiously called châteaux in France, in this case the Château de Cocquetot. It is in this forlorn place that Roland chose to die. His body was discovered by a passer-by on the next day. He had stabbed himself with Bosc's cane, and two messages were found. One bore these words: "Whoever you may be who will find me lying here, respect my remains; they are those of a man who died as he had lived, in honesty and virtue. May my country at last abhor so many crimes and return to more humane and social sentiments. J.–M. Roland." The other paper was more personal: "Not out of fear but out of indignation . . . I left my refuge as soon as I learned that they had murdered my wife; I no longer wish to remain on an earth so covered with crimes." [1]

It is in this pathetic end that the priggish and pedantic figure of Roland acquires a noble, tragic dimension and summons our compassion and sympathy. During his lifetime, he had been thrust almost unwillingly into events, with which he tried, in his earnest, conscientious way, to cope as best he could. But the Revolution required more than honest, well-intentioned administrators who expended their energy in drawing up reports and accounts. It demanded men of genius and daring who could act with decision and swiftness. Roland had been too set in his ways, too rigid and narrow-minded to oppose effectively adversaries of the caliber of Robespierre and Danton. His own personal desire had been for retirement and for the tranquillity of remote, secluded Le Clos. Yet, faced by a task beyond his scope and years, he bravely persisted in his increasingly futile efforts to stem the tide of the Terror, for he was a man of moderate feelings and decent instincts. The sentimental desertion of his wife, however, followed by her imprisonment and death, brought to him the inescapable realization that existence without her was barren, indeed unendurable. Around him, the values he had held so dear had crumbled and the woman who for him had come to mean life itself had turned away in indifference. And thus he had chosen to die, by his own hand, in a supreme gesture of protest against a world that had so poorly repaid his years of hard toil and devotion to the moral, intellectual betterment of mankind. The Terror also struck at Roland's brothers. Dominique, the Canon, had at first disapproved of the couple's revolutionary zeal. In 1791, however, a rapprochement had been effected and, in the absence of the Rolands, he ran Le Clos. After the arrest of Manon and the proscription of her husband, the Canon was imprisoned by the Lyons Revolutionary Committee. He was guillotined on December 22, 1793. His guilt: he was a relative of an "enemy of the state." [2] Another brother, Jacques-Marie, a Benedictine monk in the order of Cluny, was also arrested, but he managed to survive the storm and died in 1807, at the age of seventy-six.[3]

Shortly before her mother's execution, little Eudora was transferred from the house of the Creuzé-Latouches, where she was no longer safe, to the boarding house of Mme Godefroid. At the end of the Terror, Bosc was declared her official guardian. Eudora eventually married the second son of Champagneux, another faithful friend of the Rolands. She had two daughters and lived to be nearly seventy years old. She died in 1858, having led a very retiring existence, undisturbed by intellectual or political pursuits.[4] Mme Roland had been right in sensing that her child was quite an ordinary person with no special talent or interest. Perhaps, too, the tragic end of her parents caused Eudora to seek a measure of security and inner peace in quiet domesticity and in the consolations of religion. Only once did Eudora Champagneux emerge from obscurity while historians and writers wrote about her famous parents and new editions of her mother's *Memoirs* kept appearing. This was in 1847, on the eve of another revolution, when Lamartine published his flamboyant and highly popular *History of the Girondists,* wherein Mme Roland is accorded a prominent role. Mme Champagneux registered her protest that her mother had been glorified at the expense of her father. She even entrusted all the documents in her possession to an editor, Paul Faugère, so that he should complete a study of Roland and thus rehabilitate his memory. But Faugère died before he could complete his task.[5]

It was on November 15, 1793, that Buzot, who was hiding in the Bordeaux district with Barbaroux and Pétion, learned of Manon's execution. His grief was so violent that he remained incoherent for several days. To a confidant in Evreux, Jérôme Letellier, he wrote a sorrowful letter: "*She* is no more, *she* is no more, my friend. The scoundrels have murdered her. Consider if there is anything left for me to regret on earth!" [6] In various places of hiding, he thereafter worked on his *Memoirs,* justifying his position and repeating, in a vehement and somewhat repetitive style, charges of deceit and tyranny against Robespierre. The severe repressive measures adopted against all political opponents of the Mountain soon made the position of Buzot and his friends desperately precarious. Constantly forced to change refuge, they aimlessly roamed the Bordelais countryside, suffering from fatigue, hunger, and exposure. Sometime in June of 1794, feeling themselves hopelessly surrounded and knowing what fate awaited them if arrested, they decided to put an end to their misery. Barbaroux shot himself in the head, but succeeded only in wounding himself gravely; he was captured alive and executed on June 25. On that day, the bodies of Buzot and Pétion, half-devoured by wolves, were discovered in a wheat field. In her farewell to Buzot, Mme Roland had written: "Remain on earth if it still offers a refuge to honest men; live in order to denounce the injustice that proscribed you. But if stubborn misfortune fastens enemies to your footsteps, do not allow mercenary hands to touch you. Die a free man as you have lived." [7] In committing suicide, Buzot had faithfully carried out Manon's last wish.

Few of Mme Roland's friends managed to outlive the Terror, but those who did seem to have been haunted by her memory. Bosc published in 1795 the first edition of her *Memoirs,* which was an instant success. Champagneux, who became Eudora's father-in-law in 1796, brought out a more substantial edition of Mme Roland's works in 1800. Louvet resumed his political career after the fall of Robespierre, combining it with publishing and bookselling, but not for very long; his health had been ruined by hardships incurred and he died in 1797. Bancal des Issarts, for whom Mme Roland had in the early days of the Revolution conceived something of a sentimental attachment, was handed over to the Austrians by Dumouriez in April 1793, a betrayal which, as things turned out, saved his life. He later married and turned to mysticism, expounding his views in a book called *Of a New Social Order Founded on Religion.* In 1835, his eldest daughter, Henriette, published his correspondence with Mme Roland, with a penetrating introduction by Sainte-Beuve.[8] As for Lanthenas, who had secretly pined for Manon yet deserted her in her time of greatest need to join Robespierre's camp, he remained a forlorn, pathetic figure, forgotten or scorned by those who had once been his friends.

Mme Roland's untimely death, while endowing her with the aura of martyrdom, also kept intact the consistency of her political and moral principles. Who knows but that the Napoleonic era and ensuing Restoration might have made a different woman of her, one soberly aware that reality and ideals rarely match? The guillotine spared her the confrontation with doubt and disillusionment. For this nobly heroic end she nevertheless had to pay a price: her literary talent was not allowed to reach full fruition, and her name, in time, became dimmed by that of a more durable and influential contemporary, Mme de Staël. Yet the works she did leave behind, especially her letters and autobiography, have earned her a significant place in the history of French letters, for they testify to a sharpness of intellect and intensity of feeling of which any woman writer, including the flamboyant Mme de Staël, might well have been proud.

NOTES

PRINCIPAL ABBREVIATIONS

Corr. *Lettres de Mme Roland,* ed. Cl. Perroud (Paris, Imprimerie Nationale, 1900–1902), 2 vols. Vol. I: 1780–1787; Vol. II: 1788–1793.

Corr. N.S. *Lettres de Mme Roland,* Nouvelle série (Paris, Imprimerie Nationale, 1913–1915), 2 vols. Vol. I: 1767–1776; Vol. II: 1777–1780.

Corr. Rol. Ph. *Roland et Marie Phlipon. Lettres d'amour* (1777–1780), ed. Cl. Perroud (Paris, A. Picard, 1909).

Mem. *Mémoires de Mme Roland,* ed. Cl. Perroud (Paris, Plon, 1905), 2 vols.

Voy. A. *Voyage en Angleterre,* in *Oeuvres de J.-M. Ph. Roland, femme de l'ex-Ministre de l'Intérieur,* ed. L.-A. Champagneux (Paris, chez Bidault, An VIII [1800]), 210–85. Since an English translation of this edition appeared in London in 1800 (J. Johnson, St. Paul's Churchyard, publisher; name of translator not given), references in Chapter 9 are made to the English text. See *The Works* (never before published) *of Jeanne-Marie Phlipon Roland, Wife of the ex-Minister of the Interior,* "A Trip to England," pp. 166–222.

Voy. S. *Voyage en Suisse,* 1787, ed. G.-R. de Beer (Neuchâtel, aux Editions de la Baconnière, 1937).

W. *The Works* (never before published) *of Jeanne-Marie Phlipon Roland, Wife of the ex-Minister of the Interior* (London, J. Johnson, St. Paul's Churchyard, 1800).

Except as indicated otherwise, all references to Mme Roland's published writings are to the editions listed above, and translations are my own.

PREFACE

1. See Gita May, "Madame Roland devant la génération romantique," *The French Review* (April 1963), XXXVI, 459–68.

2. Daniel Mornet, "Deux petites bourgeoises parisiennes," in *Les Origines intellectuelles de la Révolution française; 1715–1787* (Paris, Colin, 1947), pp. 412–15; André Monglond, "Manon Phlipon," in

Histoire intérieure du préromantisme français de l'abbé Prévost à Joubert (Grenoble, Arthaud, 1929; new, unrevised edition, Paris, Corti, 1965), II, 220–31. Also see Gita May, *De Jean-Jacques Rousseau à Madame Roland: Essai sur la sensibilité préromantique et révolutionnaire* (Geneva, Droz, 1964), a study which concerns the impact of Rousseau on Mme Roland, and through her on the preromantic and revolutionary generation, but which is neither a full-fledged biography nor an analysis of her role during the French Revolution.

3. Letter to Sophie Cannet of October 2, 1776, *Corr. N.S.*, I, 492.

CHAPTER I. A CHILD OF THE SEINE

1. *Corr. N.S.*, I, 439.
2. *Mem.*, II, 79–80.
3. For a good general study of the French Enlightenment, see George R. Havens, *The Age of Ideas: From Reaction to Revolution in Eighteenth-Century France* (New York, Henry Holt, 1955; reissued in paperback edition by The Free Press, 1965).
4. *Mem.*, II, 15.
5. *Mem.*, II, 17.
6. *Mem.*, II, 11.
7. *Mem.*, II, 79. Also *Corr.*, N.S., I, 439–40.
8. *Mem.*, II, 21. J. Calemard, in *Manon Roland chez elle* (Paris, L. Giraud-Badin, 1929), gives a complete inventory of the furniture and adornments in the Phlipon household. In addition, Mme Roland gives in her *Memoirs* a loving and detailed description of her parents' home, especially of the *atelier*, where her father and the apprentices worked, and of the room her mother called the *salle*.
9. *Mem.*, II, 20.
10. It is a well-known fact that the young Rousseau read and reread Plutarch: "Plutarch, especially, became my favorite author. The pleasure I took in reading him over and over again cured me a little of my taste for novels. . . . This interesting reading, and the conversations between my father and myself to which it gave rise, formed in me this free and republican spirit, this proud and indomitable character, impatient with bondage and servitude, which has tormented me throughout my life in situations the least fitted to give it scope" (*Confessions*, Book I, *Oeuvres complètes de Jean-Jacques Rousseau*, ed. Bernard Gagnebin, Robert Osmont, and Marcel Raymond [Paris, Bibliothèque de la Pléiade, 1964], I, 9). For the impact of Plutarch on the Enlightenment, see Peter Gay, *The Enlightenment: An Interpretation; The Rise of Modern Paganism*

(New York, Alfred A. Knopf, 1966), pp. 46–47, 152–54, *et passim.*
See also Gita May, *De Jean-Jacques Rousseau à Madame Roland;
Essai sur la sensibilité préromantique et révolutionnaire* (Geneva,
Droz, 1964), chapter II, "Le Message social de Rousseau," pp. 47–
75, *et passim.* It is no coincidence that, among Mme Roland's
youthful works, as yet unpublished, there is an essay entitled *Réflexions sur Plutarque,* probably written in 1776 (Bibliothèque Nationale, MS, n.a.f. (Nouvelles Acquisitions Françaises) 6243 (fol.
90).
11. *Mem.,* II, 27.

CHAPTER 2. MYSTIC FERVOR
1. *Mem.,* II, 29–35.
2. "Madame Roland," in *Nouveaux Lundis* (Paris, Calmann-Lévy,
1896, VIII, 198–200.
3. *Mem.,* II, 41.
4. *Mem.,* II, 45–46.
5. For an analysis of French convents in the eighteenth century, see
Edmond and Jules de Goncourt, *La Femme au dix-huitième siècle*
(Paris, Charpentier, 1912), pp. 7–22.
6. *Mem.,* II, 72.
7. *Mem.,* II, 75.

CHAPTER 3. A DISCIPLE OF THE PHILOSOPHES
1. These summaries and extracts still exist today and are part of the
collection of Roland manuscripts at the Bibliothèque Nationale. For
the youthful essays and commentaries of Mme Roland, see B.N.,
Département des Manuscrits, n.a.f., 6243, 6244.
2. *Corr. N.S.,* I, 211.
3. *Mem.,* II, 108.
4. *Extrait de mon âme ou le point de vue du moment,* MS 6244, fol.
290–96, published by Cl. Perroud in his edition of Mme Roland's
correspondence, *Corr. N.S.,* I, LIII–LIV. Also see her letter to
Sophie of May 17, 1776, *Corr. N.S.,* I, 408–15.
5. *Pensées sur la morale et la religion* (essay written in 1774), MS
6244, published by L.-A. Champagneux in his edition of Mme
Roland's works, *W.,* pp. 45–50. Also see *Corr. N.S.,* I, 543–44, II,
216–19, 260, 271–72.
6. *W.,* pp. 45–46. Also see *Corr. N.S.,* II, 219.
7. *Corr. N.S.,* I, 483, 523; *Mem.,* II, 109.
8. *Extrait de mon âme, Corr. N.S.,* I, LIV.
9. *Ibid.,* LV.

10. *Ibid.*
11. *Ibid.*, LVI.
12. *Ibid.* For studies of the evolution of Mme Roland's religious ideas, see Edith Bernardin, *Les Idées religieuses de Madame Roland* (Paris, Les Belles Lettres, 1933) and Gita May, "Le Message religieux de Rousseau," in *De Jean-Jacques Rousseau à Madame Roland,* pp. 94–140.
13. *Extrait de mon âme, Corr.* N.S., I, LVI. Manon paraphrases here the following sentence in Book III, Chapter XIII, "Of Experience," of Montaigne's *Essays:* "Oh, what a sweet and soft and healthy pillow is ignorance and incuriosity, to rest a well-made head!" (*The Complete Essays of Montaigne,* transl. by Donald M. Frame, Stanford University Press, 1965, p. 822).
14. *Corr.* N.S., I, 161.
15. *Corr.* N.S., I, 178; *Mem.,* II, 102. Despite Manon's ultimate rejection of Helvétius' materialistic determinism, she was nevertheless deeply impressed by his arguments, as many a comment in her youthful essays and letters clearly testifies: see *Corr.* N.S., I, 294, 360, B.N., MS 6244, fol. 15–19, 41, 57–58.
16. *Mem.,* II, 102.
17. *Corr.* N.S., I, 240–41. Mlle Phlipon may very well have read Diderot's *Pensées philosophiques* (published in 1746), for she echoes the *Pensées* I–V: "People are forever declaiming against the passions; they attribute to them all the pains man endures, and forget that they are also the source of all his pleasures . . . it is passions alone, and strong passions, that can elevate the soul to great things. Without them, there is no sublime, either in morality or in achievement. . . . Sober passions make men commonplace. . . . Deadened passions degrade extraordinary men. Constraint annihilates the grandeur and energy of nature" (*Oeuvres philosophiques,* ed. Paul Vernière, Paris, Garnier, 1956, pp. 9–10).
18. *Mem.,* II, 108, *Corr.* N.S., I, 439–40.
19. *Mémoires de Madame d'Epinay,* ed. Paul Boiteau (Paris, Charpentier, 1865), I, 394. Also see "Troisième lettre à M. de Malesherbes, à Montmorency, le 26 janvier 1762, *Oeuvres complètes,* ed. B. Gagnebin and M. Raymond, I, 1141.
20. *Mem.,* II, 143.
21. *Corr.* N.S., I, 147.
22. *Corr.,* II, 48–49.
23. *Corr.,* II, 48.
24. *Pensées mélancoliques* (essay written in 1777), MS 6244, published

by L.-A. Champagneux in his edition of Mme Roland's works, *W.*, pp. 110–11. See Henry Vyverberg, *Historical Pessimism in the French Enlightenment* (Cambridge, Harvard University Press, 1958).

25. See note 1 of this chapter.
26. *Oeuvres choisies de Chamfort*, ed. Mathurin de Lescure (Paris, Flammarion, 1892, I, 55).

CHAPTER 4. FIRST SORROW AND NEW FRIENDSHIPS

1. See the letter to Sophie of June 3, 1775, *Corr. N.S.*, I, 306, and *Mem.*, II, 175–76.
2. *Corr. N.S.*, I, 307–8; *Mem.*, II, 181.
3. *Ibid.*, II, 181–82.
4. *Ibid.*, II, 182.
5. Letter to Roland dated June 9, 1779, *Corr. Rol. Ph.*, p. 153.
6. *Mem.*, II, 74–75. See above, pp. 26–27, and *Corr. N.S.* I, XXXV–XXXVII.
7. *Mem.*, II, 198.
8. *Ibid.*, II, 199–200.
9. *Ibid.*, II, 200–1; *Corr. N.S.*, I, 333, 336.
10. *Ibid.*, II, 202–3.
11. *Mem.*, II, 204–5; *Corr. N.S.*, I, 320, note 2, 492.
12. M. Perroud has inserted the text of this epistle in his edition of Mme Roland *Memoirs: Mem.*, II, 209–14. See the letter of May 31, 1776, to Sophie: "I beg you, my dear Sophie, to mail in the swiftest and safest way the letter contained in this package. . . . It is an anonymous letter the 'Sage' wants to send to his son" *Corr. N.S.*, I, 420.
13. *Mem.*, II, 214.
14. *Ibid.*, II, 201.
15. *Ibid.*, II, 215; also letters to Sophie of September 13 and 18, 1776, *Corr. N.S.*, I, 477, 479–81.
16. Letter of February 12, 1777, *Corr. N.S.*, II, 35–36.
17. See *Corr. N.S.*, I, XXXVII–XXXVIII.

CHAPTER 5. THE REVELATION OF JEAN-JACQUES ROUSSEAU

1. See Gita May, "Voltaire détrôné par Rousseau," in *De Jean-Jacques Rousseau à Madame Roland*, pp. 76–93.
2. *Mem.*, II, 142. Also see her letter to Sophie of March 21, 1776, *Corr. N.S.*, I, 392–93.
3. *Histoire de la Révolution française*, ed. Gérard Walter (Paris, Gallimard, 1952), I, 663.
4. See Gita May, "Le Message de *La Nouvelle Héloïse*," in *De Jean-*

Jacques Rousseau à Madame Roland, pp. 141–90. Corr. N.S., I, 392, II, 179–80.

5. Ibid., I, 392.
6. See his preface to La Nouvelle Héloïse.
7. Corr. N.S., I, 392.
8. Mem., II, 185. Mme Roland likes to link the names of these two writers, and in her essay "Réflexions sur Plutarque" (unpublished MS, BN, n.a.f. 6243, fol. 90), she underscores Rousseau's indebtedness to Plutarch.
9. W., p. 130.
10. Une Rêverie dans la forêt de Vincennes, W., p. 123.
11. Corr. N.S., I, 392.
12. Ibid. and II, 161. Also see Gita May, "Le Message social de Rousseau," in De Jean-Jacques Rousseau à Madame Roland, pp. 47–75.
13. Corr. N.S., I, 392–93.
14. Corr. N.S., II, 143.
15. Corr. N.S., I, 382–83.
16. For more details on this friend of Manon, see Corr. N.S., I, XLI–XLII and Mem., II, 111–12.
17. This was a New Year's gift; see Manon's letter of January 1, 1778, Corr. N.S., II, 170. The edition in question was no doubt the one published by Marc-Michel Rey in 1769.
18. Corr. N.S., I, 383.
19. Corr. N.S., I, 384.
20. Corr., I, 185 (letter of February 6, 1782, in which she refers to the delight she takes in reading Rousseau's description of his childhood fear of the dark).
21. See her letter of October 20, 1789, Corr., II, 71.
22. Letter written in October 1793, Mem., II, 394–95.
23. See her letters to Sophie of January 14, 1777, Corr. N.S., II, 13; of June 21, 1777, Corr. N.S., II, 84; of July 19, 1777, Corr. N.S., II, 97; of October 16, 1777, Corr. N.S., II, 151; of January 1, 1778, Corr. N.S., II, 183; and of May 14, 1778, Corr. N.S., II, 269. Also see Mem., II, 240–41. The text of this Discours has been reproduced at the end of the second volume of M.-P. Faugère's edition of Mme Roland's Memoirs and, more recently, in Madame Roland: Une Education bourgeoise au XVIIIᵉ siècle, ed. Ch. Lalloué (Paris, Union Générale d'Editions, 1964), pp. 159–81.
24. See her essay De l'Amour, W., pp. 51–62 and a charming poem she wrote on the subject, W., p. 14.
25. Corr., I, 464.

26. See Lucy Gidney, *L'Influence des Etats-Unis d'Amérique sur Brissot, Condorcet et Mme Roland* (Paris, Rieder, 1930).
27. *Corr. N.S.*, II, 133.
28. *Corr. N.S.*, II, 144.
29. *Corr. N.S.*, II, 184.
30. *W.*, pp. 107–9. Her letters to Sophie also reflect this concern. See *Corr. N.S.*, I, 235–37, 239, 294–97.
31. *W.*, p. 108.
32. *W.*, p. 109. Italics mine.

CHAPTER 6. THE ROMANCE OF MANON PHLIPON
1. See Appendix D, section 5, of *Corr.*, II, 581–86.
2. *Ibid.*, section 2, *Corr.*, II, 574–77.
3. *Ibid.*, 577.
4. *Ibid.*, section 3, *Corr.*, II, 577–78.
5. *Ibid.*, 578.
6. See G. Lenôtre (pseud. of Théodore Gosselin), "La Mort de Roland," in *Vieilles maisons, vieux papiers* (Paris, Perrin & Co., 1906), pp. 173–91.
7. See Appendix H, *Corr.*, II, 644–55.
8. Letter of January 11, 1776, *Corr. N.S.*, I, 359.
9. *Corr. N.S.*, I, pp. XXX–XXXIV; *Mem.*, II, 152, 160–62, 233–36.
10. Letter of June 25, 1776, *Corr. N.S.*, I, 428.
11. *Corr. Rol. Ph.*, p. 17.
12. *Corr. N.S.*, I, 369.
13. *Ibid.*, I, 388.
14. *Ibid.*, I, 424–25.
15. *Mem.*, II, 244.
16. *Corr. N.S.*, II, VII–IX, 196–201; *Corr. Rol. Ph.*, pp. 24–30, 105–7.
17. Letter of May 23, 1777, *Corr. N.S.*, II, 75.
18. Letter of July 1, 1777, *Corr. N.S.*, II, 92–93.
19. Letter to Sophie of July 19, 1777, *Corr. N.S.*, II, 97: *Corr. Rol. Ph.*, pp. 125–27, 154–55 (when Manon resumed her correspondence with Roland, she decided it was her duty to inform him of her relationship with Sévelinges).
20. *Ibid.*, p. 170.
21. Letter of September 17, 1777, *Corr. Rol. Ph.*, p. 37.
22. Letter of October 2, 1777, *Corr. Rol. Ph.*, pp. 39–42.
23. *Lettres écrites de Suisse, d'Italie, de Sicile et de Malthe, par M***, avocat en parlement, et de plusieurs académies de France et des Arcades de Rome, etc., à Mlle *** à Paris, en 1776, 1777 et 1778*

(not published in Amsterdam, as the title page indicates, but in Dieppe). The mysterious Mlle *** in the title is, of course, none other than Mlle Phlipon, to whom Roland addressed a very respectful and highly flattering dedication in his preface to this work. For further details on the *Lettres d'Italie* (as the book is commonly called), see *Corr.*, II, Appendix D, section 7, 588–93, and Gita May, "Voltaire a-t-il fait une offre d'hospitalité à Rousseau? Un Témoignage peu connu par Jean-Marie Roland," in *Studies on Voltaire and The Eighteenth Century*, ed. Theodore Besterman, 1966, XLVII, 93–113.

24. Letter to Sophie of February 9, 1778, *Corr. N.S.*, II, 194.
25. *Ibid.*, II, 265–66.
26. *Ibid.*, II, 279–81; *Corr. Rol. Ph.*, p. 181.
27. *Ibid.*, pp. 68.
28. *Ibid.*, p. 71.
29. *Ibid.*, p. 77.
30. *Ibid.*, p. 158.
31. *Ibid.*, p. 78.
32. *Ibid.*, p. 79.
33. *Ibid.*, p. 82.
34. Letter of April 23, 1779, *Ibid.*, p. 86.
35. Letter of May 9, 1779, *Ibid.*, p. 113.
36. See above, pp. 87–88 and note 19.
37. *Corr. Rol. Ph.*, p. 139–40.
38. Letter of June 28, 1779, *Ibid.*, p. 192.
39. Letters of September 1 and 2, 1779, *Ibid.*, pp. 253–59.
40. Letter of September 9, 1779, *Ibid.*, p. 274.
41. Letter of November 11, 1779, *Ibid.*, p. 348.
42. Letter of December 4, 1779, *Ibid.*, p. 363.
43. Letter of January 27, 1780, *Ibid.*, p. 397.
44. *Mem.*, II, 244–50.

CHAPTER 7. RETREAT INTO DOMESTICITY
1. *Mem.*, II, 36.
2. Letter to Sophie of June 16, 1780, *Corr.*, I, 13.
3. *Mem.*, II, 252.
4. For further details on Bosc, see *Corr.*, II, Appendix K, 666–87.
5. For further details on Lanthenas, see *Corr.*, II, Appendix L, 688–708.
6. *Corr.*, I, 5–7, 7–9, 9–11, 11–14, 16–18, 18–20.
7. *Mem.*, II, 255.
8. Letter of September 28, 1780, *Corr.*, I, 17.

9. *Ibid.*, 17–18.
10. *Ibid.*, 17.
11. *Ibid.*, 18.
12. See *Corr.*, II, Appendix G, section 3, 641–43.
13. Upon the extinction of the family of Orléans-Longueville (1707), which had ruled the county of Neuchâtel since 1504, it chose King Frederick I of Prussia as its prince. It became a canton of the Swiss Confederation in 1815.
14. *Histoire de la Révolution française*, ed. G. Walter, I, 661.
15. Letter of February 18, 1781, *Corr.*, I, 21–22.
16. Letter of January 28, 1782, *Corr.*, I, 173–74. Also see *Ibid.*, II, Appendix E, section 2, 612–13.
17. *Corr.*, I, 173.
18. *Corr.*, I, 15, 26, 30, 34, 39, 54, 180, 198.
19. *Corr.*, I, 44.
20. *Corr.*, I, 173; also see note 6 of Chapter 3.
21. *Corr.*, I, 55. Eudora's full Christian name was Marie-Thérèse-Eudora.
22. *Corr.*, I, 168.
23. *Corr.*, I, 57, 154, 165.
24. *Corr.*, I, 57–58.
25. For further details on Fleury, see *Corr.*, II, Appendix T, 778–84.
26. *Corr.*, I, 254.
27. *Corr.*, I, 70.
28. Letter of January 23, 1776, *Corr. N.S.*, I, 370.
29. *Corr.*, I, 256–57.

CHAPTER 8. A MISSION TO PARIS
1. See *Corr.*, II, Appendix J, 662–65.
2. Letter from Roland, MS 6240, fol. 92–93.
3. There is an exchange of letters, still unpublished, between Bosc and Roland during this period, MSS 6239 and 6240.
4. *Corr.*, I, 378, 408.
5. *Corr.*, I, 346–49, 353–55.
6. *Corr.*, I, 422.
7. *Corr.*, I, 401 (see also 319, and 385, note 3).
8. *Corr.*, I, 294, 303–4.
9. *Corr.*, I, 309, 311, 314, 334 (the first two volumes of Lavater's treatise on physiognomy had recently been translated from German into French under the title of *Fragments physiognomoniques*, The Hague, 1783). The third volume of this work was to appear only in 1787 (*Corr.*, I, 334).
10. *Corr.*, I, 307.

11. *Corr.,* I, 367, 383, 388, 402.
12. *Corr.,* I, 385–88.
13. *Corr.,* I, 363, 373.
14. *Corr.,* I, 351.
15. *Corr.,* I, 314.
16. *Corr.,* I, 313, 331.
17. *Corr.,* I, 298–99, 316.
18. *Corr.,* I, 339.
19. *Corr.,* I, 402.
20. *Corr.,* I, 388.
21. *Corr.,* I, 369, 371.
22. *Corr.,* I, 357.
23. *Corr.,* I, 398–99, note 1.
24. *Ibid.*
25. *Corr.,* I, 301.
26. *Corr.,* I, 311, 314.
27. *Corr.,* I, 292.
28. *Corr.,* I, 380, note 1.
29. *Corr.,* I, 308.
30. *Corr.,* I, 416–17.
31. *Corr.,* I, 429, note 2.
32. *Corr.,* I, 429–30.
33. *Corr.,* I, 403.
34. *Corr.,* I, 415.
35. *Corr.,* I, 442, note 1.
36. *Corr.,* I, 442.
37. *Corr.,* I, 443.
38. *Ibid.*

CHAPTER 9. A JOURNEY TO ENGLAND

The material used in this chapter is substantially the same as that presented in my article, "Eighteenth-Century England as Seen by a Disciple of the *Philosophes*," *French Studies,* July 1965, XIX, 253–65.

1. *Voy. A.,* p. 167.
2. *Voy. A.,* p. 174.
3. *Voy. A.,* p. 169.
4. *Voy. A.,* p. 172.
5. *Voy. A.,* p. 170.
6. *Voy. A.,* p. 174.
7. *Ibid.*
8. For a historical description of the London sights mentioned by Mme Roland, see Sir Walter Besant, *London in the Eighteenth Century*

—·—⊷—•—·—

(London and New York, Adam & Charles Black and the Macmillan Co., 1903).

9. *Voy. A.*, p. 192.
10. *Voy. A.*, p. 176.
11. *Ibid.*
12. *Voy. A.*, pp. 189–90.
13. *Voy. A.*, p. 214.
14. *Voy. A.*, p. 196.
15. *Voy. A.*, p. 197.
16. *Voy. A.*, p. 178.
17. *Ibid.*
18. *Voy. A.*, p. 180.
19. *Ibid.*
20. See Sir Walter Besant, *London in the Eighteenth Century*, p. 446.
21. *Voy. A.*, p. 183.
22. *Voy. A.*, p. 184.
23. *Voy. A.*, p. 185.
24. *Voy. A.*, p. 190.
25. *Voy. A.*, p. 191.
26. *Ibid.*
27. *Ibid.*
28. *Voy. A.*, p. 181.
29. *Ibid.*
30. *Ibid.*
31. *Voy. A.*, p. 205.
32. *Voy. A.*, p. 204.
33. *Ibid.*
34. *Ibid.*
35. *Ibid.*
36. *Voy. A.*, p. 182.
37. See her letter to Sophie dated December 13, 1774, *Corr. N.S.*, I, 240–42.
38. *Voy. A.*. p. 202.
39. *Ibid.*
40. *Voy. A.*, p. 201.
41. *Voy. A.*, p. 192.
42. *Ibid.*
43. *Voy. A.*, p. 193.
44. *Voy. A.*, p. 207.
45. *Voy. A.*, pp. 216–17.
46. *Voy. A.*, p. 218. Morande was to return to Paris in 1791 (*Corr.*, II, 338, 353).

47. *Voy. A.,* p. 222.
48. *Ibid.*

CHAPTER 10. RUSTIC INTERLUDE

1. See Jean Schiff, *Madame Roland et le Clos de la Platière à Theizé, village historique* (Villefranche-en-Beaujolais, J. Guillermet, 1952), and *Corr.,* II, Appendix M, section 3, 711–12.
2. *Corr.,* II, Appendix M, section 2, 710–11.
3. *Corr.,* I, 505–6.
4. For further details on the personality and background of Roland's mother, see *Corr.,* II, Appendix C, 565, 568–69.
5. *Corr.,* I, 498 and note 2.
6. *Corr.,* I, 464, 492.
7. *Corr.,* I, 492.
8. Germaine Necker's first published writing was an essay on Rousseau entitled *Lettres sur les ouvrages et le caractère de J.-J. Rousseau* (1788). J. Christopher Herold, in his *Mistress to an Age; A Life of Madame de Staël* (New York, The Bobbs-Merrill Co., Inc., 1958), makes this brief but apt comment on the question of Mme Roland and Mme de Staël: "Between the two ladies no love was lost" (p. 111). Also see Ch. Schlosser and G. A. Bercht, *Mme de Staël et Mme Roland* (Paris, Janet and Cotelle, 1830) and Sainte-Beuve, "Madame Roland," in *Oeuvres,* ed. Maxime Leroy (Paris, Gallimard, 1951), II, 1152–57.
9. *Corr.,* I, 504, 602, 640, 696.
10. *Corr.,* I, 716–18.
11. *Corr.,* I, 708 (letter to Roland dated November 22, 1787).
12. *Mem.,* II, 276.
13. *Corr.,* I, 695 (letter to Roland dated November 18, 1787).
14. *Corr.,* I, 709.
15. *Corr.,* I, 615–16.
16. See Madame Roland, *Voyage en Suisse* (1787), ed. G. R. de Beer (Neuchâtel, Aux Editions de la Baconnière, 1937) and Gita May, "La Suisse vue par une préromantique," in *De Jean-Jacques Rousseau à Madame Roland,* pp. 191–204.
17. See Daniel Mornet, *Le Sentiment de la nature en France de J.-J. Rousseau à Bernardin de Saint-Pierre* (Paris, Hachette, 1907), Paul Van Tieghem, *Le Sentiment de la nature dans le préromantisme européen* (Paris, Nizet, 1960), and Marjorie H. Nicolson, *Mountain Gloom and Mountain Glory: The Development of the Aesthetics of the Infinite* (Ithaca, Cornell University Press, 1959).
18. *Voy. S.,* pp. 58–59.

19. *Voy. S.*, p. 86.
20. *Voy. S.*, pp. 84–97.
21. *Voy. S.*, pp. 135–38.
22. *Voy, S.*, pp. 140–46. See above, p. 121 and note 9.
23. *Corr.*, I, 712, II, 20–23, 440–41, 465.
24. *Voy. S.*, p. 152.
25. *Voy. S.*, p. 173.
26. *Aperçu des causes qui peuvent rendre une langue universelle et observations sur celle des langues vivantes qui tend le plus à le devenir* (MS B.N., n.a.f., 6243, fol. 70–80).
27. *Corr.*, II, 43–49
28. *Corr.*, II, 46.
29. *Ibid.*
30. *Corr.*, II, 47.
31. *Ibid.*
32. *Corr.*, II, 48.
33. *Corr.*, II, 52–56.

CHAPTER 11. 1789 AND SOARING HOPES

1. *Mem.*, II, 74, 137; see above pp. 87–88.
2. *Corr.*, II, 62.
3. *Ibid.*
4. *Corr.*, II, 53.
5. *Ibid.*
6. *Corr.*, II, 68.
7. *Corr.*, II, 62.
8. See *Corr.*, II, Appendix P, 729–35. Also see Eloise Ellery, *Brissot de Warwille: A Study in the History of the French Revolution* (Boston and New York, Houghton Mifflin Co., 1915) and M. J. Sydenham, *The Girondins* (London, Athlone Press, 1961), pp. 61–74, 76–84, 86–89, 92–94, 100–1, 105–6, 107–9, 110–15, 149–50, 153–54, 178–79, 191–92, 208–9, and *passim*.
9. See Lucy Gidney, *L'Influence des Etats-Unis d'Amérique sur Brissot, Condorcet et Mme Roland* (Paris, Rieder, 1930).
10. *Corr.*, II, 729; *Mem.*, I, 191.
11. *Corr.*, II, 54, 55, 59–60, 268–71, 293–95; *Mem.*, I, 192. Also see Cl. Perroud, "Brissot et les Roland. Collaboration des Roland au *Patriote français*," *Révolution française* (1898), XXXIV, 403–22.
12. *Corr.*, II, Appendix N, 714–23. Also see Louis Hastier, "Un Ami de Madame Roland: L.-A. Champagneux," *Revue des Deux Mondes* (February 1, 1966), pp. 405–21.
13. *Corr.*, II, 714.

14. *Corr.*, II, 715. Also see Edith Bernardin, *Jean-Marie Roland et le Ministère de l'Intérieur* (1792–1793) (Paris, Société des Etudes Robespierristes, 1964), p. 12 and note 82.
15. *Corr.*, II, 715.
16. *Ibid.*
17. *Corr.*, II, 59–60.
18. *Corr.*, II, 60.
19. *Corr.*, II, 65.
20. *Corr.*, II, 80.
21. See *above*, pp. 145–46; *Corr.*, I, 492, II, 16, 26–27, 82, 111, 128, 155, 164.
22. *Corr.*, II, 70–71, 103, 144, 149, 155, 241, 255, 302, 307, 308, 312–13, 316, 319, 328–29, 336, 345, 351; *Mem.*, I, 88, 193, 205, 209.
23. See *Corr.*, II, Appendix Q, 736–52. Jules Michelet, in his *Histoire de la Révolution française*, ed. G. Walter, I, 666–69, gives an idealized version of the relationship between Mme Roland and Bancal des Issarts. Sainte-Beuve, on the other hand, in his introduction to a 1835 edition of the letters Mme Roland wrote to Bancal, makes a perceptive analysis of this relationship. This essay was reproduced in Sainte-Beuve, *Oeuvres*, ed. Maxime Leroy (Paris, Gallimard, 1951), II, 1133–58.
24. *Corr.*, II, 675, 732. Also see Cl. Perroud, "Un Projet de Brissot pour une association agricole," *Révolution française* (1902), XLII, 260 ff.
25. See *Corr.*, II, Appendix O, 724–28, and Camille Riffaterre, *Le Mouvement antijacobin et antiparisien à Lyon* (Lyons, A. Rey, 1912–1928), 2 vols.
26. *Corr.*, II, 122–24.
27. *Corr.*, II, 113.
28. *Corr.*, II, 133.
29. *Corr.*, II, 114–20.
30. *Corr.*, II, 165.
31. *Corr.*, II, 213, 733.
32. *Corr.*, II, 235.
33. See George Rudé, *The Crowd in the French Revolution* (Oxford, Oxford University Press, 1959; also issued as an Oxford University Press paperback, 1967).

CHAPTER 12. A REVOLUTIONARY SALON
1. *Corr.*, II, 240.
2. *Corr.*, II, 241; *Mem.*, I, 62, 193.

3. *Corr.*, II, 241.
4. *Corr.*, II, 243–44; *Mem.*, I, 194–95.
5. For a description of the attraction that the Constituent Assembly had for the public, and especially women, see Albert Mathiez, *La Révolution française* (Paris, Armand Colin, 1958), I, 108–9.
6. *Corr.*, II, 241, 255; *Mem.*, I, 62, 88, 193. See Louis Barthou, *Mirabeau* (Paris, Hachette, 1913).
7. *Corr.*, II, 239, 270, 303, 306, 310, 312.
8. See M. J. Sydenham, "Madame Roland's Salon," in *The Girondins*, pp. 86–91, and Edith Bernardin, *Jean-Marie Roland et le Ministère de l'Intérieur*, pp. 13–14.
9. *Mem.*, I, 196.
10. *Mem.*, I, 197.
11. *Mem.*, I, 199–202, M. J. Sydenham, 87–88. Also see Cl. Perroud, "Recherches sur le salon de Madame Roland en 1791," *Révolution française*, XXXVI (1899), 336–44.
12. *Mem.*, I, 140–43, II, 279–82.
13. *Corr.*, II, 304, 306, 310, 330; *Mem.*, I, 199, 202–5. See Gérard Walter, *Robespierre* (Paris, Gallimard, 1936–1940), 3 vols., and James M. Thompson, *Robespierre* (Oxford, Basil Blackwell, 1943).
14. *Mem.*, I, 200–2.
15. *Mem.*, I, 200.
16. See in particular Etienne Dumont's *Souvenirs sur Mirabeau et sur les deux premières Assemblées législatives*: "I have seen in her home several committees of ministers and the principal Girondists. A woman seemed somewhat out of place at these gatherings, but she did not take part in the discussions; during most of them she remained at her desk, wrote letters, and ordinarily appeared occupied with something else, although she did not miss a word." Quoted by Charles-Aimé Dauban, *Etude sur Madame Roland* (Paris, Plon, 1864), p. CXXXV.
17. *Ibid.*
18. See Pierre-Edouard Lemontey's portrait of Mme Roland in his *Memoirs* (Charles-Aimé Dauban, pp. CXXXIV–CXXXV).
19. *Corr.*, II, 343, 356.
20. The article is reproduced in *Corr.*, II, 271–72.
21. Letter to Brissot of April 28, 1791, *Corr.*, II, 270–71.
22. Letter to Champagneux of May 27, 1791, *Corr.*, II, 284 (also see *Corr.*, II, 274, 276).
23. Letter to Bancal of June 22, 1791, *Corr.*, II, 302–6.
24. Letter to Bancal of June 23, 1791, *Corr.*, II, 306; *Mem.*, I, 204.
25. *Mem.*, I, 204.

26. *Ibid.*

27. *Mem.*, I, 205.

28. Letter to Bancal of June 24, 1791, *Corr.*, II, 310.

29. *Corr.*, II, 310–11.

30. *Corr.*, II, 304.

31. For a detailed account of this famous episode in the French Revolution, see George Rudé "The 'Massacre' of the Champ-de-Mars," in *The Crowd in the French Revolution*, pp. 80–94.

32. *Mem.*, II, 208, note 2 (also see *Corr.*, I, 75, note 4).

33. *Corr.*, II, 336.

34. *Corr.*, II, 335, 341, 358.

35. *Corr.*, II, 334, 336, 339, 341, 344, 345.

36. *Corr.*, II, 335.

37. *Corr.*, II, 209–10.

38. *Mem.*, II, 108 (also see *Corr. N.S.*, I, 543, II, 260). For Robespierre, see his *Rapport fait au nom du Comité de Salut public, sur les rapports des idées religieuses et morales avec les principes républicains, et sur les fêtes nationales*, séance du 18 floréal (Paris, Imprimerie nationale, l'an II, mai 1794). Also see, for the question of religion and the French Revolution: Alphonse Aulard, *Le Culte de la Raison et le culte de l'Etre suprême, 1793–1794; Essai historique* (Paris, Félix Alcan, 1904), Albert Mathiez, *Les Origines des cultes révolutionnaires (1789–1792)* (Paris, G. Bellais, 1904), and "Robespierre et le culte de l'Etre suprême," in *Etudes sur Robespierre* (Paris, Editions sociales, 1958), pp. 157–84, and Pierre Trahard, "La Sensibilité religieuse," in *La Sensibilité révolutionnaire* (Paris, Boivin & Cie, 1936), pp. 155–73. And for Rousseau's impact on the religious beliefs of the revolutionaries, see Pierre-Maurice Masson, *La Religion de J.-J. Rousseau* (Paris, Hachette, 1916), III, Ch. V.

39. Albert Mathiez, *Girondins et Montagnards* (Paris, Firmin-Didot, 1930), p. 17.

40. *Mem.*, I, 203–4.

41. *Corr.*, II, 262.

42. *Corr.*, II, 311, 358; *Mem.*, I, 204–5.

43. *Mem.*, I, 269.

44. *Mem.*, I, 269–70.

45. *Corr.*, II, 349.

46. *Corr.*, II, 214.

47. Letter of September 27, 1791, *Corr.*, II, 384–85.

48. *Corr.*, II, 385.

49. *Corr.*, II, 386.
50. *Corr.*, II, 385.
51. "Hang the aristocrats!" *Corr.*, II, 386.
52. *Corr.*, II, 387.
53. See his edition of Michelet's *Histoire de la Révolution française,* I, 1417, note 5, where the letter in question is rather unfairly described as being "more obsequious than dignified and replete with excessive flattery." Jean Jaurès, for his part, while not questioning Mme Roland's sincerity in her early dealings with Robespierre, is hardly more generous in his overall evaluation of her character and political acumen (*Histoire socialiste de la Révolution française* [Paris, Editions de la Librairie de l'Humanité, 1922], IV, 5–7).
54. *Corr.*, II, 389; *Mem.*, I, 66.
55. *Corr.*, II, 393.

CHAPTER 13. UNEASY TRIUMPH
 1. *Corr.*, II, 397; *Mem.*, I, 66; M. J. Sydenham, pp. 66–67, 87; E. Bernardin, p. 15.
 2. *Corr.*, II, 397; *Mem.*, I, 227; E. Bernardin, p. 15.
 3. *Mem.*, I, 67–68; *Souvenirs de Sophie Grandchamp,* reproduced in *Mem.*, II, 474–76.
 4. *Corr.*, II, 409–12; *Mem.*, I, 68.
 5. *Mem.*, I, 67.
 6. *Corr.*, II, 398; *Mem.*, I, 67; M. J. Sydenham, pp. 77–80.
 7. *Corr.*, I, 398.
 8. *Souvenirs,* in *Mem.*, II, 474.
 9. *Ibid.*, II, 475.
10. *Ibid.*, II, 477.
11. *Corr.*, II, 417; *Mem.*, II, 140.
12. *Corr.*, II, 401, 418, 420; *Mem.*, I, 81–82, 267–68. Also see L.-A. Champagneux, *Discours préliminaire,* in *Oeuvres de J.-M. Ph. Roland* (Paris, Bidault, 1800), I, XXXIII–XXXVIII; P.-E. Lemontey, in *Etude sur Madame Roland* by C.-A. Dauban, p. CXXXV; E. Dumont, *Ibid.*
13. *Mem.*, I, 82.
14. *Mem.*, I, 70, 232 (Mme Roland must have liked this anecdote, for she repeated it twice in her *Memoirs*).
15. *Mem.*, I, 252.
16. *Mem.*, I, 235.
17. *Mem.*, I, 232–34.
18. *Mem.*, I, 238.

19. *Mem.,* I, 236.
20. *Mem.,* I, 83 and note 1.
21. *Mem.,* I, 161–63; M. J. Sydenham, pp. 67, 88–89; Dauban, p. CXIII. Louvet's novel has recently been reprinted; see *Romanciers du XVIIIᵉ siècle,* ed. Etiemble (Paris, Gallimard, 1965), II, 405–1222.
22. See A. Mathiez, "La Guerre," in *La Révolution française,* I, 179–99; L. Gershoy, "The Outbreak of the War and the Downfall of the Monarchy," in *The French Revolution and Napoleon* (New York, F. S. Crofts & Co., 1933), pp. 198–210; A. Cobban, "Fall of the Constitutional Monarchy," in *A History of Modern France* (Baltimore, Penguin Books, 1961), I, 180–95, G. Lefebvre, "Flight of the King and Declaration of War against Austria, June, 1791–April, 1792," in *The French Revolution from its Origins to 1793,* transl. by Elizabeth M. Evanson (New York, Columbia University Press, 1962), pp. 206–26.
23. *Corr.,* I, 464.
24. *Mem.,* I, 238, II, 286.
25. See Mathiez, I, 189; Gershoy, p. 203; Cobban, I, 203; Lefebvre, p. 217.
26. *Mem.,* II, 286.
27. *Corr.,* II, 418–20.
28. *Corr.,* II, 413–14.
29. *Corr.,* II, 417.
30. *Mem.,* II, 286.
31. *Ibid.* Also see M. J. Sydenham, pp. 107–9.
32. *Mem.,* II, 287. Of the two leading Girondists G. Lefebvre writes: "Certainly Brissot and Vergniaud possessed ability, but they lacked strength of character" (pp. 214–15).
33. *Mem.,* I, 156.
34. See E. Lintilhac, *Vergniaud* (Paris, Hachette, 1920); A. Mathiez, "Robespierre et Vergniaud," in *Girondins et Montagnards,* pp. 20–69; M. J. Sydenham, 58–59, 67, 77–80, 89–90; G. Lefebvre, p. 215.
35. *Corr.,* II, 398, 428, note 1; M. J. Sydenham, 77–80.
36. *Corr.,* II, 428.
37. *Mem.,* I, 241: "I wrote the famous letter" (also see *Mem.,* I, 76; C.-A. Dauban, *op. cit.,* pp. CXI–CXII).
38. This letter has frequently been reproduced. See *Le Moniteur* of June 15, 1792 and P.-J.-B. Buchez and P.-C. Roux, *Histoire parlementaire de la Révolution française depuis 1789 jusqu'en 1815* (Paris, Paulin, 1833–1838), XV, 40–45 (the text is also quoted

almost *in extenso* by Jean Jaurès in his *Histoire socialiste de la Révolution française,* "La Sommation de Roland," IV, 24–27).

39. Buchez and Roux, XV, 45.
40. *Ibid.*, XV, 40.
41. *Ibid.*, XV, 40–41.
42. *Ibid.*, XV, 42.
43. *Ibid.*
44. *Histoire de la Révolution française,* ed. G. Walter, I, 899.
45. Buchez and Roux, XV, 42.
46. *Ibid.*, XV, 43.
47. Autograph note, BN, n.a.f., MS 6241, fol. 305, reproduced in *Corr.*, II, 403; also in *Mem.*, I, 79, note 2, and 243–44, note 1.
48. Session of June 13, 1792, of the Legislative Assembly. See Buchez and Roux, XV, 33–45; *Mem.*, I, 79–80, 243–44.
49. *Mem.*, I, 87.
50. *Corr.*, II, 404 and note 2, 428–29; M. J. Sydenham, 70, 88–89.
51. *Mem.*, I, 84, 87, 158–61.
52. *Mem.*, I, 160.

CHAPTER 14. THE GATHERING STORM

1. *Corr.*, II, 405–6; *Mem.*, I, 259–79.
2. John Moore, "Roland and Danton," in *English Witnesses of the French Revolution,* ed. J. M. Thompson (Oxford, Basil Blackwell, 1938), pp. 206–7. Also see Louis Madelein, *Danton* (Paris, Hachette, 1914) and Albert Mathiez, "Danton," in *Girondins et Montagnards,* pp. 260–305.
3. *Mem.*, I, 90 (also see 213–14).
4. *Mem.*, I, 91.
5. *Mem.*, I, 213.
6. *Mem.*, I, 215.
7. See in particular Albert Mathiez, "Danton," in *Girondins et Montagnards,* pp. 260–305.
8. *Mem.*, I, 31, 216–17. Also see Leo Gershoy, "Danton and the September Massacres," in *The French Revolution and Napoleon,* pp. 210–26 and George Rudé, *The Crowd in the French Revolution,* pp. 108–12.
9. *Mem.*, I, 105. The text of this letter is reproduced by Buchez and Roux, *Histoire parlementaire de la Révolution française,* XVII, 381–86 and by the Baron de Girardot, *Les Ministres de la République française; Roland et Mme Roland* (Paris, Guillaumin, 1860), pp. 45–50.

10. *Mem.*, I, 217–18 (also *Mem.*, I, 102–3).

11. *Corr.*, II, 434; *Mem.*, I, 218–19.

12. *Corr.*, II, 434.

13. See Albert Mathiez, "Les Elections à la Convention," in *La Révolution française*, II, 40–69; Leo Gershoy, "The Convention: Jacobins and Girondins (1792–1793)," in *The French Revolution and Napoleon*, pp. 228–33; and Georges Lefebvre, "The Beginning of the Convention: Girondins and Montagnards," in *The French Revolution*, pp. 264–73.

14. *Mem.*, I, 110.

15. *Corr.*, II, 434; *Mem.*, I, 107–8.

16. *Mem.*, I, 267–68; above, p. 206.

17. *Mem.*, I, 119.

18. *Mem.*, I, 120–21. Buchez and Roux, XIX, 136–37.

19. *Mem.*, I, 120–21. Buchez and Roux, XIX, 141.

20. Buchez and Roux, XIX, 148–53.

21. *Ibid.*, XIX, 336–37.

22. *Corr.*, II, 436.

23. Buchez and Roux, XIX, 410–12 (the text of the report is reproduced *in extenso* among the supplementary documents for October 1792, XX, 103–22). Also see James M. Moore, *The Roots of French Republicanism* (New York, The American Press, 1962), pp. 226–27.

24. Buchez and Roux, XIX, 415. Also see John Moore, "Louvet and Robespierre," in *English Witnesses of the French Revolution*, ed. J. M. Thompson, pp. 210–12.

25. Buchez and Roux, XIX, 422–36. The text of the speech, entitled *Accusation contre Robespierre*, was printed by order of the Convention. Also see Albert Mathiez, *La Révolution française*, II, 119–20.

26. *Mem.*, I, 55, 162. Of Louvet's speech James M. Moore, p. 228, note 12, writes that if its "recommendations had been followed, perhaps the Girondins would have been able to maintain the republic."

27. Buchez and Roux, XX, 198–219.

28. *Mem.*, I, 272–73.

29. *Mem.*, I, 251.

30. *Mem.*, I, 251–52.

31. See Albert Mathiez, "La Trahison de Dumouriez," II, 179–89; Georges Lefebvre, *The French Revolution from 1793 to 1799*,

transl. by John H. Stewart and James Friguglietti (New York, Columbia University Press, 1964), pp. 44–48.

32. Corr., II, 442–43; Mem., II, 189–90. Also see Georges Lefebvre, The French Revolution from its Origins to 1793, p. 283.
33. Corr., II, 442.
34. Corr., II, 443.
35. Mem., II, 189–90.
36. Mem., II, 295–99. Of this famous episode Georges Lefebvre writes in The French Revolution from its Origins to 1793: "Roland committed the signal mistake of being the first to examine its compromising papers [of the iron chest] with no witnesses present" (p. 271). Mme Roland insists in her Memoirs that both the architect Heurtier and the locksmith Gamain were present when Roland examined the contents of the safe. It would nevertheless have been far more prudent to have called official witnesses before opening the safe.
37. See Albert Mathiez, II, 123–38; Leo Gershoy, pp. 233–39; Georges Lefebvre, ibid., p. 272; James M. Moore, pp. 237–46. For the actual proceedings of the trial and vote counts, see Buchez and Roux, XXIII, 98–270. Also see Albert Soboul, Le Procès de Louis XVI (Paris, Julliard, 1966).
38. See Lefebvre, The French Revolution, pp. 264–73; George Rudé, pp. 113–18.

CHAPTER 15. LOVE AND IDEOLOGY

1. See Corr., II, Appendix R, 735–66; Mem., I, 135–40, 211, II, 281–82; M. J. Sydenham, 63, 65–67, 70–72, 88–89; Charles Vatel, "Notes et documents sur Buzot," in Charlotte de Corday et les Girondins (Paris, Plon, 1864–1872), II, 279–350; Jacques Hérissay, Un Girondin, François Buzot (Paris, Perrin, 1907).
2. Mem., I, 211 and note 3. This correspondence has unfortunately disappeared (Corr., II, Appendix R, 755).
3. Corr., II, 460; Mem., II, 251.
4. See François-Nicolas-Léonard Buzot, Mémoires, ed. J. Guadet (Paris, Béchet, 1823).
5. See Albert Mathiez, La Révolution française, II, 94–95, 127.
6. Mem., II, 250.
7. Corr., II, 449–57, 703–4, 757–58; Mem., II, 253–54.
8. Mem., II, 254.
9. Corr., II, 706 and note 2.
10. Corr., II, 457.

11. Buchez and Roux, XXI, 240–41. Also see Dauban, pp. CLV–CLVIII.

12. *Mem.*, I, 116–18, 122. Also see Louis R. Gottschalk, *Jean-Paul Marat; A Study in Radicalism* (Chicago, The University of Chicago Press, 1967).

13. *Mem.*, I, 116. The letter Marat wrote to Roland in order to ask for the subsidy is reproduced in Buchez and Roux, XVIII, 24.

14. *Corr.*, II, 445.

15. This anecdote is related by Champagneux in his introduction to the 1800 edition of Mme Roland's works, *W.*, XXVI. Also see *Mem.*, I, 19, 297.

16. *Corr.*, II, 448.

17. *Corr.*, II, 447, note 4, 765, note 1. For Mlle Mignot's denunciation of the Rolands, see *Mem.*, II, 425–26.

18. *Corr.*, II, 447–48.

19. *Corr.*, II, 465.

20. Buchez and Roux, XXII, 466.

21. *Ibid.*

22. Buchez and Roux, XXIII, 364–71. MS 6243, fol. 181–91. Also see Baron de Girardot, 200–7.

23. The text of this autobiographical fragment was reproduced by Champagneux in his introduction to the 1800 edition of Mme Roland's works, *W.*, VIII–XIV.

24. *Corr.*, II, 461–62.

25. *Corr.*, II, 462–63.

26. *Corr.*, II, 462; *Mem.*, I, 6.

27. *Corr.*, II, 463; *Mem.*, I, 6–7.

28. *Mem.*, I, 7.

29. *Mem.*, I, XVIII–XIX; Albert Mathiez, "La Chute de la Gironde," in *La Révolution française*, II, 202–22; Lefebvre, "Fall of the Girondins: The Revolution of May 31 and June 2, 1793," in *The French Revolution from 1793 to 1799*, pp. 40–54; Albert Soboul, "Montagnards, Modérés et Sans-Culottes (2 juin–13 juillet 1793)," in *Les Sans-Culottes parisiens en l'an II* (Paris, Clavreuil, 1958), pp. 21–89; James M. Moore, pp. 252–89.

30. *Mem.*, I, 8.

31. *Mem.*, I, 9.

32. *Ibid.*

33. *Mem.*, I, 10.

34. *Ibid.*

35. *Mem.*, I, 11–12.

36. *Mem.*, I, 13.
37. *Ibid.*
38. *Mem.*, I, 14.
39. *Mem.*, I, 15.
40. *Mem.*, I, 22.
41. *Mem.*, I, 23.
42. *Ibid.*
43. *Mem.*, I, 26.
44. *Ibid.*
45. *Mem.*, I, 28.

CHAPTER 16. VICTORY IN DEFEAT

 1. *Corr.*, II, Appendix R, 761–62; *Mem.*, I, 238, note 2, II, 335, note 1.
 2. *Corr.*, II, 481–82.
 3. *Corr.*, II, 483.
 4. *Corr.*, II, 484.
 5. *Corr.*, II, 498.
 6. *Corr.*, II, 506.
 7. See Dauban, *Etude sur Mme Roland*, pp. 16–50; *Corr.*, II, 481–507. The fifth letter, dated August 31, 1793, was not even properly recognized in 1864 because of the subterfuges Mme Roland used to hide the identity of her correspondent (see *Corr.*, II, 507, note 1; *Mem.*, II, 369, note 1).
 8. *Mem.*, I, CXIX–CXXI; Dauban, *Etude sur Mme Roland*, p. 62, note 1; Charles Vatel, *Charlotte de Corday et les Girondins* (Paris, Plon, 1864–1872), II, 575.
 9. Dauban, *Etude sur Mme Roland*, pp. 61–62; *Corr.*, II, Appendix R, 761–62.
10. See Honoré-Jean Riouffe, *Mémoires d'un détenu*, in *Les Prisons de Paris sous la Révolution d'après les relations des contemporains*, by C.-A. Dauban (Paris, Plon, 1870), pp. 101–3; Helena-Maria Williams, "Madame Roland in Prison," in *English Witnesses of the French Revolution*, ed. J. M. Thompson, pp. 239–40; Jacques-Claude Beugnot, *Mémoires du Comte Beugnot*, ed. Robert Lacour-Gayet (Paris, Hachette, 1959), pp. 137–41; Sophie Grandchamp, "Souvenirs de Sophie Grandchamp," in *Mem.*, II, 484–94.
11. *Mem.*, II, 264.
12. See above Chapter II, p. 20 and note 2.
13. The minutes of the interrogation are reproduced in *Mem.*, II, 427–31 and in *W.*, pp. 301–4.
14. *Mem.*, I, 282. See in particular the June 20, 1793, issue of Hébert's

Père Duchesne (reproduced by Cl. Perroud in *Mem.,* II, 431–33).
For extracts of other articles in the *Père Duchesne* which concern
the Rolands, see Dauban, *Etude sur Mme Roland,* pp. CLXI–
CLXXIII.
15. *Mem.,* I, 254.
16. *Mem.,* II, 63–64.
17. *Mem.,* I, XXIV–XXVI, 284–86.
18. Dauban, *Etude sur Mme Roland,* pp. CCXVI–CCXVII; *Mem.,* I,
    285, 301, II, 65, 305.
19. *Mem.,* I, 297, 299.
20. *Mem.,* II, 107, 376, 487.
21. For further details on Grandpré, see *Mem.,* I, 30–31 and note 2.
22. *Corr.,* II, 505; *Mem.,* I, 47, 298, II, 9, 486.
23. *Mem.,* II, 266.
24. In James M. Thompson, *English Witnesses,* pp. 239–40.
25. As related by Henriette herself. See Dauban, *Etude sur Mme Ro-
    land,* p. XXXII. Mme Roland also alluded several times to this
    attempt to help her escape. See *Corr.,* II, 494 and note 2, 498 and
    note 2, 552; *Mem.,* II, 255, 321.
26. *Corr.,* II, 527.
27. *Corr.,* II, 509.
28. *Corr.,* II, 525–26.
29. *Corr.,* II, 526.
30. *Mem.,* I, 331.
31. *Mem.,* I, XXX–XXXI, II, 267–77, 273, 325.
32. *Corr.,* II, 530.
33. *Corr.,* II, 529.
34. *Corr.,* II, 534; *Mem.,* II, 310–11.
35. See Dauban, *Etude sur Mme Roland,* pp. CCXXIX–CCXXXI.
36. *Corr.,* II, 540.
37. *Ibid.*
38. *Corr.,* II, 538–39, note 5.
39. *Corr.,* II, 540.
40. *Corr.,* II, 541–42.
41. *Mem.,* II, 108.
42. *La Nouvelle Héloïse,* ed. R. Pomeau (Paris, Garnier, 1960), p. 731.
43. *Corr.,* II, 269.
44. *Corr.,* II, 277.
45. See Dauban, "La Conciergerie," in *Les Prisons de Paris sous la
    Révolution,* pp. 136–37.
46. *Mem.,* II, 313.

47. Riouffe, pp. 101–2.
48. *Ibid.*, p. 102.
49. *Ibid.*
50. *Ibid.*
51. Beugnot, p. 137 (text also reproduced in Dauban, *Etude sur Mme Roland*, p. CCXXXV).
52. *Beugnot*, p. 138.
53. *Ibid.*, p. 139.
54. *Ibid.*
55. *Ibid.*, p. 140.
56. See Dauban, *Etude sur Mme Roland*, pp. CCXXXVII–CCXXXVIII; *Mem.*, I, XXXIV–XXXV. The minutes of these interrogations have been reproduced in *Mem.*, II, 312–19, 439–46, and in *W.*, pp. 308–15.
57. *Mem.*, II, 315.
58. *Mem.*, I, XXXIV–XXXV, II, 314–15, note 2. Also see Riouffe, p. 102.
59. *Mem.*, I, XXXVI–XLIII.
60. Beugnot, pp. 140–41. For further details on Mme Roland on the day of her trial, also see Riouffe, p. 103, and Sophie Grandchamp, p. 494.
61. Dauban, *Etude sur Mme Roland*, p. CCXXXVIII; *Mem.*, I, XXXVI, 447–50; *W.*, pp. 315–18.
62. "Projet de défense au Tribunal," in *Mem.*, II, 320–27.
63. *Mem.*, I, XXXVII–XXXVIII.
64. *Mem.*, I, XLIII.
65. Dauban, *Les Prisons de Paris . . .* , p. 103.
66. "Souvenirs de Sophie Grandchamp," in *Mem.*, II, 493–97; Beugnot, pp. 140–41 (also in Dauban, *Etude sur Mme Roland*, pp. CCXXXV–CCXXXVII); Riouffe, p. 103.
67. Sophie Grandchamp., 494.
68. *Ibid.*
69. *Ibid.*, 495–96.
70. Dauban, *Etude sur Mme Roland*, p. CCXLII.
71. Riouffe, p. 103; *Mem.*, I, XLV.

CHAPTER 17. THE AFTERMATH
1. G. Lenôtre, "La Mort de Roland," in *Vieilles Maisons, vieux papiers, pp.* 173–87; Dauban, "Mort de Roland," in *Etude sur Mme Roland*, pp. CCXLIX–CCLI; Champagneux's Preliminary Discourse, in *W.*, pp. LIX–LXIII.

2. *Corr.*, II, Appendix C., 569.
3. *Corr.*, II, Appendix C., 570.
4. *Corr.*, II, Appendix T, 783–84; "Fragment de mémoires de Bosc," in *Mem.*, II, 456–61; Lenôtre, pp. 188–91; Champagneux's Preliminary Discourse, in *W.*, pp. LV–LIX.
5. *Mem.*, I, CXIV–CXVII. The recent study by Edith Bernardin, *Jean-Marie Roland et le Ministère de l'Intérieur* (1792–1793) fills this gap.
6. *Corr.*, II, Appendix R, 765.
7. *Mem.*, II, 269–70. Also see Dauban, "Les Derniers jours de Buzot," in *Etude sur Mme Roland*, pp. CCLI–CCLXI, and Charles Vatel, II, 101–370; III, 600–37, 692–736, for accounts and documents pertaining to the tragic end of Buzot, Pétion, and Barbaroux.
8. *Corr.*, II, Appendix Q, 751–52.

SELECTIVE BIBLIOGRAPHY

Primary Sources

1. MANUSCRIPTS

Bibliothèque Nationale, Paris Département des Manuscrits, "Dossier Roland," *Nouvelles Acquisitions Françaises* (*n.a.f.*):

Roland de la Platière (Marie-Jeanne Phlipon): Lettres, 12760, n.a.f. 1730; Mémoires, 13736, n.a.f. 4697; Notes, n.a.f. 7543; Papiers, n.a.f. 1730, n.a.f. 6238–44, n.a.f. 9532–34; Oeuvres de loisir et réflexions diverses de l'année 1773, n.a.f. 6244.

Roland de la Platière (Jean-Marie): Lettres, 12760, n.a.f. 1730; Papiers, n.a.f. 1730, n.a.f. 6238–44, n.a.f. 7543, n.a.f. 9532–34, 22422–24; Compte rendu à la Convention, n.a.f. 7543.

Lettres de Mme Roland à son mari, n.a.f. 6238 (1777–1791).

Lettres de Roland à sa femme, n.a.f. 6240 (1777–1791).

Lettres de Mme Roland à Buzot, n.a.f. 1730 (1793).

Lettres autographes de Mme Roland. Supplément Jany, cahiers Brissot, Danton, etc. n.a.f. 4697. In this collection are Mme Roland's published letters and memoirs, as well as a large number of unpublished letters by Roland, communications to Academies, political documents, and many other papers, including Mme Roland's youthful essays and summaries of her readings.

2. PRINTED WORKS BY MME ROLAND

Appel à l'impartiale postérité par la citoyenne Roland, ed. Louis Bosc (Paris, Louvet, 1795), 4 vols.

Oeuvres de J.-M. Ph. Roland, femme de l'ex-ministre de l'Intérieur, ed. L.-A. Champagneux (Paris, Bidault, 1800), 3 vols.

Mémoires de Mme Roland, ed. MM. Berville et Barrière (Paris, Baudouin Frères, 1820), 2 vols.

Mémoires de Mme Roland, ed. J. Ravenel (Paris, A. Durand, 1840).

Mémoires de Mme Roland, ed. M.-P. Faugère (Paris, Hachette, 1864), 2 vols.

Mémoires de Mme Roland, ed. C.-A. Dauban (Paris, Plon, 1864).

Mémoires de Mme Roland, pref. by Jules Claretie (Paris, Librairie des Bibliophiles, 1884), 2 vols.

Mémoires de Mme Roland, ed. Cl. Perroud (Paris, Plon, 1905), 2 vols.

Mémoires particuliers de Mme Roland, ed. G. Huisman (Paris, Firmin-Didot, 1929).

Une Éducation bourgeoise au XVIIIᵉ siècle (Extrait des Mémoires), par Mme Roland (suivi du Discours de Besançon), ed. Ch. Lalloué (Paris, Union Générale d'Éditions, 1964).

Mme Roland, Mémoires, ed. P. de Roux (Paris, Mercure de France, 1966).

Lettres autographes de Mme Roland, adressées à Bancal-des-Issarts. Introduction by Sainte-Beuve (Paris, E. Renduel, 1835).

Lettres inédites de Mlle Phlipon, Mme Roland, adressées aux demoiselles Cannet, de 1772 à 1780, ed. A. Breuil (Paris, W. Coquebert, 1841), 2 vols.

Lettres en partie inédites de Mme Roland (Mlle Phlipon) aux demoiselles Cannet, ed. C.-A. Dauban (Paris, Plon, 1867), 2 vols.

Lettres choisies de Mme Roland, ed. C.-A. Dauban (Paris, Plon, 1867).

Le Mariage de Mme Roland, Trois années de correspondance amoureuse. 1777–1780, ed. A. Join-Lambert (Paris, Plon, 1896).

Roland et Marie Phlipon. Lettres d'amour (1777 à 1780), ed. Cl. Perroud (Paris, Picard, 1909).

Lettres de Mme Roland, v. I (1780–1787), ed. Cl. Perroud (Paris, Imprimerie Nationale, 1900).

Lettres de Mme Roland, v. II (1788–1793), ed. Cl. Perroud (Paris, Imprimerie Nationale, 1902).

Lettres de Mme Roland. Nouvelle série, v. I (1767–1776), ed. Cl. Perroud (Paris, Imprimerie Nationale, 1913).

Lettres de Mme Roland. Nouvelle série, v. II (1777–1780), ed. Cl. Perroud (Paris, Imprimerie Nationale, 1915).

Nouvelles Lettres inédites de Mme Roland, ed. Cl. Perroud (Paris, Charavay, n.d.).

Discours prononcé par Marie-Jeanne Phelippon [sic], femme de Jean-Marie Roland, ex-ministre de l'Intérieur, aux juges du Tribunal Révolutionnaire à Paris, le 18 brumaire, l'an II (n.p., n.d.).

Copie littérale prise sur la minute, du style et de la main de Marie-Jeanne Roland, femme du ci-devant Ministre de l'Intérieur (Paris, chez la Veuve d'A.-J. Gorsas, l'an III).

Voyage en Suisse, 1787, ed. G.-R. de Beer (Neuchâtel, Editions de la Baconnière, 1937).

3. ENGLISH TRANSLATIONS OF MME ROLAND'S WORKS

An Appeal to Impartial Posterity by Citizeness Roland (London, J. Johnson, 1795), 2 vols.

An Appeal to Impartial Posterity by Madame Roland (New York, printed by Robert Wilson, for A. Van Hook, Proprietor of the Reading-Room, 1798), 2 vols.

The Works (never before published) of Jeanne-Marie Phlipon Roland, Wife of the ex-Minister of the Interior (London, J. Johnson, 1800).

The Private Memoirs of Madame Roland, ed. Edward Gilpin Johnson (Chicago, A. C. McClurg & Co., 1900).

4. WORKS BY M. ROLAND

(A) LITERARY WORKS

Voyage en France, 1769, ed. Cl. Perroud (Valence, d'Auray Fils & L. Deschizeaux, 1913).

Lettres écrites de Suisse, d'Italie, de Sicile, et de Malte, par M*** à Mlle *** à Paris en 1776, 1777 et 1778 (Amsterdam, 1780), 6 vols.

De l'Influence des lettres dans les provinces, comparée à leur influence dans des capitales. Discours lu à la séance publique de l'Académie de Lyon, le 6 décembre 1785, par M. Roland de la Platière (n.p., n.d.).

De l'un des moyens de connaître les femmes. Discours lu à l'Académie de Lyon, le 8 août 1786 (Ms. B.N., n.a.f. 6243, fol. 83–88. Also printed in Delandine's *Conservateur,* 1788, II, 247–56).

Réflexions sur Plutarque. Discours lu à l'Académie de Lyon, le 16 janvier 1787 (MS B.N., n.a.f. 6243, fol. 89–90).

Aperçu des causes qui peuvent rendre une langue universelle et observations sur celle des langues vivantes qui tend le plus à le devenir. Mémoire lu à la Société d'émulation de Bourg-en-Bresse, le 20 avril 1789 (MS B.N., n.a.f. 6243, fol. 70–80).

(B) TECHNICAL WORKS

Manufactures, arts et métiers, par M. Roland de la Platière (Encyclopédie méthodique), v. I (Paris, Panckoucke, 1784).

Manufactures, arts et métiers, par M. Roland de la Platière (Encyclopédie méthodique), v. II (Paris, Panckoucke, 1785).

Manufactures, arts et métiers. Errata (Paris, Panckoucke, 1790).

Manufactures, arts et métiers, par M. Roland de la Platière (Encyclopédie méthodique, v. III (Paris, Panckoucke, 1790).

Mémoire sur la culture de France comparée à celle de l'Angleterre. Séance publique de la Société royale d'agriculture de la généralité de Lyon, le 5 janvier 1787 (Geneva, 1787).

Notes pour servir à l'histoire de l'industrie, du commerce de Villefranche en Beaujolais. Mémoire de J.-M. Roland de la Platière, ed. J. Balloffet (Villefranche, d'Auray Fils & L. Deschizeaux, 1913).

(c) POLITICAL WORKS

Discours prononcé à la Société centrale formée des commissaires des sociétés populaires des Amis de la Constitution, le 6 janvier 1791 (n.p., n.d.).

Discours prononcé à la Société philanthropique de Lyon par Roland de la Platière, président du comité de travail de cette société (n.p., 1790).

Lettre aux membres du Conseil général de la commune de Lyon, à propos des finances de la ville. Lyon, le 30 juin 1790 (Revue du Lyonnais, XIX, 1859, 299–303).

Discours de M. Clavière, Ministre des Contributions publiques, de M. de Grave, Ministre de la Guerre, et de M. Rolland [sic], *prononcés à l'Assemblée Nationale dans la séance du 26 mars 1792* (n.p., n.d.).

Correspondance du Ministre de l'Intérieur relative au commerce, aux subsistances et à l'administration générale (16 avril–14 octobre 1792), ed. A. Tuetey (Paris, Imprimerie Nationale, 1917).

Compte rendu à l'Assemblée Nationale, par M. Rolland [sic], *le 20 août 1792* (Paris, Imprimerie Nationale, n.d.).

Concitoyens, par Roland, 1er septembre 1792 (n.p., n.d.).

Aux Habitants des campagnes, par Roland, 5 septembre 1792 (Paris, Imprimerie Nationale, 1792).

Convention Nationale. Compte rendu, le 23 septembre 1792, par le Ministre de l'Intérieur, Roland (Paris, Imprimerie Nationale, 1792).

Convention Nationale. Lettre du Ministre de l'Intérieur à la Convention Nationale, du 30 septembre 1792 (Paris, Imprimerie Nationale, n.d.).

Convention Nationale. Rapport du Ministre de l'Intérieur à la Convention Nationale sur l'état de Paris. Du 29 octobre 1792 (Paris, Imprimerie Nationale, n.d.).

Aux Corps administratifs, le 3 novembre 1792, par le Ministre de l'Intérieur, Roland (Paris, Imprimerie Nationale, 1792).

Aux Pasteurs des villes et des campagnes, par Roland, le 6 novembre 1792 (Paris, Imprimerie Nationale, 1792).

Correspondance du Ministre de l'Intérieur, Roland, avec le général Lafayette (Paris, Imprimerie du Cercle social, 1792).

De L'Esprit public. Chapitre XXVe du Compte rendu par le Ministre de l'Intérieur à la Convention Nationale, le 6 janvier 1793 (Paris, Imprimerie Nationale, 1793).

L'ex-Ministre de l'Intérieur (Roland) au président de la Convention Nationale, le 10 avril 1793 (n.p., 1793).

L'ex-Ministre de l'Intérieur (Roland) au président de la Convention Nationale, le 19 avril 1793 (Paris, Imprimerie de Gorsas, n.d.).

5. MEMOIRS, LETTERS, DOCUMENTS, AND CITED WORKS

Barbaroux, Charles-Jean-Marie, *Correspondance et Mémoires*, ed. Cl. Perroud (Paris, Société historique de la Révolution, 1923).

Barbier, Edmond-Jean-François, *Journal d'un bourgeois de Paris sous le règne de Louis XV* (Paris, Union Générale d'Éditions, 1963).

Beugnot, Edmond-Jean-François, *Mémoires*, ed. R. Lacour-Gayet (Paris, Hachette, 1959).

Buchez, P.-J.-B., and Roux, P.-C., eds., *Histoire parlementaire de la Révolution française depuis 1789 jusqu'à l'Empire* (Paris, Paulin, 1833–1838), 40 vols.

Bosc, Louis-Augustin-Guillaume, *Fragment de Mémoires*, in *Mémoires de Mme Roland*, ed. Cl. Perroud (Paris, Plon, 1905), II, 450–61.

Brissot, Jacques-Pierre, *Mémoires*, ed. Cl. Perroud (Paris, Picard, 1904).

Buzot, François-Nicolas-Léonard, *Mémoires*, ed. J. Guadet (Paris, Béchet, 1823).

—— *Convention Nationale, Rapport fait, au nom de la commission des neuf, par le citoyen Buzot, sur une loi contre les provocateurs au meurtre et à l'assassinat* (Paris, Imprimerie Nationale, n.d.).

—— *Rapport et Projet de décret sur la garde des 83 départements, par le citoyen Buzot* (Paris, Imprimerie Nationale, n.d.).

Chamfort, Nicolas-Sébastien Roch, pseud. de, *Oeuvres choisies*, ed. M. de Lescure (Paris, Flammarion, 1892), 2 vols.

Desmoulins, Camille, *Histoire des Brissotins* (Paris, Imprimerie patriotique et républicaine, 1793).

—— *Le Vieux Cordelier*, ed. H. Calvet (Paris, Colin, 1936).

—— *Oeuvres*, ed. J. Claretie (Paris, Charpentier, 1874), 2 vols.

Diderot, Denis, *Oeuvres philosophiques*, ed. P. Vernière (Paris, Garnier, 1956).

Dumont, Pierre-Etienne-Louis, *Souvenirs sur Mirabeau et sur les deux premières Assemblées législatives*, ed. J.-L. Duval (Paris, Gosselin, 1832).

Dumouriez, Charles-François, *Mémoirs du général Dumouriez*, ed. J.-F. Barrière (Paris, Firmin-Didot, 1848), 2 vols.

—— *La Vie et les Mémoires de Dumouriez*, ed. MM. Berville et Barrière (Paris, Baudouin Frères, 1822–1823).

Encyclopédie, ou Dictionnaire raisonné des Sciences, des Arts et des Métiers, ed. Diderot et d'Alembert (Paris, Briasson & Le Breton, 1751–1780), 36 vols.

Epinay, Louise Tardieu d'Esclavelles, marquise d', *Mémoires*, ed. P. Boiteau (Paris, Charpentier, 1865), 2 vols.

Epinay, Louise, *Histoire de Mme de Montbrillant,* ed. G. Roth (Paris, Gallimard, 1951), 3 vols.

Grandchamp, Sophie, *Souvenirs de Sophie Grandchamp,* in *Mémoires de Mme Roland,* ed. Cl. Perroud (Paris, Plon, 1905), II, 461–97.

Helvétius, Claude-Adrien, *De L'Esprit* (Paris, Durand, 1758).

—— *De L'Homme, de ses facultés intellectuelles et de son éducation, ouvrage posthume de M. H. publié par le prince Galitzin* (London, 1773), 2 vols.

—— *De L'Esprit,* ed. Guy Besse (Paris, Editions sociales, 1959).

La Fayette, Marie-Madeleine Pioche de La Vergne, comtesse de, *Romans et Nouvelles,* ed. E. Magne (Paris, Garnier, 1958).

Louvet de Couvrai, Jean-Baptiste, *Mémoires,* ed. F.-A. Aulard (Paris, Librairie des Bibliophiles, 1889), 2 vols.

—— *Les Amours du Chevalier de Faublas,* in *Romanciers du XVIIIe siècle,* ed. R. Étiemble (Paris, Gallimard, 1965), II, 405–1222.

Mallet du Pan, Jacques, *Considérations sur la nature de la Révolution et sur les causes qui en prolongent la durée* (London and Brussels, Flon, 1793).

Marmontel, Jean-François, *Mémoires,* ed. M. Tourneux (Paris, Librairie des Bibliophiles, 1891), 3 vols.

Mercier, Louis-Sébastien, *Tableau de Paris* (Amsterdam, 1782–1788), 12 vols.

—— *Paris pendant la Révolution (1789–1799) ou Le Nouveau Paris* (Paris, Poulet-Malassis, 1862).

—— *De Jean-Jacques Rousseau considéré comme l'un des principaux auteurs de la Révolution* (Paris, Brisson, 1791), 2 vols.

Montaigne, Michel de, *Essais,* ed. A. Thibaudet (Paris, Gallimard, 1950).

—— *The Complete Essays of Montaigne,* transl. D. M. Frame (Stanford, Stanford University Press, 1958).

Montesquieu, Charles-Louis de Secondat, Baron de la Brède et de, *Oeuvres complètes,* ed. R. Caillois (Paris, Gallimard, 1949–1951), 2 vols.

Muralt, Béat Louis de, *Lettres sur les Anglois et les François et sur les voiages,* ed. Ch. Gould and Ch. Oldham (Paris, Champion, 1933).

Pétion, Jérôme de Villeneuve, *Mémoires,* ed. C.-A. Dauban (Paris, Plon, 1866).

Raynal, abbé Guillaume-Thomas-François, *Histoire philosophique et politique des établissements et du commerce des Européens dans les deux Indes* (Amsterdam, 1770), 6 vols.

Richardson, Samuel, *Pamela, or Virtue Rewarded* (London, Hodges, 1742–1754), 4 vols.
—— *Clarissa Harlowe*, ed. J. A. Burrell (New York, The Modern Library, 1950).
—— *Lettres anglaises, ou Histoire de Miss Clarisse Harlove*, transl. Abbé A.-F. Prévost (London, Nourse, 1751), 6 vols.
Riouffe, Honoré-Jean, *Mémoires d'un détenu pour servir l'histoire de la tyrannie de Robespierre* (Paris, B. Mathé & Louvet, 1795).
Rivarol, Antoine, *Oeuvres* (Paris, Colin, 1808), 5 vols.
—— *Essai sur les causes de la Révolution française* (Paris, Boucher, 1927).
Robespierre, Maximilien-Marie-Isidore de, *Oeuvres*, ed. A. Laponneraye (Paris, chez l'éditeur, 1832–1840), 3 vols.
—— *Oeuvres complètes*, ed. M. Bouloiseau, G. Lefebvre, J. Dautry, and A. Soboul (Paris, Presses Universitaires, 1953–   ), 7 vols. published thus far.
—— *Discours de Maximilien Robespierre sur la guerre. Prononcé à la Société des amis de la Constitution*, le 2 janvier 1792 (Paris, n.p., 1792).
—— *Déclaration des droits de l'homme et du citoyen. Présentée à la Convention Nationale en 1793, par Robespierre* (Paris, Voinier Fils, 1833).
—— *Rapport fait au nom du Comité de Salut Public, par Maximilien Robespierre, sur les rapports des idées religieuses et morales avec les principes républicains, et sur les fêtes nationales. Séance du 18 floréal* (Paris, Imprimerie Nationale, l'an II, mai 1794).
—— *Discours de Maximilien Robespierre, président de la Convention Nationale, au peuple réuni pour la fête de l'Etre Suprême, décadi 20 prairial, l'an II de la République* [le 8 juin 1794] (Paris, Imprimerie Nationale, 1794).
—— *Correspondance de Maximilien et Augustin Robespierre*, ed. G. Michon (Paris, F. Alcan, 1926), 2 vols.
Robespierre, Charlotte, *Mémoires sur ses deux frères*, ed. Laponneraye (Paris, chez l'éditeur, 1832–1840), 3 vols.
Rousseau, Jean-Jacques, *Oeuvres complètes*, ed. B. Gagnebin and M. Raymond (Paris, Gallimard, 1959–1964), 3 vols. published thus far.
—— *La Nouvelle Héloïse*, ed. R. Pomeau (Paris, Garnier, 1960).
—— *Emile*, ed. F. and P. Richard (Paris, Garnier, 1961).
Saint-Just, Louis-Antoine de, *Oeuvres complètes*, ed. Ch. Vellay (Paris, Fasquelle, 1908), 2 vols.

Sévigné, Marie de Rabutin-Chantal, marquise de, *Lettres*, ed. Gérard Gailly (Paris, Gallimard, 1953–1957), 3 vols.

Staël-Holstein, Anne-Louise-Germaine Necker, Baronne de, *Lettres sur les ouvrages et le caractère de J.-J. Rousseau* (Paris, n.p., 1788).

———*De L'Influence des passions sur le bonheur des individus et des nations* (Paris, Maradan, 1818).

——— *Des Circonstances actuelles qui peuvent terminer la Révolution*, ed. J. Viénot (Paris, Fischbacher, 1906).

——— *De La Littérature considérée dans ses rapports avec les institutions sociales*, ed. Paul Van Tieghem (Geneva, Droz, 1959), 2 vols.

——— *Correspondance générale*, ed. B. Jasinski (Paris, J.-J. Pauvert, 1960).

Stendhal, Marie-Henri Beyle, pseud., *Oeuvres complètes*, ed. H. Martineau (Paris, Le Divan, 1927–1937), 79 vols.

Thompson, James M., ed., *English Witnesses of the French Revolution* (Oxford, Basil Blackwell, 1938).

Thomson, James, *The Seasons*, ed. E. Gosse (London, G. Routledge, 1906).

Voltaire, François-Marie Arouet de, *Oeuvres complètes*, ed. L. Moland (Paris, Garnier, 1883–1885), 52 vols.

——— *Romans et Contes*, ed. H. Bénac (Paris, Garnier, 1960).

——— *Dictionnaire philosophique*, ed. J. Benda et R. Naves (Paris, Garnier, 1954).

Williams, Helena-Maria, *Letters containing a sketch of the scenes which passed in the various Departments of France during the tyranny of Robespierre* (Philadelphia, Snowden & M'Corckle, 1796).

Williams, Helena-Maria, *Souvenirs de la Révolution française*, transl. C. Coquerel (Paris, 1827).

Young, Arthur, *Travels in France during the years 1787, 1788 and 1789*, ed. C. Maxwell (Cambridge, The University Press, 1950).

Young, Edward, *The Complaint, or Night Thoughts*, ed. J. R. Boyd (New York, Scribner, 1851).

Secondary Sources

I. GENERAL HISTORIES OF THE FRENCH REVOLUTION, SPECIAL STUDIES AND BIOGRAPHIES, WORKS ON THE GIRONDISTS

Aulard, Alphonse, *Etudes et Leçons sur la Révolution française*, quatrième série (Paris, Félix Alcan, 1904).

——— *Le Culte de la Raison et le Culte de l'Etre Suprême, 1793–1794. Essai historique* (Paris, F. Alcan, 1904).

———— *Histoire politique de la Révolution française. Origines de la Démocratie et de la République; 1789–1804* (Paris, Colin. 1913).

Aymard, Camille, *L'Appel de l'échafaud* (Paris, Flammarion, 1927).

Barthou, Louis, *Mirabeau* (Paris, Hachette, 1913).

———— *Danton* (Paris, P. A. Michel, 1932).

Bouloiseau, Marc, *Robespierre* (Paris, Presses Universitaires, 1957).

Bradby, E. D., *A Short History of the French Revolution; 1789–1795* (Oxford, The Clarendon Press, 1926).

Brinton, Crane, *The Jacobins: An Essay in the New History* (New York, The Macmillan Co., 1930).

———— *A Decade of Revolution* (New York, Harper, 1934).

Brunot, Ferdinand, *Révolution et Empire,* in *Histoire de la langue française* (Paris, Colin, 1937), t. IX, 2 vols.

Cabanès, Augustin, and Nass, Louis, *La Névrose révolutionnaire* (Paris, Albin Michel, 1924), 2 vols.

Carlyle, Thomas, *The French Revolution* (New York, The Modern Library, 1934).

Champion, Edme, *J.-J. Rousseau et la Révolution française* (Paris, Colin, 1909).

Cobban, Alfred, *Old Regime and Revolution; 1715–1799,* in *A History of Modern France* (Baltimore, Maryland, Penguin Books, 1961), vol. I.

Dauban, Charles-Aimé, *Les Prisons de Paris sous la Révolution, d'après les relations des contemporains* (Paris, Plon, 1870).

Ellery, Eloise, *Brissot de Warville: A Study in the History of the French Revolution* (Boston and New York, Houghton Mifflin, 1915).

Gershoy, Leo, *The French Revolution and Napoleon* (New York, F. S. Crofts & Co., 1933).

———— *The Era of the French Revolution; 1780–1799* (New York, Van Nostrand Co., 1957).

Gibbs, Philip, *Men and Women of the French Revolution* (London, Kegan Paul, Trench, Trubner & Co., 1906).

Godechot, Jacques, *La Pensée révolutionnaire; 1780–1799* (Paris, Colin, 1964).

Goncourt, Edmond and Jules de, *Histoire de la société française pendant la Révolution* (Paris, Charpentier, 1895).

Gottschalk, Louis R., *Jean-Paul Marat; A Study in Radicalism* (Chicago, The University of Chicago Press, 1967).

Groethuysen, Bernard, *Philosophie de la Révolution française. Précédé de Montesquieu* (Paris, Gallimard, 1956).

Guadet, Joseph, *Les Girondins, leur vie privée, leur vie publique, leur proscription et leur mort* (Paris, Perrin & Cie, 1889).

Hérissay, Jacques, *Un Girondin, François Buzot, député de l'Eure à l'Assemblée Constituante et à la Convention; 1760–1794* (Paris, Perrin & Cie, 1907).

Hyslop, Beatrice, *French Nationalism in 1789 according to the General Cahiers* (New York, Columbia University Press, 1934).

—— "Recent Work on the French Revolution," *American Historical Review*, April 1942, XLVII, 488–517.

Jaurès, Jean, *Histoire socialiste de la Révolution française* (Paris, Editions de la Librairie de l'Humanité, 1921–1924), 8 vols.

Kuscinski, August, *Dictionnaire des Conventionnels* (Paris, Société de l'histoire de la Révolution française, 1917).

Labrousse, Ernest, *La Crise de l'économie française à la fin de l'ancien régime et au début de la Révolution* (Paris, Presses Universitaires, 1943).

Lamartine, Alphonse de, *Histoire des Girondins* (Paris, Hachette, 1913), 6 vols.

Lavisse, Ernest, *Histoire de France contemporaine depuis la Révolution jusqu'à la paix de 1919* (Paris, Hachette, 1920–1922), vol. I: P. Sagnac, *La Révolution, 1789–1792;* vol. II, G. Pariset, *La Révolution, 1792–1799.*

Lefebvre, Georges, *La Révolution française* (Paris, Presses Universitaires, 1957).

—— *The Coming of the French Revolution,* transl. R. R. Palmer New York, Vintage Books, 1957).

—— *The French Revolution from its Origins to 1793,* transl. E. M. Evanson (New York, Columbia University Press, 1962).

—— *The French Revolution from 1793 to 1799,* transl. J. H. Stewart and J. Friguglietti (New York, Columbia University Press, 1964).

Lenôtre, Théodore Gosselin, pseud., *Le Tribunal révolutionnaire; 1793–1795* (Paris, Perrin & Cie, 1912).

—— *La Proscription des Girondins* (Paris, Hachette, 1927).

Leroy, Maxime, *Histoire des idées sociales en France de Montesquieu à Robespierre* (Paris, Gallimard, 1947).

Lintilhac, Eugène, *Vergniaud* (Paris, Hachette, 1920).

McDonald, Joan, *Rousseau and the French Revolution; 1762–1791* (London, The Athlone Press, 1965).

Madelin, Louis, *La Révolution française* (Paris, Hachette, 1910).

—— *Danton* (Paris, Hachette, 1914).

—— *Figures of the French Revolution*, transl. R. Curtis (New York, The Macaulay Co., 1929).

Martin, André, and Walter, Gérard, *Catalogue de l'histoire de la Révolution française* (Paris, Bibliothèque Nationale, 1936–1943), 5 vols.

Mathiez, Albert, *Les Origines des cultes révolutionnaires: 1789–1792* (Paris, G. Bellais, 1904).

—— *Contributions à l'histoire religieuse de la Révolution française* (Paris, F. Alcan, 1907).

—— "Les Girondins et la Cour à la veille du 10 août," *Annales historiques de la Révolution française*, 1931, pp. 193–212.

—— *Girondins et Montagnards* (Paris, Firmin-Didot, 1930).

—— *Etudes sur Robespierre* (Paris, Editions sociales, 1958).

—— *La Révolution française* (Paris, Colin, 1958–1959, 13th ed.), 3 vols.

—— *After Robespierre: The Thermidorian Reaction*, transl. C. A. Phillips (New York, Universal Library, 1965).

Meynier, Albert, *J.-J. Rousseau révolutionnaire* (Paris, Schleicher, 1912).

Michelet, Jules, *Histoire de la Révolution française*, ed. G. Walter (Paris, Gallimard, 1952), 2 vols.

—— *Les Femmes de la Révolution française* (Paris, A. Delahaye, 1854).

Monglond, André, *La France révolutionnaire et impériale. Annales de Bibliographie méthodique et description des livres illustrés* (Grenoble, Arthaud, 1930–1931), vols. I–III (1789–1796).

Moore, James M., *The Roots of French Republicanism; The Evolution of the Republican Ideal in Revolutionary France and its Culmination in the Constitution of 1793* (New York, The American Press, 1962).

Mornet, Daniel, *Les Origines intellectuelles de la Révolution française* (Paris, Colin, 1947).

Palmer, Robert R., *Twelve Who Ruled: The Committee of Public Safety during the Terror* (Princeton, Princeton University Press, 1941).

Peyre, Henri, "The Influence of Eighteenth-Century Ideas on the French Revolution," *Journal of the History of Ideas*, 1949, X, 63–87.

Ratinaud, Jean, *Robespierre* (Paris, Editions du Seuil, 1960).

Riffaterre, Camille, *Le Mouvement antijacobin et antiparisien à Lyon* (Lyons, A. Rey, 1912–1928), 2 vols.

Rivers, John, *Louvet: Revolutionist and Romance Writer* (New York, Brentano's, 1911).

Rudé, George, *The Crowd in the French Revolution* (Oxford, The Clarendon Press, 1959; paperback edition, 1967).

Rudé, George, *Revolutionary Europe; 1783–1815* (New York, Harper Torchbooks, 1966).

Soboul, Albert, *Les Sans-Culottes parisiens en l'an II; Mouvement populaire et gouvernement révolutionnaire; 2 juin 1793—9 thermidor l'an II* (Paris, Librairie Clavreuil, 1958).

—— *The Parisian Sans-Culottes and the French Revolution*, transl. G. Lewis (Oxford, The Clarendon Press, 1964).

—— "Classes populaires et rousseauisme sous la Révolution," *Annales historiques de la Révolution*, 1962, XXXIV, 421–38.

—— *Précis d'histoire de la Révolution française* (Paris, Editions sociales, 1962).

——*Le Procès de Louis XVI* (Paris, Julliard, 1966).

Sozzi, Lionello, "Interprétations de Rousseau pendant la Révolution," *Studies on Voltaire and the Eighteenth Century*, ed. Th. Besterman, Geneva, Institut et Musée Voltaire, 1968, LXIV.

Staël-Holstein, Anne-Louise-Germaine Necker, Baronne de, *Considérations sur les principaux événements de la Révolution française* (Paris, Delaunaux, 1820), 3 vols.

Sydenham, M. J., *The Girondins* (London, The Athlone Press, 1961).

Taine, Hippolyte, *Les Origines de la France contemporaine* (Paris, Hachette, 1921–1927), vol. II, *La Conquête jacobine.*

Thompson, James M., *Robespierre* (Oxford, Basil Blackwell, 1943).

—— *The French Revolution* (Oxford, Basil Blackwell, 1943).

Tocqueville, Alexis de, *The Old Regime and the French Revolution*, transl. S. Gilbert (New York, Doubleday & Co., 1955).

Trahard, Pierre, *La Sensibilité révolutionnaire* (Paris, Boivin & Cie, 1936).

Vatel, Charles, *Charlotte de Corday et les Girondins* (Paris, Plon, 1864–1872), 4 vols.

Walter, Gérard, *Marat* (Paris, Albin Michel, 1933).

—— *Robespierre* (Paris, Gallimard, 1936–1940), 3 vols.

—— *Répertoire de l'histoire de la Révolution française. Travaux publiés de 1800 à 1940: Personnes* (Paris, Bibliothèque Nationale, 1941), 2 vols.

2. WORKS ON M. AND MME ROLAND

Abbott, Jacob, *Madame Roland* (New York, Harper & Brothers, 1901).

Becker, Carl, "The Memoirs and the Letters of Madame Roland," *American Historical Review*, July 1928, XXXIII, 784–803.

Bernardin, Edith, *Les Idées religieuses de Madame Roland* (Paris, Les Belles Lettres, 1933).

——— *Jean-Marie Roland et le Ministère de l'Intérieur; 1792–1793* (Paris, Société des Études Robespierristes, 1964).

Birch, Una (Mrs. Pope-Hennessy), *Madame Roland* (New York, Dodd, Mead & Co., 1918).

Blind, Mathilde, *Madame Roland* (London, W. J. Allen & Co., 1886).

Brunetière, Ferdinand, "Lettres de Mme Roland," *Revue des Deux Mondes,* March–April 1901, CCCLXXVI, 473–80.

Calemard, Jean, *Manon chez elle* (Paris, L. Giraud-Badin, 1929).

Caro, Elme-Marie, "Deux Types de femmes de l'autre siècle: Mme du Deffand, Mme Roland," *Revue des Deux Mondes,* March 15, 1871, XCII, 256–73.

Clemenceau-Jacquemaire, Madeleine, *Madame Roland* (Paris, Plon, 1926).

——— *Vie de Mme Roland* (Paris, Editions J. Tallandier, 1929), 2 vols.

——— *The Life of Madame Roland,* transl. L. Vail (New York, Longmans, Green & Co., 1930).

Colet, Louise, "Les Dernières Heures de Madame Roland," in *Charlotte Corday et Madame Roland* (Paris, Berquet & Pétion, 1842).

Dauban, Charles-Aimé, *Etude sur Madame Roland et son temps, suivie des lettres de Madame Roland à Buzot et d'autres documents inédits* (Paris, Plon, 1864).

Dobson, Austin, "Madame Roland," in *Four Frenchwomen* (Oxford, Oxford University Press, 1923).

Doumic, René, "Le Mariage de Mme Roland," in *Etudes sur la littérature française,* deuxième série (Paris, Perrin & Cie, 1898), pp. 73–97.

Evans, Serge, "Mme Roland," in *Evocations et paysages* (Paris, Revue Moderne des arts et de la vie, 1937).

Gidney, Lucy, *L'Influence des Etats-Unis d'Amérique sur Brissot, Condorcet et Mme Roland* (Paris, Rieder, 1930).

Girardot, Auguste-Théodore, Baron de, *Etudes sur les Ministres de la République française, Roland et Mme Roland* (Paris, Guillaumin, 1860).

Hastier, Louis, "Un Ami de Madame Roland: L.-A. Champagneux," *Revue des Deux Mondes,* February 1, 1966, pp. 405–21.

Huisman, Georges, *La Vie privée de Mme Roland* (Paris, Hachette, 1955).

——— *Madame Roland, une grande laïque du XVIIIe siècle* (Paris, Cercle de la Ligue française de l'enseignement, 1957).

Lamartine, Alphonse de, "Madame Roland," in *Histoire des Girondins* (Paris, Hachette, 1913), I, 345–74, III, 132–33, 338–39.

Lenôtre, Théodore Gosselin, pseud., "The Salon of Madame Roland," in *Paris in the French Revolution*, transl. H. N. Williams (London, Hutchinson & Co., 1925), pp. 149–70.

———— "La Mort de Roland," in *Vieilles Maisons, vieux papiers* (Paris, Perrin & Cie, 1906), pp. 173–91.

May, Gita, "Stendhal and Madame Roland," *The Romanic Review*, February 1962, LIII, 16–31.

———— "Madame Roland devant la génération romantique," *The French Review*, April 1963, XXXVI, 459–68.

———— *De Jean-Jacques Rousseau à Madame Roland; Essai sur la sensibilité préromantique et révolutionnaire* (Geneva, Droz, 1964).

———— "Eighteenth-Century England as Seen by a Disciple of the *Philosophes*," *French Studies*, July 1965, XIX, 253–65.

———— "Voltaire a-t-il fait une offre d'hospitalité à Rousseau? Un Témoignage peu connu par Jean-Marie Roland," *Studies on Voltaire and the Eighteenth Century*, ed. Th. Besterman, Geneva, Institut et Musée Voltaire, 1966, XLVII, 93–113.

Michelet, Jules, "Madame Roland," in *Histoire de la Révolution française*, ed. G. Walter (Paris, Gallimard, 1952), I, 661–72, II, 619–22.

Monglond, André, "Manon Phlipon," in *Histoire intérieure du préromantisme français de l'abbé Prévost à Joubert* (Grenoble, Editions B. Arthaud, 1929), II, 220–31. In new, unrevised edition (Paris, J. Corti, 1965), II, 186–97.

Mornet, Daniel, "Deux petites bourgeoises parisiennes," in *Les Origines intellectuelles de la Révolution française* (Paris, Colin, 1947), pp. 412–15.

Perroud, Claude, "Recherches sur le salon de Madame Roland en 1791," *La Révolution française*, 1899, XXXVI, 336–44.

———— "Brissot et les Roland," *La Révolution française*, 1898, XXXIV, 403–22.

———— "Un Projet de Brissot pour une association agricole," *La Révolution française*, 1902, XLII, 260 ff.

———— "Le Premier ministère de Roland," *La Révolution française*, 1903, XLII, 511–27.

———— "La Maison de Mme Roland," *La Révolution française*, 1909, LVI, 304–17.

Poncetton, François, *Manon Roland, l'imaginaire* (Geneva, Paris, Montreal, Editions du Milieu du Monde, Imprimerie Kündig, 1947).

Robert, Henri, "Le Procès de Madame Roland," in *Les Grands Procès de l'histoire*, IIᵉ série (Paris, Payot, 1924).

Sainte-Beuve, Charles-Augustin, "Madame Roland," in *Nouveaux Lundis* (Paris, Calmann-Lévy, 1896), VIII, 190–265.

——— "Madame Roland," in *Oeuvres*, ed. M. Leroy (Paris, Gallimard, 1951), II, 1133–76.

Schérer, Edmond, "Mme Roland," in *Etudes sur la littérature contemporaine* (Paris, Calmann-Lévy, 1886), II, 283–383.

Schiff, Jean, *Madame Roland et le Clos de la Platière à Theizé, village historique* (Villefranche-en-Beaujolais, J. Guillermet, 1952).

Schlosser, Fr. and Bercht, G. A., *Mme de Staël et Mme Roland, ou la fille et la femme d'un ministre de la Révolution; mise en parallèle avec les événements et les acteurs de la Révolution* (Paris, Janet & Cotelle, 1830).

Tarbell, Ida M., *Madame Roland, A Biographical Study* (New York, Phillips & Co., 1905).

Trahard, Pierre, "Une Expérience malheureuse," in *La Sensibilité révolutionaire* (Paris, Boivin & Cie, 1936), pp. 207–27.

Wilcocks, Mary Patricia, *Madame Roland, l'idole des Girondins*, transl. J. Thérol (Paris, Hachette, 1938), English edition (London, Hutchinson, 1938).

3. WORKS ON THE EIGHTEENTH-CENTURY BACKGROUND

Abensour, Léon, *La Femme et le féminisme avant la Révolution* (Paris, E. Leroux, 1923).

Ascoli, Georges, "Essai sur l'histoire des idées féministes en France du XVIᵉ siècle à la Révolution," *Revue de Synthèse historique*, 1906, XIII, 25–57, 99–106, 161–84.

Atkinson, Geoffroy, *Les Relations de voyages du XVIIᵉ siècle et l'évolution des idées. Contribution à l'étude de la formation de l'esprit du XVIIIᵉ siècle* (Paris, Ed. Champion, 1927).

——— *Le Sentiment de la nature et le retour à la vie simple; 1690–1740* (Geneva, Droz, 1961).

Baldensperger, Fernand, *Young et ses "Nuits" en France*, in *Etudes d'histoire littéraire* (Paris, Hachette, 1907).

——— *Le Mouvement des idées dans l'émigration française, 1789–1815* (Paris, Plon, 1924), 2 vols.

Becker, Carl L., *The Heavenly City of the Eighteenth-Century Philosophers* (New Haven, Yale University Press, 1959).

Cassirer, Ernst, *The Philosophy of the Enlightenment*, transl. C. A. Fritz, Koelln, and James P. Pettegrove (Boston, Beacon Press, 1955).

——— *The Question of J.-J. Rousseau*, transl. Peter Gay (New York, Columbia University Press, 1954).

Chinard, Gilbert, *L'Amérique et le rêve exotique dans la littérature française au XVIIe et au XVIIIe siècles* (Paris, Droz, 1934).

Cobban, Alfred, *In Search of Humanity. The Role of the Enlightenment in Modern History* (New York, George Braziller, 1960).

Crocker, Lester G., *An Age of Crisis; Man and World in Eighteenth-Century French Thought* (Baltimore, Johns Hopkins Press, 1959).

—— *Nature and Culture; Ethical Thought in the French Enlightenment* (Baltimore, Johns Hopkins Press, 1963).

Etienne, Servais, *Le Genre romanesque en France depuis l'apparition de "La Nouvelle Héloïse" jusqu'aux approches de la Révolution* (Paris, Colin, 1922).

Fellows, Otis, and Torrey, Norman L., eds., *The Age of Enlightenment* (New York, Appleton-Century-Crofts, Inc., 1942).

Fusil, C.-A., *La Contagion sacrée, ou Jean-Jacques Rousseau de 1778 à 1820* (Paris, Plon, 1932).

Gay, Peter, *Voltaire's Politics. The Poet as Realist* (Princeton, Princeton University Press, 1958).

—— *The Party of Humanity. Essays in the French Enlightenment* (New York, Alfred A. Knopf, 1964).

—— *The Enlightenment: An Interpretation. The Rise of Modern Paganism* (New York, Alfred A. Knopf, 1966).

Goncourt, Edmond and Jules de, *La Femme au dix-huitième siècle* (Paris, Charpentier, 1912).

Guérard, Albert, *The Life and Death of an Ideal* (London, W. H. Allen, 1957).

Havens, George R., *The Age of Ideas* (New York, Holt, 1955; Free Press Paperback edition, 1965).

Hazard, Paul, *La Crise de la Conscience européenne; 1680–1715* (Paris, Boivin, 1934–1935), 3 vols.

—— *La Pensée européenne au XVIIIe siècle* (Paris, Boivin, 1946), 3 vols.

—— *European Thought in the Eighteenth Century from Montesquieu to Lessing,* transl. J. Lewis May (New Haven, Yale University Press, 1954).

Herriot, Edouard, ed. *French Thought in the Eighteenth Century* (London, Cassell & Co. Ltd., 1953).

Luppé, Albert de, *Les Jeunes Filles dans l'aristocratie et dans la bourgeoisie à la fin du XVIIIe siècle* (Paris, Ed. Champion, 1924).

Martin, Kingsley, *The Rise of French Liberal Thought; A Study of Political Ideas from Bayle to Condorcet,* ed. J. P. Mayer (New York, New York University Press, 1954).

Masson, Pierre-Maurice, *La Religion de J.-J. Rousseau* (Paris, Hachette, 1916), 3 vols.

Mauzi, Robert, *L'Idée du bonheur au XVIIIe siècle* (Paris, Colin, 1960).

Monglond, André, *Histoire intérieure du préromantisme français de l'abbé Prévost à Joubert* (Grenoble, Editions Arthaud, 1929; Paris, J. Corti, 1965), 2 vols.

——— *Vies préromantiques* (Paris, Société d'édition "Les Belles-Lettres," 1925).

Mornet, Daniel, *Le Sentiment de la nature en France de J.-J. Rousseau à Bernardin de Saint-Pierre* (Paris, Hachette, 1907).

Palmer, Robert R., *Catholics and Unbelievers in Eighteenth-Century France* (Princeton, Princeton University Press, 1939).

Peyre, Henri, *Literature and Sincerity* (New Haven, Yale University Press, 1963).

Sée, Henri, *La France économique et sociale au XVIIIe siècle* (Paris, Colin, 1925).

Torrey, Norman, ed., *Les Philosophes; The Philosophers of the Enlightenment and Modern Democracy* (New York, Capricorn Books, 1960).

Trahard, Pierre, *Les Maîtres de la sensibilité française au XVIIIe siècle; 1715–1789* (Paris, Boivin & Cie, 1931–1933), 4 vols.

Van Tieghem, Paul, *Le Sentiment de la nature dans le préromantisme européen* (Paris, Nizet, 1960).

Vyverberg, Henry, *Historical Pessimism in the French Enlightenment* (Cambridge, Harvard University Press, 1958).

Wade, Ira O., *The Clandestine Organization and Diffusion of Philosophic Ideas in France from 1700 to 1750* (Princeton, Princeton University Press, 1938).

INDEX

Index

Lafayette, Marie-Joseph-Paul du Motier, marquis de, 160, 170, 171; in Constituent Assembly, 191; Paris Guard and, 216

Lafayette, Marie-Madeleine Pioche de La Vergne, comtesse de, 66, 245, 246, 326

La Harpe, Jean-François de, 50

Lalande, Joseph-Jérôme Le Français de, 104

Lally-Tollendal, Trophime-Gérard, comte de, 160

Lamartine, Alphonse de, v, 291, 330

Lambert, Anne-Thérèse, marquise de, 68

Lande, France, 289

Language study, 16, 39–40, 92, 128; universalist project, 153–55

Languedoc, France, 78

Lanthenas, François, 119, 123, 124, 126, 230, 292–93; Roland meeting, 105; hypnosis and, 121; journalism of, 171–72, 209; in Paris (1791), 183; Ministry appointments (1791) and, 204; Buzot love affair and, 248

La Rochefoucauld-Liancourt, François-Alexandre-Frédéric, duc de, 160, 181

Latin, 16, 39, 135

Latour, Maurice Quentin de, 8, 9, 47

Lauze-Deperret, Claude, arrest of, 282

Lavater, Johann Kaspar, 121, 253, 303n9; visit to, 153

Law, 198; speculation and, 7; anti-clerical, 22, 31–32, 33, 192, 203, 216, 218; English, 133, 139–41, 154; trial of Louis XVI and, 189; on executive posts, 204; on divorce, 249; on arrest, 260, 271; interrogation and, 269–70, 281–82; Girondist trials and, 277, 282, 284; trial of Mme Roland and, 282–85

Le Clos de la Platière, Theizé, 76, 126, 144, 148–50, 153, 176, 306n1, 335; Dominique Roland

and, 107, 146, 290; Revolution of 1789 news at, 155, 162; Bancal des Issarts visit, 172–73, 174; Roland return (1791) to, 195–99, 201, 244; Eudora shelter at, 252–53; Roland retirement hopes (1793), 254, 255, 290

Leçons de physique expérimentale (Nollet), 42

Lefebvre, Georges, 312nn22, 25, 32, 34, 314nn13, 31, 315nn32, 36, 37, 38, 316n29, 330

Legislative Assembly, 199, 200, 204, 209; Austrian War (1792) and, 211, 212; Girondist cabinet fall (1792) and, 219; National Convention and, 220, 227, 240

Leibniz, Gottfried Wilhelm von, 128

Leopold II, emperor of Austria, 210

Leroy, Alphonse, 121

Lescot-Fleuriot, Jean-Baptiste-Edmond, Public Prosecutor, 281, 283, 284

Letters, 24, 25–26, 28, 42, 211, 244; on religion, 29; on poetry, 40; on death of Mme Phlipon, 47, 48; from Boismorel, 50, 51; on Rousseau, 57, 61–62, 63-64, 127, 146, 149, 300n20; to Rousseau, 63–64; on American Revolution, 69–70, 114–15; on Roland courtship, 82, 84, 85, 86–87, 89, 90, 91, 93–95, 96, 97–101; to Sévelinges, 87–88, 96; on Greece, 92; on Beaujolais, 106, 107–108, 148, 195; on Amiens, 111, 112; on status of women, 115–16, 117; on patent of nobility negotiations, 120–21, 124–25; on La Blancherie, 122; on Eudora, 125, 127, 146, 278; on Lyons inspectorship, 126, 145; to Lavater, 153, 253; on the English language, 154–55; on Louis XVI, 161, 162, 163–64, 169–70, 189, 208; on Revolution of 1789, 161, 162–64, 169–70,

Manufacturing (*Continued*)
81, 88, 119–20, 125–27, 199; invention rights and, 80–81, 159; guilds, 103; depression (1790–1791), 176–177, 186–87; Revolutionary souvenirs, 276

Marais sector, Paris, 26, 191, 198

Marat, Jean-Paul, viii, 56, 179, 224, 229, 316*nn*12, 13, 329; in National Convention, 222, 227, 252, 254; journalism of, 233–34, 239, 250, 251, 284; Lanthenas and, 248; assassination of, 272

Marie-Antoinette, queen of France, 133, 251, 279, 286; music lessons, 39; Mme Roland view of, 161, 162, 208; Revolution of 1789 and, 169; Austrian War and, 210

Marius, 275

Marriage of Figaro (Beaumarchais), 121, 145

Marseille, Academy of, 109

Marseille, France, 219–20

Martyrology, 33

Massillon, Jean-Baptiste, 14

Materialism, 29, 30, 35–36, 37, 298*n*14

Mathematics, 32, 44, 50

Mathiez, Albert, 191, 310*nn*38, 39, 312*nn*22, 25, 34, 313*nn*2, 7, 314*nn*13, 31, 315*n*37, 316*n*29, 331

Maupertuis, Pierre-Louis Moreau, 42

Medicine, 105, 113, 121, 147–48

Memoirs (Beugnot), 280–81, 285, 317*n*10, 319*nn*51, 52, 60, 325

Memoirs (Buzot), 246–47, 265, 291–92, 315*n*4, 325

Memoirs (Grandchamp), 205, 285, 311*n*4, 317*n*10

Memoirs (Louvet), 265, 326

Memoirs (Montpensier), 14

Memoirs (Pétion), 265

Memoirs (Mme Roland), vi, ix, x, 266–68, 291, 292; on her father, 8,

267; on education, 10, 16, 21; on Plutarch, 15, 300*n*8; on dress, 17; on sex, 19, 20, 102, 267; on Sévigné, 25; on Rousseau, 56, 58, 65, 308*n*8; on Roland de la Platière, 85, 101, 106; on class tensions, 161; on Brissot, 183, 214; on Paris salon (1791), 184–85; on Robespierre, 188, 191, 193–94, 214, 275–76; on Paine, 195; on Interior Ministry, 203–204, 206, 267; on Dumouriez, 207, 237; on foreign policy, 211; on revolution of August 10 (1792), 220; on Danton, 222, 223, 225, 226; on September massacres, 227, 228; on Condorcet, 233, 236–37; on Lanthenas, 248; on arrests, 259–61, 270–71; on Sainte-Pélagie prison, 272; on Phlipon household, 296*n*8

Memoirs (Williams), 273, 317*n*10, 328

Memoirs on the Bastille (Linguet), 142

Memoirs of a Prisoner (Riouffe), 280, 285, 317*n*10, 319*nn*60, 71, 327

Mercier, Louis-Sébastien, 169, 326

Messina, Italy, 86

Methodical Encyclopedia (Roland de la Platière), *see L'Encyclopédie*, Panckoucke edition

Meudon, France, 46, 47

Michelet, Jules, v, 57; quoted, 110, 218, 308*n*23, 311*n*53, 331

Milton, John, 40, 154

Mirabeau, Honoré-Gabriel Riquetti, comte de, 160, 171; 309*nn*6, 16, 325, 329; in Constituent Assembly, 180, 181, 191

Mississippi river, 53

Molière (Jean-Baptiste Poquelin), 44

Monarchy, 5; absolute, 15, 41, 134, 160, 162, 170, 207–208, 216, 229, 262; war and, 68–69, 115, 145, 210–14, 262; overthrow of, 71–72,